AN ILLUSTRATED HISTORY OF THE
JEWISH PEOPLE

זה המערה ואהרן הטיב שמן בנירות

AN ILLUSTRATED HISTORY OF THE
JEWISH PEOPLE

THE EPIC 4000-YEAR STORY OF THE JEWS, FROM THE ANCIENT PATRIARCHS AND KINGS
THROUGH CENTURIES-LONG PERSECUTION TO THE GROWTH OF A WORLDWIDE CULTURE

LAWRENCE JOFFE

LORENZ BOOKS

CONTENTS

Below The Damascus keter, 1260.

Below The Dead Sea in Israel.

Below Ark of the Covenant, Capernaum.

Above Auschwitz memorial.　　　　*Above Orthodox Jews in New York.*　　　　*Above Synagogue by Frank Lloyd Wright.*

INTRODUCTION

OVER A PERIOD OF 4,000 YEARS, JEWISH CULTURE HAS SOMEHOW FLOURISHED, DESPITE ENDLESS ATTACKS AND PERSECUTION. THE JEWISH STORY IS PERHAPS THE MOST INTRICATE STRAND IN HUMAN HISTORY.

The tale of Jewish survival is full of extraordinary drama – triumphs followed by setbacks, and miraculous rebirths coming after periods of near extinction. Such changes in fortune have persisted to modern times, with the devastation of the Holocaust between 1939 and 1945 followed three years later by the founding of the first Jewish State in 2,000 years.

Intrinsic to Jewish history is the theme of returning to the 'promised land', Israel, from the Diaspora, life outside Israel. As Jews have established communities throughout the world, other cultures have enriched the Jewish story and identity. In return, individual Jews have made a profound impact on civilization, from Moses and Jesus Christ to Maimonides and Albert Einstein.

Below Possible remnants of the fabled Hanging Gardens of Babylon, one of the Seven Wonders of the Ancient World.

MIDDLE EASTERN ROOTS

In a sense the Jewish story has recently returned to where it began, the Middle East, and in particular a small, pivotal area along the eastern Mediterranean, known as the Land of Israel to Jews and historical Palestine to others.

Jewish history traditionally begins with Abraham, who lived perhaps 4,000 years ago. The Hebrew Bible – what Christians call the Old Testament – encompasses the origins and moral codes of the people. Jews did not leave behind great palaces or artworks, as did the contemporaneous empires of Egypt or Mesopotamia. All that remains is the Bible itself, arguably the greatest Jewish gift to civilization. The Bible's vivid characters have stimulated and informed world literature and art for centuries. Consisting of 24 books in all, the first five, the Books of Moses, are central to Jewish faith.

Above Ezekiel prophesied the fall of the Temple in Jerusalem, and is seen here in a fresco of 1510 by Michelangelo.

BIRTH AND SURVIVAL

This book outlines the origin, religion, traditions, culture and artistic, literary, social and scientific contributions of the Jews, both as individuals and as a distinct group in history. It begins with the biblical account of how the descendants of the Patriarchs, Abraham, Isaac and Jacob, became wandering Hebrews, who evolved into 12 Israelite tribes with a belief in one God (monotheism).

Liberation from slavery in Egypt (whether mythical or not) is the pinnacle of this saga, after which charismatic rulers known as the Judges ruled a more settled population back in historic Israel. The Jews then created a briefly united Kingdom of Israel, and forged a national ethos honed by a tradition of Prophets. These men, and sometimes women, acted as a buffer against the excesses and misjudgements of the monarchy. But having disastrously lost ten of their twelve tribes to the Kingdom of Assyria around 722BCE, and the remaining Kingdom of Judah to Babylon two centuries later, their story seemed to be at an end.

LIFE BEYOND ISRAEL

In fact, the destruction of the first Jerusalem Temple in 586BCE and the second in 70CE actually took Judaism and the Jewish people to new places, to explore new directions. The exiles that followed disasters at home invariably sent Jews into the world to form new communities. Throughout Jewish history there is a fascinating tension between its core identity and an ethos that grew through exposure to and opposition to the cultures that Jews found themselves living in: Persian influence, Hellenistic philosophy and Roman rule being only the earliest. Running parallel to this history is the story of anti-Semitism, a virulent and ever-evolving hatred of Jews and their beliefs.

Gradually, the centre of Jewry shifted to Babylon and Persia, and then to western Europe (Ashkenazi), North Africa and Spain (Sephardi). While Jews were everywhere a minority, they formed networks that linked vast areas and thus contributed immensely to the advancement of host societies.

Below Jews who resisted Nazis in the Warsaw Ghetto Uprising are rounded up by the SS, 1943.

Right Anti-Semitic or pro-Jewish? Arguments still rage over Shakespeare's fictional Shylock, seen with his daughter Jessica in Sir James Dromgole's artwork.

CONFLICTING FAITHS

This book explains how Christianity sprang from Judaism, and how this new faith, and later Islam, came to challenge Judaism for dominance. The faith survived, partly thanks to new institutions, not least the compendium of writing called the Talmud, which helped unite Jews in their particular faith and traditions.

It was in the 'Golden Age' of Spain that interfaith cooperation triumphed, producing an era of unprecedented creativity and cultural progress. Sadly, the Golden Age ended when Jews were perceived as a threat by Christian leaders and expelled in 1492. Similar patterns were repeated elsewhere in Europe.

NEW DISASTERS

Some Sephardi Jews fleeing Spain in 1492 were welcomed by eastern Europe, which became the new hub of Jewish life. During the Emancipation and Enlightenment periods, Jews emerged from the physical and

notional ghettos that had cordoned them off from the rest of society. Now, many experienced a crisis of faith, which sharpened an existing divide between traditional and Reform versions of Judaism, or led many to abandon Jewish life altogether.

An explosion of creativity in the late 19th century coincided with extraordinary mass immigration from Europe to America and a proliferation of new ideologies, including Zionism – a movement to reclaim the 'promised land'. However, the catastrophe of the Nazis' World War II Holocaust seemed set to end all such dreams. Miraculously, the Jewish people survived to see the birth of Israel in 1948 and its development, if troubled, as a new axis of Jewish identity.

The Jewish story that emerges is one of survival despite adversity, dreadful miscalculations and remarkable innovations; of a people as tenacious as they are talented; and of individuals who have shone as beacons of hope and inspiration. Timelines and a guide to Jewish festivals introduce readers to the culture, then evocative photography and instructive text bring the narrative to life, telling one of history's most exciting, and devastating stories of human survival.

TIMELINE

THIS IS A CHRONOLOGICAL HISTORY OF THE JEWISH PEOPLE FROM THE TIME OF ABRAHAM AND THE PATRIARCHS, THROUGH THE EXILE AND THE DIASPORA, TO THE MODERN STATE OF ISRAEL.

Above Expert Assyrian archers like these confronted Israel in 722BCE.

2000–600BCE

*c.*2000–1700BCE According to tradition, the age of the Patriarchs starts with Abraham. The Bible records how the Israelites leave Canaan for Egypt when famine strikes.
*c.*1700BCE Joseph is sold into slavery. He later welcomes his family to Egypt.
*c.*1700–1300BCE Enslavement of the Israelites.
*c.*1300–1200BCE Moses leads the Israelites from Egypt.
*c.*1280BCE Torah, including the Ten Commandments, received by Moses at Mount Sinai.
*c.*1240BCE The Israelites under Joshua conquer Canaan.
*c.*1200–1000BCE Time of Judges.
1050BCE Philistines vanquish Shiloh and win the Ark of the Covenant. The time of Samuel, prophet and last judge.
1020BCE Saul is first King of the united Kingdom of Israel and Judah; rules until 1007BCE.
*c.*1004–965BCE King David crowned in Bethlehem. He makes Jerusalem his new capital and installs Ark of the Covenant.
*c.*965–928BCE Solomon is crowned. The Kingdom expands. First Temple is built.
*c.*928BCE Kingdom splits into Judah under Rehoboam, and Israel under Jeroboam.
918BCE Shishak of Egypt invades Israel.
*c.*900–800BCE Time of prophet Elijah.
722BCE Assyrians take over Israel. Ten tribes disperse. Time of prophet Isaiah.
727–698BCE King Hezekiah of Judah introduces major religious reforms.
639–609BCE King Josiah makes religious reforms in Judah. Dies at Battle of Megiddo fighting Egyptian forces and their Assyrian allies.

600–100BCE

586BCE Babylonians conquer Judah and destroy Jerusalem and the Temple. Most Jews are exiled to Babylon (the first Diaspora).
*c.*580BCE Jews establish a colony on the River Nile island of Elephantine, Egypt.
538–445BCE Persian King Cyrus defeats the Babylonians. Jews return to Israel, led by Zerubbabel and scribes Ezra and Nehemiah. Jerusalem Temple and city walls rebuilt. Canonization of the Torah.
536–142BCE Persian and Hellenistic periods.
*c.*500–400BCE Canonization of Book of Prophets. Presumed period of Queen Esther and the Purim saga in Persia. Elephantine Temple destroyed in Egypt.
347BCE Time of the Great Assembly, end of kingship.
332BCE Land conquered by Alexander the Great; Hellenistic rule.
285–244BCE 72 Jewish sages in Egypt translate Torah into Greek; called the Septuagint.
219–217BCE Rival Hellenistic dynasties fight for control of Israel. Seleucids finally displace Ptolemaids in 198BCE.
166–160BCE Maccabean (Hasmonean) revolt against Seleucid rule.
142–129BCE Jewish autonomy under Hasmoneans. In Jerusalem the zugot, or pairs of sages, acquire more power.
138BCE Rededication of the Second Temple. Foundation of Dead Sea Jewish sect at Qumran.
129–63BCE Hasmoneans achieve complete independence and expand national borders.

100BCE–300CE

76-67BCE Reign of Queen Salome Alexandra.
63BCE Romans invade Judea. Jerusalem captured by Pompey who names Judea a Roman vassal.
37BCE–4CE Herod the Great rules Judea. Temple in Jerusalem refurbished. Sanhedrin acts as Jewish legislature and judicial council.
*c.*30BCE–30CE Time of rabbis Hillel and Shammai.
6CE Judea becomes Roman province with capital at Caesarea.
*c.*20–36CE Ministry of Jesus of Nazareth.
30–100CE The birth of Christianity.
66–73CE The Great Revolt of Jews against Rome.
70CE Jerusalem conquered by Romans who destroy Second Temple.
70–200CE Age of the Tanna'im, rabbis who organized the Jewish oral law.
115–117CE Abortive Jewish revolt against Rome, the Kitos Wars.
131CE Hadrian renames Jerusalem Aelia Capitolina and forbids Jews to enter.
132–135CE Rebellion of Bar Kochba against Rome. Rome defeats rebels and Emperor Hadrian renames Judea 'Syria Palestina'.
*c.*210CE Mishnah, standardization of Jewish oral law, compiled by Rabbi Yehuda Ha-Nasi.
212CE Jews accepted as Roman citizens.
245CE Dura-Europos synagogue built in northern Syria.

300–600CE

220–500CE Period of the Amora'im, the rabbis of the Talmud. The main redaction of Talmud Bavli (Babylonian Talmud) is mostly completed by 475CE.

305CE Council of Elvira forbids Spanish Christians to socialize with Jews.

313–37CE Constantine converts Roman empire to Christianity. Empire is split into two, and Jews come under the rule of the more powerful Eastern, Byzantine empire in 330CE.

313–636CE Byzantine rule.

351CE A Jewish revolt in Galilee directed against Gallus Caesar is soon crushed.

361–3CE The last pagan Roman Emperor, Julian, allows Jews to return to Jerusalem and rebuild the Temple. The project lapses when he dies and his successor Jovian re-establishes Christianity as the imperial religion.

c.390CE Mishnah commentary, written form of oral traditions, is completed. Hillel II formulates Jewish calendar.

400–50CE Redaction of Talmud Yerushalmi (Talmud of Jerusalem).

425CE Jerusalem's Jewish patriarchate is abolished.

438CE The Empress Eudocia removes the ban on Jews praying at the Temple site.

489CE Theodoric, King of the Ostrogoths, conquers Italy and protects the Jews.

502CE Mar Zutra II establishes a small Jewish state within Babylon.

525–9CE End of Himyar Jewish Kingdom in southern Arabia. Byzantine Emperor Justinian I issues anti-Jewish legislation.

550–700CE Period of the savora'im, sages in Persia who finalized the Talmud.

556CE Jews and Samaritans revolt against Byzantines. Midrashic literature and liturgical poetry developed.

600–750CE

7th century CE Foundation of the Khazar kingdom in Caucasus, southern Russia.

608–10CE Anti-Jewish pogroms break out from Syria to Asia Minor. Jews riot in Syria against Christians.

613–14CE Persian invasion of Palestine ends Byzantine rule of Syria and Palestine and brings the Byzantine period to an end.

614CE Jews gain autonomy in Jerusalem after a Persian-backed revolt.

622CE Migration of Prophet Mohammed to Medina, marking the start of the Islamic calendar. His new faith, Islam, comes to dominate the Arabian Peninsula. Many Jewish communities there are dispersed, though Jews in Yemen mostly unaffected.

629CE Byzantines retake Palestine and kill many Jews.

632CE Death of Islamic Prophet Mohammed.

636–1099CE Arab rule in Palestine.

638CE Islamic and Arab conquest of Jerusalem. Arabs permit some Jews to return to Jerusalem, including immigrants from Babylon and refugees from Arabia.

640–2CE Arabs conquer Egypt.

691CE Dome of the Rock built on Temple Mount by Caliph Abd el-Malik on the site of the former Temples in Jerusalem.

694–711CE The Visigoths outlaw Judaism in Spain.

700–1250CE Period of the Ga'onim, heads of rabbinical colleges in Sura and Pumbedita, Babylon. New Jewish academies arise in Kairouan, Tunisia, and Fez, Morocco.

711CE Muslim armies invade and within a few years occupy most of Spain.

c.740CE Khazar Khanate royals and many Khazars convert to Judaism.

750–950CE Heyday of the Masoretes in Tiberias, Palestine, who codify Torah annotations and grammar.

Above Isaiah's utopian vision captured in Edward Hicks' painting of c.1840.

750–1050CE

760CE Karaite Jews reject the authority of the oral law and split off from rabbinic Judaism.

763–809CE Reign of Persian-born Harun al Rashid in Baghdad, fifth and most fabled Abbasid Caliph. Jewish diplomat Isaac forges bonds between Harun and Frankish King Charlemagne.

807CE Harun al Rashid forces Jews to wear a yellow badge and Christians to wear a blue badge.

808CE Idris II makes Fez (Morocco) the capital of his Shia dynasty and allows Jews to live in their own quarter (mellah) in return for an annual tax.

809–13CE Civil war in Persia.

900–1090CE The Golden age of Jewish culture in Spain.

912CE Abd-ar-Rahman III becomes Caliph of Spain.

940CE In Iraq, Saadia Gaon compiles his siddur (Jewish prayer book).

953CE Jewish historical narrative, Josippon, written in southern Italy.

960–1028CE Rabbenu Gershom of Germany, first great Ashkenazi sage, bans bigamy.

1013–73 Rabbi Yitzhak Alfassi writes the Rif, an important work of Jewish law.

1040–1105 Time of Rashi of France, Rabbi Shlomo Yitzhaki, who writes commentaries on the Hebrew Bible and Talmud.

1050–1250

1066 Jews enter England in the wake of the Norman invasion.

1090 Muslim Berber Almoravides conquer Granada, ending the period of tolerance. Jews flee to Toledo.

1095–1291 Christian Crusades begin, sparking war with Islam in Palestine. Thousands of Jews are killed in Europe and Middle East.

1099 Crusaders temporarily capture Jerusalem.

1100–1275 Time of the tosafot, medieval Talmudic commentators on the Torah carrying on Rashi's work.

1107 Moroccan Almoravid ruler Yusuf Ibn Tashfin expels Jews who do not convert to Islam.

1135–1204 Rabbi Moses ben Maimon, aka Maimonides, is the leading rabbi of Sephardic Jewry. He writes the Mishneh Torah and the *Guide for the Perplexed*.

1141 Death of Yehuda Halevi, who calls on Jews to emigrate to Palestine.

1144 First blood libel, in Norwich, England. The trend spreads to Europe.

1179 Third Lateran Council in Vatican establishes Jewish-Christian relations.

1187 Arab leader Saladin (c.1138–1193) takes Jerusalem and most of Palestine; many Jews arrive.

1200–1300 Zenith of the German Jewish Hasidei Ashkenaz pietist movement.

1240 Paris Disputation. Monks publicly burn the Talmud.

1244–1500 Successive conquest of Palestine by Mongols and Egyptian Muslims. Many Jews die or leave.

1249 Pope Innocent IV in Italy forbids Christians to make false blood libels against Jews.

1250–1480

1250–1300 The time of Moses de Leon of Spain, reputed author of the *Zohar*. Modern form of Kabbalah (esoteric Jewish mysticism) begins.

1250–1516 Mamluk rule.

1250–1550 Period of the Rishonim, the rabbinic sages who wrote commentaries on the Torah and Talmud and law codes.

1263 The Disputation of Barcelona, where Nahmanides (Ramban) defends the Talmud against Christian accusations.

1267 Nahmanides settles in Jerusalem and builds the Ramban Synagogue.

1270–1343 Rabbi Jacob ben Asher of Spain writes the Arba'ah Turim (Four Rows of Jewish Law).

1290 Jews are expelled from England by Edward I.

1290–1301 Mamluk rulers allow attacks on churches and synagogues, and segregate Jews and Christians from Muslims.

1300 Time of Rabbi Levi ben Gershom (1288–1344), aka Gersonides, a French philosopher.

1306–94 Jews are repeatedly expelled from France and readmitted. Last expulsion lasts 150 years.

1343 Persecuted in west Europe, Jews are invited to Poland by Casimir the Great.

1348–50 The Plague kills 30 to 60 per cent of Europe's people, and some blame Jews.

1391 Massacres in Spain; Jewish refugees find sanctuary in Algeria.

1415 Pope Benedict XII orders censorship of Talmud.

1458 Jews welcome Ottoman Turks, who conquer Byzantine Constantinople.

1475 First Hebrew book printed, in Italy, Ben Asher's *Arba'a Turim*.

1478 The Spanish Inquisition begins.

1480–1550

1486 First Jewish prayer book published in Italy.

1487 Portugal's first printed book is a Pentateuch in Hebrew.

1488–1575 Life of Joseph Caro, born in Spain, who writes the *Shulkhan Arukh*, the codification of halakhic law and Talmudic rulings.

1492 The Alhambra Decree – 200,000 Jews are expelled from Spain. Ottoman Sultan Bayezid II sends ships to bring Jews to safety in his empire. Many Jews survive as conversos (converts) or flee. Columbus reaches America.

1493 Jews are expelled from Sicily.

1495 Jews are expelled from Lithuania.

1497 Jews are forced to convert or leave Portugal.

1501 King Alexander of Poland readmits Jews to the Grand Duchy of Lithuania.

1516 Ghetto of Venice established

1517 Martin Luther starts the Protestant Reformation.

1517–1917 Ottoman rule in Palestine.

1525–72 Rabbi Moses Isserles (The Rama) of Krakow writes a gloss to the *Shulkhan Arukh* for Ashkenazi Jews.

1525–1609 Life of Rabbi Judah Loew ben Betzalel, called the Maharal of Prague.

1534 First printed Yiddish book published in Poland.

1547 First Hebrew Jewish printing house in Lublin, Poland.

Below Maimonides, the greatest Jewish genius of medieval Spain.

1550–1720

1534–70 Isaac Luria founds the new school of Kabbalists.

1550 Moses ben Jacob Cordovero founds a Kabbalah academy in Safed.

1564 First printed version of Joseph Caro's code of Jewish law published.

1567 First Jewish university yeshiva founded in Poland.

1577 Hebrew printing press in Safed, the first of any kind in Asia.

1580–1764 First session of the Council of Four Lands (Va'ad Arba' Aratzot) in Lublin, Poland. Seventy delegates from local Jewish kehillot meet to discuss issues important to the Jewish community.

1626–76 Time of false messiah Shabbetai Tzvi of Smyrna, Turkey.

1632-77 Life of Baruch Benedict Spinoza, Dutch Jewish philosopher.

1648–55 Ukrainian Cossack Bogdan Chmielnicki leads a massacre of Polish gentry and Jewry that leaves an estimated 130,000 dead. The total decrease in the number of Jews is estimated at 100,000.

1654 The first Jews go to North America.

1655 Jews are readmitted to England.

1675 The world's first Jewish newspaper is printed in Amsterdam.

1700 Rabbi Yehuda He-Hasid immigrates to Palestine with hundreds of followers.

1700–60 Israel ben Eliezer, known as the Ba'al Shem Tov, founds Hasidic Judaism in eastern Poland.

1701 Foundation of Bevis Marks Synagogue, London, the oldest British synagogue still in use.

1720 Unpaid Arab creditors burn the unfinished synagogue built by immigrant followers of Rabbi Yehuda and expel all Ashkenazi Jews from Jerusalem.

1720–97 Time of Rabbi Elijah of Vilna, the Vilna Gaon.

1720–1800s

1729–86 Moses Mendelssohn and the Haskalah (Enlightenment) movement.

1740 Ottomans invite Rabbi Haim Abulafia (1660–1744) to rebuild Tiberias.

1740–50 Mass immigration to Palestine under Messianic predictions.

1747 Rabbi Abraham Gershon of Kitov is the first immigrant of the Hasidic Aliyah, migration to Palestine.

1759 Time of Jacob Frank, who claimed to be the reincarnation of Shabbetai Tzvi and King David.

1772–95 Partitions of Poland between Russia, Kingdom of Prussia and Austria where most Jews live. Old Jewish privileges are renounced.

1775–1781 American Revolution, which guaranteed freedom of religion.

1789 The French Revolution leads France in 1791 to grant citizen rights to Jews, under certain conditions.

1790 In the USA, George Washington writes to the Jews of Rhode Island that he wants a country 'which gives bigotry no sanction ... persecution no assistance'.

1791 Emancipation of Jews begins in Europe. Russia creates the Pale of Settlement.

1799 Failed attempt by the French to seize Acre in Palestine.

1800–1900 The Golden Age of Yiddish literature, the revival of Hebrew as a spoken language and in literature. First major Yiddish theatre founded in Romania in 1876.

1810 Reform Movement in Germany opens first synagogue in Seesen.

1820–60 Orthodox Judaism emerges in response to Reform Judaism and Enlightenment movements, characterized by strict adherence to Jewish religious law.

Above Touro Synagogue RI, built 1763, is the USA's oldest still operating today.

1800s–1870

1806 Nathan Mayer Rothschild starts his business in Manchester, England.

1810 Birth of Rabbi Israel Salanter, founder of the Mussar Movement.

1830 First Jewish wedding celebrated in Australia.

1841 David Levy Yulee of Florida is the first Jew elected to Congress. The *Jewish Chronicle* is printed in the UK.

1850s Positive-Historical Judaism begins in Germany. Later known as Conservative Judaism, it advocates a middle path between Reform and Orthodoxy.

1851 Norway allows Jews entry. They are emancipated in 1891.

1858 Jews emancipated in England.

1860 Alliance Israelite Universelle is founded in Paris to protect Jewish rights as citizens.

1860–1943 Time of Henrietta Szold, founder of Hadassah.

1861 The Zion Society is formed in Frankfurt am Main, Germany. The first Haskalah Russian journal, *Razsvet*, is founded.

1862 Jews gain equal rights in Congress Kingdom of Poland. Moses Hess writes *Rome and Jerusalem*.

1867 Jews emancipated in Hungary. Karl Marx publishes Das Kapital.

1868 Converted Jew Benjamin Disraeli becomes UK Prime Minister.

1870–90 Russian Zionist groups Hovevei Zion and Bilu set up Jewish settlements in Palestine, aided by Baron Edmond James de Rothschild. Eliezer Ben-Yehuda revives Hebrew as a spoken modern language.

1870–1900

1870-1 Jews are emancipated in Italy and then Germany.

1875 Reform Judaism's Hebrew Union College is founded in Cincinnati.

1877 New Hampshire becomes the last US state to give Jews equal rights.

1881–84, 1903–6, 1918–20 Three waves of pogroms kill thousands of Jews in Russia and Ukraine.

1882–1903 First Aliyah (large-scale immigration) to Palestine, mainly from Russia.

1886 Jews fleeing pogroms in Lithuania swell South African Jewish community.

1887 Conservative Jewish movement founded in America. Birth of Marc Chagall, leading 20th-century artist.

1890 The term 'Zionism' is coined by Nathan Birnbaum.

1891 Jewish Colonisation Organisation founded, prompts Jewish agricultural colonies in Argentina.

1892 Israel Zangwill publishes *Children of the Ghetto* in England.

1894 Alfred Dreyfus, French army captain and a Jew, is falsely convicted of treason.

1897 Theodor Herzl writes *Der Judenstaat* (The Jewish State). The Bund (General Jewish Labor Union) is formed in Russia. Zionist Congress meets in Switzerland and founds a Zionist Organization.

Below 'Work sets you free' – the cynical motto that greeted Jews at Auschwitz.

1900–1922

1902 The Jewish Theological Seminary becomes the flagship of Conservative Judaism. Herzl publishes utopian Zionist novel *Altneuland*.

1903 The Kishinev Pogrom is caused by accusations that Jews practise cannibalism.

1904–14 The Second Aliyah, mainly from Russia and Poland.

1905 Russian Revolution, accompanied by pogroms.

1909 The first kibbutz and Tel Aviv are founded.

1914 American Jewish Joint Distribution Committee founded.

1915 Yeshiva College and Rabbinical Seminary is established in New York.

1917 British troops drive Ottoman Turks from Palestine. Balfour Declaration gives official British support for 'a national home for the Jewish people'. Russia's October Revolution abolishes the Pale of Settlement and grants Jews equal rights. Russian civil war leads to more than 2,000 pogroms.

1918–48 British Rule of Palestine.

1919–23 Third Aliyah, mainly from Russia.

1920 Histadrut (Jewish labour federation) and Haganah (Jewish defence organization) founded in Palestine. Jewish community (yishuv) sets up National Council. Britain receives the League of Nations' British Mandate of Palestine.

1921 Civil administration of Palestine closes land east of the Jordan River to Jewish settlement. Polish-Soviet peace treaty in Riga. First moshav (cooperative village) founded in Palestine. Albert Einstein wins Nobel Prize.

1922 Transjordan set up on three-quarters of Palestine. Jewish Agency is established. Birth of Reconstructionist movement in USA.

1922–60

1923 Britain awards Golan Heights to Syria.

1924–32 Fourth Aliyah, mainly from Poland.

1929 Major Arab riots in Palestine.

1931 Etzel (Irgun) right-wing, 'revisionist' Jewish underground organization founded.

1933 Hitler takes over Germany and begins imposing race laws against Jews.

1933–9 Fifth Aliyah, mainly from Germany.

1936 World Jewish Congress founded.

1938 9-10 November: Kristallnacht (Night of Glass) – Nazi violence against Jews.

1939 Britain strictly limits Jewish immigration to Palestine.

1939–45 World War II. Holocaust and the murder of six million Jews.

1946–8 Haganah, Irgun and Lehi militants resume struggle for a Jewish state in Palestine.

1947 Discovery of Dead Sea Scrolls.

1947 29 November: The United Nations approves creation of a Jewish State and an Arab State in Palestine. Violence erupts between Jews and Arabs.

1948 14 May: The State of Israel declares independence.

1948 15 May: Arab–Israeli War erupts. Israel survives Arab attacks, expands borders. Jerusalem divided, influx of Holocaust survivors, flight of Palestinian Arab refugees.

1949 Armistice agreements with Arab states.

1949-50 'Operation Magic Carpet' brings Yemenite Jews to Israel.

1949–54 Mass immigration to Israel of Jews from Arab states.

1952 Prague trials revive anti-Semitic fears in Communist eastern bloc.

1953 Establishment of Yad Vashem Holocaust Memorial in Israel.

1955 David Marshall, son of Baghdadi Jews, becomes Singapore's first Chief Minister.

1956 The Suez War.

1960–80

1962–5 Jewish–Christian relations improve with Vatican II.

1964 Palestine Liberation Organization (PLO) founded

1966 Shmuel Yosef Agnon (1888–1970) becomes the first Hebrew writer to win the Nobel Prize in literature; jointly with German Jewish author Nelly Sachs.

1967 5–11 June: Six Day War fought between Israel versus Egypt, Syria and Jordan. Israel gains control of East Jerusalem, West Bank, Sinai Peninsula and Golan Heights.

1967 1 September: Arab Leaders in Khartoum reject recognition of Israel. UN 242 offers 'land for peace' formula and underpins most future peace plans.

1968–70 Egypt's War of Attrition against Israel. Jewish settlers occupy houses in Hebron, amid more than 100,000 Palestinians.

1972 Soviets clamp down on 'refusenik' Jews wishing to leave the USSR. Palestinian terrorists kill Israeli athletes at Munich Olympics.

1973 6-24 October: Yom Kippur War. Israel surprised by Egyptian–Syrian attack, retains 1967 territories.

1974 Foundation of Gush Emunim, religious settlers movement. Golda Meir, Middle East's first woman leader, resigns.

1975 USA ties Soviet trade benefits to freedom of emigration for Jews. United Nations resolution equates Zionism with racism. Rescinded in 1991. Israel becomes an associate member of the European Common Market.

1977 Rightist Likud party wins Israeli elections, ousting Labour for the first time since independence.

1978 18 September: Israel and Egypt sign comprehensive peace accords at Camp David. Leftist Israelis found Peace Now.

1979 Israel–Egypt Peace Treaty signed. Prime Minister Menachem Begin and President Anwar Sadat are awarded Nobel Peace Prize.

1980–2000

1982 Israel's withdrawal from Sinai completed. Operation Peace for Galilee removes PLO fighters from southern Lebanon.

1982 June–December: The Lebanon War. Anger in Israel and abroad over Sabra and Chatilla massacre.

1983 American Reform Jews formally accept patrilineal descent. Menachem Begin resigns as prime minister, replaced by Yitzhak Shamir.

1984–5 Operations Moses and Joshua: Rescue of Ethiopian Jewry by Israel. Inconclusive elections result in Labour–Likud coalition.

1987 Beginning of the First Intifada Palestinian uprising against Israeli occupation.

1989 Fall of the Berlin Wall. Leonard Bernstein conducts a celebration concert in a free East Berlin.

1990 The Soviet Union relaxes emigration laws. Thousands leave for Israel.

1990–1 Iraq invades Kuwait, triggering a war between Iraq and allied United Nations forces.

1991 Operation Solomon rescues most remaining Ethiopian Jews. The Madrid Peace Conference starts first bilateral talks between Israeli and Jordanian, Syrian and Palestinian delegations since 1949.

1992 New government headed by Yitzhak Rabin of the Labour party.

1993 13 September: Israel and the PLO sign the Oslo Accords.

1994 26 October: Israel and Jordan sign peace treaty.

1994 10 December: Arafat, Rabin and Peres share Nobel Peace Prize. Palestinian self-government in Gaza Strip and Jericho area.

1995 Broadened Palestinian self-government is implemented in West Bank and Gaza Strip.

1995 4 November: Israeli Prime Minister Yitzhak Rabin is assassinated.

1999 Ehud Barak elected Prime Minister of Israel.

Above Itzhak Perlman, one of the best-loved violinists of the modern era.

2000–

2000 24 May: Israel withdraws its forces from southern Lebanon.

2000 Camp David II peace talks between Israel, PLO and America end in failure.

2000 29 September: Start of the second Palestinian uprising, al-Aqsa Intifada.

2001 First Holocaust Memorial Day in Britain. Ariel Sharon elected Israeli Prime Minister.

2002 Spate of suicide attacks on Israeli towns. Israeli military reoccupation of Palestinian urban centres.

2003 US President George W Bush proposes Israeli–Palestinian roadmap to peace. Arab League re-airs Saudi Plan for peace.

2005 31 March: Israeli government recognizes the Bnei Menashe people of north-east India as one of the Ten Lost Tribes of Israel. Mahmoud Abbas elected Palestinian president.

2005 August: The Government of Israel withdraws military and Jewish settlers from the Gaza Strip.

2005 December: Prime Minister Ariel Sharon falls into a coma.

2006 Prime Minister Ehud Olmert forms new Israeli government. Islamist Hamas wins Palestinian elections. New war with Hizbollah in Lebanon.

2008 Israel celebrates 60 years of independence.

2009 Barack Obama becomes first US President to host Passover seder in the White House, Washington DC.

Jewish Traditions and Festivals

Inseparable from their faith and history, the traditions of feasting, fasting and prayer on special days help to define what it means to live as a Jewish person today.

The Jewish year follows the 354/5-day lunar calendar, as opposed to the more usual 365/6-day solar year, so while each Jewish festival falls on precisely the same date in each year of the Jewish calendar, the dates will differ on the Gregorian calendar. For synchronicity, and also to keep the months in their appropriate season, a 13th month is added to the Jewish calendar every two or three years. In the northern hemisphere, Rosh Hashanah will always be celebrated between summer and autumn, while

Below This 18th-century Mizrah scroll, hung on the west wall of the house to indicate the direction of Jerusalem, also illustrates major Jewish festivals.

Hanukkah always heralds winter and Pesach ushers in the spring, regardless of how different the actual dates will be on Christian calendars.

Jewish holidays always begin at sundown on the day before. The year of celebrations starts around September, with Rosh Hashanah, the Jewish New Year, and progresses through Yom Kippur, the Day of Atonement, which is marked nine days later. Sukkot, the harvest festival of thanksgiving, follows, ending with Simchat Torah, the festival of the Torah. Around December comes Hanukkah, the festival of lights, when gifts are traditionally exchanged. Tu b'Shevat, the Holiday of the Trees, falls around February,

Above Adam and Eve are tempted by the serpent, an immortal biblical scene from the Golden Haggadah, 14th-century Spain.

and this is followed by Purim, a festival that involves dressing up in colourful costumes, and is considered a kind of Jewish Mardi Gras.

Pesach commemorates Israel's deliverance from Egypt. During this eight-day festival, Jews consume particular foods and drinks, eschewing those that contain leaven. Shavuot celebrates the Giving of the Torah, while Tisha B'Av is a day of fasting, when the Destruction of the Temple is mourned.

Many communities also observe Yom Hatsma'ut, Israeli Independence Day, which is celebrated on 14 May with various festivities. Yom Ha Shoah, the Holocaust Remembrance Day, is observed shortly after Pesach.

ROSH HASHANAH

The Jewish year begins in September or October with Rosh Hashanah, which means the head of the year. This is the start of the Ten Days of Penitence, also called the Days of Awe, which end with Yom Kippur. Jews are encouraged to spend these days in retrospection, considering their behaviour and how to make amends, improving their own lives and the lives of those around them.

The holidays of Rosh Hashanah and Yom Kippur are often referred to as the High Holy Days, and many Jews consider them so important that even if they observe no other festivals in the year, at this time they will go to synagogue, partake of a festive meal, and recite the prayers and blessings.

BLESSINGS FOR ROSH HASHANAH

Several blessings and benedictions attend this festival, which marks the beginning of the Jewish year. In addition to the blessings printed below, parents give thanks for their children, the challah is blessed as for Shabbat, and a slightly longer Kiddush (sanctifying blessing) is recited over the wine before it is drunk.

Candle Lighting

If Rosh Hashanah falls on the same day as Shabbat, then the blessing is modified and added to accordingly.

Baruch Ata Adonai Elohaynu Melech Ha'olam, asher Kid'shaynu b'mitzvotav, v'tzivanu l'hadleek neir shel Yom Tov.
Blessed are You, Lord God, Eternal One, who enables us to welcome Rosh Hashanah, by kindling these lights.

Benediction

This prayer – Shehehayanu (the Hebrew for 'Who has given us life') – is recited on Rosh Hashanah and other important occasions.

Baruch Ata Adonai Elohaynu Melech Ha'olam, shehehayanu, v'keeyomanu v'higeeyanu lazman hazeh.
Blessed are You, Lord God, Eternal One, who has kept us alive and sustained us, enabling us to celebrate this New Year.

Honeyed Apples

Apples and honey represent a sweet new year. Apple slices are dipped in honey, and this blessing is recited.

Baruch Ata Adonai Elohaynu Melech Ha'olam, boray p'ree ha aytz.
Blessed are You, Lord God, Eternal One, who creates the fruit from the earth.

The Ram's Horn

A ceremonial shofar (ram's horn) is blown on Rosh Hashanah, as it is on Yom Kippur. The sound reminds Jews of their history and the covenant between the people of Israel and God.

One tradition (tashlich) calls for penitents to throw all their sins of the previous year into a body of running water. The gesture symbolizes a fresh start for the new year.

Rosh Hashanah begins, as usual, at sundown on the evening before. Candles are lit, the bread is blessed, and the Kiddush is recited over the wine. A festive meal is prepared.

Different Customs

Various ethnic groups have different customs for the holiday. Sephardim eat a fish with the head left intact,

Left The ceremonial shofar (ram's horn) is blown at Rosh Hashanah to welcome in the New Year.

expressing their hopes for a year rich with wisdom, with Israel as the head of the nations rather than the tail.

No sour or bitter foods are eaten at Rosh Hashanah, as no sharp flavours may interfere with the sweetness of the festival. All the new season's fruits are enjoyed.

YOM KIPPUR

The 10th of Tishri, the first month in the Jewish calendar, is Yom Kippur – the Day of Atonement. It also marks God's forgiveness of early Israelites after they worshipped the golden calf while Moses received the tablets of the law on Mount Sinai.

It is a day devoted to spiritual life, when the physical is set aside. Sex is forbidden, as is wearing leather shoes, brushing the teeth, spending money, using perfumes or soap and wearing make-up. Everyone, other than children, pregnant women, and the ill or infirm, is expected to fast.

Making Amends at Yom Kippur

Jews are urged to take stock of their sins, to make amends for any wrongs, and to repent. The ancient Kapparot (expiations) ceremony is still observed in some circles. A live chicken is passed over the head of an individual, so that his or her sins may be transferred to the bird. Many prefer to use a coin instead. The coin symbolizes giving to charity.

On the day of Yom Kippur, Jews go to synagogue, greeting each other with 'Have an easy fast'. Much time is then spent in quiet retrospection as individuals examine their consciences with honesty, aiming to make amends for past misdeeds, and promising to do much better in the year ahead. The Yom Kippur devotions include chanting the Kol Nidre, and the Yizkor, the memorial service at which the dead are remembered and respected. Kaddish, the prayer for the dead, is recited for deceased family members and friends of participants, and for the Jewish martyrs. Candles are also lit for the deceased.

All foods eaten before the fast must be light and simple and not too salty or spicy as it is terribly difficult to fast with a raging thirst. It is intended that penitents should feel a few hunger pangs while they are fasting, but nothing more serious.

A Day of Purity

At Yom Kippur the synagogue is decorated in white, the Torah is draped in white and the rabbi wears a kitl (a white robe), as a symbol of purity. Observant Jews also wear white in the synagogue, and shoes made from cloth rather than leather.

Unlike at other festivals, the candles are lit after rather than before the meal – before the start of Yom Kippur and the festival observances. A pure white tablecloth is draped on the dinner table, and a Bible, prayer book and other sacred religious texts are placed on the table until the observance has been completed.

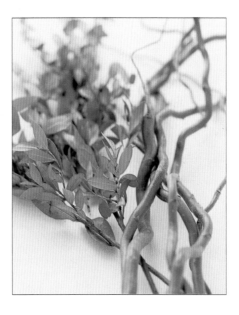

Families and friends gather together for celebrations to break the fast after Yom Kippur. It is a happy occasion after the solemnity of the day's observance. Sephardim serve eggs, the symbol of life.

SUKKOT

This festival is observed by building a sukkah, which is a little three-sided hut or booth. The Mishnah (the first code of Jewish Law) lays down how this must be done. There must only be three sides, and the roof must be covered with schach, or branches of trimmed greens or palm leaves, with enough open space to permit those inside to see the stars. A sukkah must be a temporary building. Sometimes a few families get together to share the task of building, starting at one house and then moving to the next until all the structures are complete.

If the weather permits, meals during the seven-day festival are eaten in the sukkah. The mood of Sukkot is festive. Friends and family drop by, and if the weather is mild enough, families sleep in the sukkah, too. It is wonderful to catch sight of these sukkahs in big cities where you can see their greenery perched on terraces and in courtyards and gardens.

Right Children spin the dreidel as part of the Hanukkah celebrations.

Left Myrtle and willow branches are placed in the sukkah along with the etrog (citron) and lulav (palm branch).

Celebrating Sukkot

The proper greeting for Sukkot is 'Chag Sameach', which translates as happy holiday. Celebrants give thanks for the previous year, and express hopes for the year to come. At the end of the festival, prayers are offered for rain and the Hebrew dance Mayim may be performed.

Four plants – Arba Minim – decorate the sukkah, and are held in the hands during the blessings each evening. They are: the etrog (a lemon-like citron); the lulav (palm branch); the arava (willow branch); and the myrtle. Each of these has a deep significance. The etrog is shaped like a heart and symbolizes the hope of divine forgiveness for the desires of our heart; this should be held in the left hand. The right hand holds the lulav, which symbolizes Israel's loyalty to God, while the myrtle is shaped like an eye, and represents the hope that greed and envy will be forgiven. Finally, the arava, considered to be shaped like a mouth, symbolizes forgiveness for idle talk and lies. Bright cut-outs are pinned up and fresh and dried fruits are hung from the roof.

HANUKKAH

Throughout the world, beginning on the eve of the 25th of Kislev (which falls in November or December), Jews celebrate Hanukkah, the festival of lights, by lighting an oil lamp or menorah filled with candles. They light one every night for eight nights until all are lit. A shamash (helper candle), is used to light each candle.

The festival commemorates the Maccabean victory over Antiochus IV, who was known as Epiphanes of Greece, in the year 165BCE.

At Hanukkah, Jews eat foods cooked in oil, to remind them of the sacred lamp in the synagogue that burned miraculously without oil for the Maccabees. On the first night, the Shehehayanu (the benediction of thanks) is recited. Each evening a blessing is said over the candles.

Customs and Traditions

Jewish children often make ceramic or papier-mâché menorahs (candelabras) or dreidels (spinning tops) with which to celebrate the holiday. Jews will gather together socially throughout the festival of Hanukkah, greeting each other with 'Chag Sameach', meaning happy holiday, drinking spirits, exchanging gifts or giving money (Hanukkah gelt), and

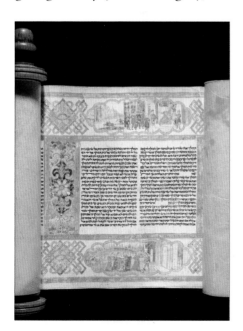

singing songs such as 'Ma-oz Tzur' (Rock of Ages) or the Dreidel Song. This last will often accompany a game of dreidel, when small coins or nuts are gambled away on the outcome of the spinning of the four-sided top. Hebrew initial letters marked on the top signify 'A Great Miracle Happened There', or, if one lives in Israel, 'A Great Miracle Happened Here'.

Hanukkah is a joyous celebration. Indeed, the *Shulkhan Arukh* – the code of law – forbids mourning and fasting during this time, and instead encourages merry-making and feasting.

PURIM

This festival is one of joy, feasting and drinking. It falls on the 14th Adar, around February or March, and reminds Jews of the triumph of freedom and goodness over evil.

The story that Purim celebrates took place in Shushan (now Iran). The main characters are Queen Esther, her cousin Mordecai and the evil First Minister of King Ahasuerus, Haman. The tale relates how Haman, irate that the Jew Mordecai did not show him proper respect, plotted to kill the Jews. Esther went to her husband pleading for the lives of her people. And so, at a banquet designed to honour Haman, the tables were turned. The king hanged Haman on the gallows intended for Mordecai, and the Jews were saved.

Celebrating the Story of Esther

During Purim, children come to the synagogue dressed in costume, often as Haman, Mordecai or Esther. The Megillah, the Scroll of Esther, is read

Left Scrolls of Esther, like this beautifully decorated example from Italy, 1781, are read aloud on Purim.

Above Masks are often worn as part of the Purim festivities.

aloud, and when Haman's name is uttered, all make as much noise as they can, by twirling the grogger (noise-maker) or banging things together.

Wine is a sign of happiness and inaugurates many Jewish religious ceremonies, but at Purim it is essential. Indeed, the Talmud exhorts Jews to 'drink so much that you can't tell the difference between Mordecai and Haman'. This is because Esther served huge quantities of wine at the banquet she gave at the palace, when Haman was exposed as a villain.

Special foods are eaten for Purim. In Ashkenazi cultures, triangular pastries filled with nuts, seeds or dried fruit are served. This commemorates Esther, who ate only fruits and nuts in the palace, as the kitchen was not kosher. North African Sephardim eat pastries drenched in honey called oznei Haman (the ears of Haman).

Gifts to Share at Purim

The giving of sweet pastries and fruit, known as shaloch manot, is a Purim observance. Charitable donations are given to at least two individuals or causes. Some Jews observe the fast of Esther, in honour of the queen's fast before she pleaded with the king.

PESACH

The Passover festival, Pesach, is one of the biggest in the Jewish year. Pesach falls sometime around March or April, following the Jewish calendar. It commemorates the story of the exodus of the Hebrew slaves from bondage in Egypt, a flight that turned a tribe of slaves into a cohesive people. It celebrates the fight for freedom of all humanity – the freedom of spirit as well as personal, religious and physical freedom.

'Why is tonight different from all other nights?' asks a small child, quoting from the Haggadah, the narrative read at the Pesach feast. And so the story unfolds.

The word 'pesach' means passing over, and represents the passing over of the houses whose doorways the Israelites had splashed with lamb's blood, so that those inside remained unharmed when the angel of death ravaged Egypt, slaying the first-born sons. This was Egypt's final agony, which convinced Pharaoh to, in the much-quoted words of Moses, 'Let my people go!' And go they did, into the desert to wander for an entire generation until Moses led them to the Promised Land. The festival of Pesach takes Jews on that journey via the Haggadah; the story is relived as the ritual meal is eaten.

For eight days special foods are eaten, and foods that are customarily eaten at other times of the year

Left Two 18th-century Pesach cups from Germany and an embellished Haggadah from Hamburg, 1760s.

are taboo. No leavened foods are permitted, which rules out any food allowed to rise or ferment, such as dough containing yeast and flour.

In the weeks prior to the Pesach feast, the entire house is cleaned from top to bottom, especially the kitchen. The day before the Seder or Pesach feast, the head of the household searches for anything that might contain leaven – usually there are napkins filled with crumbs left here and there for the purposes of symbolic removal. Then he or she recites a blessing on the hametz (leavening) that has been gathered which is then burned. In addition to bread, all flour or leavened products are forbidden, as are beer and other alcoholic drinks made with yeast. Observant Jews are very careful about the dairy products that they eat during Pesach. Milk should come from animals that have only eaten grass, not grain, and there must be no risk of contamination with leaven.

Sephardim eat all vegetables and some eat rice, though Ashkenazim eschew many vegetables on the grounds that they could be considered grains or ingredients to make breads or cakes. The list includes corn, green beans, peas, lentils, chickpeas, and other dried beans.

Above A ritual Seder plate.

The Seder

On the first night of the festival (and the second night too, unless the participants are Reform or living in Israel) a ritual meal called the Seder is served. The word seder means order, referring to the fact that the meal has a specific order of events. The meal revolves around the reading of the Haggadah, the story of the exodus from Egypt and slavery. The foods eaten often have symbolic significance and represent elements of the story.

The Seder Plate

Maror (bitter herbs) are placed on the Seder plate to remind Jews of the bitterness of slavery. Horseradish is usually used as maror, but any bitter herb can be eaten. Haroset comes next. Also known as charosses, harosses and halek, this is a blend of sweet fruit and nuts. Mixed with wine to become a sludge, it symbolizes the mortar used by the Hebrews.

The cycle of life is represented by a roasted egg. It is also a symbol of the sacrifices brought to the ancient Temple and a symbol of mourning for the destroyed Temple. A bowl of boiled eggs is usually served with salt water as the first course. Salt water represents the Hebrews' tears.

Also to be dipped in the salt water are spring greens such as parsley or lettuce, which recall the oppression of the Israelites and the renewal of spring.

A roasted shank bone of lamb is placed on the plate as a reminder of the paschal sacrifice at the Temple. Some individuals refuse to eat lamb at the Seder until the Temple is rebuilt. There are no specific rules about what must be on the Seder menu, apart from the restrictions of Pesach itself. Each community has developed its own traditions. A Persian custom commemorating the beating of the slaves, involves hitting each other with spring onions (scallions). Four cups of wine must be poured during the Seder. A fifth is left for the prophet Elijah, the harbinger of the Messiah, who is said to visit every Jewish house on the night of the Seder, drinking from every cup.

SEFIRAH

Between Pesach and the next major festival, Shavuot, is a period called Sefirah. It is a solemn time of observance rather than a festival. Beginning at the end of Pesach, it commemorates the day when a sheaf of young barley – the Omer – was traditionally brought into the Temple in Jerusalem. Observing this period is called Counting the Omer. The solemnity of this period is thought to stem from an ancient superstition. Partial mourning was observed in the hope it would ensure a good harvest of grain.

During this time, the observant do not celebrate weddings, have other celebrations or even cut their hair.

Left When the Omer (a sheaf of young barley) was brought into the Temple in Jerusalem the day after Pesach ended, the period of Sefirah began.

Right Prayers for Shavuot include reading from the Book of Ruth.

LAG B'OMER

This happy day falls on the 33rd day of counting in the month of Lyar and is the one break in the solemn time of Sefirah. It is a day made for celebrating out of doors and picnicking. For observant Jews, Lag b'Omer is the day in spring when you could schedule a wedding or have a haircut.

TU B'SHEVAT

This festival is known as the Holiday of the Trees. It is one of the four holidays that celebrate nature, as mentioned in the Mishnah (part of the Talmud). Tu b'Shevat occurs in early February, when the sap begins to rise in the fruit trees of Israel. Tu b'Shevat is often celebrated by planting trees and collecting funds for reforestation. An old custom of holding Tu b'Shevat Seders has recently been revived. The meal progresses from fruits and nuts, through various juices, all symbolizing the awakening of nature after its slumber during winter.

The Tu b'Shevat Seder contains three different categories of fruits and nuts: hard, medium and soft, which are said to represent the different characteristics of the Jews. Certain fruits also have specific meanings. For example, pomegranates represent fertility, apples represent the splendour of God, almonds represent divine retribution (because the almond tree blossoms before other trees) and carob represents humility and penitence.

Enjoying a meal made up entirely of fruits and nuts, or simply adding fruits and nuts to a braided loaf of challah are all traditional ways of celebrating the festival of Tu b'Shevat.

SHAVUOT

The word 'shavuot' means weeks in Hebrew, as this festival comes seven weeks after Pesach. In English it is known as Pentecost, from the Greek for 50 days.

It is also sometimes referred to as the Festival of the Torah, because it tells the story of the Israelites wandering through the desert and commemorates the giving of the Jewish scriptures, the Torah, and the Ten Commandments to Moses on Mount Sinai. And it is the Feast of the First Fruits, when the first fruits and grains of the season were brought to Jerusalem as offerings.

Shavuot is celebrated for one day among Israeli and Reform (Progressive) Jews and for two days in other Jewish cultures throughout the world. As with Shabbat, the holiday begins at sundown the night before. The table is set with a fine, festive cloth, wine and challah, as well as fresh spring flowers.

Shavuot is also a time to enjoy meals based on dairy products, although there are no rules that say this must be done. The Book of Ruth is read on Shavuot and provides a dramatic story of a woman devoted to her adopted faith, choosing it over her own family upon the death of her husband.

Shavuot is one of the four times of the year that Yizkor, the memorial prayers in which the dead are respected, are recited.

THE SHABBAT

THE SABBATH OR SHABBAT IS A WEEKLY DAY OF REST FOR JEWS, HONOURING GOD'S DAY OF REST AFTER CREATION. SHABBAT IS OBSERVED FROM BEFORE SUNSET ON FRIDAY UNTIL NIGHTFALL ON SATURDAY.

The Jewish calendar is punctuated by holidays, festivals and observances, which are shared by the entire community. Personal milestones in the lives of individuals such as bar or bat mitzvahs, weddings and celebrations attending the birth of a baby are also celebrated. Each festival has a special significance, and is accompanied by its own songs, stories, admonitions, activities, food and prayers.

The most important festival and observance of them all is the Sabbath or Shabbat. This is celebrated every week, and forms a model for all the other holidays.

SHABBAT

This is the sabbath, the day of rest. It is arguably the pre-eminent Jewish holiday, and it comes not once a year, but once a week. It is the weekly island of peace amid the sea of hectic life. Shabbat is a day for refraining from work, escaping the chaos of the ordinary working week, focusing on the spiritual, appreciating nature and enjoying family life. Even those who are not observant in other ways will often enjoy keeping Shabbat. The word 'shabbat' means cessation of labour and it is treasured time to relax with the family.

The origins of Shabbat are related in Genesis, the first book of the Bible, which describes how God created the world in six days and rested on the seventh. In the fourth of the Ten Commandments, it is decreed that Shabbat is a day that must be kept holy (Exodus 31:17).

A set of rules has been laid down, encompassing what it means to keep Shabbat. Observant Jews do not do any work, handle money, carry loads, light fires, tear paper, watch television or listen to the radio. They also may not cook.

Above Shabbat begins with the blessings being said over a loaf of challah and a cup of wine.

The Festive Meal

On the eve of Shabbat a festive meal is served. It begins with the lighting and blessing of the candles before sundown. Further blessings are then said over the challah (braided bread), and the Kiddush (sanctifying blessing) is said over the wine.

The lighting of the candles marks the dividing line between the rest of the week and the start of Shabbat. When the candles are lit, traditionally by the woman of the household, she passes her hands lightly over the flame in a movement that seems to gather up the light, then she covers her eyes.

The greeting on Shabbat is 'Shabbat Shalom', often accompanied with a kiss on the cheek, as participants wish each other a Shabbat filled with peace.

Different families have different customs or rituals regarding the blessing of the challah loaf. It is traditional in a number of households for everyone to gather around the table, with their hands on the challah during the blessings, after

Left A Californian family praying before the Sabbath meal.

which they pull it apart, making sure that each person has a bite of the blessed bread.

A welcoming song might be sung, for example 'Shalom Aleichem', and/or 'Shabbat Shalom', a light and evocative melody that welcomes the holiday and puts everyone in a mellow mood.

The meal on Friday night often includes chicken soup. Guests will often be invited, and the table set with white linen, flowers and the finest china and cutlery. Meanwhile, the next day's meal will be simmered slowly in a low oven, as no cooking is allowed on the Shabbat itself. This is usually a dish of beans and meat taken from the Sephardi or Ashkenazi tradition.

MORNING SERVICES

Services of prayer and worship are held on Saturday mornings in the synagogue; this is also a popular time for bar and bat mitzvahs, for boys and girls respectively. If one of these ceremonies is taking place, then a light celebration meal will often be served at the synagogue for the whole congregation.

Shabbat is over when the first three stars are visible in the night sky. At this time Havdalah will be observed. The Havdalah ceremony comes from the word 'hevdal', which means different, to signify the difference or separation between Shabbat and the other days.

The ceremony consists of the blessing over the wine (the Kiddush), inhaling the fragrance of sweet spices and lighting a braided candle, which is then extinguished by a few drops of wine – and so the new week begins.

SHABBAT BLESSINGS

Candle Lighting
This signifies the start of Shabbat and a blessing is recited:

Baruch Ata Adonai Elohaynu Melech Ha'olam, asher Kid'shanu b'mitzvotav, v'tzivanu l'hadleek neir shel Shabbat.
Blessed are You, Lord our God, Eternal One, who lets us welcome Shabbat by kindling these lights.

If children are present, a blessing is said over them. The head of the household places his or her hands on the children and asks that they strive to carry on the traditions of the Jewish people and faith.

A plea is always offered for God's blessing, safety, warmth and protection, and peace.

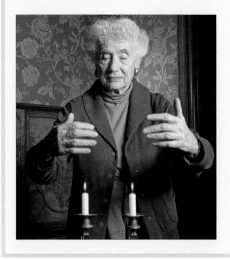

Friday Night Kiddush
Kiddush means 'sanctification'. The blessing that follows is said over the goblet of Kiddush wine.

Baruch Ata Adonai Elohaynu Melech Ha'olam, boray p'ree hagafen.
Blessed are You, Lord God, Eternal One, who creates the fruit of the vine.

Baruch Ata Adonai Elohaynu Melech Ha'olam, asher Kid'shanu b'mitzvotav, v'rahzah banu, v'Shabbat Kodsho b'ahavah oov'rahzon heen'heelanu, zeekahron l'maasay b'raysheet. Kee hoo yom t'heela l'meekrah-ay kodesh, zaycher l'tzeeat meetzraheem. Kee vanu vacharta ohtanu keedashta meekol ha'ahmeem v'Shabbat kodshecha b'ahavah oov'ratzon heenaltanu. Baruch Ata Adonai M'kadesh HaShabbat. Amen.
Blessed are You, Lord God, Eternal One, who sanctifies us with holy acts and gives us special times and seasons to rejoice. Shabbat reminds us of the times for celebration, recalls the days of Creation of the world and how God rested from that work. Shabbat commemorates the Exodus from Egyptian slavery. God has distinguished us from all people and given us the Shabbat full of joy and love. Blessed are You, Lord God, Eternal One, who sanctifies the Shabbat.

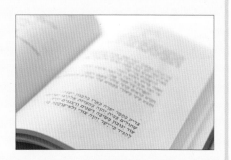

Saturday Midday Kiddush
This blessing is said over the wine to begin the Shabbat meal.

Al ken bayrah Adonai et Yom Hashabbat v'kodsho. Baruch Ata Adonai Elohaynu Melech Ha'olam, boray p'ree hagafen.
Behold, the Eternal blessed the seventh day and called it a holy time. Blessed are You, Lord God, Eternal One, who created fruit from the vine.

Blessing over the Challah
This blessing is said over bread: challah, rye bread, matzo etc.

Baruch Ata Adonai Elohaynu Melech Ha'olam, hamotzi lechem meen ha'aretz.
Blessed are You, Lord God, Eternal One, who creates bread from the earth.

The Birkat Hamazon is the grace said after a meal in which bread or matzo has been eaten.

LIFE EVENTS

CIRCUMCISION, COMING-OF-AGE CEREMONIES KNOWN AS BAR OR
BAT MITZVAHS, AND FUNERALS ARE AN INTEGRAL PART OF JEWISH LIFE
FROM THE CRADLE TO THE GRAVE.

From birth to death, Judaism offers ceremonies and observances to mark the rites of passage and key events in the lives of individuals, many of which take place in the synagogue. Each event is always accompanied by abundant festive food and drink.

BRIT MILAH
Male children are ritually circumcised on the eighth day after birth unless they have are at birth, ill or premature; if any of these occur, the circumcision will be delayed until the child is healthy and has achieved a specific weight so as not to endanger his health.

The ritual circumcision is called brit milah in Hebrew, bris in Yiddish. It is usually performed in the home by a community specialist called a mohel, although some Reform Jews

Below A 19th-century painting shows a rabbi tying the phylacteries to a boy's arm.

have the baby circumcised in hospital by a doctor. In a traditional ceremony, the baby is given no more than a few drops of wine as painkiller and the operation is swift. The baby scarcely gives more than a little cry, but the adults often need a bit more wine or something stronger to fortify themselves after the baby's ordeal.

After the ceremony, which includes blessings and prayers, there is a party, because this is a very happy occasion, when the newborn baby becomes part of the world's Jewish community. At the brit milah, the male child is given a Hebrew name. He is often named after a favourite relative; in Sephardic tradition it is a favourite living relative, in Ashkenazic tradition it is a revered deceased relative.

A girl child will usually be given her Hebrew name at the synagogue, at the age of about a month. In observant families, there is a ceremony for the first-born child –

Above Circumcision, from a 15th-century Jewish manuscript.

Pidyon ha Ben for a boy and Pidyon ha Bat for a girl. This means redemption of the first born and marks the start of the new family.

BAR OR BAT MITZVAH
The next milestone in the life-cycle is a child's bar or bat mitzvah. This coming-of-age ceremony marks the time when the child takes on the religious obligations of an adult.

Bar mitzvah – the ceremony for a boy – means the son of the commandment; bat mitzvah, the equivalent ceremony for girls, means daughter of the commandment. After bar or bat mitzvah the child may be counted as part of a minyan (quorum of ten people required to hold a religious service). In Orthodox communities, ten men are still required to make up a minyan, while in others, such as Reform (Progressive), it is simply ten people – either male or female.

A bar mitzvah ceremony takes place any time after the boy's 13th birthday, while a bat mitzvah takes place after the girl's 12th birthday.

MARRIAGE
Weddings have a special role in Jewish life. They are grand, festive and full of hope. The chatan (groom) and kallah

(bride) fast from dawn until after the ceremony. The chatan wears the traditional white robe that is also worn on Yom Kippur. They greet their guests separately, and in Ashkenazi families the mothers of the bride and groom smash a plate, to show that no broken relationship can ever be fully mended. The ceremony takes place under a huppah, a canopy with open sides, symbolically open to friends and family. The marriage is official once the chatan has given an object of value, traditionally a ring) to the kallah. After the reading and signing of the contract, and recital of seven blessings, a glass is broken to remind the couple of their sadness, even on a day of joy, at the destruction of the Second Temple in Jerusalem. There follows a feast and party with foods such as smoked salmon, chopped liver, herring and rye breads, and lots of dancing of the hora.

BEREAVEMENT

Even at the end of life, food plays an important role for Jews. The period of mourning is known as Shiva. Each night during the period of mourning there is a gathering for the purpose of prayer, a minyan. Members of the community bring prepared foods with them when they come to offer support and comfort. Usually these will be traditional, homely foods that warm the soul and are easily digested, for grief is hard on the body. Food, and the act of giving food, sustains the mourners through their ordeal, for even when there is no strength for the task it is still necessary to eat to survive. The preparing, bringing and eating of food is all about survival.

The dead may not be cremated, as this speeds the natural disposal of the body, or embalmed, as this preserves it artificially. They must be

Right: A Jewish couple marry under the huppah (canopy with open sides) at a wedding in Israel.

FEATURES OF SYNAGOGUE LAYOUT

The synagogue's basic structure is quite simple: a rectangular room, an ark to contain the Torah scrolls (*aron ha-kodesh* or *heikhal*) and a platform from where the Torah is read, called *bimah* by Ashkenazim, *almemar* (after the Arabic *al-minbar*) by central European Jews, and *teba* by Sephardim. Customarily, synagogues allow worshippers to pray in the direction of Jerusalem. Orthodox synagogues segregate male and female worshippers, either by a *me chitza*, or 'low barrier', or a women's gallery overlooking the men.

Reform temples and 19th-century Orthodox United Synagogue buildings in Britain copied Protestant custom by placing pulpits at the front of the congregation to impose decorum. Stained-glass windows are another Christian trait. They illustrate months, zodiac signs or the 12 tribes of Israel, the most dazzling examples being Marc Chagall's windows at the Abell Synagogue in Jerusalem.

Some synagogues in Morocco and Italy deliberately introduce errors, either by misspelling a word in a Hebrew inscription or inserting a false beam, thus acknowledging that only God is perfect.

Today the world's largest synagogues belong to the Ger and Belz Hassidim in Jerusalem, seating 8,500 and 6,000 respectively. Their lavish arks and crystal chandeliers testify to renewed Orthodox vigour. However, the essence of Judaism resides in people meeting, praying and debating, as they have done for 4,000 years. Most Hassidim prefer to pray in humble *shtieblach*, or 'backrooms' given over to daily services.

---

buried in a simple wooden casket, and all Jews should be buried wearing a simple white shroud, as a symbol their earthly wealth is unimportant and all are equal in death.

Flowers are seen as a Christian tradition and not encouraged. At the funeral, seven relatives over the age of 13 each tear an outer garment to symbolize their loss.

מכתב מיראד
ויומרו
הרטשיב אל פרעה ויבא
אליה הוא ויעל הם מהו
אויחא ישרא אתהריה
מדילה אשר עשת
במניהם ויריא העם אתה ויאמינו ומשה
עבדו

CHAPTER 1

ORIGINS OF A PEOPLE, BIRTH OF A FAITH

Are the Jews a people, a race, a nation or a religion? Their early story is encapsulated in the Hebrew Bible, arguably the Jews' greatest gift to civilization. Biblical ideas spawned three faiths, Judaism, Christianity and Islam. In the biblical account, miraculous rebirths followed near extinctions, a cycle that has typified Jewish history to the present day.

Jews trace their origins to ancient Hebrews who emerged in the Middle East some 4,000 years ago. Traditionally, they were descended from Abraham, who followed God's command to leave his native Iraq and settle in Canaan. For four centuries they lived as slaves in Egypt until Moses led the Jews to the 'promised land'. After rule by judges, the Jewish tribes united under kings Saul, David and Solomon, but soon divided into the rival kingdoms of Israel and Judah. Eventually the Assyrians broke Israel around 722BCE.

Opposite Moses leads the Children of Israel across the Red Sea.
From the manuscript of a Jewish prayer book from Hamburg, 1427.

Above Abraham Sacrifices Isaac, *Persian School, 18th century. The Torah tells how Abraham proved his faith by his willingness to sacrifice his son, and how God showed mercy in return.*

25

INTRODUCTION TO THE PATRIARCHS

JUDAISM, CHRISTIANITY AND ISLAM ARE THE SISTER FAITHS OF 'ETHICAL MONOTHEISM' (BELIEF IN ONE GOD), WHOSE FOUNDING FATHER, ABRAHAM, MAY HAVE LIVED AROUND 2000-1700BCE.

The history of the Jewish people begins with the tale of Abraham's family. They became a clan, which grew into a tribe and then set down roots to become a nation. Over time this nation spawned world religions and sacred texts that together make up the most widely read tome in history. The Torah (Old Testament) inspires 14 million Jews, 2 billion Christians and, through the retelling of its tales in the Koran, has reached 1.5 billion Muslims.

ABRAHAM'S VISION

As the Jews were the first to speak of Abraham, he has a special significance for them. In Hebrew he will always be *Avraham Avinu*, 'Our father

Below The wanderings of Abraham from the ancient city of Ur through Harran and Damascus to Hebron.

Abraham'. Abram, relates the Torah, was a descendant of Noah's son Shem. According to Genesis, Abram and his father left Ur, a town near the Persian Gulf in present-day Iraq, for Harran, 1,600km (1,000 miles) to the east. There Abram had a vision of God, who demanded that Abram and his clan should worship Him alone.

Abram and his wife Sarai took new names – Abraham, 'father of many', and Sarah, 'princess'. In return, God was to lead them to a 'promised land' in Canaan. In the Torah, this was *Eretz Yisrael*, 'the Land of Israel'. The Hebrews (later called Israelites, then Jews) deemed themselves specially chosen to spread the word of God's unity to the world as a 'light unto the nations'. If the Jewish people disobeyed their faith, God would see them punished by disaster or enemy–nation attacks.

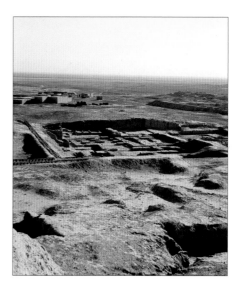

Above View of the ruins of Ur in southern Mesopotamia, where Abraham lived before his family departed for Harran.

TO THE PROMISED LAND

Departing from Harran (in today's south-east Turkey), Abraham and his band travelled south across the Euphrates River. This may explain the name 'Hebrew', meaning 'from the other side'. They then passed through the ancient cities of Damascus in Syria and Hazor in Canaan (a land also later historically known as Palestine). At Shechem Abraham built a small altar and he eventually bought land in Hebron. It was a burial plot, signalling that this was to be his resting place and the heritage of his descendants.

Neither Abraham nor, later, his son Isaac came close to conquering Canaan. Many other nations already lived there. Apart from Canaanites, there were Hittites and Phoenicians to the north, Moabites to the west (in today's Jordan), Midianites in the south (Negev and Sinai) and smaller groups in the central plain. Canaan also hosted wanderers, including the Semitic Amurru (Amorites or 'westerners'). Occasionally erupting into Palestine were the two major powers of the ancient Middle East: Egypt and Mesopotamia. Ultimately, says the Torah, the Jewish people were to

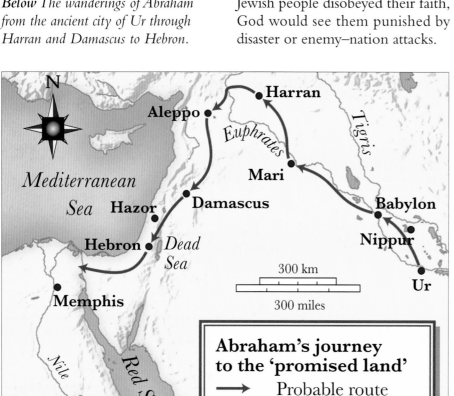

Abraham's journey to the 'promised land'
→ Probable route

Above 6th-century mosaic of the Sacrifice of Isaac from the Beit Alfa synagogue, Heftziba, Israel.

forge their identity in exile in Egypt, and it took another 400 years before Moses led them back to Canaan.

THE SONS OF ABRAHAM

Abraham had two sons: first Ishmael, by Sarah's handmaid, Hagar, and then Isaac, by Sarah. Sarah made Abraham banish Ishmael and Hagar to the desert, but God protected Ishmael, who eventually founded a major branch of the Arab nation. Isaac, meanwhile, continued the Jewish line. Some trace the rivalry between Jews and Arabs to these figures.

In Genesis, the ancestors of the Jews emerge as semi-nomadic rural wanderers. Abraham's existence cannot be verified outside the Torah, and some regard him as legendary. Even so, he appears a credible 'type' of the age – a tribal patriarch and charismatic trader and diplomat who galvanized his followers into a distinct people.

While Abraham's band was weak compared to the powers of Egypt or Mesopotamia, he was probably not a poor wastrel. In the book of Genesis, for example, he musters a fighting force of more than 300. He was evidently a born leader, who commanded great respect.

Primarily, Abraham is portrayed as a man of faith, who uniquely rejected the worship of idols. He had to make hard decisions: travelling into unknown country, circumcising himself and his sons as a sign of the 'covenant' (promise of obligation between his people and God), and finally obeying God's demand to sacrifice his son Isaac. The binding of Isaac on Mt Horeb forms one of the Torah's abiding motifs. Abraham passes the test of faith by showing his willingness to obey God, while God shows mercy by placing a goat in a thicket as a substitute sacrifice.

JACOB'S SONS OF ISRAEL

'Hebrews' came to form a people with a single language, culture, religion, and sense of historical mission. Yet 'Israel' is the name early Jews preferred. It is bound up with Jacob, the third patriarch. Abraham's son Isaac married Rebecca, and they had twin boys, Jacob and Esau. Jacob duped Esau into surrendering his birthright. Thus Jewish lineage passed through Jacob, while the furious Esau went on to found the Edomites. Poetic or Divine justice was at work, however: for seven years Jacob worked for his uncle without pay, only to be married to the wrong sister – Leah instead of Rachel.

In a dream, Jacob wrestled with an angel, who turned out to be a personification of God and gave Jacob the new name Israel, translated as 'He who contends with God'. Jacob had 12 sons and one daughter by his wives and concubines. His descendants duly adopted the name *Bnei Yisrael*, 'Sons of Israel', or Israelites.

Below Jacob and Esau by a follower of Caravaggio, c.1625. Esau sells his birthright for a dish of lentils.

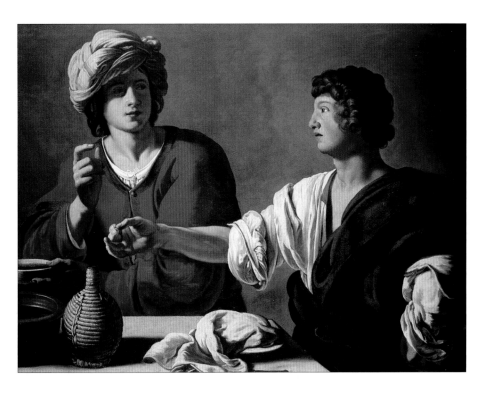

CANAAN AND THE BIRTH OF A CIVILIZATION

CANAAN LAY AT THE CROSSROADS OF CIVILIZATIONS, CONNECTING THREE CONTINENTS. IF MANKIND ORIGINATED IN AFRICA, AS IS NOW BELIEVED, THE ANCESTORS OF ALL ASIANS AND EUROPEANS MUST HAVE CROSSED THIS LAND.

Precious goods travelled north and south along the King's Highway: from Egypt across the Sinai, through Jordan into Syria and ending at the Euphrates River, the southern border of Mesopotamia. Another route moved east to west, from Arabia to Petra in Jordan, or from India by ship through the Red Sea to the Gulf of Aqaba. Traders then moved on to Beersheva, today in southern Israel, eventually arriving at Gaza, from where they shipped their silks and spices across the Mediterranean Sea.

Canaan was thus a crucial thoroughfare. Its location drew the attention of great empires. Some of the fiercest battles of ancient history took place on or near its soil – including the clash between Egypt's Ramses II (1304–1237BCE) and the Hittites of Anatolia, fought in Kadesh, southern Syria, in 1274BCE.

Naturally this interest made Canaan as much a curse as a blessing to the smaller peoples who lived there! Among those peoples were the ancestors of the Jews.

Below A limestone statue of the Ur goddess Narundi, made c.2100BCE – perhaps one of the gods that Jewish legend says young Abraham destroyed in his father's idol-selling shop.

MYSTERIES OF JEWISH ORIGIN
Material evidence of the first Israelites is scant. The first extra-biblical reference to 'Israel' comes in the Victory Stele obelisk inscribed in the name of the Egyptian king Merneptah (ruled c.1204BCE). Mostly we know of the Israelites through the Bible/Torah, which as a historical reference is potentially flawed.

The existence of the Canaanites of Palestine can be verified, as can the Moabites, Amorites and Edomites to their east, and a kingdom of Aram to the north, of which the Bible/Torah speaks. As early as 2350BCE, inscribed tablets from Ebla in northern Syria refer to Canaanites. The Babylonian Mari letters (18th century BCE) and Egyptian Amarna letters (14th century BCE) both refer to wanderers called *Habiru* or *Apiru*, quite possibly the same as 'Hebrew'.

Above A 4th-century BCE bronze plaque shows the Phoenician alphabet, from which early Hebrew was derived.

Archaeological evidence shows that indigenous Canaanites had a basic yet sturdy material culture, and the Victory Stele speaks of the Canaanite city-states Gezer, Ashkelon and Yanoam. Yet it only refers to Israel as a people, not a place, which may confirm the biblical version of the patriarchs as being essentially semi-nomadic.

One theory says that the Israelites were a blend of Canaanites and Habiru, or Shasu Bedouin marauders, who later claimed descent from Ur (Abraham's place of origin). Over time it seems they acquired the trappings of civilization, including a sophisticated native tongue. Hebrew belonged to the same Semitic linguistic family as Canaanite, Phoenician and Punic, yet only Hebrew survives. Canaanites also developed the world's first consonantal alphabet in the 18th and 17th centuries BCE. Spread by the Phoenicians through trade, this alphabet formed the template for the Hebrew lettering system, and later for Greek, Latin and Arabic as well.

All strata of Israelite society seem to have been literate, which may explain their remarkable endurance. For while Israelites left few impressive edifices, their literacy encouraged story-telling and debate, trade and communication, and an intricate system of law, taboos and ethical codes, which are characteristic of Jewish civilization to this day.

EARLY SUPERPOWERS

Abraham, Isaac and Jacob were small players politically, who variously fought against or allied themselves with nearby tribes. Their neighbours were in turn dwarfed by stronger forces. For most of the 2nd millennium BCE, Canaan was a province of one or other of the great powers of the day: Egypt to the south, or Babylon and Mesopotamia to the north. Both were phenomenally well-organized river-fed civilizations that towered over potential rivals. They boasted

Below The Middle East, c.1500BCE, showing the extent of the empire of Hammurabi, the sixth Babylonian king.

advanced systems of governance, employed the latest military technology, traded far and wide and controlled vassal states beyond their borders. No one could escape their influence, either materially, in terms of art and architecture, or spiritually.

Mesopotamian legends and social norms clearly coloured early Jewish customs. For example, the Great Flood story appears in many traditions and probably recalls an actual event. Also, the Jews' covenantal relationship with God resembles in structure Mesopotamian legal contracts, such as Ur-Nammu's constitution or the code of Hammurabi (*c.*1792–1750BCE), except the Torah says that man was created in God's image, so human life has special value.

SMASHING IDOLS

While the people of Ur worshipped images of as many as 3,000 deities, the Hebrew patriarchs rejected the idolatry that had formerly been part of their culture. Abraham's father, Terah, sold idols for a living, states the Bible. One Jewish fable, repeated in the Koran, tells how Abraham precociously destroyed his father's wares. Child sacrifice was another

Above A terracotta carving depicting the idol goddess Astarte or Ishtar from Ur, 2100BCE.

typically Canaanite custom that the Torah expressly forbids. The scriptures state: 'I give before you life and death: therefore choose life'. Certainly the patriarch's beliefs were revolutionary in their day.

In Canaan the patriarchs built altars in harsh central hill country, such as Bethel and Shechem, situated on a backbone of mountains running from north to south. To their west was the more fertile coastal area, dominated by Canaanites, later by Philistines; to their east, the Jordan River valley, and beyond, desert. Yet before a genuine new faith and nation could be established, the Israelites had to move once more – this time from Canaan to the well-watered pastures of Egypt.

Major centres of the Middle East, *c.*1500BCE
Hammurabi's Babylonian Empire 1792BC–1750BC

THE ISRAELITES MOVE INTO EGYPT

THE RIVER NILE'S BANKS TRACE A GREEN STRIP OF FERTILE LAND THAT 7,000 YEARS AGO HELPED CREATE THE LONGEST-LASTING AND AT TIMES MOST POWERFUL CIVILIZATION OUTSIDE ASIA – EGYPT.

Pharaoh Djoser (*c.*2650–2575BCE) built the first pyramid, a step-like structure at Saqqara, as long ago as 2650BCE. He launched the so-called Old Kingdom, centred on Memphis, which succumbed to anarchy around 2180BCE. For nearly 200 years Egypt was split into two kingdoms – Upper and Lower, or southern and northern – until it was reunited as the Middle Kingdom around 2000 BCE and ruled from Thebes.

Reinvigorated, successive dynasties of pharaohs spread their influence northwards to the still embryonic civilizations of the Greek lands and through the Sinai to Palestine, or Canaan, and Syria. Egyptians never settled in these lands in large numbers. Yet their officials built

Below A 19th-dynasty Egyptian sculpture of Pharaoh Ramses II between god Amun and goddess Mut.

palaces and outposts at places including Beit She'an and Megiddo in ancient Palestine. Egypt was determined to keep trade routes open and hold sway politically. Often this proved a daunting task, given the patchwork nature of Canaan's ethnic divisions, and threats from encroaching northerners.

After 1800BCE, an economic boom in Egypt drew in thousands of foreign sojourners, including Palestinians. They paid taxes and enjoyed certain privileges, but they were never naturalized. Many formed their own distinct communities and had their own kings. Increasingly, as recently discovered papyri show, Egyptian governors must have been drawn from these communities, as they bore foreign and often Semitic names (Semites were the descendants of Shem, the eldest son of Noah).

Above Hebrew slaves building cities for the Egyptian Pharaoh, from the 14th-century Barcelona Haggadah.

HEBREWS IN EGYPT

During the years 1700–1550BCE, one group, known as the Shepherd Kings, or Hyksos, appears to have ousted the indigenous rulers altogether. Exactly who the Shepherd Kings were remains a mystery; some say Semites, others say Indo-Europeans from Anatolia (modern Turkey). Many historians, going back to the Egyptian historian Manetho

WHAT IS IN A NAME?

When Orthodox Jews want to thank God they say *Baruch Hashem*, 'blessed is the name'. But what is the name of God? Until Moses appears in the Book of Exodus, the Bible uses a plethora of names to denote the One God. Mostly we find the name *El*, which was originally a deity worshipped in Canaan, and which finds later resonance in the Arabic word for God, Allah. Often El is qualified: like '*El-Elyon*', God on High; or '*Elohim*', literally 'gods' (possibly an afterglow of polytheism). Another name used in early passages is '*Shaddai*', God of the Hills, or, in another interpretation, the suckling breasts. There is also '*Melekh ha-Olam*', king of the world; '*Ha-Rachamim*', the merciful one; and a female name for God: '*Shekhina*', denoting the indwelling spirit of the creator. Torah redactors apparently reconfigured names of pagan gods other than El: for instance Adonis, or Adon, from Lebanon, becomes '*Adonai*', Lord. The one name that cannot be said aloud – the true name of God as revealed to Moses – is approximated by the letters YHWH, and rendered in English as Jahweh or Jehovah. Jews pray daily for the world to recognize 'God as one, and his name as one.'

(2nd century BCE), deduce that they must have been Hebrews. According to the biblical account, Joseph's envious brothers sold him into Egyptian slavery, but he exploited his gift as a dream-interpreter to become a vizier in the pharaoh's court. Joseph eventually got his revenge on his siblings by terrifying them in his guise as an Egyptian potentate; but then relented and granted them and their father, Jacob, a new home in Egypt.

Egypt was the nearest metropolis to Canaan, so assuming that drought did strike – as happens in the water-starved Middle East – the story makes eminent sense. But could it be, ask scholars, that Joseph symbolizes a historical process: the temporary usurpation of Egyptian government by foreigners? Likewise the later enslavement of the Hebrews and their subsequent departure under Moses has been read as mirroring the toppling of the Hyksos monarchs by a resurgent New Kingdom. Under pharaohs such as Tutenkhamen and Thutmose

Below Prisoners of Ramses III, 1187–1156BCE, who used slaves to rebuild Karnak and Luxor.

Above Joseph interpreted Pharaoh's dreams and became a vizier in his court. From a painting by Raphael, c.1515.

III, the Egyptian empire expanded south into Nubia and fought the Hittites in Syria.

Egyptian records never refer to Hebrews along the Nile. Even the Bible falls silent about the 400 years between Joseph and Moses. Yet that does not disprove their presence. The proto-Israelites may have been one of the many foreign communities living in Egypt around this time, even if the bulk of the Israelites (as some scholars believe) never left Canaan. Furthermore, Egyptian culture had an impact on the Israelites: for instance, some see ties between the Instructions of Amenemopet of 1200BCE Egypt and the later biblical work the Book of Proverbs.

It is known that the Egyptian king Seti I (1290–79BCE) moved his capital to Avaris at the north of the Nile Delta, where he built huge garrisons. Naturally, building a new capital required significant labour. So while there is no specific mention of Jewish slaves in Egyptian texts, Seti may well have enslaved Hyksos and Jewish and other Semites and forced them to build barricades against any

attack from the East. Later, Ramses III (r.1186–1155BCE) used slaves to rebuild Karnak and Luxor, and experienced the first recorded labour strike in history.

EGYPTIAN INFLUENCE

Some scholars believe a theological revolution in Egypt influenced the Jewish faith. Amenhotep IV (1353–1336BCE) suddenly outlawed polytheism and insisted on praying to a single deity, Akhen. He even renamed himself Akhenaton. Might this ruler have re-inspired the monotheism of his Hebrew subjects? It remains a theory. What is undeniable is that after Akhenaton's death, Egyptians reverted to worshipping Ra, Isis, Osiris, Ptah, Bes, Toth and other nature- or animal-based gods. And the Egyptians continued to deify their pharaohs, one of whom, says the Bible, so feared the growth of the Hebrew people that he tried to eliminate them entirely.

MOSES

UNTIL MOSES' DAY, A FEW SIMPLE BELIEFS AND PRACTICES DEFINED THE NOMADIC HEBREW CLANS. BUT AFTER MOSES RECEIVED THE HOLY LAW AT MOUNT SINAI, JUDAISM EMBARKED ON ITS PATH TO BECOME A WORLD FAITH.

According to the biblical account, Moses was formidable: a national leader, sage, social engineer and dreamer, a practical teacher, a compassionate man of principle, a radical and sometimes a despot. He led the Israelites' Exodus from Egypt, which experience, at once political and religious, became the prototype for all future redemption. Moses was also the first Hebrew to make an impact on the ancient world. Greeks conflated him with their own gods and heroes.

MOSES IN THE TORAH

The only first-hand source we have for Moses' life is the Torah (the first five books of the Old Testament to Christians). There is no explicit mention of the Exodus in Egyptian texts, yet Moses' centrality to Judaism is undeniable. Strictly speaking, the Torah denotes the Five Books of

Below This 6th-century CE mosaic of the crossing of the Red Sea is at Dura-Europos synagogue, Syria.

Moses, or the Pentateuch. Four of them – Exodus, Leviticus, Numbers and Deuteronomy – concern Moses and the Israelites' 40 years in the Sinai desert. The Hebrew for Exodus is *Bamidbar*, 'in the Desert', where Jewish lore says God fed the Israelites manna from heaven.

Moses apparently enjoyed a rapport with God, and he presided over numerous miracles, yet he was never deified, nor were his flaws hidden: his humanity, including his fiery temper, are well-recorded.

ORIGINS IN EGYPT

The name Moses may be Egyptian in origin. To summarize the biblical account, Moses was born the son of Amram, a Levite, and his wife Jochebed. Hebrews had lived for nearly 400 years in relative harmony with Egyptians in the Land of Goshen, in the eastern part of the Nile Delta. When a new Pharaoh came to power, and ordered all newborn Hebrew boys killed, Moses' sister Miriam hid

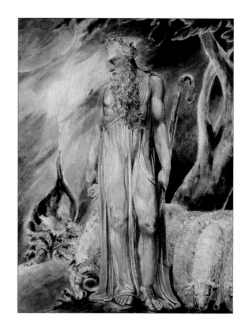

Above Moses heard the voice of God in a burning bush, as in this painting by William Blake (1757–1827).

the baby in bulrushes, until Pharaoh's daughter, Thermuthis, discovered him there. The princess named the baby and took him back to the royal court. There he was raised as a prince, and nursed by his real mother, Jochebed, at the entreaty of Miriam. Meanwhile, Pharaoh forced the Hebrews into slavery. The ruler is unnamed in the Bible, but he may be Ramses II (r. 1279–1213BCE), who launched huge building projects.

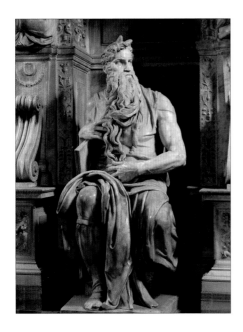

Above *Freud believed Michelangelo's* Moses *showed him about to break the tablets of the Ten Commandments.*

One day Moses killed a taskmaster who was beating a Hebrew slave. Fearing punishment, he fled to Ethiopia, where he became a military leader. Later he moved to the Jordanian desert and worked as a shepherd for Jethro, high priest of the Midianites. In time Moses married Jethro's daughter, Zipporah, and they had a son, Gershom.

MOSES AS A LEADER

Forty years later, relates Exodus, Moses encountered a bizarre sight while tending his flocks near Mount Horeb. He saw a bush that burned yet was not consumed, and from the bush came a divine voice: 'I appeared to Abraham, to Isaac and to Jacob as El Shaddai (God Almighty) but by my name YHWH I did not make myself known to them.' (Exodus 6:3). The use of this previously unutterable name – Yahweh or Jehovah – signals a new stage in the maturation of Judaism.

Chosen to redeem the 'lost sheep of Israel', says Exodus, Moses returned to Egypt and instigated a slave revolt, possibly the first in history. Pharaoh was punished by ten

plagues and eventually allowed the Hebrews to leave. They numbered some 600,000 and they crossed the Reed Sea (incorrectly known as the Red Sea) for the Sinai Peninsula, led by miraculous pillars of fire and smoke. Exodus calls the liberated flock an *erev rav*, mixed multitude, so perhaps slaves of other nationalities joined the Hebrew revolt and left Egypt with them.

THE TEN COMMANDMENTS

Just weeks later, dissatisfied Hebrews began demanding to return to the 'fleshpots of Egypt'. Worse followed when they began worshipping a golden calf idol. Moses brought the Hebrews to Mt Sinai, where he received the Ten Commandments and the oral law from God, says the Bible. This covenant reaffirmed the earlier vows that God had made with Abraham and Jacob. All the myriad laws that govern Orthodox Jewish life stem from the laws derived from the Torah.

Later rabbis identified 613 '*mitzvot*', or commandments: 248 positive ones, and 365 prohibitions, covering almost all human actions, from eating and drinking to hygiene, belief, sex, trade, ethics and keeping the Sabbath holy.

THE SPIES

After less than a year in the desert the Israelites approached the perimeter of the 'land of milk and honey'. Moses sent 12 spies into the territory, one from each tribe. Most reported back that Canaan's cities were heavily fortified and its countryside populated by giants and ghouls. Only Joshua of Ephraim and Caleb of Judah said it was safe to invade. The Israelites were obliged to wander in the desert for 40 years until a new generation was ready to attack Canaan.

FROM MOSES TO JOSHUA

According to Deuteronomy, Moses sent diplomats to the kings of Moab and Edom, south and east of the Dead Sea, who allowed him free passage through their territory. The Pentateuch closes with the poignant image of Moses surveying Israel from Mount Nevo, but denied entry for his failings. So he passed on the mantle to Joshua, son of Nun, his former camp guard. More than a military leader, Joshua now had prophetic powers because of Moses' blessing – but could he hold the tribes together?

Below *The Sinai Desert in Egypt, home to Mount Sinai, the site where Moses received the commandments.*

RETURN TO CANAAN

THE DRAMATIC FALL OF JERICHO, THE OLDEST WALLED CITY IN HISTORY, REPRESENTED THE ISRAELITES' FIRST BREACH INTO CANAAN, BUT THE FULL CONQUEST MAY HAVE TAKEN YEARS, EVEN DECADES, TO ACHIEVE.

Above Dante's Vision of Rachel and Leah, *Rossetti 1855. The Italian poet saw the sisters as symbolizing contemplation and action respectively.*

The Book of Joshua tells how the invaders, led by Joshua and Caleb, crossed the River Jordan, encircled the fortified town, blew their trumpets and brought the walls tumbling down on the seventh day.

ISRAELITE INVASION – TRUTH OR FICTION?

So goes the biblical story, but did the siege really happen this way? Archaeological evidence suggests that Jericho's walls had fallen long before the Israelites arrived. Some scholars question whether a military conquest took place at all, and believe that Israelites infiltrated Canaan over two centuries. Biblical accounts of the conquest, from the books of Numbers, Joshua and Judges, show discrepancies.

Left Map of Joshua's conquest of Canaan, showing the route taken by his army as they moved north.

Yet the biblical portrait might have some merit. Excavations show that the Canaanite cities of Lachish, Kiryat-Sepher and Eglon in the south, Bethel in the centre and Hazor, a town of 50,000 citizens in the far north, were all destroyed in the late 13th century BCE. Other evidence confirms that occupation of the hill country took place from east to west, which tallies with the biblical version.

The shrine of Shechem, where Abraham was promised Canaan a millennium earlier, showed no sign of destruction. The Book of Joshua confirms that Israelites were not hindered there. Piecing together evidence from archaeology, biblical sources and the geopolitics of the time, the following reconstruction of events seems possible.

Israelites emerged from the Sinai into Transjordan and prepared to enter Canaan from the east. They were lightly armed and weary after their 40 years in the desert. An assault on Canaan's well-defended cities seemed set to fail. Moreover, the Canaanites had field armies, so conventional battle-field engagements were best avoided.

However, the Israelites used stealth. They took Bethel, Ai and Gibeah by means of feigned retreats and posted spies in Jericho before the siege. Often the Israelites used diplomacy to exploit divisions among Canaan's diverse peoples. For instance, they formed a treaty with the Hivites of Gibeon and neighbouring cities, and helped defend them when four Canaanite city-states attacked.

WAVES OF ATTACK

The Israelites advanced in two broad waves. The first consisted of the Rachel tribes (Rachel was Jacob's chief wife), headed by Ephraim and Manasseh of the house of Joseph. They advanced through the Transjordanian kingdoms of Moab and Edom. After fording the River Jordan and taking Jericho, they climbed the mountain range and, once over Mt Ephraim, they fanned out in different directions.

Perhaps a generation later came the second wave; the Leah (Jacob's second wife) tribes led by Judah. After defeating the Amorites, they entered Canaan north of Jericho and moved towards the Judean Hills and the Shefelah Plain nearer the coast. Meanwhile, non-Israelite clans related to Judah, the Calebites, Kenites and Kenizzites, helped them seize Hebron and the Negev Desert.

The Book of Joshua says that the Israelites destroyed 12 fortress towns, but admits that subjugation was far from total. After the initial victories the Israelites suffered reverses, and were forced out of the coastal plains and on to barren hill country.

Right A 14th-century French illumination by Guiart Desmoulins, showing the 12 tribes of Israel.

MULTI-ETHNIC CANAAN

The Israelites lived cheek by jowl with other peoples in Canaan. On the northern borders were Phoenicians; to the east, Arabs and other Semitic nomads, such as the Ammonites. Around 1175BCE a new group arrived to upset Canaan's already fragile ethnic balance. These were the Philistines, an advanced race who settled along the southern coast of Canaan.

TRIBAL DEMARCATIONS

Temporarily weakened by internal strife, and disturbed by a spate of earthquakes, Egypt began withdrawing from Canaan around 1150BCE. Each Israelite tribe was allocated an area to settle. Reuben, Gad and Manasseh chose to remain east of the River Jordan. In Canaan proper, four tribes were located north of Shechem: Asher by the coast, Naphtali stretching towards Mt Lebanon, Issachar between Mt Tabor and Mt Gilboa, and Zebulon just east of Mt Carmel. The five remaining tribes all settled south of Shechem. These were Ephraim in the centre, Dan nearer the coast, Benjamin near the northern shore of the Dead Sea, Judah in an arc

around Hebron, and Simeon to the south west of the Dead Sea. Members of the priestly Levite caste were not allocated any territory of their own, and instead lived amid all the tribes.

LIFE IN THE PROMISED LAND

The books of Joshua and Judges vividly describe a poor, agrarian, clan-based and egalitarian society, which Late Bronze Age archaeological findings confirm. The Israelites settled on a loosely republican system of government, called the *edah*, congregation or assembly. Its basis was theocracy – politics governed by a religion. Tribal borders shifted over time, depending on battles against or agreements with neighbours. Internal frontier disputes were rare, but the Book of Joshua hints at a growing cultural schism between north and south.

Left This section of a 5th-century CE mosaic map from Madaba, Jordan, shows the city of Jericho and the River Jordan near the Dead Sea.

THE AGE OF JUDGES

BETWEEN THE RE-ENTRY OF ISRAELITES INTO CANAAN AND THE START OF
MONARCHY SOME 200 YEARS LATER, A NEW TYPE OF RULER EMERGED, CALLED
THE *SHOFTIM*, OR JUDGES — CHARISMATIC LEADERS FOR PERILOUS TIMES.

Sometimes the Book of Judges hints at a truly national leader. Mostly, though, *shoftim* were local figures, imbued with great charisma. Some came with a pedigree, such as Othniel. As the nephew of Joshua's chief spy, Caleb, he represented continuity from one era to the next. The majority, however, had lowly, even semi-criminal backgrounds.

The Israelites were a Bronze Age people adapting to the new Iron Age, bound together by common ethnicity and beliefs, yet overall remarkably decentralized. The Ark of the Covenant was based at Shiloh in central Palestine, and Israelites held occasional pan-tribal assemblies there, but it was not their capital.

Perhaps one reason for the looseness of the tribal confederation is that Canaan, or historic Palestine, is an amazingly varied locale. The very nature of their environment exacerbated tribal divisions. No one tribe dominated, and even the smallest contributed leaders.

ETHNIC DIVERSITY

Unlike the Book of Joshua, which says all foes were vanquished, Judges presents a more confusing, though probably more realistic, picture. Canaan appears as a multi-ethnic patchwork quilt in which Israelites are one people among many. The Book of Judges 3:5 states: 'The children of Israel dwelt among the Canaanites, the Hittites, the Amorites, the Perrizites, the Hivites, and the Jebusites.'

The stories in Judges share a familiar pattern: every time a judge died the people backslid into bad ways, shirking the one God and worshipping alien deities, especially the Canaanite Baal and his female consort Asherah.

DEBORAH

The only female judge was Deborah, a prophetess who led the Israelites during one of their darkest hours. For 20 years Canaanites under King Javin of Hazor had

Above The Israelite judge Deborah (1209–1169BCE) invokes her people to battle in this painting by Salomon de Bray, 1635.

oppressed her people. Their commander, Sisera, mustered 900 chariots and stood poised to crush the Israelites. Just when all seemed lost, says the Bible, Deborah received a visitation from God promising victory. On hearing the news, the Israelite general, Barak, of the tribe of Naphtali, insisted that she accompany him into battle. The laws of warfare forbade women from participating in war, so Barak's decision showed how exceptional Deborah's personality was.

Spying the Canaanites near the Kishon River, Barak's small force attacked from Mount Tabor, 17 kilometres west of the Sea of Galilee. They then destroyed the enemy by taking advantage of a rainstorm, which caused Sisera's chariots to sink in the mud.

Deborah's song of praises to the Lord is in the Book of Judges, chapter five, and is thought to be one of the most ancient passages in the Bible.

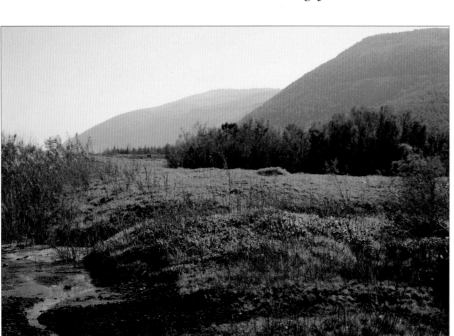

Left The Plain of Jezreel was the site of many battles, including those of Deborah and Gideon. Saul and his sons died here fighting the Philistines.

Above A bronze and gold statuette of a Canaanite god, probably Baal, dated 1400–1200BCE.

GIDEON AND SAMSON

Deborah was succeeded by the particularly martial Gideon, who 'threshed wheat by the winepress' yet grew into a 'mighty man of valour'. Aided by a cohort of just 300 men, he defended the Israelites from two fearsome besieging groups: camel-borne Midianites from the southern Jordanian desert, allies in Moses' day, turned bitter foes; and Amalekites, distant relatives of the Israelites. When Gideon beat them, the Israelites implored him to be their king. He refused, insisting that 'only the Lord will rule over you'. This was just as well, as his son and would-be successor, Abimelech,

Right Samson, probably the most famous and flawed of the judges, fighting a lion, in this image from a Hebrew Bible and prayer book.

turned into a monster who butchered 70 of his brothers and half-brothers.

Most famous of the judges, and probably the most flawed, was Samson. He was a member of the Nazirite sect, puritans who avoided drink and frivolities, and who probably influenced later Jewish strains, like the Essenes, Zealots and Rechabites. Much about the Samson story is mythical, like his superhuman strength derived from his long hair. His tale evokes the romance of a hero, a sinner put to service for good. When he brought down the Temple of Dagon in Gaza, he instilled pride in fellow Israelites. But he was never a conventional ruler, nor did he eradicate the Philistine threat.

THE PHILISTINES

The Israelites and Canaanites had just worked out spheres of influence and fashioned a tense truce, when the Philistines arrived to threaten them both. Today 'philistine' has become a byword for anything boorish, yet the real Philistines were artistically gifted. In fact, they may have been an offshoot of the Mycenean and Minoan civilizations of Crete, Cyprus and the Aegean Islands, or present-day Turkey. Almost certainly they were Indo-European 'Sea People' and not Semitic – a thesis that tallies with the biblical account of the family of nations.

The Philistines were also wise in the arts of war. They used the latest iron swords and 'helmets of brass', as the Book of Samuel reports of the feared warrior Goliath. Evidently the Philistines jealously guarded their

Right This chapter title page from Maimonides's Mishneh Torah gives the title of the Book of Judges – Shoftim.

technology and prevented ironsmiths from working in enemy territory. But in an early instance of industrial espionage, Israelites captured enemy arms in battle and copied them.

SEARCHING FOR A KING

From their coastal locations of Gaza, Gath, Ashkelon, Ekron and Ashdod, the Philistines began encroaching on Canaan's hinterland. Frustrated at being the butt of attack, undermined by myriad schisms and rivalries between the tribes, the Israelites began longing for a national leader who could unite them. So they turned to Samuel, the last of the judges, and asked him to break with tradition and find them a king.

SETTLING ON A MONARCHY

JEWISH TRADITION REGARDS SAMUEL AS THE LAST OF THE JUDGES AND FIRST OF THE PROPHETS. HE WAS A CRUCIAL TRANSITIONAL LEADER AS ISRAEL MOVED FROM TRIBAL CONFEDERACY TO MONARCHY.

Samuel arose at a time of crisis when the Israelites, especially the southern tribe of Benjamin, were facing constant attack from the Philistines (c.1180–1150BCE). Samuel's mother, Hannah, was a religious woman of advanced years who came from the remote town of Ramah, and longed for a child. Eventually, Samuel was born in answer to her prayers. So grateful was Hannah, that she entrusted her boy to Eli, high priest at the sanctuary of Shiloh.

When Samuel was 12, the Philistines defeated Israelites at Eben-Ezer and stole the holy Ark of the Covenant. To Samuel this was a seminal moment, after 20 years of Philistine oppression, he summoned an army at Mitzpah and repelled the foe. Now a true national figure, Samuel toured the country dispensing advice. He set up a guild of ecstatic prophets and eventually passed leadership to his sons. But when they proved corrupt, the Israelites begged him to give them a king.

Samuel insisted that choosing a king represented blasphemy against the rule of God. Furthermore, there were many dilemmas: Which tribe should the king come from? Should the monarch be hereditary or popularly chosen? Could a queen be a monarch? And should the king rule on religious matters?

SAMUEL ANOINTS SAUL

In the end Samuel relented, and chose for the Israelites Saul, a farmer from the tribe of Benjamin. Saul seemed modest and principled and, as a Benjaminite, a people who suffered the most from Philistine attack, he knew better than most what it was like to be oppressed.

At first Saul did not want the job and hid when Samuel came looking for him. He was called *nagid* (military commander), and not *melekh* (king), perhaps indicating his unwillingness to fully embrace the monarchic idea. However, Saul proved his mettle when he saved the Benjaminite city

Above King David enthroned. From a Spanish Hebrew manuscript of the Book of Kings, Kennicott Bible, 1476.

of Jabesh Gilead from Ammonite attack. Anointed with oil and crowned king at Gilgal, on the Jordan, he built his capital at his birthplace, Gibeah, from where he ruled for 38 years. Shiloh is believed to have been his alternative capital.

Saul, says the biblical Book of Samuel, successfully fought 'enemies on every side', including Philistines, Edomites and Ammonites, urbanized Gibeonites and nomadic Moabites. He and his chief general, Abner, created Israel's first standing army, comprising units based on tribe and territory. He granted land to those close to him, a common practice in the ancient Levant, but until then unknown among Jews.

A tragic figure, Saul grew to be wracked by insecurity and obsessive envy. Increasingly he made arbitrary confiscations and violent arrests. Samuel withdrew his favour when the king disobeyed his orders, thought to come from God, and when Saul lapsed into despotism.

Left Hannah presents her son Samuel to the High Priest Eli. A painting by 17th-century artist Lambert Doormer.

Left Saul resented the harp-playing youth, and this 1646 painting by Guercino shows Saul attacking David.

RISE OF DAVID, FALL OF SAUL

To soothe his melancholia, Saul employed a talented troubadour from the tribe of Judah, David, who befriended Saul's son and chief lieutenant, Jonathan.

David was born in Bethlehem, the son of Jesse and grandson of Ruth, a Moabite convert to Judaism. In time he married Saul's daughter, Michal. According to the familiar story, he killed the Philistine giant Goliath armed only with a slingshot. David's distinctive six-pointed star later became the Jewish national symbol, and the most beautiful psalms are attributed to him.

However, David's triumphs aroused Saul's murderous envy. When David fled, Saul executed Ahimelech and 85 other priests of Nob who gave the young courtier refuge. Often the biblical account hints at social rifts within a still-maturing tribal society. At times it speaks of Jonathan leading Hebrews, as distinct from Israelites. Likewise it says David accepted a fiefdom from the enemy Philistines when he was hiding from Saul.

Another recurrent theme is mercy versus duty. Jonathan, for instance, felt torn between loyalty to his father and love for David. The prophet Samuel rebuked King Saul for not slaying Agag, the defeated Amalekite king. And twice David had Saul in his sights on the battlefield, but chose not to kill him.

Determined to exploit Israelite divisions, the Philistines launched a westward invasion, slaying Jonathan in the opening skirmishes. Saul ultimately took his own life after Philistines defeated his army at Gilboa. When his body was draped on the walls of Beth She'an, the men of Jabesh remembered his earlier service and buried him in their town.

ISH-BOSHET AND DAVID

Saul's captain, Abner, proclaimed Ish-Boshet, Saul's son, king *c.*1007BCE. His two-year reign was undistinguished. David, meanwhile, was crowned rebel king of Judah. Even Abner deserted Ish-Boshet for David's side, and in 1005BCE David's partisans defeated the formal king's forces. Ultimately Ish-Boshet was murdered by two of his own captains, after which David was anointed, allegedly by Samuel, as king of Judah and the northern tribes of Israel.

David immediately executed Ish-Boshet's treacherous killers. Disloyalty was not to be tolerated as he began his major task, the consolidation of a truly united Kingdom of Israel. And Jewish history was to enter a new phase under his reign, the crowning glory of which would be the taking of Jerusalem.

Below Samuel anoints David. A 2nd-century fresco from Dura-Europos, Syria, one of the world's oldest synagogues.

THE GREAT KINGS

DAVID AND SOLOMON TRANSFORMED TRIBES INTO A NATION. THEY
MADE JERUSALEM THE CAPITAL OF A UNITED ISRAEL, ESTABLISHED
PEACE AND BUILT THE TEMPLE AS JUDAISM'S SPIRITUAL FOCAL POINT.

The biblical account of King David's life is probably unique in early Near Eastern literature. Few sagas contain so much personal detail, psychological insight or information about contemporary society. David almost certainly existed: in 1993 archaeologists working in Tel Dan, northern Israel, uncovered an ancient basalt artefact bearing the words 'House of David' and 'King of Israel'. The books of Samuel and Chronicles describe how after fleeing Saul's court, David recruited a roving army of general malcontents who terrified the tribal elders of Judah. David convinced Judah's elders that only he could protect them.

JERUSALEM IS CAPITAL

In his eighth year David attacked and overwhelmed Jerusalem, making it his new capital. The original Jebusite inhabitants were not massacred or expelled, but continued to live in the city. David even purchased land from Jerusalem's former ruler, Melchizedek, to house the Ark, repository for the commandments.

King David was to rule Jerusalem for the 33 remaining years of his 40-year monarchy. He completed the process begun by Saul in pacifying Canaanite enclaves, and then established Israelite control over Moab, Edom, Ammon and Aram–Damascus in the north-east. Yet he ended his reign with a sense of incompletion, because he never built his desired temple for the Ark.

DAVID'S SONS

Absalom was David's favourite son, and just as David proved a thorn in the side of his mentor, Saul, so Absalom grew to defy his father. He harnessed the ten northern tribes against Judah, but he lost the battle and was stabbed to death by Joab. David chose as his heir his surviving

Above Reputed exterior of David's Tomb. It became a synagogue, later incorporated into a Crusader church.

son, Solomon, a scholar-judge, whom he instructed on his deathbed to 'walk in God's ways'. Other Israelite leaders had fought and won battles, but none had so thoroughly stymied Israel's foes as David. The Philistines could not dent Judah's borders for hundreds of years, and Solomon (whose name means 'his peace') enjoyed the luxury of governing for decades without ever having to fight a war.

Solomon was no great military general, but he proved that he could be ruthless. On taking power he replaced all his father's ministers (murdering some) and stopped recruiting conscripts from the northern tribes of Israel, whom he never really trusted. Next, Solomon divided Israel into 12 tax districts, and expanded trade by marrying daughters of all the neighbouring

Left An illumination from a Jewish manuscript of 1728–9 showing the Temple of Jerusalem.

Above A Muslim miniature from Persia showing Solomon surrounded by courtiers, angels, demons and wives, c.1570.

princes. His best-known dalliance was with the beautiful Queen of Sheba, from Yemen or Ethiopia. One result was Israelite control over trade in the valuable myrrh, frankincense and spices from Arabia.

TEMPLE AND EMPIRE
The honour of building the Temple passed from David to Solomon in 973BCE. He chose the highest point in the city, what Jews call '*Har ha-Bayyit*', the Temple Mount, and Muslims call the Noble Sanctuary. The biblical account is remarkably explicit about the Temple's dimensions. It also details how King Hiram of Tyre, south Lebanon (969–936BCE) helped to fund and build the structure.

Solomon probably won more acreage by negotiation and diplomacy than his predecessors had done

Right Map showing Phoenician trade routes from Solomon's kingdom to Europe and northern Africa.

by warfare. His imperial borders stretched from the Nile to the Euphrates and encompassed former enemies, including Philistines. Proof of the kingdom's extent was found in 1902 with the discovery of the remains of Ir Ovot, a plateau fortress in the Negev Desert. Now in southern Israel, the site dates back to the 10th century BCE.

ECONOMIC GENIUS
Trade was the essence of Solomon's economic success, especially trade by sea. From his Mediterranean ports of Akko (Acre) and Jaffa he shipped goods to and from Tarshish in Spain and Chittim in Cyprus. He built a vast merchant fleet at his southernmost port, Etzion-Geber, near present-day Eilat on the Gulf of Aqaba. Solomon also became an arms dealer, and traded Cilician horses for Egyptian chariots.

However, power corrupted Solomon in his later years. He built chariot cities and royal depots, a sumptuous palace and three new royal fortress cities, at Hazor, Gezer and Megiddo (Armageddon), but these were expensive to fund. So he raised taxes and instituted a corveé on Canaanite and northern Israelite subjects, who laboured for no pay. Northerners resented his Temple

cult, as did religious purists, who saw Jerusalem as absolutist and dictatorial, veering towards idolatry. He was also intolerant of local shrines at Bethel and Shechem. So when Solomon died, in 925BCE, northern Israelites insisted that his son Jeroboam be crowned in their area, Shechem.

PSALMS AND PROVERBS
The scriptures include numerous passages ascribed to David and Solomon, the most famous being the psalms, where David's poetic genius and religious passion come across powerfully. Rabbis believe the Book of Proverbs is Solomon's handicraft, and perhaps the famously erotic and spiritual 'Song of Songs', too.

David and Solomon also greatly influenced Judaism's sister faiths. The Book of Matthew, for instance, traces the lineage of Jesus back to David to prove Christ's messianic claim. In Islam *Tawrat* refers to the Torah, but a separate name, *Zabur*, denotes the Psalms of David. Likewise Solomon (as Suleiman) is popular in Persian Muslim art, and the king features in numerous fables. David and Solomon have been immortalized in the three monotheistic faiths but, in historical terms, their deaths created a void that swiftly led to the splitting apart of their united kingdom.

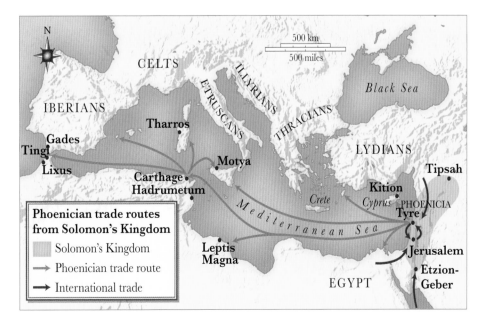

THE ROYAL HOUSES OF ISRAEL AND JUDAH

AFTER KING SOLOMON DIED IN 927BCE THE UNITED KINGDOM OF ISRAEL SPLIT INTO ISRAEL IN THE NORTH AND JUDAH IN THE SOUTH. AT TIMES THEY EVEN FOUGHT EACH OTHER, AND BOTH SUFFERED RELIGIOUS BACKSLIDING.

For decades the ten tribes in the north had felt uneasy about accepting the family of David as their overlords. Only the wisdom and guile of Solomon had managed to hold the squabbling tribes together.

CAUSES OF STRIFE

The immediate cause of the rift was a clash between Rehoboam, Solomon's son and heir, and Jeroboam, an Ephraimite rebel from Solomon's court. Jeroboam fled to Egypt and became a protégé of Pharaoh Shoshenq I (945–924BCE). When Solomon died, Rehoboam took advice from younger counsellors to increase taxes, and thereby stamp his authority over all Israelites.

Below Jeroboam's Idolatry, *1752, by J.-H. Fragonard. To distinguish his reign from Judah, Jeroboam set up a rival temple cult worshipping golden calves.*

The northern tribes revolted and Jeroboam agreed to lead them. He rebuilt Shechem (near modern-day Nablus) as his capital. But while the smaller southern kingdom consisted only of the tribes of Judah and Benjamin, it had three winning assets: the city of Jerusalem; its Temple; and a healthy economy.

Jews from the north enjoyed travelling to Jerusalem three times a year, for Passover (*Pesach*), Tabernacles (*Sukkoth*) and Weeks (*Shavuot*). Jealous of Jerusalem, Jeroboam fired his Levite priests, replaced them with his own priesthood and built golden calves to be worshipped at Dan in the north and Bethel in the south.

Jeroboam's plans backfired: Judah thwarted the northern Israelites and many died. Ahijah, formerly Jeroboam's prophetic mentor, foretold that his entire dynasty would be exterminated. Jeroboam died soon

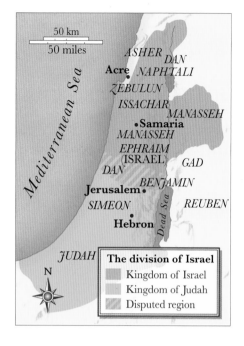

Above Map showing the division of the kingdom between Israel in the north and Judah in the south.

afterwards, leaving the throne to his son Nadab. Two years later the prophet Ahijah's prophecy came true when a soldier called Baasha murdered Nadab and made himself king.

JUDAH'S GOOD KING ASA

Meanwhile, conditions were far from perfect in Judah. Asa inherited a backlog of inefficiency when he took Judah's throne around 908BCE. Asa's stable rule contrasted dramatically with the chaos of northern Israel, and thousands immigrated southwards to Judah, especially from the tribes of Ephraim and Manasseh.

During the years of peace, Asa strengthened Judah's fortifications. His wisdom was proven when a massive force of Egyptian-backed Ethiopians attacked. Asa's army defeated them, thus safeguarding Judah from Egyptian interference for nearly 300 years.

In Asa's 36th year King Baasha of Israel attacked his kingdom. A desperate Asa took gold and silver from the Temple to pay off Ben-Hadad I (died *c.* 841BCE), King of Damascus and Israel's ally. The ploy worked, as

Ben-Hadad began to attack cities belonging to the northern tribes of Dan and Naphtali. Diverted by this Syrian assault, Baasha had to call off his invasion of Judah.

BAASHA TO THE OMRIDS

A military dictator who sealed his borders to prevent immigration to Judah, Baasha built vast fortifications at Ramah from which to raid his enemies. Born into the tribe of Issachar, he ruled for 23 years.

Baasha's descendants fell into vicious infighting until in *c.*882BCE the military commander Omri took over and launched a new dynasty. Israel's new king immediately moved

Right Athaliah killed all the royal children, except her grandson Joash, in revenge for her son Ahaziah's murder.

his capital from Shechem to Samaria (Shomron). Though condemned in the Bible for heresy, Omri was a statesman of some talent. He ruled for 12 years and his son, Ahab, for 20. Economic prosperity returned as the Omrid dynasty nurtured peace with Judah and the Sidonites of Lebanon.

AHAB AND JEZEBEL

Often the Omrids sealed diplomatic pacts with dynastic marriages, the most famous being the union of Ahab and Queen Jezebel (died

*c.*843BCE), daughter of Sidon's King Ethbaal. The prophets railed against Jezebel for introducing the worship of the pagan god Melkart. She in turn had many of them killed.

Under Omri and Ahab, Israel increased its territory and created new cities. Judah, under King Jehoshaphat (*c.*873–849BCE), reconquered Edom. Together, the Jewish kingdoms knew prosperity.

ALLIANCE AND REVOLT

Jehoshaphat fought against the Baal cult and sent Levites to instruct common folk in the law. A pragmatist who reigned for 25 years, he allied himself with successive Israelite kings – Ahab, Ahaziah and Joram – though with mixed military results.

The only queen of Judah was Athaliah, who succeeded her husband, Jehoram, and their son, Ahaziah, on the latter's death. She revived Baal worship after Jehu killed her extended family in Israel. Athaliah also killed all but one of the House of David. That survivor was her one-year-old grandson, Joash, who was hidden and raised secretly by the priest Jehoiada.

Six years later Joash was placed on the throne and Athaliah was slain before she could quell the revolt. Joash ruled for 35 years, although Jehoiada acted as his regent in the early years. When Jehoiada died, though, Joash turned to pagan habits. Judah faced constant threat from the Aram Syrians, and hopes of reform receded.

 THE KINGS OF ISRAEL AND JUDAH

A UNITED KINGDOM
Saul *c.*1047–1007BCE
Ish-Boshet *c.*1007–1005BCE
David *c.*1005–967BCE
Solomon *c.*971–928BCE

DIVIDED KINGDOMS

ISRAEL	JUDAH
Jeroboam I 928–906BCE	Rehoboam 928–911BCE
Nadab 907–905BCE	Abijam 911–908BCE
Baasha 906–882BCE	Asa 908–867BCE
Elah 883–881BCE	
Zimri 881BCE	
Tibni 881–876BCE	
Omri 882–870BCE	
Ahab 871–851BCE	Jehoshaphat 870–845BCE
Ahaziah 851–850BCE	Jehoram 851–840BCE
Joram 850–839BCE	Ahaziah 840BCE
Jehu 839–811BCE	Queen Athaliah 839–833BCE
Jehoahaz 812–795BCE	Joash 833–794BCE
Joash 797–781BCE	Amaziah 795–764BCE
Jeroboam II 792–751BCE	Uzziah 797–735BCE
Zechariah 750–749BCE	Jotham 794–733BCE
Shallum 749BCE	
Menahem 749–739BCE	
Pekahiah 738–736BCE	
Pekah 736–730BCE	Ahaz 732–716BCE
Hoshea 731–722BCE	
Fall of Samaria 722–721BCE	
Fall of Israel 718BCE	Hezekiah 715–686BCE

THE AGE OF PROPHETS

THE WORDS AND DEEDS OF PROPHETS RUN LIKE A GOLDEN THREAD THROUGH JEWISH LORE. THEY ALSO ACTED AS A COUNTERBALANCE TO CORRUPT RULERS AND REFLECTED THE CONSCIENCE OF THE PEOPLE.

One third of the Old Testament/ Tanakh is devoted to the Prophets' writings. Taken literally, *nevi'im*, the Hebrew word for prophets, means proclaimers, probably a reference to visionaries who roamed the country-side shouting predictions and praise for God. Apart from being mystics and channellers of divine messages, prophets often played political roles, as royal advisers, promoters of national feeling or moral compasses.

MAJOR AND MINOR PROPHETS

Some regard all the patriarchs, judges and other early figures, such as Job, Joshua, Samuel and Moses, as prophets. In Islam even Adam is called a prophet. However, the Jewish consensus is that the term 'professional prophet' refers to three

Above The Vision of the Prophet Ezekiel *by Raphael, 1510. Ezekiel lived in Babylonian exile c.500BCE.*

major prophets, each with a book in the biblical division Nevi'im/Prophets, and 12 minor prophets, whose writings constitute one book. The major figures are Isaiah, Jeremiah and Ezekiel. The minor ones, so called only because their writings are shorter, are Hosea, Joel, Amos, Obadiah, Jonah, Micah, Nahum, Habbakuk, Zephaniah, Haggai, Zechariah and Malachi. Other prophets, like Neriah, Baruch and Huldah, are just quoted among other biblical writings.

One of the most human stories in the Bible concerns the northern Israelite prophet Jonah. He was born near Nazareth and lived around the years 780–740BCE. Jonah's short book is read on Yom Kippur, the Jewish Day of Atonement. It describes what seemed like an impossible mission, when he was told to persuade the evil-doing people of Nineveh, capital of the Assyrian empire, to mend their ways. After surviving a storm at sea and being swallowed by a whale, Jonah finally did convince the citizens of Nineveh to repent; only to lambast God for so easily forgiving these former sinners while making his own life so difficult!

ADVOCATES OF JUSTICE

Time and again prophets would chide the monarch of the day for neglecting the poor and the weak. In the words of Jeremiah: 'Thus says the Lord, "Do justice and righteousness, and deliver the one who has been robbed from the power of his oppressor. Also do not mistreat or do

Left A late 16th-century Islamic Ottoman miniature shows the story of Jonah and the whale.

violence to the stranger, the orphan, or the widow; and do not shed innocent blood in this place."'

Prophets wielded huge influence and acted as a counterbalance to an often overbearing monarchy. Put another way, the prophet represented God's conscience, and advocated the welfare of the common people. It would be too much to liken the prophet to an 'official opposition' in the parliamentary sense. However, if anyone could remind the king that he was not above the law, it was the prophet. The priests of Judah were not immune from prophetic criticism either. One of the last prophets, Malachi (c.420–400BCE), explicitly condemned Jerusalem's priests for failing in their duties. Elijah went as far as leading an insurrection against the false priests of Mount Carmel, when he inspired a mob to kill dozens of them at the Kishon River. Born into poverty, a member of the fundamentalist Rechabite sect, the revolutionary Elijah none the less wrote that God's true spirit was 'not in the earthquake, nor in the fire, but in the still, small voice' (1 Kings

19:12). His disciple, Elisha, continued his mission to even greater effect against Ahab's heir, Joram.

The Bible speaks of prophets having special powers. Some, like Elisha, could revive the dead; many anointed kings; and most were adept at predicting the future, as well as describing the messianic age to come. Certain prophets seem to argue directly with God, like Habbakuk; others, such as Obadiah, specialize in attacking the enemies of 'God's people'; and social prophets, like Micah and Amos, target the avarice of the rich.

ISAIAH

The most prolific and oft-quoted prophet, Isaiah, lived during a particularly difficult era in Jewish history, the 8th century BCE. From Judah, he witnessed Assyria's destruction of the northern kingdom of Israel, a tragedy that is reflected in his poignant verses. Isaiah prophesied during the reigns of four kings of Judah – Uzziah, Jotham, Ahaz and Hezekiah. Owing to the long time-span of this period, some imagine

that there must have been two Isaiahs. Of aristocratic birth, yet deeply concerned for the downtrodden, Isaiah advised King Ahaz to trust in the Lord and not seek help from Assyria. Ahaz ignored him, though Hezekiah wisely heeded his warning in 711BCE to stay out of a conflict between Assyria and Egypt.

Isaiah strongly condemned idolatry, yet he went further than other prophets in asserting that God rejected even Jewish rituals if the practitioners were cruel and unjust.

Above The coming of Elijah at Passover, from the Washington Haggadah, created in north Italy by Joel ben Simeon, 1478.

When Israel forgets her mission, he wrote, she is like a wife deserting her husband, God. At the same time he saw God as king of the world, not only of Israelites. To Christians, Isaiah's repeated phrase 'the holy one of Israel' is a prediction of Jesus. Perhaps his most powerful words concern making God's kingdom on earth, when peace reigns and 'swords are beaten into plough shares'. The United Nations has adopted this as its unofficial motto.

Prophetic writings abound in dazzling poetry and stirring polemics that have inspired thinkers well beyond their immediate Jewish audience. The prophets had varying approaches, but all saw a divine purpose underlying history. They spoke to the individual, helping him or her make sense of life. In short, the prophets broadened Judaism from tribal concerns and rituals. In Babylonian captivity they were to embrace the idea of a universal God who heeds human suffering.

Left The Peaceable Kingdom *by Edward Hicks depicts the messianic age, when, as the prophet Isaiah predicted, the lion would lie down with the lamb and men would learn war no more.*

THE NORTHERN KINGDOM FALLS

FOLLOWING THE DEVASTATION OF THE NORTHERN KINGDOM OF ISRAEL BY THE ASSYRIANS IN 722BCE, TEN OF THE TWELVE ISRAELITE TRIBES WERE ASSIMILATED OR BANISHED, AND LOST TO HISTORY.

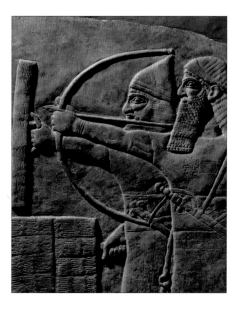

Above Assyrian archers. Assyria was a world power and Israelites were just one of the many peoples they deported.

Seen in context, the northern kingdom's destruction was a subtext of a larger story of two empires, Assyria and Babylonia, battling for control of Mesopotamia. Paradoxically, the sacking of northern Israel resolved an ongoing battle between the ten tribes in the north and the two tribes of the south. If the Assyrians had not triumphed, suggest some scholars, Jews may never have refined their faith, written the Bible or survived as we know them today.

ASSYRIAN EXPANSIONISM

The story begins with Ashurnasirpal II (884–859BCE), who developed the Assyrian war machine by using heavy chariots, the latest iron weaponry and fearsome discipline. Shalmaneser III (859–824BCE) continued Assyria's westward thrust but faced a formidable pact headed by Damascus and Hamath (present-day Hama). One

Below Map of Assyrian conquests at the time of the defeat of the northern kingdom of Israel, c.722BCE.

key member of this alliance was Ahab the Israelite, who, according to the historian of the document known as the Kurkh Monolith had 2,000 chariots and 10,000 men. In 853BCE the two sides fought the largest battle in history to date at Qarqar. The clash proved indecisive, but apparently disabled the alliance, which spelt trouble for Israel.

ISRAEL'S YEARS OF DECLINE

After King Ahab's death, his son Joram (r. 850–839BCE) took over Israel's crown and began a string of disastrous military campaigns. He lost control of Edom (today, southern Jerusalem) and was defeated by the Arameans from Syria at Ramoth-Gilead. Eager to restore order, the prophet Elisha backed a popular Israelite military revolt in 842BCE led by Jehu ben Nimshi (r. c.842–815BCE). Jehu soon killed off the entire Ahab/Joram dynasty and eliminated all worship of Baal. The prophets praised Jehu's purge for its spiritual purity, but in political terms it weakened Israel

dreadfully. Judah soon broke its alliance with Israel and when Assyria turned its attention to northern ventures, Aram's leaders Hazael and Ben-Hadad III turned Jehu's son and heir, Jehoahaz (735–720BCE) into little more than a vassal.

Some relief came in the form of a decisive Assyrian blow against Damascus in 796BCE. Israel's new king, Joash, recovered lost cities from a weakened Aram and acknowledged Assyria as Israel's protector. Joash went on to capture Jerusalem, plunder the Temple, and briefly imprison King Amaziah of Judah.

ISRAEL REVIVES

Israel enjoyed its greatest period just before the fatal Assyrian blow. By the time Jeroboam II (792–751BCE) succeeded Joash, as King of Israel, Aram was losing its grip over Syria–Palestine. Jeroboam took advantage of Assyria's Armenian campaigns in the far north to attack and take Damascus and Hamath.

Military success paid economic dividends. Israel controlled the trade routes connecting Anatolia and Mesopotamia to Egypt, and, when it conquered Bashan and Hauran,

The end of the Kingdom of Israel, 722BCE

Assyrian expansion 883–824BC
Assyrian expansion 745–705BC
Assyrian expansion 705–669BC

300 km
300 miles

it recovered access to 'the wheat granary of Israel'. Jeroboam opened up new territories to Israelite settlement. Chronicles speaks of Reubenite tribesmen grazing their flocks as far north as the River Euphrates.

JUDAH'S NEW PROSPERITY

Jeroboam's counterpart in Judah, Uzziah, son of Amaziah, became ruler and later king 784–733BCE. Judah conquered the southern port of Eloth, near modern-day Eilat on the Red Sea, which allowed Uzziah to control the two great trade routes of historic Palestine. International commerce boosted Judah's economy to an extent not seen since the united kingdom days. Where Uzziah fatally erred was in attempting to participate directly in Temple services, for which sin, says tradition, he contracted leprosy and died. Even so, his son Jotham continued his father's expansive policies, this time into transjordan.

Below This obelisk marks the triumphs of Shalmaneser III (859–824BCE) and his defeat of Israel's king Jehu.

LOST TRIBES

Above A Beta Yisrael synagogue in Ethiopia, whose people claim descent from the tribe of Dan.

What happened to the ten 'lost tribes' of Israel remains a mystery. Most exiles were settled near Gozan on the Khabur River, today near the Syrian border with Turkey. Others served as Assyrian garrison troops in Medea. A few maintained Jewish practices but most were assimilated with surrounding Arameans within Greater Assyria.

Jewish folklore speaks of lost Jews who await the Messiah's arrival, but remain marooned across the mythical Sambatyon River, which stops flowing every Sabbath. Less fancifully, many refugees from Israel fled south to Judah. Others probably mixed with gentiles in Samaria and became Samaritans or blended into the gene-pool of today's Kurds.

Supposed descendants of the ten appear in all places: David Reuveni, a false messiah, swore he was from the tribe of Reuben. The Ethiopian Jews (Beta Yisrael or Falasha) claim descent from the tribe of Dan, as do some Yemenite Jews. Evidence suggests the priestly sect of the Lemba of southern Africa has a gene marker typical of Cohens. A group from India called Shimlung say they are the offspring of Manasseh.

Even among non-Jews, people claim Lost Tribe ancestry: the Yousefzai clan of Pathans in Afghanistan, for instance, wear side-locks and ritual tassels, like Orthodox Jews. Others who claim such descent include the Celtic Irish and Cornish, the Japanese Makuya sect, a distinctive Ghanaian community, Muslim Kashmiris, certain Native American tribes, and the Ibo of Nigeria.

ASSYRIA ATTACKS SOUTHERN RIVALS

King Jeroboam II's death in 751BCE marked the beginning of Israel's ultimate decline. A power-hungry usurper named Menahem massacred an entire village and crowned himself king of Israel in 747BCE. Two years later, in 745BCE, Tiglath-Pileser III (r. 745–727BCE), one of the most effective military commanders in history, took over the Assyrian kingdom. In 739BCE, Tiglath defeated Judah's King Uzziah in battle. Six years on, he conquered the Philistine-ruled Mediterranean coastline, then turned inland, defeating Damascus, occupying Israel and annexing Galilee.

ISRAEL'S ENDGAME

Israel's new ruler, Hoshea, was king in name only: he controlled little more than Samaria (the ancient capital of Israel). All seemed lost when in 729BCE Tiglath crushed Assyria's greatest foe, Babylon, and assumed control over all of Mesopotamia. After Tiglath's death in 727BCE, King Hoshea chose to revolt by ceasing payment of tributes to Assyria, and turned to Assyria's old enemy, Egypt, for help. But it was too late: Tiglath's successor, Shalmaneser V (726–721BCE), devastated Samaria, took Hoshea captive and deported him to Assyria.

In 721BCE Sargon II seized power in Assyria, crushing a series of regional revolts, and defeating an Egyptian army. He rebuilt Samaria as capital of the Assyrian province of Samerina. He deported 27,290 Samarian Israelites, and resettled the land with colonists from other parts of his empire. Some scattered Israelites remained, but the Kingdom of Israel was no more.

CHAPTER 2

EXILE, RETURN AND DISPERSAL

The year 721BCE seemed to mark Judaism's demise. Ten of Israel's twelve tribes were driven out and lost forever, and the kingdom of Assyria stood poised to destroy Jerusalem. Somehow the little kingdom of Judea survived. But 136 years later its rulers were marched off into Babylonian captivity. Curiously this apparent nadir marked a rebirth of sorts. In exile, Jews developed new scribal and proto-rabbinical traditions. Once Persia allowed them to return after 539BCE, sages rebuilt the Jerusalem Temple and compiled the final version of the Hebrew Bible. Dual rule by king and prophet gave way to more democratic if theological bodies. Two centuries later, Hellenism challenged Jews politically and culturally, until Hasmonean 'kings' reasserted Judean autonomy. Direct Roman control after 37BCE spawned new sects, of which the Jesus followers were one. Finally an ill-fated revolt led to the Second Temple's destruction in 70CE and the collapse of Judea as the centre of Jewish life.

Opposite Ezra in Prayer *by Gustave Doré, 1865. Born in Babylonian exile, Ezra's return to Judah with the blessing of Persia marked a crucial turning point in ancient Jewish history.*

Above *Exotic animals swirl around the word melekh, 'king' in Hebrew, taken from a Hebrew prayer book, late 13th-century Germany.*

JUDEA ALONE

WITH NORTHERN ISRAEL SHATTERED, JUDAH WAS LEFT VULNERABLE
TO ASSYRIAN ATTACK. THE LITTLE KINGDOM SURVIVED FOR 136 YEARS,
UNTIL POLITICAL AND MORAL BLUNDERS INVITED NEW DISASTERS.

The dispersal and loss of the ten tribes of northern Israel in 722BC represented a devastating blow to the Jewish people. Arguably, however, Assyria's destruction of northern Israel rescued Judaism. For with the Israelite capital Samaria vanquished, Jerusalem regained its status as the centre of Jewish devotion and the House of David regained its status.

The very name *yehudim*, or Jews, derives from the tribe of Judah (Yehuda). Benjamin, Judah and remnants of Simeon and the priestly tribe of Levi were the only Israelites to survive the Assyrian conquest of 721BCE intact. Today, most Jews trace their lineage from the southern tribes of Judah and Benjamin. The name 'Israel' lingered on in religious passages and medieval poetry, but only regained political expression with the creation of the State of Israel in 1948.

Below Attacking through the Judean desert, Assyrians laid waste to northern Israel and nearly took Jerusalem too.

SURVIVING DEVASTATION

Hezekiah (c.715-686BCE), son of King Ahaz, was the 13th king of an independent Judea when Assyria took the Israelites into captivity. He felt that the Israelites' annihilation had been divinely ordained because they had strayed from the true path. Unwilling to see Judea suffer a similar fate, he set about reforming his small kingdom. Hezekiah railed against unethical behaviour, banned idolatry and foreign gods, and even threw Moses' 'brazen serpent' from the Temple, as people had begun praying to it. Another challenge was how to cope with the influx of Israelite refugees who had escaped the Assyrian dragnet. Some say as many as 70 per cent fled south to Judea where they were absorbed into the surviving southern kingdom. But how could Hezekiah accommodate these newcomers in a crowded Jerusalem whose population was set to increase fivefold over the next century? Adopting a pragmatic approach, the

Above Hezekiah's Tunnel, built c.701BCE, linked the Gihon Spring to the Pool of Siloam and saved besieged Jerusalemites from dying of thirst.

king expanded city boundaries to the west, and made engineers build a canal to deliver water from the spring of Siloam to the city. This venture also provided work and housing for Israelite migrants.

HOLDING ASSYRIA AT BAY

The Assyrian tyrant Sennacherib (d. 681BCE) grew angry when Hezekiah allied himself with rebellious Ekronites, Egyptians and Arabs. He besieged Jerusalem in 701BCE. Hezekiah stood fast, reports the biblical Book of Kings, and prayed to the Lord, who the next morning 'smote 185,000 in the Assyrian camp'. Assyrian records state that Hezekiah paid off the invaders with a tribute purloined from his temple. The Greek historian Herodotus suggests, conversely, that a horde of mice spread plague in the Assyrian camp and thus halted their assault on Jerusalem. Yet another view says that black African Kushite soldiers, fighting under the Egyptian banner, stormed through the Sinai and devastated the Assyrians.

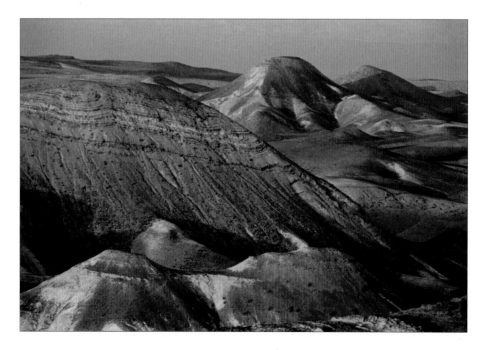

On the hexagonal Taylor prism, dated 689BC, Sennacherib, 'perfect hero, mighty man, first among princes', boasts of levelling with battering rams 46 walled Judean cities. After 'diminishing the land of Hezekiah', he shut up the king 'like a caged bird in Jerusalem, the royal city'. Eventually, though, Sennacherib abandoned his Judean vendetta and sent his troops home to counter more pressing rebellions by Elam and Babylon.

JUDEA UNDER KING JOSIAH

Assyria's departure was a welcome respite for Hezekiah, who continued building, consolidating and

Below A sight that Judeans dreaded: two Assyrians riding a chariot, 8th-century BCE stone relief.

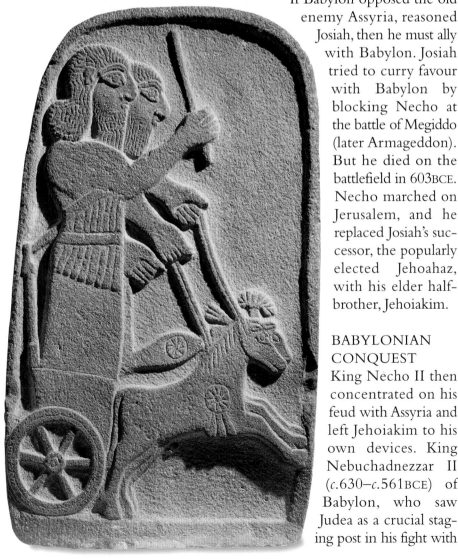

reforming Judea. Unfortunately his son and successor, Manasseh (687-642BCE), undid much of his hard work, and it was left to Manasseh's grandson, Josiah, to restore order to Judea. In his 18th year in power he cast out idols to Baal and Ashterah, restored the long-neglected Temple, and seems to have rediscovered the lost scroll of Deuteronomy (the last of the Five Books of Moses).

Praised by the prophetess Huldah and the prophet Jeremiah, Josiah also extended Judean control over most of what had been northern Israel. Unfortunately for him, a new power was rising in the north – Chaldea, which adopted the ancient name 'Babylon'. King Necho II of Egypt set off northward with a mighty army, determined to nip this rival in the bud. Judea lay in the way.

If Babylon opposed the old enemy Assyria, reasoned Josiah, then he must ally with Babylon. Josiah tried to curry favour with Babylon by blocking Necho at the battle of Megiddo (later Armageddon). But he died on the battlefield in 603BCE. Necho marched on Jerusalem, and he replaced Josiah's successor, the popularly elected Jehoahaz, with his elder half-brother, Jehoiakim.

BABYLONIAN CONQUEST

King Necho II then concentrated on his feud with Assyria and left Jehoiakim to his own devices. King Nebuchadnezzar II (c.630–c.561BCE) of Babylon, who saw Judea as a crucial staging post in his fight with

Above Found in Nineveh and dated to 689BCE, the Taylor prism luridly describes Sennacherib's destruction of Judean cities and siege of Jerusalem.

Egypt, promptly invaded Jerusalem. Jehoiakim was taken captive, along with the prophet Daniel, and later returned to the Judean throne as a mere vassal. An inept ruler, Jehoiakim famously tore up parchments bearing the prophet Jeremiah's criticisms and then rebelled against Babylon. Nebuchadnezzar's response was swift: Chaldean, Amorite, Moabite and Ammonite troops attacked and pillaged the whole of Judea.

In short, mediocre Judean rule frittered away the advantages won by Hezekiah and Josiah, and prepared the way for the fall of Judea and Jewish exile in Babylon. It looked as if Judah's 200-year interregnum had been a mere prelude to national annihilation. In fact, banishment to Babylon was to prove a catalyst in the maturation and survival of both the Jewish people and their faith.

BY THE RIVERS OF BABYLON

EXILE PROFOUNDLY ALTERED JEWISH LIFE. ONCE OVER THE SHOCK OF EXPULSION, JEWS LEARNT HOW TO PRESERVE THEIR IDENTITY AND SURVIVE, WHILE SYNAGOGUES MADE FOR A MORE EGALITARIAN FAITH.

Above A 5th-century CE terracotta tile from Tunisia, North Africa, showing Daniel in the lions' den.

For centuries the Assyrians dominated the northern Middle East. They boasted fine libraries, intricate legal structures, advanced cities and lavish royal courts. But all great empires attract rivals, and over a period of 150 years the Chaldeans, or neo-Babylonians, contested Assyrian supremacy.

After King Ashurbanipal died in 627BCE, the Babylonians and Medeans (probably ancestors of today's Kurds) wrested Nineveh from Assyria in 612BCE. Seven years later Babylon defeated superpower Egypt at the battle of Carchemish. Babylonian King Nebuchadnezzar II added the former Assyrian provinces of Phoenicia and Syria to the rump of his empire in Mesopotamia.

In 597BCE, when Judah's King Jehoiakim rebelled, the Babylonians plundered Jerusalem. They killed the king, banished his son Jehoiachin to Babylon, and placed his brother, Zedekiah, on Judah's throne.

THE TEMPLE DESTROYED

The Bible relates that Zedekiah, too, ignored prophetic warnings and joined a new insurrection led by Egypt. An enraged Nebuchadnezzar destroyed the Temple after an 18-month siege and annexed Judah in 587BCE. So began a second mass deportation of Judah's social elite to Babylon. Others fled east to Moab, Ammon and Edom in modern Jordan.

A Jewish governor, Gedalia, persuaded many refugees to return. But chaos followed when a Judean royal murdered him, and thousands of Jews now sought asylum in Egypt. A third and final expulsion to Babylon in 581BCE sealed the fate of the once-independent Kingdom of Judah. For the first time since Joshua's days, Jews lost political control over even the smallest part of historic Palestine.

It seemed as if a new Jewish state within a state might develop by the rivers of the Tigris and Euphrates –

ironically not far from ancient Ur, birthplace of the patriarch Abraham. Egypt formed another pole in what became known as the Diaspora, Greek for 'dispersal'.

After 50 years of exile, a few Jews began to return to Judah. However, their stay in Babylon profoundly altered their religion and identity. And large numbers chose to remain, thus giving birth to the 2,500-year-old Jewish communities of Iraq and Iran.

IN THE LIONS' DEN

Some of the Bible's most moving verses describe the shock and the dislocation of exile. 'By the rivers of Babylon, there I wept when I remembered Zion. For how can we sing the Lord's song in a strange land?' runs Psalm 137. The Lamentations of the prophet Jeremiah, include a powerful depiction of Jerusalem's desolation. And centuries later talmudic authors used the term 'Babylon' to denote the condition of Diaspora and Exile.

By contrast, the Book of Daniel expresses hope. It enriched the English language with some compelling

Left A detail from Belshazzar's Feast by Rembrandt. At the banquet, Daniel predicted Babylon's fall.

Above A 693BCE Assyrian relief shows Ashurbanipal and his queen feasting in the gardens of Babylon.

phrases. An exile himself, Daniel survived a night in the lions' den. According to Daniel, his fellow Jews, Shadrach, Meshach and Abednego, emerged unscathed from the tyrant's furnace. At Belshazzar's feast God places strange 'writing on the wall'. Daniel tells the arrogant rulers the words mean: 'You have been weighed in the balance and found wanting'. These mystical signs suggested that Jews would survive exile, return home and outlast their enemies. As Daniel's interpretation of Nebuchadnezzar's dream explains, even great emperors have 'feet of clay'.

LESSONS FROM BABYLON

Jews saw their exile as divine punishment, but life in Babylon was not as harsh as slavery in Egypt. Many Jews became merchants, bankers, artisans and land owners. Former King Jehoiachin of Judah had a seat at the table of Merodach, son of Nebuchadnezzar; and Daniel rose to high rank in the imperial court.

Jews learnt a great deal from the Babylonians. New theological elements filtered into Judaism – migration of souls, celestial angels, and the first notions of a messianic age to come. Jews also absorbed Gnostic ideas of the clash of good and evil, and they adopted a new square script based on local forms. Called *ashuri*, or 'Assyrian', it is still used for writing Hebrew today.

Babylonian Jews were allowed to practise their faith freely, so scribes began writing down the holy texts. In time the scribes displaced the prophets in importance, and the first rabbis and synagogues appeared.

Exile encouraged social change: old tribal divisions that made sense in Israel now dissolved and created, arguably for the first time, a unified sense of 'Jewishness'. In addition, Jews learnt it was possible to live as Jews in exile. If they were treated civilly, advised the prophet Jeremiah, they

Left Ezra flies over Jerusalem's destroyed Temple. From a 1583 Muslim Ottoman work, the Fine Flower of Histories.

Above From a French Christian Bible, 1364, a depiction of the prophet Daniel in the lions' den.

should offer their gentile rulers their loyalty. As he told fellow Jews: 'Seek the peace of the city whither I have caused you to be carried away captive, and pray unto the Lord for it'.

RISE OF CYRUS THE GREAT

Babylon, like Assyria before it, seemed impregnable. Nebuchadnezzar II created in Babylon, his capital, the most astonishing urban civilization of the day. His hanging gardens were considered a wonder of the world.

But soon a new Indo-Iranian contender arose from the East to challenge Babylonia's primacy. In 539BCE Cyrus the Great of Persia won over disgruntled Medes, then conquered Babylon and absorbed its territories.

While the exact reason for Babylon's collapse remains a mystery, for Jews the Persian victory was a godsend. Wishing to demonstrate his tolerance for his neighbours, Cyrus ordered captive populations to return to their ancestral lands. However, Cyrus' generosity carried a political price: from now on Judah was to be Persia's subject-province. Also, returning Jews found Samaritans, whose Jewish claims they rejected, occupying swathes of their former land.

REFORM UNDER EZRA

THANKS TO PERSIAN LIBERALITY, JEWS RETURNED TO JERUSALEM AND
REBUILT THEIR TEMPLE. OLD TRIBAL DIVISIONS MATTERED LESS NOW
THAN SETTING UP A LEGISLATURE AND CODIFYING THE BIBLE.

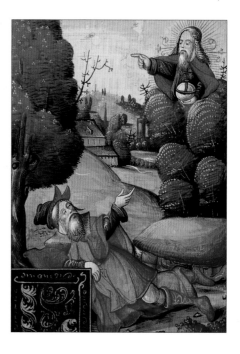

Above God appearing to Ezra, from a
French Christian Bible, 1526.

The prophet Isaiah described Persia's
King Cyrus as the 'shepherd of God'
and 'the anointed one' because of his
role in delivering Jews from exile.
Restoration of a temple in Jerusalem
was central to his imperial policy,
and in 538BCE, the same year that he
proclaimed liberty for his non-
Persian subjects, a party of 42,360
Jews returned to Judah. However,
the newcomers faced many troubles,
and Judah only truly stabilized when
Ezra and Nehemiah arrived several
generations later. These charismatic
figures reformed the Jewish faith,
organized a proper system of government and law, and determined
the final shape of the Bible – an
'institution' more crucial than the
Temple itself.

A NEW TEMPLE

In 536BCE Judah's governor,
Zerubabel, laid a foundation stone
for the second Temple in Jerusalem.
The actual building of the new
shrine was to prove more problematic than they first imagined.

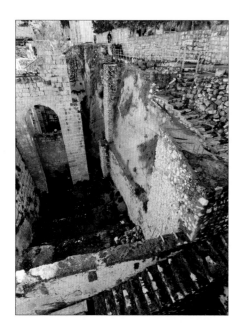

Those Jews who had never gone
into exile, the humbler, indigenous
Jews, resented the privileges that
Persia bestowed on the aristocratic
newcomers. Together with neighbouring Arabs and Edomites, they
interrupted building work in protest.
Zerubabel offended the Samaritans
when he rebuffed their offer to help
construct the Temple. Persia froze
funding when rebellions broke out
in the empire, and work stopped after
Cyrus the Great died in 529BCE.
The Temple was only finished at the
instigation of the prophet Haggai in
516BCE. It was smaller and lacked
the ark of the covenant of the first.
But it had the required two courts,
twin towers, altars and inner sanc-
tum for the high priest.

EZRA ESTABLISHES ORDER

The arrival of Ezra in 458BCE shook
up Judah's Jewish community.
Renowned among Babylonian
Jews and Gentiles alike, he brought
with him a party of 1,500 Levites,
priests, singers and other Temple
functionaries. A teacher, scribe and
ally of Persia's ruler Xerxes, Ezra
was sent to Judah in part to guard
against an anti-Persian revolt in
neighbouring Egypt turning into a
region-wide conflagration.

Likened to a 'second Moses', he
addressed himself to the 'people of
exile', and largely ignored the humbler indigenous Jews. He asked that
Jewish nobles and priests separate
from their non-Jewish wives. He also
began the custom of determining
Jewishness through one's mother.

Left The Pool of Bethesda in
*Jerusalem, a reservoir dating to the
Second Temple period.*

Ezra summoned a *Knesset ha-
Gedolah*, or 'Great Assembly', which
effectively became Judah's legislature
and the high court of Jewish people
everywhere. This body ruled until
the 2nd century BCE, in lieu of a
monarch. Jews did not wish to run
the risk of questioning Persian royal
authority. Nonetheless, they hoped
that one day a new king would arise
from the House of David. The
Assembly's 120 members canonized
the Hebrew Tanakh (Bible), which
Christians call the Old Testament.
Several members wrote biblical texts,
such as Ezra and his ally Nehemiah,
and the last prophet, Malachi.

NEHEMIAH'S REFORMS

In 445BCE, 13 years after Ezra
arrived in Judah, Nehemiah, formerly cup-bearer to King Ataxerxes
of Persia, became governor of
Jerusalem. A skilled statesman as well
as a social radical, Nehemiah persuaded Persia to allow Jews to
rebuild Jerusalem's city walls. He
enlarged the capital's population by
insisting that 10 per cent of the populace of Judah lived there. He also
provided for regular payment of a

Temple tithe and ensured that its benefits spread to the poorer Levites. Judah paid substantial taxes to the Persian court, yet also enjoyed fiscal autonomy and had a small army.

Ezra and Nehemiah were contrasting figures, one conservative and pious, the other radical and worldly wise. They cooperated, however, in galvanizing society in Judah and purging it of 'impurities'. Significantly, they read out the entire Torah in one public sitting, effectively proclaiming it as the constitution of the Jewish people. They established the essential structure of Jewish life that has arguably lasted to the present day.

Ezra was not unique in having ties to both Jerusalem and Babylon: many rabbis crossed between the two up to the late medieval period. However, centuries of separation also moulded distinct identities and encouraged a sense of rivalry between the two great Jewish centres.

Jews in the Persian province of Trans-Euphrates are thought to have enjoyed a decentralized leadership based around the first synagogues. They worked in agriculture, fishing and minor government service,

Below Illuminated heading from a book of Hebrew prayers for the Day of Atonement, Germany, c. 1320–5.

though little extra detail is known, except for what can be gleaned from Book of Esther in the Bible. This book has themes that would reappear in Jewish history, namely assimilation, acceptance, dissimulation, survival and political influence.

STRUCTURE OF THE BIBLE

The Jewish biblical canon is called Tanakh, an acronym for Torah (Law), Nevi'im (Prophets) and Ketuvim (Writings). Sometimes the whole is referred to as Torah, and the first section – the Five Books of Moses – is called Humash (The Five) in Hebrew, or Pentateuch, in Greek.

The most sacred parts of the bible are the Books of Moses. These are, in order: Genesis, Exodus, Leviticus, Numbers and Deuteronomy. Orthodox Jews believe that the Hand of God wrote all but the last.

The Book of Prophets is divided into Early and Later Prophets. The first contains four books: Joshua, Judges, Samuel I and II, and Kings I and II. Later Prophets has Isaiah, Jeremiah, Ezekiel, and a book devoted to the 12 Minor Prophets.

Writings comprise the three Books of Truth – Psalms, Proverbs and Job; five Megillot (Canticles): Song of Songs, Ruth, Lamentations,

Above The feast of Purim celebrates the lives of the Persian Jew Mordechai and his niece, Queen Esther; here painted by Aert de Gelder, 1685.

Ecclesiastes, Esther; and three 'other writings': Daniel, Ezra-Nehemiah, and Chronicles I and II (also by Ezra).

According to a model established by Ezra 2,500 years ago, the Torah is read in synagogues in yearly cycles, on Mondays, Thursdays and Saturdays (Sabbaths). Alongside the Torah portion, Jews also recite a *haftorah* (excerpts from the other books, Prophets and Writings). These readings were chosen to tally with the Torah portion, and often give the rabbi material upon which to base his sermon.

On festivals there are also readings from other parts of the Bible. For instance, Lamentations is read on the Fast of Tisha B'Av and Jonah on Yom Kippur (Day of Atonement). Quotations from the Psalms, Prophets, Proverbs and later from medieval poetry, outside the Bible, appear in the three Jewish daily services, *shacharit*, or 'morning', *mincha*, or 'afternoon', and *ma'ariv*, or 'evening'. One work that was not accepted into the Tanakh, *The Wisdom of Ben Sira*, became the basis of the most important daily Jewish prayer, the Amidah.

HELLENISM

GREECE POSED A FORMIDABLE INTELLECTUAL CHALLENGE TO JEWS EVEN BEFORE ALEXANDER CONQUERED THE LEVANT. NOW JEWS WERE TORN BETWEEN DYNASTIES, AND SUBJECT TO CULTURAL TENSIONS.

Above Roman mosaic of Alexander, who spread Hellenism across the Middle East. Jews hailed him as a liberator.

Until the 4th century BCE the main axis of Middle Eastern power politics ran north to south – essentially, a struggle for influence between the poles of Egypt and whoever controlled Mesopotamia. That pattern was shattered by the arrival of a potent new force from the West: Greece, or more precisely, Greek-derived Hellenism.

BEFORE ALEXANDER

Greek culture had seeped into the Middle East through trade and culture long before Alexander the Great (336-323 BCE). Greeks brought an entirely new way of looking at the world, one that challenged all Levantine peoples, including the Jews. Politically, there was the innovation of democracy, introduced in

Below Ptolemy II of Egypt, shown in a painting by Vincenzo Camaccini, 1813, asked Jewish sages to translate the Hebrew Bible into Greek.

Athens under Pericles in the 5th century BCE. Greek playwrights first posited the idea of moral choices facing the individual. Philosophers echoed the call that 'man was the measure of all things'. Successive schools, from the Stoics and followers of Socrates, Plato and Aristotle, down to the Cynics and Skeptics, applied rational techniques to the most profound ethical, political and metaphysical questions.

Greece did not conquer the Middle East until the Hellenic period. One reason might be that Greece lacked a single central authority, much like the pre-monarchy Israelites. Greek *polis*, or 'city-states', cherished their autonomy. They would unite in bodies like the Achaean or Hellenic Leagues when fighting a common enemy (invariably Persia), only to dissolve into divisive turf battles, most famously between Sparta and Athens. Even

when Persia was outmanoeuvred, successive kings, such as Darius the Great (522–486BCE) and Xerxes (485–465BCE) blocked the Greeks from encroaching into the Middle East. Meanwhile, Greeks established cities along the coastal rim of Anatolia (present-day Turkey).

Xerxes spent much of his reign battling the Greeks. A century after he died, Greek civilization in the guise of Macedonia overwhelmed Xerxes' heirs. This titanic clash between East and West was to have profound ramifications for Jewish history, thought and culture.

IMPACT ON JUDAISM

Many aspects of Greek culture alarmed Jews: tolerance of public nakedness and homosexuality; the proliferation of 'graven images'; a rational spirit which doubted claims of divine revelation; and democracy, which questioned the priestly right to govern. There were certainly Jews who resisted the Hellenic embrace, fearing the authentic core of Judaism was being lost. Assimilation, they argued, would eradicate the Jews as a distinct people. Other Jews, however, welcomed Hellenic sophistication.

Above Proof positive of Hellenic influence: a Greek stele, c.50CE, from the Jerusalem Temple exterior wall.

In time, Jews adopted Greek names, and Greek rationalism informed Jewish thinkers. Under Ptolemy II (285–246BCE), 70 Jewish sages in Alexandria translated the Hebrew Bible into Greek. This Septuagint, meaning 'seventy' in Greek, became the main scriptural source for Greek-speaking Jews. The Septuagint also opened Hebrew wisdom to gentiles: many became 'God-fearers', while several thousands converted to Judaism outright. Traditionalist Jews protested that only *ha-lashon kodesh*, or the 'holy language', Hebrew, was valid. However, paradoxically, the 'alien' Greek tongue was now spreading the ancient faith to new adherents, and bolstering the beliefs of Jewish communities in the Diaspora (from the Greek for dispersal, literally 'scattering of seeds').

ALEXANDER THE GREAT

The chief disseminator of Hellenic culture was Alexander. He was not Greek, but was the son of Philip, King of Macedon, a Greek subject province in the Balkans. Philip conquered Greece in 338BCE and was assassinated two years later.

Alexander, aged 22 and a student of the Greek philosopher, Aristotle, vowed to fulfil his father's dream of eastward expansion. In four years he defeated the entire Persian empire. By 332BCE Hellenic Macedonians controlled all of Asia Minor (Anatolia), Mesopotamia, Persia, Egypt, Syria and Palestine. Next, Alexander led his troops through Afghanistan, up to the Indus River in northern India, and north into south Russia and Uzbekistan. Within ten years he had created the largest empire ever seen.

CONTENTIOUS PALESTINE

Alexander died in Babylon in 323BCE – of fever, poison or heavy drinking – before he could designate an heir. Immediately his *diadochi*, or 'generals', started fighting over the spoils. By 315BCE the empire had been split into four zones. Generals Ptolemy Soter and Seleucus won control of Egypt and Syria respectively. Each founded a dynasty.

Palestine became a bone of contention between the two dynasties. Jerusalem changed hands seven times during 319–302BCE. The Ptolemies prevailed until in 200BCE Palestine fell to the Seleucids. By then, Hellenic governors had populated much of the land with military and later civilian Greek settlers, in cities such as Akko (renamed Ptolemais) and Beit She'an (Scythopolis). Canaanite nobles generally adopted Greek ways, though Jews initially kept their distance.

NEW LIFE IN EGYPT

Generally the first three Ptolemies were good to their Jewish subjects. They allowed the high priest and his council of elders to run affairs in Palestine, as long as they paid an annual tribute. The Ptolemies also encouraged Jews to settle in Egypt, where they largely prospered, built synagogues, and increasingly began speaking Greek. From Alexandria in the north to the Nile island of

Right Alexander, or Iskander, with seven sages, from the Quintet *or* Khamsa *by Nizami. Persian, 1494.*

Above Aristotle teaching Alexander, a detail from the French manuscript Romance of Alexander.

Elephantine in the south, Egypt became the second great centre of the Jewish Diaspora after Babylon.

Jews fared considerably less well under the fourth Ptolemy, Philopater (221–203BCE), who persecuted them mercilessly and tried to storm the Temple's holy of holies and defile it. In 198BCE a dynamic Seleucid ruler, Antiochus III (223–187BCE), defeated Epiphanes, successor to Philopater, at Panion in the Jordan Valley and won control of all of Palestine.

THE MACCABEES AND HASMONEANS

THE SELEUCID RULER ANTIOCHUS III TOOK PAINS NOT TO UPSET THE JEWISH PRIESTS OF JERUSALEM. HOWEVER, HIS ILL-CONSIDERED FOREIGN ADVENTURES ULTIMATELY LED TO REVOLUTION IN PALESTINE.

Goaded on by Hannibal, the defeated Carthaginian ruler, Antiochus III decided to invade Greece itself – a foolhardy move, as the rising power of Rome was Greece's ally. In 190BCE a Roman force inflicted a humiliating defeat on Antiochus and took his son hostage. The Seleucids had to pay reparations, and Antiochus' successor, Seleucus IV (187–175BCE), taxed his subjects to meet the bill.

Onias, the high priest in Jerusalem, condemned such payment as sinful. By contrast his brother,

Below A Roman bronze sculpture of Antiochus IV, whose insensitivity sparked a revolt by pious Jews.

Jason, wanted to pay, hoping that the Seleucids would then grant him the priesthood. When Antiochus' son Epiphanes returned from exile in Rome, he took over the dynasty after Seleucus IV was murdered in 175BCE. He called himself Antiochus Epiphanes, 'the illustrious one'. He immediately removed Onias from office and installed Jason in his stead. Jason built Greek *gymnasia*, or 'schools', in a city that he renamed Antioch-in-Jerusalem. Three years later Epiphanes replaced him with Menelaus.

REVOLT OF THE PIOUS

The *hassidim*, or Jewish 'pious ones', were disgusted that Antiochus Epiphanes nurtured a priesthood open to the highest bidder. Not averse to punning in Greek, they renamed Antiochus IV *Epimanes*, or 'the madman'. Soon farce turned to tragedy. On hearing Antiochus had died, Jason overthrew Menelaus but the rumours proved false, and Antiochus sacked Jason and reinstated Menelaus. This prompted a civil war between partisans for Jason and those for Menelaus, who were backed by the Tobiads, fabulously wealthy Hellenized Jewish tax collectors. Worse followed when Rome thwarted Antiochus' attack on

Above King Antiochus receiving the Judean leaders, from the Book of Maccabees, 11th-century Latin Bible.

Ptolemaic Egypt in 168BCE. In revenge Antiochus tore down Jerusalem's city walls, massacred thousands, ordered the Jewish scriptures destroyed, brought prostitutes to the Temple, and executed anyone caught practising circumcision. The final outrage came in December, when Antiochus entered the Temple and sacrificed a pig in honour of the Greek god Zeus.

THE MACCABEE BROTHERS

What followed was probably the first successful guerrilla war in history. In Modi'in, outside Jerusalem, a priest named Mattathias the Hasmonean killed a Jew who was about to sacrifice to a Greek idol. Mattathias and his five sons then fled to the hills of Judea, and became folk heroes. One son, Judah ha-Maccabee, or 'the hammer', led their makeshift dissident army after Mattathias died and harried Seleucid forces up and down the country. By 165BCE the Maccabee brothers took Jerusalem itself. General Lysias, preoccupied

Above A 13th-century Spanish Hebrew Bible shows implements and vessels of the Temple.

with strife in the Seleucid capital, Antioch, granted the Jews religious freedom. The Maccabees then cleansed the Temple, reinstituted Jewish worship, and named Judah's brother Jonathan as high priest. According to legend, there was only enough oil to light the Temple lanterns for a day, but it lasted for eight. This small miracle symbolized the greater miracle of national redemption and is still commemorated in the joyous eight-day-long wintertime festival of Hannukah.

THE HASMONEAN DYNASTY

No sooner had victory been achieved than divisions emerged. Judah was imbued with holy fervour and continued fighting. Others wanted to consolidate their gains and sign pragmatic treaties with neighbouring powers.

Judah died in battle in 160BCE, and his successor, Jonathan, was recognized as civil governor in 150BCE. With his brother Simon, Jonathan conquered Jaffa in 147BCE, thus winning Judea a desperately needed outlet to the sea. The biblical book 1 Maccabees praises Jonathan for making peace in the land: 'Israel

rejoiced with great joy, for every man sat under his vine or his fig tee, with none to disturb him.'

When Jonathan died in 142BCE, Simon Maccabee, Mattathias' last surviving son, became both high priest and army commander. That same year Syria's King Demetrius II granted Judea political independence. The Roman Senate confirmed this status a few years later. From then until 37BCE, a Hasmonean dynasty governed the first truly autonomous Jewish state since the Babylonian conquest 500 years before.

A HOUSE DIVIDED

Simon Maccabee's son and successor, John Hyrcanus (134–104BCE) proved energetic, able and resourceful. Calling himself nasi, or 'president', not king, he fended off an attack by Antiochus VII of Syria who besieged Jerusalem in 130BCE. John also converted the Idumeans (Edomites) to Judaism, crushed the Samaritans and expanded the kingdom's borders. Hasmonean rulers failed to live up to expectations, however. They adopted Hellenistic customs and Greek names and usurped the post of high priest, hitherto reserved for the tribe of Levi.

Above From the same Spanish Bible, the menorah, which the Maccabees relit after cleansing the defiled Temple.

Also, they quarrelled among themselves, some supporting the Ptolemies, others the Seleucids.

After John died, his son, the high priest Aristobolus, imprisoned his mother and brothers and titled himself king. After his death his widow, Salome Alexandra (*d.* 67BCE), freed the prisoners. One of these, Alexander Yannai, reigned from 103 to 76BCE. He further extended national borders, repelled invaders, introduced new coinage and formed a pact with Egypt's Queen Cleopatra (51–30BCE). He persecuted the Pharisee sect and during 94–86BCE he fought a civil war against them that claimed some 50,000 lives.

Internal divisions made Judah vulnerable to the ever-growing regional power of the Roman empire, which had initially favoured the Jews as an ally against their mutual enemies. Now Rome feared that Judah's aggressive policies of conversion and land acquisition east of the Jordan might impede their own imperial growth.

Left Judah ha-Maccabee gives money for sacrifices, from the Hours of Constable Anne de Montmorency, France, 1549.

Pharisees, Sadducees and Messianism

MASS POLITICAL PARTIES DID NOT EXIST IN THE ANCIENT WORLD. INSTEAD, RIVAL FACTIONS CONTENDED FOR CONTROL OVER UNDEMOCRATIC LEADERS. IN JUDEA, REFORMERS CLASHED AGAINST ALOOF PRIESTS.

In the 2nd century BCE Judea was more a theocracy than a monarchy. Its chief factions – Pharisees and Sadducees – grew out of differing theological trends. Both groups belonged to the Great Sanhedrin (assembly), a religious as well as a legislative body.

Over time Pharisees and Sadducees clashed over how they regarded the outside world. Generally, Sadducees favoured accommodating Persia, Ptolemaic Egypt, Seleucid Syria and later Rome. This remained true even when Judea gained formal independence after 142BCE. The Pharisees, by contrast, despised Hellenistic influence and preferred to assert Jewish autonomy, even at the risk of causing war with neighbouring gentile powers.

SADDUCEES, GUARDIANS OF THE TEMPLE CULT

Exactly when the Sadducees and Pharisees emerged as identifiable groups remains uncertain. Probably named after Zadok, King Solomon's high priest, the Sadducees claimed lineal descent from Aaron and officiated over the Temple cult.

Gradually the Sadducees grew into a hereditary aristocratic caste with a conservative outlook. In religious

Above Horseman of the apocalypse, a Christian vision of the messianic age from a Mexican church, 1562.

terms they sought to preserve their divinely ordained privileges. They read the Torah literally, distrusted innovation, denied the legal force of oral traditions and stressed ritual aspects of faith. Politically the Sadducees favoured a centralized state where priests, administrators and generals all gathered in Jerusalem. Sadducees also became pivotal to Judea's economy. Yet while they regarded their wealth as a sign of blessedness, their enemies called them corrupt and venal.

Sadducees accepted foreign rulers as long as they tolerated priestly customs. Excessive nationalism was dangerous, they reasoned, as past rebellions against Assyria and Babylon had proven. While Judah ha-Maccabee had been willing to risk a holy war, his surviving younger brother, the high priest Simon, preferred accommodating Judea's stronger neighbours. By the 2nd century BCE Sadducees began associating with the Hasmonean dynasty and also with Hellenism, some out of pragmatic calculation, some out of genuine admiration.

MESSIANISM

From the 2nd century BCE onwards a new theme emerged in Judaism. Called messianism, it drew on the prophetic writings of Isaiah, Elijah and Ezekiel, and gained political impetus as a backlash against Hellenism. Messianism articulated the dream of better days ahead. Its central figure was a moshiach, 'one anointed in oil', a saviour drawn from the Royal House of David. According to the belief, he will restore divine sovereignty to Israel and usher in a golden age of universal peace when God rules the earth. The notion gradually developed of two messiahs – one to redeem the Jews, followed by another to save all mankind. Messianism also promised the revival of the dead at the 'end of days', when an apocalyptic battle between good and evil was followed by a final judgement. The belief revolutionized Jewish thought and comforted Jews wary of the flawed secular world. A potentially dangerous ideology, it spawned many false messiahs during the 2,000 years of exile. It also influenced Kabbalah mysticism. Christians see Jesus as the promised messiah; to Jews, the messiah has yet to come. Though he will come, insisted the medieval sage Maimonides – 'even though he tarries'.

Above The anointing of David, from the Macclesfield Psalter, c. 1330.

Right Jewish Maccabees fight the Greek followers of Bacchus. 15th-century illustration by Jean Fouquet.

PHARISEES, INTERPRETERS OF A LIVING FAITH

Literally meaning 'the separated ones' (from the Hebrew *perushim*), the Pharisees were initially a small group of religiously learned laymen. Sincere worship and social justice mattered more to them than Temple rites. Spiritually they harked back to the prophet Isaiah, who wrote: 'To what purpose is the multitude of your sacrifices unto Me? saith the Lord. Bring no more vain oblations; it is an offering of abomination unto Me. Cease to do evil; learn to do well; seek justice, relieve the oppressed, judge the fatherless, plead for the widow'.

Pharisees owed much to the scribal tradition of Ezra, yet politically they grew out of the anti-Seleucid *hasidic* movement. At first the Pharisees supported the Hasmoneans, until they felt the revolution was being betrayed. On the religious plane, Pharisees interpreted an oral law which they said was delivered to Moses at Mt Sinai,

alongside the written Torah. Unlike Sadducees, they believed in human free will and divine retribution, as well as resurrection and the afterlife, and a conviction that a messiah would come. Pharisees believed that God was everywhere, not just in the Temple. Their preferred institution was the synagogue, decentralized and open to participation by all. Hence many consider them to be precursors of the rabbis.

BATTLE FOR POWER

Ultimately Rome's destruction of the Second Temple in 70CE removed the Sadducees' raison d'être. Even without a Temple, Jews today maintain a Sadducee ritual when Cohens or Levis recite the priestly benedictions – daily in Orthodox Israeli and Sephardi communities, only on high holy days for Ashkenazi Jews in the Diaspora. But the Pharisees provided the model for Judaism's development, and were the true precursors of today's rabbis.

Left Roman destruction of the Second Temple as imagined by the 19th-century Italian artist Francesco Hayez.

ISRAEL AND THE ROMAN EMPIRE

FROM A BACKWARD PROVINCIAL ITALIAN KINGDOM, REPUTEDLY FOUNDED BY TWIN BROTHERS IN 753BCE, ROME GREW INTO THE MIGHTIEST POWER THE WORLD HAD SEEN. AND IT SOON SET ITS SIGHTS ON JUDEA.

Rumours of Rome's prowess swept the Middle East when, in 202BCE, Scipio vanquished the Semitic Carthaginians of Tunisia. So when the Roman Republic signed a treaty with Judea in 161BCE, Jews thought they had a powerful ally in their battle against the Seleucids.

MASTER OF THE MEDITERRANEAN

Rome clearly wanted to own the Mediterranean region. It quelled Macedonia and imposed crippling terms on the Seleucid Antiochus III (223–187BCE) with the Treaty of Apamia (188BCE) after beating him in battles at land and sea.

By 168BCE Roman consuls were ensconced in Egypt; in 100BCE Rome crushed Jugurtha of Numidia (Algeria). Rome's eastern commander, Pompey, defeated Tigranes II of Armenia in 66BCE. The next year Rome overwhelmed its most dogged

Right Pompey the Great (106–48BCE), the general who made Judea a client of Rome.

foe, King Mithridates VI of Pontus, northern Anatolia, and Pompey cleared the eastern Mediterranean of pirates.

The gateway now lay open to the Middle East. Civil strife and attacks by Persian Parthians had severely weakened the Seleucid realm. Finally Pompey deposed Antiochus XIII and turned Syria into a Roman province in 64BCE.

POMPEY ENTERS JERUSALEM

Most Jews regarded Rome's triumph over Syria as divine comeuppance. They also hoped that Rome might help a benighted Judea. For ever since the Hasmonean queen Alexandra Salome died in 67BCE, her two sons, Hyrcanus II and Aristobolus II (reg. 66–63BCE), had

waged a ruinous battle for succession. The latter was triumphant in battle and took the crown.

The grievances took an ideological turn when the Pharisees supported Hyrcanus, and the Sadducees, Aristobolus. During Passover of 63BCE, Hyrcanus and his ally the Arab sheikh Ametas of Petra trapped the Sadducees in the Jerusalem Temple. Somehow, Aristobolus smuggled out a message to Pompey's consul in Syria, Marcus Aemilius Scaurus, promising him 6,000kg in silver if he could help. Aemilius duly ordered Ametas of Petra to lift the siege. When Pompey himself arrived in Jerusalem in 62BCE, Aristobolus gave him 800kg in gold. But when Aristobolus rashly accused the consul Aemilius of theft, Pompey switched sides and backed Hyrcanus. Roman forces then joined Pharisees in attacking the Sadducees. Following a three-month siege, they breached the Temple sanctuary with battering rams and catapults.

Now it was Pompey's turn to miscalculate: he entered the Holy of Holies and allowed his soldiers to

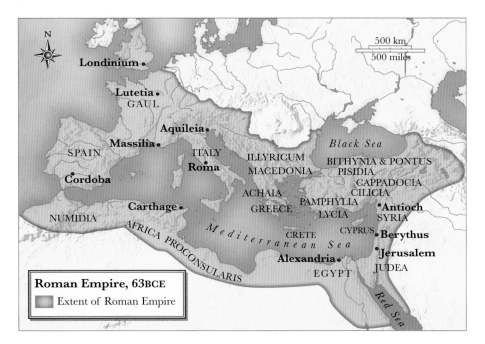

Roman Empire, 63BCE
Extent of Roman Empire

Left The Romans called the Mediterranean 'our sea'… their writ ran from Morocco in the west to Palestine and Egypt in the east.

Right Romulus and Remus, the twin brothers who legend says founded Rome. Sculpture dated c.500–480BCE.

make a sacrifice to their standards. Jews saw this as blasphemy, and the incident cast a pall over future relations with Rome.

Having turned Judea into a client kingdom, Pompey left to pursue his duties as joint ruler of Rome. Hyrcanus was enthroned as Judea's high priest and *ethnarch*, or 'national leader'. Aristobolus was banished and Roman forces annexed some 30 Judean cities that were exclusively populated by ethnic Greeks.

CAESAR AND ANTIPATER

Initial Jewish optimism for Roman rule turned sour in 57–55BCE, when Syria's governor, Aulus Gabinius, retrenched Hyrcanus' powers and favoured Judea's Greeks over Jews. One beneficiary of Roman rule was Antipater, an Idumean of Arab stock

Below A focal point of Rome's 2,200-year-old Jewish community, the Great Synagogue blends classical Italian and neo-Babylonian styles.

and a Jewish convert. Decades earlier Alexander Yannai had appointed him general of all Judea. Antipater later became chief aide to Hyrcanus, advisor to Pompey and governor of Idumaea. He then helped Gabinius thwart Aristobolus' last attempt to regain power in 55BCE, and steadily encroached on Hyrcanus' authority. Antipater then ingratiated himself with Julius Casear after he defeated Pompey's armies. He persuaded Egyptian Jews to back Caesar and recruited Jewish and Nabatean soldiers to the fight. In 47BCE Caesar made Judea a direct subject of Rome. Having crushed revolts by two Hasmonean aspirants, Antipater became Judea's regent, procurator (chief minister) and tax collector.

Caesar restored Jewish confidence by granting Jews greater political autonomy. He reduced their taxes, exempted them from army service, guaranteed freedom of worship and returned some land to Judea. The shock of his assassination in 44BCE threw the future into doubt. Antipater now switched allegiance to the equally canny Cassius, administrator of Syria, against Rome's new emperor Mark Antony. A Syrian–Judean alliance seemed imminent, until Antipater was poisoned by a rival and died in 43BC.

Wisely, Antipater had guaranteed his legacy by ensuring that his sons, Herod and Phasael, were governors of Galilee and Jerusalem. Herod was to found a dynasty that supplanted the Hasmoneans and changed the course of Jewish history.

SONS OF ROME

There is a curious twist to this story. Pompey had taken thousands of Judean prisoners to Rome in 62BCE. After they were freed they settled beyond the River Tiber. There they formed the hub of a unique Diaspora Jewish society called Benei Roma (Sons of Rome), or Italkim. They were led by *archontes*, or 'rulers', and *gerousiarchoi*, or 'synagogue presidents'. Despite thriving in Rome, resentment simmered under the surface. In 55BCE the orator Cicero called Judaism barbaric, and defended a proconsul of Asia accused of seizing Temple gold donated by Jews. A fraud case saw Jews temporarily expelled from Italy in 19CE. But the community was enhanced when a new influx of Jewish prisoners came to Rome after the destruction of Jerusalem's Temple in 70CE. The community still exists, and its liturgy and cantorial techniques may preserve the closest approximation of original Judean tradition today.

HEROD'S DYNASTY

HEROD DISPLACED JUDEA'S HASMONEAN DYNASTY WITH ROME'S
APPROVAL. HIS NOTORIOUS CRUELTY BLIGHTED HIS REPUTATION AS
A MASTER BUILDER AND REGIONAL POTENTATE.

Pax Romana, or the 'peace of Rome', took an unexpected blow in Judea when Parthians overran Asia Minor, Syria and Judea in 40BCE. Working in cahoots with renegade Roman commander Labienus, the Parthians deposed Judea's Hyrcanus II, cut off his ears, and replaced him with his nephew Antigonus who was fated to be Judea's last Hasmonean ruler. In Rome, Mark Antony met Herod, recently deposed as governor of Galilee, and crowned him 'king of the Jews'. Herod then headed a Roman army that recovered Jerusalem after a five-month siege in 37BCE. Antigonus was overthrown and beheaded.

HEROD THE GREAT
The controversial new king became known as Herod I the Great (37–4BCE). The Christian Gospels tell of his 'massacre of the innocents' in his quest to kill the newborn 'king of the Jews', Jesus Christ. Jews recalled

Below A genius of construction, Herod built Herodium as his hilltop palace and fortress south-east of Bethlehem.

how he had also slain religious rebels in Galilee while governor. During Herod's reign he killed 47 members of Judea's Sanhedrin soon after his enthronement. He married Mariamne, daughter of the Hasmonean queen, Alexandra, but put her to death, as well as her mother and brother, and even his two sons, as his paranoia took grip.

Herod saw himself as monarch of all Jews and not just those in Judea. He appointed Hananel, a descendant of Zadok, as high priest, and funded synagogues, libraries, baths and charities for burgeoning Jewish communities in Antioch, Babylon, Alexandria and Rome itself. Generally he favoured Pharisees over Sadducees, and fellow Hellenized (Greek-influenced) Jews over traditionalists.

A MASTER BUILDER
A financial genius, Herod monopolized the extraction of asphalt from the Dead Sea and relieved drought in Judea by importing grain from Egypt. Herod was fanatically loyal to Rome and cleverly heeded non-Jewish concerns beyond Judea's borders. He single-handedly revived the Olympic Games, refurbished Antioch and Byblos, built a forum in Tyre and theatres in Sidon and Damascus.

Certainly the greatest Jewish builder since King Solomon, Herod sought to modernize what he saw as a backward Judea. He recast Samaria as 'Sebastia' and he created a mountain villa-fortress overlooking the Dead Sea at Masada, and another, Herodium, just south of Jerusalem. He also built the sumptuous port of Caesarea, complete with a vast artificial harbour.

Above Herod captures Jerusalem with his Roman allies, 38BCE. From Jean Fouquet's 15th-century French manuscript, Antiquites Judaïques.

In Jerusalem Herod built an amphitheatre and the imposing Antonia fortress, and vastly expanded and ornamented the second Temple, drawing millions of visitors, Jewish and gentile alike. He encouraged lavish Temple sacrifices and the three pilgrimage festivals, yet confined the Sanhedrin to purely religious matters.

A ROYAL DYNASTY
Herod established a hereditary dynasty, but his successors were weak. Herod Archelaus (*b.* 22BCE–*d. c.*18CE), his son and heir by the Samaritan queen, Malthace, proved so unpopular and incompetent that in 6CE Rome deposed him as national leader of Judea. Rome now chose to rule through procurators in Caesarea, answerable to the Roman legate in Antioch. Herod the Great's grandson, Herod Agrippa, raised in elite circles in Rome, proved more able and governed Judea from 37CE until his death in 44CE. (His brother, Herod III, ruled southern Lebanon over the same period.) Agrippa was allegedly assassinated by Romans who feared his growing power. Rome then re-imposed direct rule, sowing the seeds for Jewish revolt.

ROME AND IUDAEA

INEPT RULE BY HEROD'S SUCCESSOR INVITED ROMAN INTERVENTION AND THE CREATION OF IUDAEA. HERE, JEWS REJECTED TAX, BATTLED THE GREEKS AND ADOPTED MILITANCY AGAINST THE OCCUPIERS.

Long dormant troubles surfaced after Herod the Great died in 4BCE. Rioting broke out and only ceased when Roman authorities crucified 2,000 rebels. Eventually opposition to Rome combined with religious and class schisms and led to nationwide uprisings, the Temple's destruction and the end of Jewish statehood. Amidst the turmoil a new religion was born – Christianity.

DIRECT RULE AND TAXES
In 6CE Emperor Augustus heeded calls from Jews and Samaritans and ousted the inept Herod Archelaus. What followed was less welcome: Rome fused Judea into a directly governed province called Iudaea, which included Idumea (Edom) and Samaria but excluded Galilee, the Golan Heights and Perea. So Galilean Jews were cut off from their kinsfolk in a policy of 'divide and rule'.

Below The ruins of Masada, last outpost of the 66-73CE Jewish Revolt. Here some 960 Jewish Zealots and their families took their own lives, it is said, rather than surrender to Roman forces.

Publius Sulpicius Quirinius became governor of Syria, and Coponius ruled Iudaea as its first prefect (based in Caesarea). Judas of Galilee, driven as much by cultural and theological motives as by economic ones, led a violent revolt when Quirinius ordered a regional census for the purposes of taxation. Of all Rome's subject peoples, Jews especially refused to accept Roman culture as superior.

ZEALOTS
Jerusalem's high priest Joazar condemned the tax revolt, which Rome anyway soon crushed. Nonetheless, wrote the contemporary Jewish historian Flavius Josephus, Judea now had a fourth sect after the Pharisees, Sadducees and Essenes. These 'Zealots' drew on messianic rhetoric and sent vigilantes, the Sicarites, to kill Romans, Greek colonists and suspected Jewish collaborators with their sicus, or 'short sword'. Zealots saw Rome as a kingdom of arrogance, the antithesis of what God had promised his 'chosen people'.

Above Pontius Pilate, Roman procurator at the time of Jesus, by an unknown Italian painter, 1510.

Roman procurators, or prefects, governed Iudaea until 41CE, the most infamous being Pontius Pilate (26–38CE). King Herod Agrippa I, a favourite of emperors Caligula and Claudius, reigned over Iudaea from 41 to 44CE and managed to placate Romans and Jews to some extent. Direct Roman rule returned after Agrippa's assassination. Immediately two sons of Judas of Galilee, Jacob and Simon, led another abortive Zealot revolt.

ONE IN TEN ROMANS...
Some seven million Jews lived in the Roman empire by 44CE; another million were located outside the imperial borders, mostly in Babylonia. Thus the vast majority of the world's Jews came under the Roman ambit. They constituted fully 10 per cent of the empire's population.

Of that number, fewer than 2.5 million Jews dwelt in Judea itself. Thus when Herod the Great claimed to speak for all Jews, not just Judeans, he gained influence out of proportion with the size of his kingdom.

JESUS

OUT OF 1ST-CENTURY JUDEA A PREACHER EMERGED WHO WAS TO
MAKE A MASSIVE IMPACT ON CIVILIZATION. JESUS WAS BORN, RAISED
AND ARGUABLY DIED A JEW, BUT HIS STORY SPAWNED CHRISTIANITY.

Above The Tree of Jesse, from a 13th-century psalter, demonstrates Christ's lineage from Jesse, father of David, and hence his claim to messianic inheritance.

Jesus of Nazareth is the most famous man in history. He is the inspiration of the world's largest religion, Christianity. To Christians he is the messiah promised in the Book of Isaiah, and the Son of God. No other figure has been so celebrated in art, and his teachings have been translated into virtually every known language. Jesus profoundly affected the development of Western civilization. Christians, moreover, see Jesus as the saviour of humanity.

Jesus' story – as told in the four Gospels, Matthew, Mark, Luke and John – is deeply rooted in the Jewish narrative. 'Jesus', an anglicized form of the Greek Iesous, is Greek for Joshua (*Yehoshua* in Hebrew, which means 'YHWH is salvation'). 'Christ', from the Greek *Christos*, or 'anointed one', is equivalent to the Hebrew messiah. He was born to a Jewish family in Bethlehem, David's royal city. He studied under rabbis, preached almost exclusively to fellow Jews and often quoted Jewish scriptures. Apart from one trip to Egypt, his life and mission was located within historic Palestine. His followers sought to prove that his arrival fulfilled Old Testament prophecies. Matthew traces his descent from David, as a Jewish readership would expect such lineage before they could consider him as messiah.

JESUS THE MAN

Despite some discrepancies in the gospels and folklore that attached to later accounts, the historic Jesus is fairly well documented, although precise dates are not certain. He was probably born in 4BCE, shortly before Herod the Great died. His parents were Joseph and Mary (Miriam); Matthew and Luke affirm a virgin birth. The family came from Nazareth but went to Bethlehem for Herod's census.

When Jesus was eight his family fled to Egypt to escape persecution by Herod Archelaus. In 7CE, say the Gospels, the 12-year-old Jesus amazed the Jerusalem Temple priests with his knowledge. After this he returned to Nazareth to help his carpenter father. There then follow several missing years. Jesus' ministry began in around 26CE, after John the Baptist anointed him messiah in the River Jordan. Around that time Pontius Pilate became prefect of Judea, and Caiaphas was appointed high priest in Jerusalem.

JESUS' GOSPEL

In autumn 26CE Jesus cleared the money changers out of the Temple in Jerusalem, and in summer 27CE four Galilean fishermen became his first followers. By winter 28CE he had 12 disciples; in the spring he preached his 'sermon on the mount', as found in Matthew 5-7, in which he laid down the foundations of the new teaching ethic founded on the law of love in contrast to the old law of retribution. He also began conducting miracles. Soon the disciples were also spreading Jesus' gospel and performing healing.

Left Christ praying on the Mount of Olives as his disciples rest. From a painted panel, Hohenfurth Monastery, Bohemia, 1350.

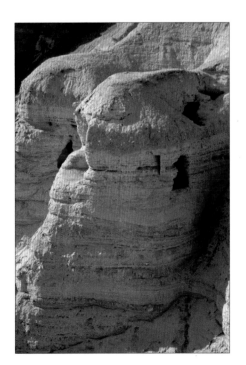

The Essenes emerged in the 2nd century BCE when anti-Hellenist Jews, furious that Maccabeans had usurped the high priesthood, left Jerusalem and lived monastically in the wilderness, seeing themselves as the 'True Israel'. Essenes lacerated the Pharisees in stronger terms than Jesus. The Dead Sea Scrolls contain one Essene psalm that promises salvation to 'the humble, oppressed in spirit and those who mourn', echoing Jesus' word. But while Essenes were reclusive and refused female company, Jesus preached to all.

Jesus predicted his own death in 29CE. The next year he entered Jerusalem. Betrayed by his disciple Judas Iscariot during the Passover festival, Jesus was arrested in the Garden of Gethsemane, tried by the Sanhedrin, or Temple officials, for blasphemy, and sentenced by Pilate, seemingly for insurrection. He was then crucified at Golgotha.

ORIGINS AND INFLUENCES

The Gospels famously condemn both Pharisees and Sadducees as hypocrites. On closer inspection, suggest some scholars, Jesus himself

Above An early Christian painting of Christ and the Samaritan woman at the well, Roman catacombs, c.320BCE.

might have been a Pharisee, albeit a radical one. Certainly he was no Sadducee: he damned excessive wealth and corrupt Sadducean practices. Jesus apparently resembled one Pharisaic strain, the *hakhamim*, or 'itinerant wise men'. Like them he was a populist rabbi, or teacher; he delivered lessons through parables, akin to rabbinic *midrashim*. Jesus never refuted the Torah's law and commandments in the Gospels. He did, though, stress that faith, love, hope and charity are in God's eyes superior to the legalism ascribed to by Pharisees.

Some scholars define Jesus as an Essene (see box), but he rejected their ascetic tendencies. His use of messianic imagery recalls the Zealots. But his message – 'turn the other cheek' – clashes with their militancy. Jesus chided disciples who wanted to attack Rome; he paid the

Temple tax and said 'render unto Caesar what is Caesar's'. Whether he can be subsumed into a sect or not, Jesus certainly drew on his Jewish heritage. After his death a new religion emerged, one that both spread Judaic principles and clashed with the parent faith.

Left Scrolls from this cave at Qumran have intrigued scholars ever since they were found in 1947.

Right Similar jars from Qumran held the Dead Sea Scrolls, whose Essene writings call to mind Jesus' teachings.

THE RISE OF CHRISTIANITY

PAUL HELPED FORM CHRISTIANITY INTO A DISTINCT RELIGION. 'JEWISH CHRISTIANS' WITHERED AWAY AS GENTILES ACCEPTED THE NEW FAITH AND JEWS BAULKED AT GOSPEL ACCOUNTS OF CHRIST'S DIVINITY.

At first the 'Jesus movement' was basically another Jewish sect. Gradually, though, the two separate religions emerged and by 150CE Judaism and Christianity were competing faiths, heading in different directions.

SISTER FAITHS DIVIDED

Three factors may explain this schism. First, St Paul's mission of spreading Christ's words to gentiles (non-Jews) accelerated the process of absorbing 'alien' Hellenistic customs into the faith. Core Christian texts were written in Greek and Latin, which further divorced the religion from its Hebrew, Aramaic and Jewish roots. Second, the notion of a resurrected Jesus and the developing doctrine of God's incarnation

Below St Stephen's stoning to death in Jerusalem c.34CE typified the Jesus sect's tribulations. Painting by Francesco Bissolo, 1505.

in human form tested Christianity's ties with Judaism to breaking point. Third, Jews considered that the Christian New Testament depicted Jews as enemies of God's will. Christian dogma spoke about their followers replacing Jews as the 'true elect of Israel'. And when the Roman empire adopted Christianity in the 4th century CE, the faith became a religion of power. This seems ironic, given Christ's stress on humility, modesty and the meek. By contrast, after the destruction of the Temple, Judaism seemed like a credo of the dispersed and dispossessed.

CRACKS APPEAR

Initially, Jesus' mission seemed over when he died on the cross in 30CE. The Gospels, however, related that Jesus then reappeared to his disciples before being recalled to heaven. He had died in a bodily sense but was reborn to eternal life. Most Jews understood that a messiah should herald an age of universal peace, or at least expel the Romans from Judea. Christians replied that Christ planned a second coming and ultimate redemption.

The Gospels were completed around 90CE, long after Christ's death. Their passages speak of how the Temple shuddered when Christ was crucified. Christians interpreted this as predicting that the Temple would fall because of Jewish complicity in the Lord's death. However, because the texts were finalized after Jerusalem's destruction, some scholars suppose that these 'predictions' may have been added to 'prove' the superiority of Christianity.

Above St Peter holding the keys to the Kingdom of Heaven. Austrian altarpiece panel by Friedrich Pacher, c.1508.

JERUSALEM CHURCH

Members of the early Jerusalem Church considered themselves fully Jewish. Led by James (Jacob) – the first Christian bishop and reputedly the brother of Jesus – they prayed in the Temple, observed the Jewish Sabbath and obeyed Torah commandments. Certainly they differed from fellow Jews in seeing Jesus as the Messiah. Yet most stopped short of calling him the Son of God and questioned the doctrine of virgin birth.

While open to proselytes, the Jerusalem Church wanted gentiles to convert to Judaism before they could become Christian. Gradually, distinctive elements entered their practice. Initiates were baptized, as Christ was by John. The church became a community that shared possessions, heard reports from the apostles and stressed the virtues of love, repentance and charity. It also spread tidings of 'Christ's Way' and his return. Allied congregations in Galilee survived after a Sadducean priest killed James in 62CE. Yet the Roman sacking of Jerusalem in 70CE decimated the sect.

CHRISTIANITY'S FOUNDERS.
Some scholars regard Paul, not Jesus, as the real founder of Christianity. He was born Saul, a Pharisee from Tarsus in Cilicia, southern Turkey; a rabbi and tent-maker by trade, yet also a Roman citizen. Paul was about to persecute dissident Christ-believers in Damascus in 34CE when, he wrote, he was struck blind and saw Jesus in a revelation.

Paul preached Christian doctrines during 45–57CE, initially to Diaspora Jews in Antioch, Ephesus, Sardis, Iconium and Philadelphia (all in modern Turkey) as well as in Jerusalem, Corinth, Rome and Alexandria.

He went a step further by promoting Christianity among gentiles. Hitherto, gentile males wishing to convert to Judaism would have to undergo circumcision. Paul argued that Christ's 'new covenant' – a term originally used by the prophet Jeremiah – entirely replaced the old Mosaic code. Christians no longer needed to obey Judaism's laws of kashrut, or 'kosher food', or observe Jewish festivals, or circumcise their male children. Gentiles would thus find conversion more attractive. Further, Paul said, one could only enter the Kingdom of Heaven through personal faith in Jesus as the messiah. Such views were anathema to normative Jews.

Born at Bethsaida on the Sea of Galilee, Peter was one of the original 12 disciples. He changed his name from Simon to Peter, Greek for rock, as Jesus told him: 'Upon this rock I will build my church'. In time, Peter was hailed as the first bishop of Rome. The Jewish sage Gamaliel the Elder persuaded fellow Sanhedrin members to spare Peter's life when they threatened to execute him. Peter and Paul were partners in propagating the new faith, although Paul accused Peter of 'Judaizing' the religion. Some say Paul resented Peter for knowing Jesus.

MARTYRS AND *MINIM*

Both Roman and Jewish authorities sporadically persecuted Christians. Many apostles were martyred, beginning with Stephen, stoned to death

Above Caravaggio's dramatic depiction of St Paul's conversion on the road to Damascus, 1601.

by a Jerusalem mob around 34CE at the behest of a pre-Paul Saul. Christian tradition relates that Emperor Nero blamed Christians for the great fire of Rome in 64CE and consequently had Peter crucified and Paul beheaded.

Jewish Christian sects called Ebionites, or the 'poor ones', and Nazirites survived for a while in Judea. In the mid-2nd century CE, however, Gamaliel II, son of Gamaliel, ruled that Christians of any ilk were *minim*, or 'dissidents' who could no longer pray with other Jews.

It is known that Ebionites largely fled Judea for Pella, across the Jordan, when Judea revolted in 66CE. So some ascribe a political element to Gamaliel's charge. Put simply, Jewish Christians voluntarily dissociated themselves from the Jewish people. As Pauline Christians saw them as heretics, too, they quickly disappeared from history.

Left Jesus with James the Less, from a 12th-century column capital, Cathedral of St Lazare, Autun, France.

RABBIS ASCENDANT

JUDAISM MAY NEVER HAVE SURVIVED AS WE KNOW IT HAD A RABBINICAL TRADITION NOT BEEN ESTABLISHED. BUT WHO EXACTLY WERE THE FIRST RABBIS, AND WHAT DOES THE TERM MEAN?

'Rabbi' derives from the Hebrew for 'great teacher'. As a professional title it was first applied to Judah the Prince (Yehuda Ha-Nasi), in the Mishnah, the summary of oral law. Judah compiled the Mishnah around 200CE and based it on nearly 350 years of scholarship and debate by people we would call rabbis.

According to Jewish tradition, custodianship of the Torah passed down an ancient chain of wisdom, from patriarchs to the elders, then to the prophets, the Great Assembly, the Pharisees, and finally to the sages or rabbis. The Great Assembly's creed became the rabbis' motto: 'Be patient in judgement, raise up many students and build a fence around the Torah'. This aphorism is one of many encapsulated in the Mishnah's *Pirkei Avot*, or 'Ethics of the Fathers'.

THE SANHEDRIN

The bedrock of the rabbinic tradition were the *zugot*, or 'pairs' of rabbis, who presided over each generation, starting in 142BCE when the Maccabeans re-established Judean independence. Convention decreed that one of the *zugot* was the *nasi*, or 'president of the Great Sanhedrin', while his partner was the *av beit din*, or 'chief justice and vice-president'.

Above A simple yet stark image of the Temple menorah, from a 2nd–3rd-century CE synagogue near Tiberias.

The Great Sanhedrin combined the functions of supreme court and legal assembly. Its 71 members debated in the Temple's Hall of Hewn Stones.

Each city could have its own Lesser Sanhedrin of 23 members. Hence power was devolved and local customs respected. Lower courts encouraged independence from the Temple cult, yet only the Great Sanhedrin could put the king on trial, extend the borders of Jerusalem or act as final arbiter in any controversy. While hardly democratic in the modern sense, the Sanhedrin enjoyed considerable powers of scrutiny. Shemaya and Abtalion, Pharisees who presided during the rule of Byrcunas II, even summoned Herod, then governor of Galilee, to answer charges of murdering the rebel leader Hezekiah. Shemaya is quoted in *Pirkei Avot*: 'Love work, hate authority and don't get friendly with the government'.

HILLEL AND SHAMMAI

Under the *zugot* system, each issue tended to generate two viewpoints. The Mishnah recorded which was accepted yet preserved the minority decision for future scholars to ponder. *Zugot* often represented different approaches, too. The most famous

Left A rabbi teaches Hillel's golden rule. Depicted by Samuel Halevi in the Coburg Pentateuch, Bavaria, 1395.

duo was Hillel the Elder and Shammai, active in King Herod the Great's reign. Hillel was universalistic and innovative; his lenient rulings stressed the spirit of the law and tried to make compliance easier. Shammai, a builder by trade, was stricter, conservative and more concerned about detail.

Hillel's views usually prevailed over Shammai's. Once, goes the legend, a sceptic challenged Hillel to explain the whole Torah while he stood on one leg. 'Whatever is hateful to you, do not do to your fellow', replied the sage. 'The rest is commentary. Now go and study'. Hillel was born in Babylonia and left for Jerusalem to learn under Shemaya and Abtalion. The story is that he could not afford to pay the academy's entrance fee, so he perched on the roof and listened in. One cold Sabbath the determined student had

to be rescued from under a layer of snow. Eventually he became the *nasi*, and is thought to have taught Jesus.

Many Hillel parables and sayings appear in *Pirkei Avot*, including his three rhetorical questions: 'If I am not for myself, who will be for me?' 'If I am only for myself, what am I?' And 'If not now, when?'

THE SANHEDRIN'S POWER

Over time the Great Sanhedrin became in effect a political counterweight to the *cohen ha-gadol*, or the Temple High Priest, an office that was increasingly dominated by wealthy Hellenized appointees.

In Roman times charismatic rabbis advised and sometimes criticized secular Jewish rulers. Often they ruled on sensitive political matters. For example, Gamaliel I (the elder) of the House of Hillel persuaded the Sanhedrin to accept Christians

Above Rabbi Yehuda Ha-Nasi led Judea's Jews during late 2nd century CE Roman rule. Entrance to his burial catacomb, Beit She'arim, Israel.

within the Jewish fold. The new sect's messianic claims, he suggested, had yet to be proven or disproven. Johanan Ben Zakkai was probably the most politically effective rabbi; he rescued the Sanhedrin from Jerusalem as the Temple was about to fall and negotiated with Rome to re-establish the institution in Jabneh.

TEMPLE TO SYNAGOGUE

Alongside the rabbis, one other institution allowed Judaism to survive beyond the soon-to-be-destroyed Temple. This was the synagogue, a Greek word that means the same as the Hebrew *beit ha-knesset*, or 'house of assembly'. The first probably arose in Babylonian exile, but it truly developed in Second Temple Palestine, at Caesarea, Capernaum, Dor and Tiberias. Unlike temples, synagogues require no expensive priestly rites. Religious services could be held as long as the Torah and a *minyan*, or 'quorum', of ten adult men were present. Jews throughout the Diaspora copied the model, with the synagogue in Alexandria being the most lavish. Only one Diaspora community – a military colony of Jews on the Nile island of Zeb, or Elephantine, near Aswan in Egypt – built an alternative temple. But it withered when the 29th Egyptian dynasty replaced Persian rule in 399BCE.

PHILO OF ALEXANDRIA

Philo was a contemporary of Hillel and the first major Jewish contributor to Western philosophy. Born into a respected Egyptian Jewish family *c.* 20BCE, he still excites controversy in orthodox Jewish circles. Philo's synthesis of Judaism and Hellenism built on foundations laid by Aristobolus of Paneas. He left behind a vast literary output: philosophical works, a legal explanation of the Pentateuch, a biography of Moses, a book on the Creation, 18 treatises of allegorical interpretations, an investigation into biblical dreams, and rhetorical analyses of several Jewish texts.

Philo aimed to show that Judaism formed a coherent ethical system. He

Above Known as the Jewish Plato, Philo pioneered the blending of Greek and Judaic learning.

blended universalism with a conviction that Jews should be 'priests of humanity'. In his view the Jewish deity was identical to Plato's form of the good. Philo greatly influenced Hellenized Jews. His concept of God interceding in the world via the *logos* (word or idea) also coloured Christianity: John's Gospel opens with 'In the beginning was the word'. Philo anticipated later Jewish thinkers who engaged with the secular world, like Spinoza, Marx and Freud. Unlike them, he believed in the intrinsic truth of the Torah.

THE FALL OF THE SECOND TEMPLE

THE JUDEAN REVOLT OF 66–73CE WAS A DISASTER FOR THE JEWISH PEOPLE, YET IT MARKED A NEW BEGINNING. JEWS CHANGED THEIR SELF-DEFINITION AND ESTABLISHED THE STATUS OF THE DIASPORA.

Anger at colonial rule certainly contributed to the Judean revolt. Tiberius, who became Caesar in 14CE, had upset Jews by stealing Temple treasures to pay for an aqueduct. After he died in 37CE his successor, Caligula, provoked rioting when he tried to place a statue of himself as Jupiter in the Temple.

Another factor was the dashing of expectations raised during the reign of Herod Agrippa I, an independent Jewish king whose reign coincided with the first years of Emperor Claudius. Agrippa ruled Galilee after 38CE and also Judea, Samaria and the Golan after 41CE. A friend to Caesars

Below This map of revolts against Rome 66–74CE shows Judean rebels wrested power from Rome, but eventually imperial forces crushed all resistance.

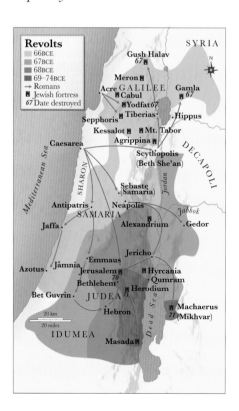

and fluent in Roman ways, he championed Jewish interests while generously funding Hellenized towns. When he died in 44CE – possibly murdered – Rome re-imposed direct rule, and replaced military prefects with harsher civilian procurators.

ROMAN PREJUDICE

More broadly, Roman rulers resented Jews' refusal to bow to imperial superiority, and feared an empire-wide conflagration as pagans, Jewish proselytes and new Christians locked horns in theological battle. Apion, Tacitus, Lysimachus and other Greek and Roman writers derided Jewish practices as bizarre and outdated. Some chastized Jews as enemies of mankind, and Emperor Claudius warned Alexandrian Jews against 'spreading a general plague throughout the world'.

In Judea, Greek settlers dominated the province's civil service, merchant class and Roman cohorts, while ordinary Jewish farmers suffered from taxation and banditry. Ethnically mixed cities such as Caesarea, Sephoris and Joppa (Yaffo) represented islands of wealth in a sea of growing poverty, and were also focal points for clashes between rival Greek and Jewish communities. The previously marginal Zealots benefited from these tensions, and their messianic fervour began attracting a formerly cautious and moderate Jewish middle class.

Opportunism also played its part in the timing of the revolt. Rome was battling Persian Parthia on its eastern flank, so Jews saw a chance to strike when the empire seemed

Above The iconic image of Jewish defeat: soldiers carry away Temple vessels. From Rome's Arch of Titus.

weak. They expected Parthia to rally to their side, and recalled how in 166BCE the Greco-Syrians had crumbled before the Maccabeans. Finally, the uprising sprang from long-simmering divisions within Jewish society. In 50CE, Herod Agrippa II became a Roman vassal-king. In 63CE he completed Temple restorations; but Judeans knew that true power resided with the procurators who colluded with wealthy priestly families of Diaspora origin.

THE SPARK

Eventually in 64CE, the notoriously megalomaniac Caesar, Nero, replaced procurator Albinus with the even more bigoted Gesius Florus. Having encouraged anti-Jewish riots by Greeks in Caesarea, in May 66CE Florus marched into Jerusalem, a city already choking with Jewish refugees from the countryside. It proved a fatal miscalculation. Roman troops massacred Jews in the market, prompting a ferocious counterattack by street-fighting rebels. After a stunned Florus withdrew his men, rebels toppled the hapless Agrippa, and by June Jerusalem had an independent aristocratic government.

DIVIDED REVOLUTION

The loss of first the city of Jerusalem and then Joppa alarmed Rome, as other subject nations might well rise up if the revolt were not crushed soon. So, in October 66CE, the Syrian legate, Cestius Gallus, invaded Palestine. After initial success he was repulsed at Jerusalem and defeated at Beit-Horon.

Agrippa's supporters attacked Eleazar ben Simon, the Jewish victor over Cestius. Galilean Zealots then captured Jerusalem's Antonia fortress before a former high priest, Anan ben Anan, declared a second aristocratic government in November 66CE. Soon Jews were fighting each other: northern guerrillas under John of Giscala battled 40,000 troops loyal to Simon bar Giora, a radical of Edomite origin.

JOSEPHUS

The leader of Galilee's rebels, Joseph ben Matthias, proved particularly mercurial. Galilee was a crucial buffer province as 60,000 Roman and allied troops and cavalry advanced from Syria. But Joseph neglected war preparations, whether

Below Nero, Vespasian and Titus are shown battling Jews in a 15th-century Histoire des Juifs *by Flavius Josephus.*

out of incompetence or deliberate treachery. General Vespasian's men massacred thousands of Jews at the fort of Yodfat (Jotapata) in July 67CE; all remaining defenders killed themselves, except Joseph and one other.

Joseph then passed on military intelligence to Vespasian and his son Titus, both future Roman emperors. Today Joseph is better known as Flavius Josephus, author of *The Jewish War*, *Against Apion* and *Jewish Antiquities*. Notwithstanding his tendency to self-promotion, he was a brilliant Latin stylist, a fascinating example of a Jew straddling two cultures, and one of the greatest historians of his age.

THE TEMPLE FALLS

After 67CE three Roman legions retook Tiberias, Gamla, Mount Tabor, Giscala, Azotus, Jamnia, Jericho and Qumran. Neither Parthia nor the Jewish Diaspora supported what seemed like a lost cause, especially given Judea's political instability. Jerusalem changed hands in 68CE when John of Giscala overthrew the aristocrats, and again in April 69CE when Simon bar Giora ousted him in turn.

Above End of an era – Titus Destroys the Temple in Jerusalem *by Nicolas Pouisson (1594–1665).*

Vespasian left Judea in 69CE, and between April and September 70CE his successor Titus besieged Jerusalem. At first rebels burnt the Roman assault ramps, but the legionaries blockaded the city and starved its inhabitants. Eventually they captured the fortress, torched the Temple, hunted down fugitives and sacked the rest of Jerusalem.

To celebrate his victory Titus toured the east and later constructed the Arch of Titus in Rome. It shows soldiers carrying the menorah and other Temple artefacts, and stands next to the Coliseum, a building probably funded by Judean loot and built by Jewish slave labour.

The Judean revolt finally ended in 73CE with the mass suicide of Zealots holed up in besieged Masada, an imposing Herodian-built fortress overlooking the Dead Sea. Agrippa II reassumed Judea's throne for another 17 years, and Rome re-established respectful relations with surviving Jews, but genuine Jewish statehood was no more.

THE FINAL REVOLT

THE YEARS FOLLOWING THE FALL OF THE TEMPLE SAW ROME BARRING
JEWS FROM JERUSALEM, AND JEWISH RISINGS AGAINST ROMAN RULE,
CULMINATING IN THE BAR KOCHBA REVOLT OF 132–5CE.

*Above The façade of the Temple in
Jerusalem on a bronze coin that dates
from the Bar Kochba revolt, 132–5CE.*

The fall of Jerusalem was not quite the end of the Jewish revolt. Ringleader Simon bar Giora was executed in spring 71CE, but Roman 'mopping up' operations dragged on for at least two more years. Finally, the cities of Herodian, Machereus and Masada fell, the last after a fearsome attack and the supposed mass suicide of its inhabitants: Sicarite fighters as well as women and children. Certain Israeli army combat units still use Masada as a site for swearing in graduates, because of its emotional symbolism.

SANHEDRIN SAVED
While some contemporary Jews hail Masada's commander, Eleazar ben Ya'ir, as a hero, others see him as a dangerously misguided extremist. By contrast, they regard Yohanan ben Zakkai as the only figure to emerge from the revolt debacle with any

*Below Ruins of the Jewish camp at
Masada where Jewish Zealots
succumbed to Rome in 73CE.*

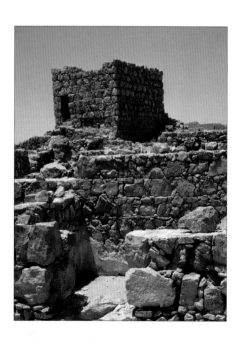

dignity. Yohanan was a revered rabbi in Jerusalem who, though initially affiliated with the Zealots, soon realized that the revolt was a hopeless cause. According to Talmudic legend, Yohanan had himself smuggled out of the besieged city of Jerusalem in a coffin. He then struck a deal with the Romans allowing him to reconstitute the Sanhedrin, formerly located in the Temple precinct, in Jamnia (Yavneh) on the southern Palestinian coast. So when Jerusalem fell in 70CE, the central authority for Jewish law survived. In 80CE, Gamaliel II replaced Yohanan and further bolstered the strength of the institution.

ROMAN PRAGMATISM
Rome barred Jews from Jerusalem after its destruction but otherwise adopted a moderate policy towards them, if only for pragmatic reasons. It was imperative to keep open the trading routes that carried grain from Egypt, through Palestine, to Rome. Likewise, Rome was determined to prevent its main enemies, the Parthians, from exploiting unrest in Palestine. If Parthia was to capture Palestine, as it had briefly managed to do earlier, this could drive a wedge through the Roman empire.

Around the year 95CE the Emperor Diocletian agreed to recognize a Jewish patriarch in Galilee as spokesman for Jews throughout the empire. This office, invariably held by a Pharisee, lasted until 425CE. In addition, Jews were granted exemption from the customary Roman demand that all subject peoples participate in the official imperial cult of emperor-worship.

DIASPORA UNREST
Despite these concessions, the Temple's destruction had nonetheless shocked Jews in the Diaspora to the core. Between 115 and 117CE, Jews revolted against both Roman rule and antagonistic Greek neighbours in several major centres: Alexandria, Cyprus, Mesopotamia and northern Africa. All were quelled, and extremely brutally in the case of Alexandria, where Trajan's forces destroyed the city's synagogue.

*Below Aerial view of Betar in the
Judean hills, Bar Kochba's headquarters
and last stronghold to fall in 135CE.*

Above This Second Revolt era coin shows a palm frond that Jews brought to the Temple on the festival of Sukkot.

Collectively the uprisings are known as the Kitos Wars after a Moorish general in Roman service, Lucius Quietus. Having crushed Jewish rebels in Mesopotamia, Quietus became procurator in Judea, where he razed several towns, encouraged idol worship on the Temple Mount and killed troublesome Jewish leaders.

With hindsight these upheavals were a prelude to the final revolt, but Jews initially welcomed Hadrian when he replaced Trajan as emperor in 117CE. Hadrian recalled Quietus to Rome and had him executed. He promised Roman subjects throughout the empire that he would respect their cultures and rehabilitate their cities. In 130CE Hadrian toured the ruins of Jerusalem and Jews understood – or rather, misunderstood – that he would allow them to rebuild the Temple. Their mood soon changed when he outlawed circumcision as a bodily mutilation. Then in 131CE Hadrian mandated Judea's governor to start work on Aelia Capitolina, a new pagan city to be built on the ruins of Jewish Jerusalem.

THE BAR KOCHBA REVOLT

The sage Rabbi Akiva persuaded the Sanhedrin in Yavneh that Simon ben Kosba was the messiah who would finally rid Judea of the Roman scourge. Simon changed his name to Bar Kochba, 'son of a star' in Aramaic, thus fulfilling a prophecy in the Book of Numbers. He then launched a full-scale revolt from Modi'in.

Bar Kochba proved to be a military genius. He trapped a Roman garrison in Jerusalem and soon conquered the entire country. This time, unlike in 66CE, the Jewish forces were united. Jewish volunteers from the Diaspora helped overrun coastal towns. Rome's desperate Emperor Hadrian summoned troops from Britain and the Danube. Eventually ten legions arrived in Palestine, a third of the entire imperial forces, and considerably more than Titus had commanded. One whole Roman legion was exterminated, and Jewish naval forces even engaged the mighty Roman fleet.

Simon Bar Kochba was crowned Nasi (Prince) of a sovereign Jewish state, while a Sanhedrin headed by Rabbi Akiva revived sacrifices. Proudly, the Nasi minted coins with a Temple image and star on one side, and on the other the inscription 'Year one of Israel's redemption'. However, to follow was one of the most vicious wars in antiquity. Roman forces gradually subdued Galilee, expelled rebels from Jerusalem, and cornered them in the fortress of Beitar. So furious was this last siege, relates the Jerusalem Talmud, that the Romans 'went on killing until their horses were submerged in blood to their nostrils'. The Romans suffered huge losses, while according to the Roman historian Cassius Dio, 580,000 Jews were killed, and 50 fortified towns and 985 villages were razed. As for Bar Kochba, legend says he held out with rebels in desert caves.

The Romans put Rabbi Akiva to death, drove Jewish survivors into slavery, ploughed Jerusalem under and renamed the land 'Syria Palestina' after the virtually extinct Philistines. In this way they deliberately effaced the name of Judea. Somehow Jewish life continued in Galilee, but the south was a wasteland. Jewish fugitives crammed every Mediterranean port, and thousands of Jews were sold into slavery across the empire. Later generations wondered whether Bar Kochba had been a false messiah.

In the Diaspora, Jewish communities quickly learnt that cooler heads than Bar Kochba's should prevail if the Jewish people and faith were to survive.

Below The Ecce Homo Arch, once part of Aelia Capitolina, the Roman city built on the ruins of Jerusalem, 136CE.

CHAPTER 3

THE DIASPORA AND THE RISE OF CHRISTIANITY

The Jewish Diaspora began to dominate Jewish life after the revolts of 68–73 and 130CE decimated Judea. Bereft of the Temple, rabbis transcribed the Talmud, which became a portable constitution for Jews in exile. The Talmud fostered debate and study and remains a unique repository of Jewish folklore, ethics, law, history and literature. Gradually, Babylon replaced Galilee as Jews' cultural and religious epicentre.

Meanwhile, the related faiths of Judaism and Christianity went their separate ways. Acrimony grew when the Roman empire adopted the new religion around 314CE, and after Visigoths overran Rome in 476CE, the surviving Eastern Roman empire, called Byzantium, increased persecution of non-Christians. Still, Jewish communities displayed remarkable resilience in Libya, Greece, Turkey, Syria, Yemen and newly Christianized Europe.

Opposite This sculpture from the Arch of Titus in Rome shows the treasures of the Temple being carried in procession to honour the victory over the Jews in 70CE.

Above The Colosseum, or Flavian Amphitheatre, in Rome may have been constructed by Jewish slaves, and partly funded by the destruction of Jerusalem's Temple.

SURVIVAL IN THE DIASPORA

AFTER TWO FAILED REVOLTS, THE LOSS OF JERUSALEM AND DREAMS OF STATEHOOD DASHED, JEWS NONETHELESS SURVIVED AND AT TIMES EVEN THRIVED IN THE LANDS TO WHICH THEY FLED.

Initially, the failure of the Bar Kochba revolt against the Romans seemed like the end of the world to most Jews. An estimated million lost their lives during Judea's two uprisings; tens of thousands were taken into slavery. With their focus of worship, the Second Temple, destroyed, and most of Judea devastated, Jews wondered if they could survive.

However, Jewish life continued in the burgeoning Diaspora, which had been largely shielded from the worst effects of the Judean upheavals. Even in Palestine, once the initial trauma abated, there were signs of survival and rebirth.

THE DEMISE OF SECTS

In religious terms, the Sadducees were all but decimated as a caste when they could no longer perform their Temple rites. Evidently some assimilated into the Roman aristocracy;

Below The remains of a 5th–6th century CE synagogue in the Golan Heights.

others, hereditary Cohens and Levis, rejoined the general Jewish population; yet others left Judaism altogether. Similarly, little more is heard of the Essenes. Perhaps their tendency to monasticism, celibacy and separation of the genders simply reduced them to unsustainable numbers.

Revolutionary Zealots also suffered. Although a few Zealots fled to the Diaspora, where they helped revive moribund communities, as a distinct political movement they were finished. After 135CE the number of Jewish Christians also fell. They found themselves doubly ostracized: conventional Jews accused them of lack of patriotism and 'heresy' regarding the Torah, while Pauline Christians (followers of St Paul) shunned them for rejecting the divinity of Jesus.

By contrast with Sadducees, Zealots, Jewish Christians and Essenes, the Pharisees enjoyed a new lease of life as rabbis. They dominated the Sanhedrin, which was re-established at Yavneh. Under Gamaliel II they

Above Josephus, 1st-century CE Romano-Jewish historian, whose books have invaluable information about Jewish sects.

moved up to Galilee. Having learnt the bitter lessons of two failed revolts in 66–73CE and 132–5CE, Jews concentrated on quiet self-government according to religious law. By the early 3rd century the Sanhedrin head, Judah the Prince ('Hanasi'), had established cordial relations with Palestine's Roman administrators.

NEW SOCIAL STRUCTURES

The absence of meaningful Jewish sovereignty over Palestine deprived the old landed aristocracy of communal respect and access to wealth. Merchants, traders and artisans could more easily emigrate and start life anew in the established Diaspora.

Most Jews, though, belonged to the group that sages called *am ha'aretz* (people of the land). They proved remarkably adaptable. Some returned to Palestine or gravitated to other Jewish outposts. And while Judea itself remained largely a war-ravaged wasteland, many *am ha'aretz* reconstituted their life in Galilee.

JEWS IN A ROMAN WORLD

Once the threat of Judean nationalism had been crushed, the Roman empire tolerated and even welcomed Jewish minorities. Jewish commerce and industry benefited the ports and

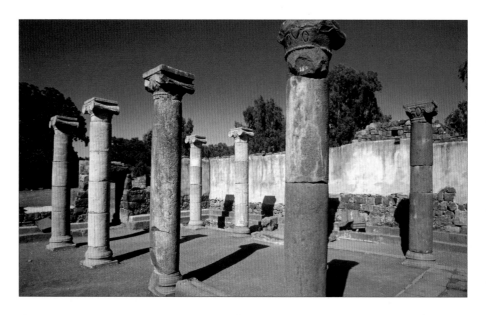

cities; their literacy and multi-lingualism were useful assets. Roman law absolved them from military service and usually granted them religious freedom and a measure of civic autonomy.

In 212CE Jews shared the new citizenship rights that Emperor Caracalla (198–211CE) bestowed on all non-slave subjects of the Roman empire. What was once the privilege of a few, and hence the cause of envy and strife, was now widely available. Citizenship improved access to travel, trade, education and professional advancement. Paradoxically, Jews only began suffering serious reverses with the rise of their sister faith, Christianity.

The long-established Jews of Alexandria in Egypt were probably the wealthiest, best educated and most politically independent of Diaspora communities. Successive Ptolemies had assigned them two of the five city districts to safeguard their customs from pagan influence. Mostly relations with the Hellenistic Ptolemies were amicable; Jewish scholars tutored the kings, and Jews excelled as perfumers, jewellers, silversmiths and fine weavers.

Alexandrian Jews paid dearly, however, when they rioted against Roman governors, first in 66CE, in sympathy with the great Judean revolt, and next in 115–17CE. In putting down the second uprising, wrote the great historian Josephus, Roman forces under Trajan killed up to 50,000 Egyptian Jews. The community then atrophied when some members became Christians.

After a long decline, Jewish life in Egypt revived in the 4th century CE. They rebuilt synagogues, forged ties with Palestinian Jews, and increasingly spoke and wrote in Hebrew, not Greek. They still enjoyed secular pastimes, however, especially theatre, and their writings and artefacts suggest a continued blend of Jewish, Hellenic and local Egyptian features.

ASIA MINOR AND BABYLON

On the north side of the Mediterranean, significant Jewish communities were already well established in Asia Minor, modern-day Turkey; and in Delos, Athens and Corinth on the Greek mainland. Both Jews and Samaritans built synagogues in Ptolemais (Akko, on the Palestinian coast) and the three Greek sites. Asia Minor and the Aegean peninsula were under Roman rule, although they remained Hellenistic in culture. The ever-shifting border in eastern Turkey represented a crossing from the Roman empire into Persian-ruled territory. The Persian realm included the ancient cradle of civilization, Babylon, which grew in status as a Jewish centre after Jewish institutions in Palestine began to wither after 400CE. Babylon became a haven for Jews fleeing economic hardship and political turmoil elsewhere in the Roman empire.

Bar Kochba's debacle had seen many Jews literally sold into slavery, and as Rome settled a depleted Judea with foreigners, the centre of Palestine's Jewish population moved to Galilee. For a while Emperor

Above Trajan's Column, commemorating the Roman emperor who crushed a Jewish revolt in Egypt after 114CE.

Hadrian prohibited the practice of Judaism itself. Almost everywhere else Jews formed a minority. While they survived as a religion and ethnicity, they no longer constituted a single political entity. The breach with Christianity, too, became final.

All these factors would shape Jewish history for nearly two thousand years. Yet Jews proved impressively resilient and disciplined. They drew sustenance from their tradition and veneration for scholarship, even when they replaced Hebrew with Greek as their everyday language. Their population shifted dramatically, westward towards Spain, Gaul and the Rhineland, and eastward towards Babylon. Jewish communities bargained for and won a measure of internal independence; and fugitives who fled Judea actually strengthened Judaism in the Diaspora. For in Babylon, in tandem with the work of the Jabneh sages, the Talmud emerged as a pinion of Jewish culture and identity.

THE TALMUD

THE PALESTINIAN AND BABYLONIAN TALMUDS ARE INTRINSICALLY RELIGIOUS BUT ALSO EMBODY A PORTABLE CONSTITUTION THAT HELPED JEWS SURVIVE FOR NEARLY 2,000 YEARS IN THE DIASPORA.

The Talmud can be understood in two senses. More narrowly, it refers to two specific books each called the Talmud: the shorter and earlier Jerusalem or Palestinian Talmud, written around 400CE, and the longer and much more detailed Babylonian Talmud, dated 500CE.

Literally, Talmud means 'learning'. Yet it is so much more than that. To many the Talmud represents the religious and civil constitution of the Jewish people, a portable constitution that helped them survive for nearly two millennia in the Diaspora. Others consider it the summation and repository of all traditional Jewish knowledge.

More broadly, 'talmud' stands for a centuries-long process, a way of life for its scholars and a guide to living for all observant Jews. It encapsulates strict law, ethical debates, sayings of the sages, history and philosophizing, questions and responses, commentaries on hidden meanings in the Bible, even folktales and aphorisms. Within this immense

oeuvre, which continues to the present and by definition will never end, the actual books named Talmud form only one, albeit pivotal, part.

WRITING THE ORAL LAW

The Palestinian and Babylonian Talmuds, narrowly defined, are themselves explications of the Oral Law. Jewish tradition says Oral Law accompanied the Written Law, or Torah/Hebrew Bible, at Mt Sinai and was then conveyed orally by prophets, elders, Pharisees and rabbis to their pupils down the generations.

The bedrock of all Jewish legal rulings are the 613 *mitzvot*, or 'commandments', that appear in the biblical books of Deuteronomy and Leviticus. They acquire additional meaning when allied with the Oral Law. So, for instance, where the Torah simply says 'thou shall not cook the calf in its mother's milk', the Oral Law builds on this edict a whole edifice of legislation determining how and why one should not cook milk and meat products together.

Above Ha'ari synagogue, Safed, Israel. Ha'ari means lion and was the nickname of the great Talmudic scholar Joseph Caro of Safed.

The first summary of Oral Law to be written down is called the Mishnah. Rabbi Yehuda Ha-Nasi, head of the Sanhedrin, edited this compilation *c.* 200CE. Essentially the Mishnah summarizes the debates of past centuries and from these it defines the obligations of Jews in all spheres of life. Rabbi Akiva (50–135CE) is credited with devising the process of linking each traditional practice to a basis in biblical text. This process is called exegesis in Greek. Akiva also helped systematize the vast amounts of material that went into the Mishnah.

But why did Rabbi Yehuda decide to write down the Oral Law in the first place? Some say that because so many scholars died during the two Judean revolts, including Akiva, the old system of a rabbi instructing his pupils would no longer suffice.

MISHNAH

In structure the Mishnah consists of six 'orders' or 'divisions'. Another name for the book is Shas, an acronym

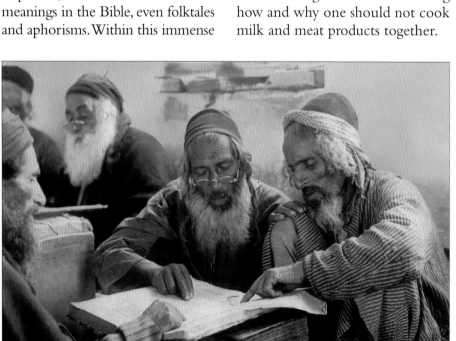

Left Yemenite rabbis studying the Talmud, 1906. The shortage of books meant the book was read from all sides.

of the Hebrew expression *shisha sidrei mishnah*, the six orders of the Mishnah: *Zera'im*, or 'seeds', *Mo'ed*, or 'festivals', *Nezikin*, or 'damages', *Nashim*, or 'women', *Kodashim*, or 'holy things', and *Taharot*, or 'purifications'.

Each order contains numerous tractates (63 in all) some of which veer from the subject matter of the order's title. For instance, under *Zera'im*, which is meant to explain the agricultural rules of ancient Palestine, the most famous tractate is *Brakhot*, or 'blessings'. Orthodox Jews believe the whole world is a sacred gift from God. Hence they feel obliged to bless apparently mundane actions, like eating, drinking, going to sleep or waking up. (Jesus' blessing of the bread and wine shows the prevalence of the custom.)

FESTIVALS AND MARRIAGE

The order called *Mo'ed*, or 'festivals', specifies in its 12 tractates the oral laws for *Pesach* (Passover), *Purim* (the festival of lots), *Rosh Hashana* (New Year), *Yom Kippur* (Day of Atonement), and *Sukkot* (Feast of Tabernacles). Its longest tractate is called *Shabbat*, and consists of 24 chapters, detailing 39 types of 'work' that are forbidden on the Sabbath. Many of the smaller

tractates have odd titles: *Beitza* (egg) deals with general practices on festive days; *Megillah* (scroll) refers to the Scroll of Esther, which contains the story of Purim; *Shekkelim* (coins) considers Temple tithes.

The ten tractates of *Nezikin* (damages) essentially summarize Jewish civil and criminal law. *Nashim* (women) covers issues between the

Left An early copy of Maimonides' Mishnah Torah, dated 1351, which summarized the subject divisions and conclusions of the earlier-written Talmud.

Above A page of the Talmud, showing the typical pattern of text conveying an ongoing dialogue. In the middle, a short Mishnah section with Gemara below. Surrounding this, Rashi, Tosafists and other commentators in each margin.

sexes, including laws of marriage, *kiddushin*, and divorce, *gittin*. *Kodashim* outlines the laws of ritual slaughter and sacrifices, which ceased when the Temple was destroyed, but have been studied since, along with other tractates and orders, by students in *yeshivas* (rabbinical academies).

Above The Semag, a 14th-century book of Halakha, *showing God creating his world.*

Finally comes the order *Taharot*, which details the laws of purity and impurity. It encompasses decisions as to which food is *kosher* (clean), or *tereif* (unclean). Eminently practical in purpose, its tractates include Hebrew titles that translate as vessels, tents, cow (concerning the rare red heifer required for Temple sacrifices), ritual baths and seminal emissions.

MORAL GUIDANCE

At first glance most of the Mishnah can appear dry, legalistic, even pedantic and didactic. However, Rabbi Yehuda wisely added minority viewpoints as an aid to future debate. He also included some extraordinary statements of universal ethics.

One tractate in particular – *Pirkei Avot*, or 'Ethics of the Fathers' – is entirely devoid of law, and comprises instead much-loved aphorisms attributed to the earliest rabbis. It focuses on character development and universally applicable moral principles.

GEMARA AND TALMUD

The Mishnah marked the end of one process and the start of another. It set in written form what had previously been conveyed orally. It also stimulated intense discussion among rabbis, and these debates were later compiled as a detailed commentary on the Mishnah, called *Gemara*, derived from the Aramaic word for 'study'. Whereas Mishnah is in Hebrew, the Gemara is overwhelmingly written in Aramaic, which was the secular lingua franca of the region.

The Talmuds that emerged, the Palestinian and Babylonian, are essentially a repetition of Mishnah tractates followed by passages of Gemara. Both books cover similar ground, although the longer, clear and detailed Babylonian version is considered the essential Talmud.

Scholars date the Palestinian version to the years 350–400CE; it emerged from the school of Johanan ben Napaha in Tiberias, and was annotated by Rav Muna and Rav Yossi. Its Gemara component consists of discussions between rabbis mainly from Tiberias and Caesarea.

The Babylonian Talmud is four times the size of the Palestinian, runs to 5,894 folio pages and is usually printed in 12 volumes. The leading debaters quoted are Abbaye and Rava; two other Babylonian sages, Ravina and Rav Ashi, are credited with completing the work around 550CE. It probably took centuries to finish entirely. Although it covers only 36 of the 63 Mishnaic tractates, most subject matter is addressed in the Gemara to other tractates.

The rabbis cited in the Mishnah are called *Tanna'im*, Aramaic for 'teachers'; those quoted in the Gemara are known as *Amora'im*, 'interpreters'. If there is a dispute on an issue commented on by both Tanna'im and Amora'im, Jews regard the former as authoritative. This is based on the principle that they were closer in time to Moses.

Right A Jewish family reads sacred texts at Passover. From Agada Pacatis, *a 15th-century Hebrew manuscript.*

WALKING AND TALKING

Within the Talmud there are essentially two types of subject matter. *Halakha* – derived from a Hebrew root for 'walking', as in, on a path – refers to legal rulings and associated discussions. This material makes up nearly 90 per cent of the Talmud. Whatever does not count as Halakha – whether ethics, business and medical advice, history or folklore, even mystical poetry – is collectively called *Aggada*. The name comes from the Hebrew for 'narrative', and relates to the word Haggadah, the traditional telling of the Exodus story around the Passover table.

Closely linked to Aggada is Midrash – the custom of adding to familiar biblical stories, or retelling them in allegorical guise. Some *midrashim* appear separately, others in the Talmud itself.

STUDY

One notable feature of Talmud study is its method. There is a fourfold way of analysing a text, especially when applied to Midrash and Aggada. This method is often summarized in the word *pardes*, which means 'orchard' or 'paradise' (the name entered Hebrew from Persian). Pardes forms an acronym for four components:

Above The tomb of Rabbi Meir, Baal ha-Nes, the miracle-maker, at Tiberias on the coast of the inland Sea of Galilee.

pashut, or 'the basic meaning'; *remez*, or 'the hint of something deeper'; *darash*, or 'discussion and interpretation', where the passage's words are compared with similar usages elsewhere; and finally, *sodi*, or 'the secret, hidden or mystical element of a passage'. Some say that the redactors of the Midrash concentrate on *remez* and *darash*, leaving the *sodi* approach to the mystical writers of the Kabbalah.

TALMUDIC PERSONALITIES

The Talmud abounds with engaging personalities. One was Bruriah, a much-quoted sage and the sharp-witted wife of Rabbi Meir. According to a midrash on Psalm 118, she once chided her husband for praying for the destruction of the wicked, rather than for their repentance. If that story were true, Rabbi Meir was probably acting out of character. He was famously generous towards the destitute, even though he was poor himself. Meir, reputedly the grandson of Emperor Nero, insisted that people should bless God for good things and bad. Even the holiest people, he warned, had to guard against the *netzer ha-rah*, or 'evil impulse'.

Meir's real name was Nehora'i and he was also called 'master of miracles'. For example, when his sister-in-law was falsely imprisoned, he reputedly sprang her from jail by mollifying guard dogs when he invoked God's name. Roman authorities launched a huge manhunt to catch him after the ill-fated Bar Kochba rebellion, which he supported. Meir left Palestine, died in Asia and was buried in Tiberias, today in Israel, where pilgrims still visit his tomb.

In Babylon there was friendly rivalry between two great sages. Abba Arika, best known simply as 'Rav', was the first Babylonian *Amora*, or 'interpreter'. He led the yeshiva at Sura, and enjoyed genuine respect in the Persian royal court. Rav's counterpart was Samuel, who re-established the famous Nehardea yeshiva in Pumbedita, after the former was overrun when Palmyrene Arabs fought Parthian Persians. Samuel was an astronomer and doctor. He established that *Dina d'malchuta dina* – essentially, 'the law of wherever you live (your kingdom or government) should be your law'. This enlightened principle enabled Jews to live securely in non-Jewish countries. It served as a retort to Jews who refused to obey secular authorities on spurious nationalistic or religious grounds. Samuel's ruling probably curbed messianic excesses and tailored Jewish political expectations to the reality of Diaspora life.

CONTINUITY AND CONTROVERSY

Between 550 and 700CE Babylonian rabbis called *Savora'im* (explainers) put the Talmud in its final form. Oppressive Byzantine rule in Palestine hampered their counterparts from similarly rationalizing the Jerusalem Talmud. Between 700 and 1250CE, after the Arab conquest of Babylon and Persia, Jews throughout the world consulted the *Ga'onim* (heads of the yeshivas) at Sura and

Pumbedita about legal and theological matters. Their *responsa* informed further glosses in the Talmud.

For the last thousand years the Talmud has faced heavy criticism. Christian medieval clerics feared the Talmud as a demonic work and either censored it heavily – especially after the invention of printing – or publicly burned the books. Among Jewish sects, Karaites rejected the Talmud as a deviation from the Torah. Centuries later, Reform Jews questioned the relevance of studying the minutiae of Temple sacrifices, which have had no practical application for 2,000 years. Others say the Talmudic method encourages *pilpul*, or quibbling.

Certainly the Talmud has enormously influenced Jewish life, providing liturgy used in synagogues and subject material for rabbinical sermons. Talmudic exegesis inspired Christian and Muslim theologians in both form and content. For Orthodox Jews the Talmud approximates a living constitution. Secular Jews feel less positively, yet welcome the *dina malchuta* ruling that limits the Talmud's remit over civil society.

Below Students at the Beit Shmuel (House of Samuel) Yeshiva in Israel studying and discussing the Talmud.

PALESTINE AFTER THE ROMAN CONQUEST

AFTER THE ROMAN CONQUEST OF PALESTINE, JEWS GAINED LIMITED AUTONOMY. GREAT CHANGE OF THE EMPIRE BEGAN UNDER EMPEROR DIOCLETIAN, WHICH WERE TO AFFECT JEWISH CULTURE IN PALESTINE.

Palestine's Jewish population fell sharply after the Bar Kochba revolt of 132–5CE. Many thousands had died; many more emigrated. Rome, meanwhile, encouraged Greek and Roman colonists to repopulate the country. Southern Judea remained largely a wasteland, and Jews were barred on pain of death from visiting Jerusalem, except on *Tisha B'Av*, the 9th of the month Av. That date marks the fall of both Temples, and it is still observed as a festival of mourning.

CLINGING TO POWER
Jews tentatively renewed communal life and re-established the Sanhedrin assembly. By the late 2nd century it had branches in Tiberias on the Sea of Galilee, Sephoris, the old Galilean capital, and Lydda in northern Judea.

Below The synagogue of Dura-Europos, a Hellenistic, Roman and Parthian border city above the Euphrates River.

The Sanhedrin sage Judah instituted the office of *nasi* (prince). In effect he became Judea's executive administrator, if not ruler. Roman authorities turned a blind eye to the fact that his supposedly civil courts judged and sentenced criminal cases.

The Roman empire reached its zenith under Trajan (reg. 98–,117CE). Rival peoples – Goths, Gauls, Parthians – beset the realm from every quarter. So it made sense to allow the Jews limited autonomy, if only to ward off another unwelcome Judean rebellion. And while Palestine raised little revenue, it remained valuable as a trade thoroughfare and bulwark of imperial defence.

Militarily weak though the Jews were, they could still wield political leverage. In the late 2nd century CE war broke out between two Roman generals, Lucius Septimius Severus and the cruel governor of Syria and Egypt, Niger Pescennius. Jews sided with the half-Berber half-Phoenician

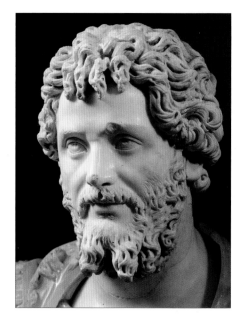

Above Septimius Severus, Roman emperor 193–211CE, who enjoyed his Jewish subjects' support.

Severus, who won the contest and was crowned Caesar in 193CE. He remembered his Jewish supporters and set up a dynasty that established good relations with the community. Severus banned conversion to Judaism or Christianity but allowed Jews to acquire whatever office they merited. One successor, Alexander Severus (222–35CE), was particularly praised in the Talmud for allowing Jews to visit Jerusalem. A number settled there with informal Roman approval. Lydda and western Judea experienced something of an urban boom. And the oldest synagogue complex in western Europe, at Ostia, Rome's port, was renamed in Alexander's honour.

DIVIDED PALESTINE
Outside Palestine the Severan tendency towards military autocracy fostered political and economic instability. Determined to rectify this situation and facilitate easier management, Diocletian (284–305CE) divided the empire into two zones, east and west. He applied a similar model of reorganization to Palestine, by attaching to it to the southern part of the Roman province of Arabia.

Diocletian's process culminated around 400CE, when Palestine was split into three distinct zones. Palestina Prima, with its capital at Caesarea, covered Judea, Samaria, Idumea, Perea and the coastal plain. Palestina Secunda consisted of Galilee, Golan, and the Decapolis – ten largely autonomous Hellenistic cities, including a rebuilt Damascus, in southern Syria and today's Kingdom of Jordan. Palestina Tertia incorporated the Negev Desert and took the ancient Nabatean city of Petra, hewn out of red rock, as its capital.

CONSTANTINE AND THE JEWS

Life grew harder for Jews when the Roman empire under Constantine legalized Christianity in the Edict of Milan of 313CE. Christianity became

Below Palestine,c. 400CE, showing the district capitals of Scythopolis, Caesarea and Petra.

Divided Palestine c.400CE
- ○ District capital
- — Province boundary
- — Administrative division
- † Centre of Christianity

the state religion. Pagan Romans had tolerated other religions; Christians, however, wanted all to convert. They had particularly strong feelings about Palestine, where their saviour Jesus had lived and died.

In 324CE Constantine took control of both halves of a divided empire and marched into Aelia (Jerusalem) to open the city to Christian pilgrimage. Two years later he built the Church of the Holy Sepulchre in Jerusalem. Palestine's Jews felt ambivalent about such developments. Christian pilgrimage benefited all locals, and a massive influx of capital transformed the area. But Christian appropriation of ancient sacred sites troubled Jews, many of whom moved to the Upper Galilee and Golan Heights to secure a realm separate from the emerging Christian Terra Sancta (Holy Land).

In Sephoris and Horazin, Jews revolted unsuccessfully against the harsh governor, Gallus, after he was made 'Caesar of the East' in 351CE.

A brief reprieve arrived when Julian the Apostate ruled as Rome's last pagan emperor in 360–3CE. In 362CE he declared that all religions were equal before the law. In 363 he ordered the Jewish Temple rebuilt, which Alypius of Antioch set about doing. What happened next is unclear: some say an earthquake

Above Hellenistic and Jewish culture combine in this zodiac mosaic in Sephoris, once Galilee's largest city.

destroyed the foundations, others, that Christian arsonists sabotaged the project. Julian died in battle against the Sassanid Persians in 363CE and his successors broadly returned to Constantine's Christian path, leaving the Jewish Temple unbuilt.

MOVING FROM PALESTINE

In 395CE Palestine was absorbed within the ambit of the Byzantine or Eastern Roman empire. Limited Jewish autonomy continued until 415CE, when Rabban Gamaliel VI, the *nasi*, was condemned to death by emperors Honorius and Theodosius II for building a synagogue without authorization, and defending Jews against Christians. After Gamaliel died in 426, imperial officials decreed that moneys once owed to the nasi would go to the Roman treasury.

By the 6th century CE, 43 Jewish communities remained in Palestine: 12 on the coast, in the Negev and east of the Jordan, and 31 in Galilee and the Jordan valley. Jewish life in Palestine was ebbing away. The Jewish centre of gravity was moving to other centres, such as Asia Minor, Babylon and the Mediterranean rim.

THE JEWISH–CHRISTIAN SCHISM DEEPENS

ROME'S UNEXPECTED ADOPTION OF CHRISTIANITY AS ITS IMPERIAL RELIGION MARKED A HISTORICAL WATERSHED — AND INSECURITY FOR JEWS AT THE HANDS OF A NEWLY EMPOWERED RIVAL FAITH.

The closeness of Christianity and Judaism provoked problems from the outset. Christians venerated the Hebrew Bible as their Old Testament, yet they interpreted the text as prefiguring Jesus. Increasingly they called themselves the 'New Israel', which antagonized Jews. Eusebius, bishop of Caesarea (c. 264–340CE), said he loved the ancient Hebrews yet hated the present-day Jews who rejected Christ. During this period most Jews and Christians lived in a slowly crumbling Roman empire. They competed for converts among Rome's pagan majority, and Christians won over poorer artisans and slaves with the simplicity of their beliefs – compared with Judaism – and the promise of eternal salvation in the afterlife.

Below A 1530 fresco shows Christians persecuted by the imperial authorities, as they often were before Rome adopted Christianity as a state religion.

CHRISTIANS PERSECUTED

Until Emperor Constantine's conversion to Christianity in 312CE, Christians had actually been more victimized than Jews. Rome accepted Judaism as a *religio licita* (a legitimate religion), whereas they considered Christianity a bizarre cult. They blamed Christians for the plague, fed believers to the lions, and threatened to kill them for not sacrificing to Roman gods.

Many Christians hid in subterranean catacombs, and most of the early saints were martyred. Roman viciousness reached its zenith under Emperor Diocletian (ruled 284–305CE) and his successor Galerius. Churches and scriptures were destroyed and Christians subjected to punishments such as blinding, mutilation and castration. Outside the empire, pagan Gothic rulers also persecuted Christians, whom they saw as a threat.

Above The Emperor Constantine and his mother, Helena, in a 7th-century fresco from Elmali Kilise, Turkey.

ROME TURNS TO CHRIST

Thousands of Jews had been enslaved after the failed Judean revolts of 68–74CE and 132–5CE. Some were forced to build Rome's Coliseum, itself funded by riches looted from Jerusalem's Temple. After Rome regained political superiority, however, most slaves were freed and Jews were tolerated, even prized, as contributors to the imperial economy and cosmopolitan culture.

Their circumstances began to change when Constantine legalized Christianity with the Edict of Milan of 313CE. The hitherto despised faith gained power and new followers as Christian bishops targeted non-believers. In 315CE Constantine denounced Jews as 'Christ killers', thus shifting blame for the crucifixion from his own imperial predecessors. In 323CE Christianity replaced paganism as Rome's favoured religion. And in 337CE Constantius outlawed Jewish proselytizing, forbade Jews to own non-Jewish slaves, banned intermarriage with Christians, and stopped rabbis meeting.

The pagan emperor Julian (360–3CE) interrupted this trend when he promised to rebuild the

Jerusalem Temple; and his Arian Christian successor, Valens (364–78CE), strengthened the Jewish patriarch. However, Theodosius I (379–95CE) confirmed mainstream Christianity as Rome's sole state religion in 380CE, and imposed a deluge of statutes on non-conformists.

While most emperors still upheld the religious rights of Jews, Christian clerics sought to curb their influence. When in 388CE a mob burned down a synagogue along the Euphrates River, Theodosius ordered it rebuilt at Christian expense, only to rescind his order under church pressure.

THEOLOGICAL RIVALRY

According to St Augustine (354–430CE), Jewish survival was part of God's design, as their travails bore witness to the truth of the new religion. Christians felt that God had spurned the former 'chosen people' and wanted Palestine transformed into a Christian Terra Sancta, or Holy Land.

Not all contact between Jews and Christians was negative. Origen, the 2nd-century Egyptian Christian theologian had spent long hours

Below St Jerome translating the Bible from Hebrew into Latin. A 15th-century Netherlandish painting on panel.

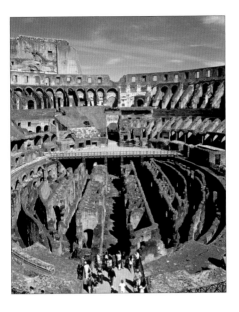

Left Rome's Colosseum, 70–82CE, was probably built by Jews, taken as slaves after the Palestine revolt.

debating with rabbis. St Jerome (347–420CE) translated the Old Testament from Hebrew into Latin, and his scriptural commentaries show the influence of Philo and the Alexandria Jewish school.

Conversely, a 4th-century archbishop of Constantinople, John Chrysostom, is credited with pioneering a specifically Christian brand of anti-Semitism, called synagogues the dens of scoundrels and warned against 'Judaizing' Christians who observed Jewish fasts and feasts. It seems his views bore political fruit in 418 when Jews were barred from Roman public office.

During 419–422CE Syrian monks raided Palestine, burned synagogues and destroyed Jewish villages. Less violent missionaries sought to 'save Jewish souls' through conversion, a venture that only partly succeeded. Churchmen especially resented the Palestinian office of the nasi, or Jewish patriarch. His status as 'remnant of the house of David' undermined their idea of Jesus as David's rightful heir. Some Jews countered with polemic of their own, including veiled references in the Mishnah to Jesus as an impostor, a magician, or even the illegitimate son of a Roman centurion.

In 429CE Byzantium abolished the 350-year-old patriarchate, and, with Palestinian Jewry duly weakened,

Samaritans offered the only real armed resistance to the spread of Christianity in Palestine.

Although the Western Roman empire ended in 476CE, Christianity survived in the Eastern Byzantine empire. By now it had taken root among Rome's barbarian conquerors too. There were moments of reprieve in Christian–Jewish relations. But harsher laws were to follow; and outside Christendom, the Jews of Babylon enjoyed better conditions.

SAMARITAN FORTUNES

Christ's 'Good Samaritan' parable in the New Testament hints at the traditional enmity between Jews and Samaritans in Palestine. Although religiously and ethnically related to Jews, many Samaritans helped Rome crush the Jewish Bar Kochba uprising of 135CE.

Samaritans were later punished by Rome when they refused to worship Roman gods, and the triumph of Christianity merely sharpened the conflict.

In the 4th century CE, Baba Rabbah revived the Samaritan sect and repeatedly defeated Roman invaders with his armies. In 483CE, Samaritans massacred Christians and burned churches after Theodosius II extended anti-Jewish statutes to their community.

In 529CE, Emperor Justinian I crushed an uprising to establish a Samaritan state, after which many converted to Christianity. Thousands fled when Muslims conquered Palestine in 634CE.

The Samaritans once numbered millions; today some 600 remain, divided between Nablus in Palestine and Holon in Israel.

BABYLON – THE NEW CENTRE OF JEWRY

FROM THE TIME WHEN PERSIANS CONQUERED BABYLON, JEWS REMAINED IN THE ANCIENT REGION. GENERALLY THEY FLOURISHED, AND THEIR RELIGIOUS CENTRES RIVALLED THOSE IN PALESTINE.

After the fall of Jerusalem, the central focus of Jewish life gradually shifted from Palestine to Babylon, a region under Persian rule since the 6th century BCE. The core of Babylon's Jewish community was formed by exiles from the Kingdom of Judah. Over time, immigrants replenished their population, including Jews fleeing turmoil within the Roman empire and Jewish farmers from Palestine, who suffered from heavy taxes, currency devaluation and military requisitions to billet Roman soldiers.

BABYLONIAN JEWS
In the 1st century CE the Jewish historian Josephus wrote: 'The Jews beyond the Euphrates are an immense multitude and not estimated by numbers.' Their rulers were Parthians, a north-east Persian clan which in 129BCE had conquered Babylon and the rest of Mesopotamia, including most of present-day Iran and Iraq.

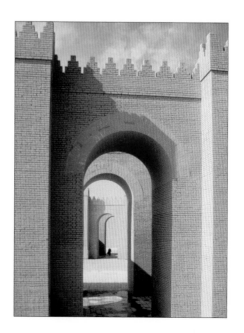

Left Modern rebuilding of Babylon, where Jews flourished under Persian rule until persecution returned c.400CE.

Babylon's Jews were furious when Romans desecrated Jerusalem in 70CE. So when the Parthians fought Rome, the community lent its protectors full support. The Parthians reciprocated by funding anti-Roman zealots in Judea, and raising the status of local Jewish communal leaders in Babylon.

Jewry received a boost when Queen Helen of the satrapy of Adiabene and her son Izates converted to Judaism in the mid-1st century CE. Helen contributed greatly to the second Temple in Jerusalem, and the royal family supported a notable yeshiva in Arbela (modern Irbil, in Iraqi Kurdistan). The Parthians already prized their Jewish subjects as revenue collectors and in 140CE they permitted them an exilarch or *resh galuta*, Head of the Exile. He interceded with the royal court on his community's behalf, and often directly influenced Persian foreign policy. Even so, he still had to contend with the authority of the yeshivas, especially in Sura, Nehardea, and later Pumbedita. The yeshivas benefited immensely from an influx of Palestinian Pharisees, such as the students of Rabbi Ishmael, a great sage of Yavneh.

THE RISE OF THE SASSANIDS
In 224CE Ardashir, an ambitious Persian provincial governor, overthrew the Parthians and crowned himself Shahanshah, 'king of kings'. His Sassanid dynasty promoted Zoroastrianism and gave their empire a more centralized structure. Ardashir

Above Relatives of Sanatruces I, 1st century BCE king of Parthia, whose descendants gave Jews honoured status.

and his successor, Shapur, conquered Roman lands in Asia Minor, such as Antioch, though not Palestine.

Rome's nadir came when the Sassanids captured Emperor Valerian in 260CE. That same year Sassanid armies killed some 12,000 Hellenized Jews defending Mazaca-Caesarea in Cappadocia. Babylon's own Jews feared that the Sassanids might end their political autonomy and religious freedom. However, Talmudic Jewish scholars Abba Arika and Samuel won security for Jews living under the new regime.

RIVALRY WITH PALESTINE
In earlier days Babylonian Jews regularly paid their Temple tax to Jerusalem; after the destruction they continued to fund the rabbinate in Palestine. Rivalry between the two centres grew, for while Palestinian rabbis were influenced by Roman and Greek culture; the Babylonians were oriented more to Eastern traditions. New influences emerged in the 4th century, however, when Persia's neighbour Armenia adopted Christianity, and Jews arrived from a crumbling Roman empire.

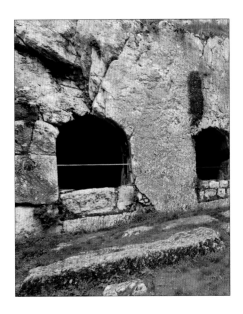

In 1935 a remarkable synagogue was discovered in Dura–Europos in northern Syria. The city was founded by Seleucids in 303BC. Its synagogue is dated to 245CE, and is the earliest preserved example to survive. It features walls of mosaics that charmingly depict the Torah's best-known characters and stories. Dura–Europos was originally Hellenistic, yet as a border town it changed hands several times. The city came under Parthian control in the 2nd century BCE, was captured by Romans in 165CE, and fell to the Sassanid Persians in 257.

It is tempting to extrapolate a sense of Persian or Babylonian Jewish culture from Dura–Europos, whose synagogue remains are now in Damascus. Strictly speaking, the city lay outside the Babylonian orbit and its mosaics defy the biblical stricture on graven images. Even if atypical of the period and region, it shows previously unimagined artistic creativity and bolsters the view that the earliest churches were modelled on Jewish houses of worship.

Above The remains of Queen Helen of Adiabene's residence. She converted to Judaism and lived in Jerusalem.

The Palestinian school claimed precedence, partly because they remained in the Holy Land and partly through such personalities as Johanan, Akiva and Yehuda Ha-Nasi, who determined the sacred calendar. Babylonian rabbis claimed a purer Davidic lineage than the Palestinians. They argued that their interpretations were less sullied by outside influence. And Jews from Palestine and beyond sought guidance from the Babylonian exilarch after the Palestinian Jewish patriarchate fell in 429CE.

Around 500 Babylonian sages produced the *Talmud Bavli*. Unlike the Palestinian Talmud, it concentrated less on rites connected to the Land of Israel and became the paramount version in all Jewish yeshivas, whether of European Ashkenazim, Spanish-origin Sephardim or Middle Eastern *mizrakhim*.

The Babylonian Talmud vividly records the real life of Jews in Babylon. It tells that the second Sassanid king, Shapur I (241–72CE), reinstated religious tolerance and befriended such sages as Samuel and his disciple, Judah. Shapur II, whose mother was Jewish, rescinded earlier oppressive legislation. Yazdegerd I (399–421CE)

married a Jewish noblewoman, Shushandukht, and habitually hosted Talmudic sages in his royal court.

Jews flourished as date cultivators, fishermen, artisans and river navigators. And for two months each year – when fieldwork ceased – ordinary farmers would pour into the academies to study Torah.

MIXED FORTUNES

Unfortunately this halcyon period did not last: fanatic Zoroastrian priests, threatened by Byzantine inroads from the west, forced King Yazdegerd III to persecute Jews, Christians and Manicheans. In 455CE Persia's rulers passed an edict

banning the Sabbath. Eventually this prompted a full-scale Jewish rebellion in 511 when the Jewish exilarch Mar Zutra usurped power from Kavadh I (ruled 488–531CE) for seven years.

Kavadh's successor, Khosrau I (531–79CE), restored Persia to its former glory, repelled Byzantium and improved conditions for his Jewish subjects, which may explain why Jews so enthusiastically backed Persia's invasion of Byzantine-ruled Palestine in the early 7th century CE.

Below 3rd-century CE relief of Shapur I of Persia, whom the Talmud praises as a friend to Jews and patron of scholars.

JEWS UNDER BYZANTIUM

JEWS EXPERIENCED A CHEQUERED EXISTENCE UNDER BYZANTINE RULE – PRECARIOUS IN PALESTINE AND PROSPEROUS IN THE CITIES. BUT, AS THE EMPIRE FALTERED, JEWS WERE INCREASINGLY OPPRESSED.

'Byzantine' has become a byword for anything unnecessarily complex. The notion probably originated when rough-hewn Crusaders encountered the sophisticates of Byzantium. Modern medievalists now argue that Western European prejudice obscured the truth – the Byzantines outlasted the Roman empire by a thousand years.

BYZANTIUM GROWS

Greek colonists founded Byzantium at the Anatolian gateway to the Black Sea in the 7th century BCE. It grew in stature after Emperor Diocletian reconfigured the Roman empire as a tetrarchy (led by four people) in 292CE. In 330CE his successor, Constantine, built a 'second Rome' on its site, which seven years later became Constantinople, capital of the Eastern Roman empire. The east–west split became permanent

Below By the 3rd century CE, Jewish communities had spread throughout southern Europe and northern Africa.

after the death of Theodosius I in 395CE, the last emperor to rule both zones simultaneously.

Rome and Byzantium shared a faith, but political, cultural and religious schisms grew as Byzantium became the seat of Greek Orthodoxy, while Rome championed Latinate Catholicism. The final rift came when Byzantium rejected the authority of the pope in 1054.

Byzantium came to dominate much of the Middle East and all of Asia Minor, and influenced the Jews who lived in those regions. In 330CE – the same year that Byzantium became Nova Roma – Constantine made Jerusalem part of his realm. Christian pilgrims began flocking to Jerusalem, and successive emperors built churches in the city, including on the former Temple Mount. Other great ancient cities of the region – like Antioch, Damascus and Alexandria – became Christian archbishoprics under the Byzantine aegis. Meanwhile, Byzantium and Sassanid Persia fought over border territories.

Above A Byzantine mosaic from 1210 showing the construction of the Tower of Babel, as told in the Hebrew Bible.

FROM PRIVILEGE TO PERSECUTION

The Byzantine age was certainly chequered for its Jewish subjects. Palestine's Jewish patriarchate was abolished less than a century after Jerusalem became Byzantine. While Palestinian Jews suffered, those Jews already living under Byzantine rule in Asia Minor and Egypt appeared to fare better, at least at first. They were granted leave from having to join civic associations; and the Emperor Arcadius reinforced privileges for their patriarchs and communal elders. But rioting by Jews in Palestine fuelled anti-Jewish feeling in Constantinople, and things worsened under Emperor Theodosius II (408–50CE), who bowed to clerical pressure and enforced anti-Jewish laws.

Despite legal restrictions, Jews maintained important positions in Byzantine society. They controlled half the shipping fleet in Alexandria, and evidently dominated the dyeing industry from the 6th to the 15th

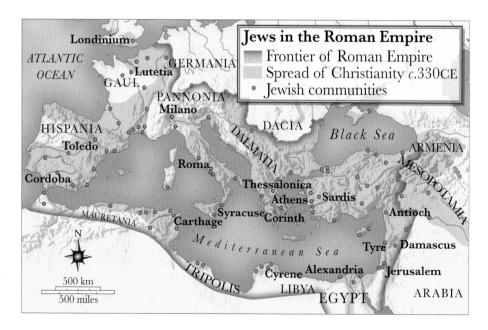

Jews in the Roman Empire
▨ Frontier of Roman Empire
▨ Spread of Christianity *c.*330CE
∘ Jewish communities

Londinium
ATLANTIC OCEAN
GERMANIA
Lutetia
GAUL
PANNONIA
Milano
HISPANIA
Toledo
DACIA
Black Sea
ARMENIA
Roma
DALMATIA
Cordoba
Thessalonica
MESOPOTAMIA
Athens · Sardis
MAURETANIA
Syracuse Corinth
Carthage
Antioch
Mediterranean Sea
Tyre · Damascus
TRIPOLIS
Cyrene Alexandria
Jerusalem
LIBYA
EGYPT
ARABIA
500 km
500 miles

centuries. Culturally, Jewish life influenced Byzantine Christianity: Hebrew poetry (*paytanim*) blossomed in Palestine, and one monk, Romanos, an apostate from Judaism, introduced Jewish poetic modes into Byzantine liturgy.

The Byzantine appointee Bishop Cyril of Alexandria (*c.*375–444CE) demanded the expulsion of the city's Jews. Ten years later, in 425CE, Theodosius II issued his Code of Law, which limited where Jews could live and what they could wear and subjected them to extraordinary taxation. Jews could no longer build synagogues or own slaves, which ruined Jewish farmers. Intermarriage with Christians was punishable by death. In 439CE, Theodosius prohibited Jews from holding public office or positions involving control of money; he also re-enacted a defunct law outlawing the building of new synagogues.

JUSTINIAN, PHOCAS AND HERACLIUS

Justinian I (527–65CE) also deprived Jews of civil and religious privileges. In 535CE he outlawed Judaism in the re-conquered lands of North Africa; in 553CE he banned the recitation of Hebrew in synagogues, and forbade the use of the Mishnah to help congregants understand the Torah. As the empire weakened under the blows of enemies within and without, successive emperors used Jews as scapegoats. Eventually, in 608CE, when Emperor Phocas (602–41CE) initiated a new wave of forced conversions, the Jews of Antioch revolted and killed the city's bishop.

Desperate to revive Byzantine fortunes, Emperor Heraclius (610–41CE) promised to protect the Jews

in Palestine as he launched a counter-attack against Persia. When Heraclius took Jerusalem in 629CE, he went back on his word. He barred Jews from living within a three-mile radius of the holy city, and allegedly allowed Byzantine troops to kill any Jew they could find.

BYZANTIUM FALTERS

Within the Byzantine realm, indigenous Christians of minority sects (Nestorians, Assyrians, Monophysites, Copts and others) resented the arrogance of Greek Orthodox clerics. Seemingly endless battles eventually exhausted all parties, effectively leaving the door open for the Muslim Arab conquests of the early 7th century CE. Byzantium's loss of swathes of land to Muslim Arabs then spelt the end of Christian patrimony over the Middle East.

Jews faced repeated attempts at conversion to Christianity by the emperors Basil I (in 873CE) and Romanus I Lecapenus (in 943CE). In 1204 Latin Crusaders sacked Constantinople and burned down the Pera district, today Beyoglu in Istanbul, south of the Golden Horn and home to Genoan, Venetian and

Jewish merchants and silk weavers. Byzantium eventually fell to Muslim Turks when the Ottoman Sultan Muhammad II took Constantinople on 24 April 1453.

Below Tiberias, major port on the Sea of Galilee, where Jews launched their final revolt against Byzantine rule in 614CE.

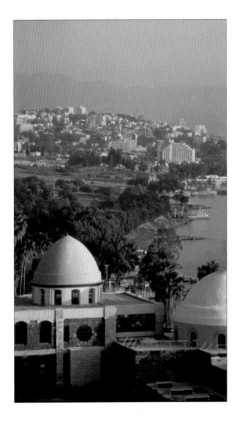

JEWISH COMMUNITIES OF THE MEDITERRANEAN

UNDISTURBED BY THE RISE AND FALL OF EMPIRES, JEWS FROM LIBYA, SYRIA, GREECE AND TURKEY FORMED A NETWORK THAT TRADED IN GOODS, SERVICES AND IDEAS ACROSS THE MEDITERRANEAN.

Outside Egypt and the Middle East, Jewish communities played a huge role in the life of the Mediterranean basin, a position they maintained after the Roman empire collapsed in the late 5th century CE. These included outposts in Morocco and Tunisia – especially the cities of Kairouan, seat of a noted yeshiva; and the island of Djerba. Other sites included Spain, Greece, Anatolia, southern France and Cyrenaica, in what is now Libya, west of Egypt.

CYRENAICA

The region of Cyrenaica consisted of five main Hellenistic cities – Cyrene, Berenice, Appolonia, Teucheria and Ptolemais – known collectively as a pentapolis. In *The Antiquities of the Jews*, Josephus writes that Jews first came to Cyrenaica from Egypt, under Ptolemy I (323–285BCE). Originally, it seems, they were regarded as the fourth 'class', after citizens, peasants

and metics (later settlers). Rome acquired the territory from the Ptolemies in 96BCE, and, after an interim of civil strife, turned it into a Roman province in 74BCE. One Cyrenaican Jew was Jason of Cyrene, whose five volumes in Greek on the Maccabean revolt were summarized in II Maccabees. Jason later helped instigate the failed Egyptian Jewish rebellion against Trajan in 115CE.

DAMASCUS

A Jewish community has probably existed in Damascus for millennia, and it lays claim to being the oldest continually inhabited city on earth. Egyptian Mari documents of the 18th century BCE call it the Land of Apum, ruled by Western Semites, and the name Damascus occurs often in the biblical books of Chronicles and Kings and in the Dead Sea Scrolls. Given Syria's geographical proximity, the city formed a natural place of refuge for Jews fleeing trouble in Palestine or the Land of Israel. (One known 'refugee' was King Herod, who hid in Damascus when the Sanhedrin accused him of treating Galilean Jewish rebels brutally.)

The Talmud speaks of Damascus as 'the gateway of the Garden of Eden', such was its economic renown. And we know of Damascus' importance from the books of Paul, who as a rabbi was sent to punish the recalcitrant 'heretical' Christ-believers among the Jews who dwelt

Left A shiviti, *a contemplative artwork traditionally placed on the eastern wall of a room or synagogue, facing Jerusalem, which reminds Jews of God's presence.*

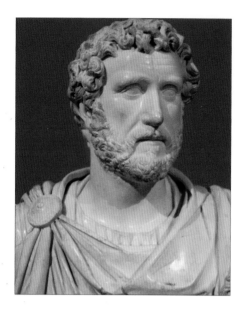

Above A bust of Jason of Cyrene, a Jew who wrote a history of the Maccabees up to the victory against Greco–Syrians.

in Damascus' Straight Street. Scholars believe that Damascene Jews farmed and traded, but they were not noted as religious sages, unlike Jews in Aleppo, north Syria.

Both indigenous Christians and Jews suffered under Byzantine rule. There also seems to have been rivalry between the two communities. When Damascene Jews helped Persia oust local Byzantine rulers in the early 7th century CE, they suppressed the Christians of Tyre (now in Lebanon), the main port outlet for landlocked Damascus.

GREECE

Documentary evidence shows that Jews lived on the Greek mainland from 300BCE; some possibly arrived as early as the Babylonian exile. Over time they formed a community called Romaniotes which was distinct from both Sephardi and Ashkenazi Jews. They had their own *minhag*, or 'local customs', and a unique language called Yevanic, a Greek dialect written in Hebrew characters. The early medieval Jewish traveller Benjamin of Tudela wrote that the largest Romaniotes community was in Thebes, where Jews

Above A ruined synagogue at Sardis, ancient capital of the Lydian kingdom and known for its fabulous wealth.

were respected as cloth-dyers and makers of silk garments. They also lived on the islands of Corfu and Aegina, and in Corinth, Athens and Thessaloniki, which became the largest Greek Jewish city when Sephardi Jews arrived from Spain after 1492. Later the fortified *kastro* section of Ioannina, a town in north-west Greece, south of Albania, became the Romaniote centre.

ASIA MINOR

Vast in size and opulent in its decoration, the marble-floored, two-tiered synagogue of Sardis was truly a wonder of ancient Anatolia. Its rediscovery in the 1960s overturned previous theories about Jewish life in Asia Minor and indicated that Jews had formed a prosperous and confident minority long after Christianity had supposedly eclipsed all other faiths.

Formerly capital of the Lydian kingdom, Sardis was known for its fabulous wealth, as captured in the expression 'as rich as Croesus', its

Right Paul preaching to the Jews in the synagogue at Damascus, 12th-century Byzantine mosaic.

6th-century BCE king. Jews had lived in Lydia since the 4th century BCE, and traded extensively along routes that passed through Sardis to Persia and beyond. Their great synagogue was built in 3rd-century CE Sardis, the metropolis of the Roman province of Lydia, the city having been previously ruled by Athenians, Persians and Macedonians. Located on a street full of elegant shops, many of them Jewish-run, the synagogue was attached to a magnificent bath-gymnasium and contained 80 Greek and seven Hebrew inscriptions.

All these facts indicate Jews were thoroughly integrated into the life of a mainly pagan and later Christian city.

Jewish mercenaries in the Greco-Syrian army of Seleucus were among the first inhabitants of Antioch, an Anatolian port created in the 3rd century BCE. From then on Jews wielded enormous influence, whether as wealthy merchants in the suburb of Daphne, rice-growing farmers to the north east, or bakers, metal workers and weavers within the city itself. Rome conquered Antioch in 64BC, and 100 years later Titus, returning in triumph after crushing the Judean revolt, imposed on its Jewish population a special tax called a *ficus Judaicus*. In effect that meant that Antioch's Jews had to pay two denarii to Rome instead of to Jerusalem as before. However, the city's Jews still enjoyed high status after the empire became Christian. In 391CE they helped fund a new synagogue in Apamea, 50 miles away. Fourth-century sources reveal that Jews, pagans and Christians lived and worked harmoniously together, while the Jews still worshipped separately and maintained strong links with their Palestinian brethren.

CHANGING FORTUNES IN EUROPE

JEWS TRADED ACROSS GERMANY, FRANCE, SPAIN AND ITALY AFTER THE ROMAN EMPIRE COLLAPSED. SOME BEFRIENDED EMPERORS AND POPES, BUT OTHERS WERE PERSECUTED BY NEWLY CHRISTIANIZED PAGANS.

Above Pope Gregory I (reg. 590–604CE) called Jews blind to Christ's truth, yet he also allowed them freedom to worship.

Jews fleeing Palestine naturally gravitated to colonies of fellow Jews who already lived in the Diaspora. Although the actual Jewish population of the world appears to have dropped markedly, from eight million around 50CE to 1.5 million around the year 1000, Jews managed to carve out new roles for themselves on the back of Roman colonization. Equally remarkably, they survived and even expanded after the Western Roman empire itself collapsed, despite being vulnerable to the whims of the rulers of the day, and certain zealous priests.

MOVING INLAND

Jews had followed the Roman empire's military encampments into inland Europe. It is known that

Below A 15th-century woodcut from Munich of the Judensau or Jewish pig, which anti-semites said suckled Jews.

Jews established trading posts in Germanic frontier towns, such as Bonn, Triers and Cologne, as testified by an imperial decree of 321. Here they first encountered the 'barbarians' who were encroaching on Rome. Conceivably these Jews were the first Ashkenazim, who make up some 90 per cent of Jews today. The name Ashkenaz derives from an obscure biblical location. It was used during medieval times to denote the lands of Germany and northern France which earlier Jewish sources called Allemania.

For the most part, Jews were welcomed in German towns as international traders to the East. New communities emerged in southern central Germany in the 11th century. There then followed a period of persecution during the 12th to 14th centuries, when Jews moved north and east, and began practising money-lending.

JEWS IN ITALY AND SPAIN

Increasingly, pagan rulers and their peoples converted to Christianity, which often led to persecution of Jews – but not always so, as in the case of Theodoric the Great. In 500CE Theodoric safeguarded the right of the Jews of Italy to determine civil disputes and worship freely. In 519, Christians in Ravenna burned the local synagogues, and he ordered the town to rebuild them at their own expense.

By contrast, the Visigoth King Recared of Spain (586–601CE) renounced Arianism in favour of Catholicism in 587CE and with the Third Council of Toledo in 589CE proceeded to persecute Jews. He banned intermarriage, forbade Jews to own slaves or hold positions of authority and ordered that children of mixed marriages be raised as Christians. Defenders of Recared's record say he rejected bribes from wealthy Spanish Jews and that he rescinded the death penalty for Jews who proselytized.

EARLY POPES AND THE JEWS

Several of the first popes were martyred, sometimes with their congregations, and it was only really

Above In this 14th-century manuscript, Entree d'Espagne, *Charlemagne (742–824) gives audience to his subjects.*

with the Edict of Milan in 313CE that the papal institution began to acquire its later power. Essentially the pope is the bishop of Rome, bishop meaning 'overseer' in Greek. Rome was one of four central cities for Christians, the others being Antioch, Jerusalem and Constantinople.

Popes often proved more tolerant than local bishops, presumably because they had to consider the economic and political well-being of the empire and not just populist concerns. The most influential early pope, Gregory the Great, formulated official church policy towards Jews in 590CE. He banned forced conversions and granted Jews the right to worship freely. Gregory thus set a standard for successors to follow – not that they always did – and Jews felt they could appeal to the pope when threatened by local bigotry.

Formally, the schism between Roman Catholics and Greek Orthodox occurred in 1054, but the two churches had been moving in different directions for centuries. By and large, the 'barbarians' who now ruled different parts of the former Western Roman empire adopted Christianity; they followed the pope in Rome as their spiritual guide, rather than the patriarch in the still-surviving Eastern Roman or Byzantine empire.

CHARLEMAGNE AND JEWISH LIFE IN FRANCE

One barbarian convert was Charlemagne, King of the Franks, who was crowned emperor of the west in 800CE. Credited with being the first true 'European', he expanded his realm from northern France to include all of Germany, northern Italy, Holland, Austria and the zone between France and Muslim Spain. While he forced other barbarians to adopt Christianity, he showed a rare respect for Jews and Judaism, borne as much by appreciation of their economic utility as by ethical considerations. Militant priests chafed at the privileges he gave Jewish traders – especially the Radhanites from Persia – but he resisted clerical attempts to curtail Jews' rights.

Generally, anti-Jewish rhetoric from the pulpit found little traction among ordinary Christian Franks, and Charlemagne was happy to keep it that way. As the borders of the 'Holy Roman empire' expanded, it encompassed such Mediterranean locales as Massalia, the first Greek outpost in western Europe. Later called Marseilles, it began attracting Jews soon after it was founded c.600BCE. (Today it houses the third-largest urban community of Jews in Europe.) Another French port with a significant Jewish presence was Narbonne, whose loyalty to the Frankish monarch won them the right to be ruled by their own Jewish 'king' of his community and effective city treasurer.

The security that was enjoyed by Charlemagne's Jews might have been exceptional. Recared's successor in Spain, Sesbut, prohibited Judaism in 610CE. Although exiled Jews returned to Byzantine Spain under his successor, Swintilla, a new law 18 years later decreed that only Catholics could live there – an edict that many Jews clearly ignored. Christianity had largely united post-Roman Europe, yet it was to prove extremely problematic for Jews who had long lived there.

Below A German woodcut showing the alleged ritual child murder of Simon by Jews in 1475 in Trent, Italy.

JEWS OF PRE-ISLAMIC PERSIA AND ARABIA

OVER TIME, JEWS FLEEING PALESTINE CAME TO LIVE AND WORK ALONGSIDE THEIR ETHNIC COUSINS, THE ARABS, AND THE YEMENITE KINGDOM OF HIMYAR EVEN BRIEFLY ADOPTED THEIR FAITH.

Above An 18th-century Persian painting of the Sacrifice of Abraham, showing the angel with the ram.

In 614CE the Persians conquered Jerusalem and ruled it until 629CE. The two former centres of Jewish life, Palestine and Babylon, were briefly reunited. However, both the Persians and their rivals, the Byzantines, were about to face a potent new threat from Arabia.

Mobilized by the monotheistic faith of Islam, Arabs conquered large parts of Sassanid Persia in 634CE. Damascus fell in 635CE, Jerusalem in 637CE, and by 650CE all of Persia and Iraq was in Arab hands.

COUSINS DIVIDED?

A broad definition of the word 'Arab' denotes any speaker of Arabic, which today covers most of the population of the Middle East and North Africa. A narrower usage applies only to the so-called 'pure' Arabs of the Arabian desert and Persian Gulf area, often referred to as Bedouin (literally, 'those who dwell outside'). However, both definitions are fraught with complexities. After the Arab and Muslim conquests of the 7th century, Syrians, Egyptians, Amorites, Berbers and Greek settlers, among others, adopted the new language. Some kept their original faith, invariably Christianity, yet still proudly called themselves Arab.

The Bible only occasionally uses the term Arab. Usually Arabs are referred to as Ishmaelites, the descendants of Abraham's firstborn son by Hagar, Ishmael. The Bible and the Koran agree that the Jewish line runs through Ishmael's younger half-brother, Isaac, so that would make Jews and Arabs first cousins. Certainly the Bible refers to both Arabs and Jews, or their Israelite ancestors, as the progeny of Noah's son, Shem – hence the word Semites. Linguistic and genetic research appears to confirm this commonly accepted tradition.

One minority view even states that the words Hebrew (*Ivri* in the Hebrew language) and Arab (*Aravi*), stem from the same Semitic root, and may once have been interchangeable. *Ivri* broadly means 'those who dwell across [the river]'; *aravi* suggests either 'of the desert' or 'those who mingle', like the blending of daylight and darkness at dusk. In all cases, there is a suggestion of the nomadic ways of the earliest biblical patriarchs and the Bedouin Arab sheikhs.

JERUSALEM UNDER PERSIA

After Jerusalem's fall in 70CE, many Jews migrated to Perea and Arabia Felix, Roman provinces east of Judea. Proto-Arabs such as the Idumeans (Edomites) had already been converted to Judaism, and to a limited extent this happened further

Left A 10th-century Arabic geography, Book of Routes and Provinces, *showing the Mediterranean.*

Right Islamic Palestine in the 7th century CE, showing the Persian conquest, the Byzantine reconquest and the Arab invasion.

east. Mostly, though, Arabic-speaking Jews of the vast Hijaz area dwelt alongside pagan Arabs, but separately, and they were respected as traders.

THE INDEPENDENT KINGDOM OF HIMYAR

Jews evidently reached southern Arabia, around Yemen, in the 1st century BCE, and Herod the Great sent a Jewish brigade to the region in 25BCE. The Arabic Kingdom of Himyar, founded in 115BCE, was centred around Yemen and the southern Najd area (of today's Saudi Arabia). It controlled most of southern Arabia by the 4th century CE. Successive Himyarite kings, Ab Karib As'ad in the 5th century CE and Dhu Nawas in the 6th, adopted Judaism. Jewish affiliation intensified among the populace when Christian Abbysinians (Ethiopians) and Byzantines threatened to capture the economically

Below A modern Yemenite Jewish girl in traditional ceremonial dress. Goldsmiths are among the craftworkers who emigrated to Israel from Yemen.

Islamic Palestine
→ Persian conquest, 610–619CE
→ Byzantine reconquest, 622–9CE
→ Arab invasion, 633–40CE

strategic region. Ultimately, declining trade destroyed Himyarite power and the Jews lost an ally.

JEWS OF PERSIA AFTER THE 5TH CENTURY CE

Between 614 and 629CE, Jerusalem and all of Palestine came under Persian rule. Most Jews at the time were suffering under the yoke of the Byzantines and thus welcomed the new invaders. The Jews of Damascus had already helped the Persians to attack and occupy that formerly Byzantine-ruled city in 613CE. In Jerusalem, the Persian conquerors destroyed many Christian churches, and later reneged on promises to re-establish Jewish sovereignty. Jews – who numbered 150,000 in all of Palestine – were barred from the holy city to a radius of three miles. Within decades, however, Arabs had control of Jerusalem and the entire Levant, which opened up new challenges and opportunities.

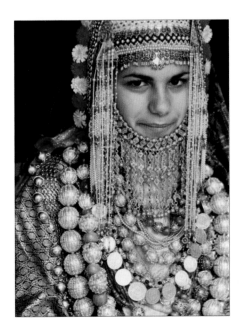

THE RADHANITES

Long before Marco Polo 'discovered' China, Jewish traders from Persia used the Silk Road to the East. Up to 1,000 merchants, the Radhanites, dominated trade in China and Europe, between Muslim and Christian worlds.

Some say their name refers to a Babylonian province; others think it is from the Persian for 'those who know the way'. Others believe that it points to the River Rhône, where the major routes to the East began.

Radhanites travelled by boat down Russia's Volga River, across the Mediterranean, or by sea from the Persian Gulf to India. They also carried goods by camel-back to Egypt, or from Khazaria across deserts to China. They traded beaver skins, slaves, eunuchs, brocade and swords from the West and from the East came musk, camphor, cinnamon, silk, oils and jewellery. The Radhanites spoke Persian, Greek, Arabic, Spanish, Frankish and Slavonic. Some say they introduced Chinese papermaking to the West, and that their use of credit notes inspired early banking systems.

CHAPTER 4

JUDAISM AND ISLAM

Early in the 7th century CE, Islam was born. Islam was the third of the three great monotheistic religions that were to arise in the Middle East, this time from Arabia. Much of the Islamic Koran, a text considered by its adherents to be the verbatim word of God, revisited the Hebrew Bible, and Jews and Muslims share remarkably similar beliefs and practices. Islam's rapid rise profoundly affected Jewish history. A rift during Mohammed's lifetime led Muslims to expel Jews from Arabia, but generally Jews were to find relations with Muslims easier than their encounters with Christians.

The encounter of the three faiths in Spain after 712CE, known as the Golden Age of Spain, spawned a period of religious tolerance when arts, sciences and trade flourished. Meanwhile, dramatic events included the Khazar Kingdom's conversion to Judaism; a Jewish rebellion against the rabbis, which resulted in the new Karaite sect; and the first stirrings of a distinctively European Ashkenazi culture of Judaism in France.

Opposite A painting of Noah's Ark, from The Fine Flower of Histories, *a work of political and religious world history by Ottoman historiographer Seyyid Loqman Ashuri, 1583.*

Above The Dome of the Rock was built on the Temple Mount of Jerusalem, on the presumed site of the Second Temple, thus making the area sacred for both Muslims and Jews.

THE BIRTH AND RISE OF ISLAM

LITERALLY MEANING SUBMISSION TO GOD'S WILL, AND DERIVED FROM THE ROOT WORD FOR PEACE, ISLAM CLAIMS TO COMPLETE THE DIVINE MESSAGE RECEIVED BY JEWS AND CHRISTIANS.

According to Muslims, the Angel Gabriel relayed the Koran, Islam's holiest text, to Mohammed. Today there are more than 1.6 billion adherents of Islam, making it the world's second largest faith.

The rise of Islam and defeat of Persia in the 7th century CE ended polytheism in most of the known world. Judaism now faced two competing monotheistic faiths. Arab victories in the Middle East and North Africa also re-united formerly split poles of Jewish life, and by 732CE Islam ruled Spain and reached Tours in France. Now 90 per cent of the world's Jews lived within the Islamic ambit, a factor that profoundly influenced Jewish history.

THE LIFE OF THE PROPHET

Born in the southern Arabian town of Mecca in 570CE and orphaned at five, Mohammed was raised by his uncle and worked as a shepherd. Legend says that when he was 12 he visited Syria, where his first encounters with Jews and Christians gave him respect for these *ahl al-kitab*, or 'People of the Book'. Illiterate yet canny, in 594CE he acted as a caravan agent for a wealthy, older tradeswoman, Khadija, whom he married.

Mohammed reported his first revelation, of being visited by the Angel Gabriel, in 610CE and began preaching in 613CE. His beliefs won him some converts, but the powerful Quraysh tribal confederation felt

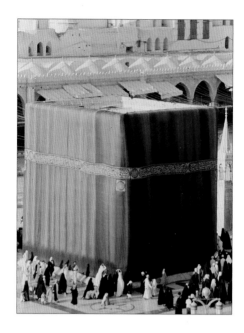

Above The Ka'bah is a granite building that, according to Islamic tradition, dates back to the time of Abraham. Muslims all over the world turn towards it in prayer.

threatened. Mohammed had damned the Quraysh as oppressors, even though he belonged to the Banu Hashim, a minor clan in the tribe. They dominated Mecca's lucrative trade routes and also controlled the Ka'bah, a cube-shaped shrine and object of pagan pilgrimage.

As a trader Mohammed often travelled to the desert oasis of Yathrib – later called Medina – where he encountered Jewish tribes, possibly descendants of refugees from Palestine in Roman times. In 622 Mohammed settled in Medina with his muhajiroun, or 'migrants', after Meccan authorities threatened to kill him. He converted the Aws and Khazraj, local majority pagan tribes; founded the first Muslim community; and skilfully arbitrated between rival factions. The Muslim calendar actually begins at 622CE, the year of the *hijra*, or 'immigration';

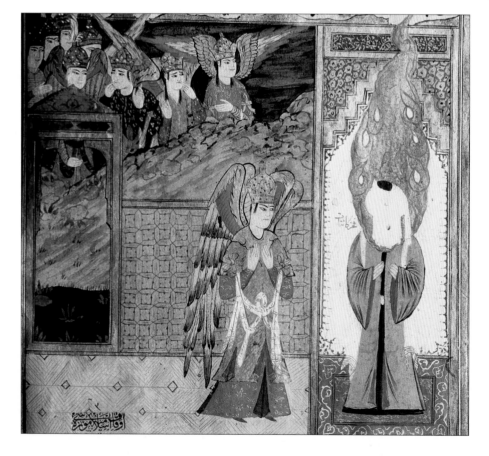

Left A 16th-century Turkish painting shows the Archangel Gabriel inspiring Mohammed. Traditional Muslim strictures on showing the face of the prophet means his face is flooded with white light.

later Muslim scholars defined the pre-*hijra* period as *jahaliya*, or 'the age of ignorance'. From a Jewish viewpoint, Medina's new constitution allowed them to maintain their religion and guaranteed their financial autonomy. It also decreed that Jews and 'believers' (Muslims) were part of a single community and pledged mutual support if either were attacked. Only Mohammed, though, could authorize war.

Mohammed expected to win over Medina's Jews to his cause. He urged Muslims to pray in the direction of Jerusalem and to assemble on Friday afternoons as Jews prepared for the Sabbath. The *Koran*, or 'reading', affirms strict belief in one God, Allah in Arabic, and is full of ethical precepts partly derived from the Ten Commandments. Islam and Judaism had and still have much in common in terms of practices such as regular prayer, fasting, circumcision and shunning certain foods.

Most of the tales in the Koran are familiar to readers of the Hebrew Bible and Midrash. It was probably first compiled in 650CE during the early caliphate, 18 years after Mohammed died. The Koran is divided into 70 *suras*, or 'chapters', one of which is called Bani Israil (Children of Israel). Moses, or Musa in Arabic, is mentioned in 176 verses, and according to Muslim belief Abraham (Ibrahim) was the first Muslim – literally, 'one who submitted to Allah'. The Koran often repeats that God first revealed Himself to the sons of Israel. All but one of the Koran's chapters opens with 'In the Name of Allah, most merciful and most compassionate'. To believing Muslims, the Koran is perfect and free from contradictions.

RIFT WITH JEWS OF MEDINA
The Jews of Medina initially sided with Mohammed, but then some reputedly mocked him for his imperfect grasp of Jewish texts. Ultimately

they rejected his claim to be the last prophet and preferred to keep their original faith. Mohammed changed the direction of prayer, or *qibla*, to Mecca, although Jerusalem was to become the third holiest site in Islam after Mecca and Medina. Mohammed had a number of disputes with Jewish tribes, including the Banu Qunayqa (who he expelled from Medina), the Banu Nadir and the Banu Qurayza. After conquering the oasis of Khaybar, he married Saffiya bint Huyay bin Akhtab, daughter of the executed Jewish sheikh of the Banu Nadir.

Mohammed also overcame many non-Jewish tribes. In 630CE he attacked Mecca and stripped the Quraysh of power. The Koran reports several alliances between Jews and early Muslims. One Hadith, or 'saying of the prophet', praised a brave Jewish general who fought for Mohammed. In another Hadith, the prophet upbraided Muslims who mocked Jewish converts over their origins. Later Muslims often invoked Khaybar, whenever tension rose with Jewish subjects. Jews were largely expelled from central Arabia after the Khaybar battle yet remained untouched in other areas where Arabs adopted Islam, especially in Yemen.

Mohammed died suddenly in 632CE, without an obvious successor in place. Widespread tribal rebellion erupted, although it was stemmed when Abu Bakr was chosen as caliph (*khalif*, or 'God's deputy') and re-imposed Islamic government over Arabia. Omar ibn al-Khatib succeeded Abu Bakr in 634, and over ten years subjugated Syria, Palestine, Egypt, Mesopotamia and Persia. Vastly more Jews than had ever lived in Arabia now found themselves under Arab rule.

The pace of the Arab conquest was astonishing. Desert nomads forced the Byzantine empire back into its Anatolian heartland, while

Above Mohammed, the founder of Islam, with his father-in-law Abu Bakr, who became caliph when Mohammed died.

Persia dissolved entirely as an independent political unit. Most of all, Islam galvanized the Arab people and gave them a sense of unity, pride and identity that they never had before.

Some Jews and Christians converted, but most kept their original faiths. Formally, Muslims tolerated them as 'people of the book' and held them in higher esteem than pagans and idolaters. Moreover, the Koran stated that there should be 'no compulsion in religion', though certain overzealous Arab commanders ignored this stricture.

In practice, Arab leaders probably considered Jews less threatening than Christians, who they feared harboured loyalties to the Byzantine foe. Generally the Arabians were pragmatic; instead of antagonizing local populations, they employed them as builders, administrators, teachers and traders. They sought to consolidate their expanded borders and came to respect the more settled and refined cultures of the Levant. Overall, Jews fared better under early Islam than they did in the Europe of the day.

JEWS BETWEEN RIVAL CALIPHATES

THE DRAMATIC ARAB CONQUEST OF PALESTINE, PERSIA AND NORTH AFRICA UNITED MOST OF WORLD JEWRY UNDER MUSLIM RULE. GENERALLY, JEWS WERE PROTECTED, PROVIDED THEY PAID TAXES.

From the outset, Muslims were uncertain how to treat Jews and Christians. 'To you be your religion, and to me my religion', runs one Koranic verse. On the other hand, certain Koran verses suggest that Muslims should fight non-believers, including Jews and Christians. The Koran also chides Jews for spurning the prophets.

MILITARY TRIUMPH

The question of other monotheist religions sharpened when Muslims came to rule over millions of Christians and Jews after Mohammed's death in 632CE. In fact, the second Caliph, Omar, acquired more territory more quickly than anyone before in history. His camel-borne fighters struck north and conquered large parts of Sassanid Persia in 634CE. He then swung south and took Damascus in 635CE and Jerusalem in 637CE. Egypt fell in 640CE and by 650CE all of Persia and Iraq were in Arab hands. Within decades warriors from the Arabian

hinterland controlled the entire Middle East and North Africa, and by 717CE had added northern India and most of Spain to their realm.

Jews in Palestine and Babylonia were glad to be rid of Byzantine domination and Persian caprices, yet they also recalled how severely Mohammed had treated Arabian Jews in Khaybar. Most, though, welcomed Arabs as fellow Semites and followers of a monotheistic faith.

DIVISIONS IN ISLAM

The size of the Arab victory dissuaded defeated peoples from rebelling. Meanwhile, the Muslim *umma*, or 'community of believers', was divided over how to choose a successor to Mohammed. They settled on having a caliph, literally God's 'deputy', as a combined spiritual and political leader.

Sunni Muslims, Islam's majority trend, called the first four caliphs – Abu Bakr, Omar, Othman and Ali ibn Abi Talib – the righteously guided ones. However, the latter's followers

Above A 7th-century CE mosaic from a shrine in the courtyard of the Umayyad Mosque in Damascus. The date palm may represent the tree of life in the garden of Paradise.

claimed that the Sunni were impostors, and spawned a dissident Shia party after Ali was murdered in 661CE and his son in 680CE, both in Iraq. This clash began the Sunni–Shia schism that persists today.

Another division was cultural and geographic in nature. After Ali died, Mu'awiya, governor of Damascus, established the Umayyad Caliphate and moved Islam's centre from the Arabian Peninsula to Damascus. He employed Christian officials and set up *diwans*, 'Byzantine-modelled bureaucracies', to run a realm from Egypt to Iran. He also introduced hereditary leadership, which earlier Muslims had rejected.

PACT OF OMAR

The 622CE constitution of Medina protected Jews but did not cover rule by Muslims of non-Muslim majorities adequately. One of the first caliphs,

Left Map of the Umayyad Caliphate showing how the centre of Islam moved from Arabia to the old 'fertile crescent', traversing the edge of the Mediterranean.

Early Caliphates: Muslim territory
under the Umayyads 661–750
under first four Caliphs 632–661
until Mohammad's death 632
• New town and date founded

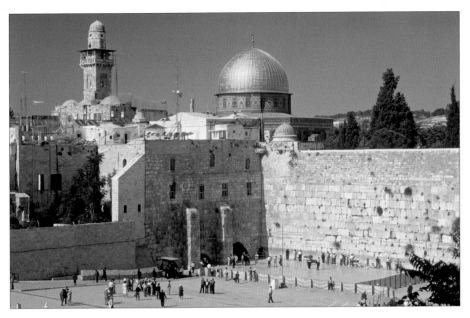

Above A 15th-century Syrian artwork of the Umayyad mosque, Damascus, built by Caliph al Walid I, 706–15CE.

Above The Dome of the Rock, built on the Temple Mount, rises behind the Western Wall in Jerusalem.

Omar, conquered Jerusalem, then humbly entered the city on foot and in 637CE signed a treaty with Patriarch Sophronius guaranteeing Christian freedom of worship. The caliph overturned Christian restrictions by allowing 70 Jewish families to move to the city. Omar's successors built the magnificent Dome of the Rock in 692CE and completed the nearby Al Aqsa mosque in 715CE.

The Umayyad Caliph Omar II in 717CE issued a second 'Pact of Omar', which formalized the concept of the tolerated *dhimmi*, or 'protected ones', essentially Jews, Christians and Zoroastrians. *Dhimmi* gained military protection in return for paying a *jizya* (poll tax).

POLITICS AND ECONOMICS

Islamic jurists began dividing the world conceptually into *Dar al-Harb*, or the non-Muslim 'house of war', and *Dar al-Salam*, or Muslim-ruled 'house of peace'. As conditions changed, so did the law. Intermediate categories emerged, like *Dar al-Ahd*, or 'abode of agreement'; and *Dar al-Dhimmi*, or 'zone of tolerance'. These formulations allowed Muslims to live

in peace within Christian majority societies, and also permitted Muslim rulers to forge pacts with non-Muslim regimes.

Under the Umayyad Caliphate, which began in 661CE, the ruler became a more political and less spiritual figure. Practically speaking, Umayyads worried that tax revenue from the *jizya* would fall if too many *mawali*, or 'non-Arabs', converted. The land tax forced most Jews to abandon farming and flock to cities, where they were continuing to prosper as officials and craftsmen.

ABBASID RULE

Eventually the Umayyad Caliphate was overturned in 750CE by the Abbasids, a coalition of religious revivalists and *mawali* non-Arabs, who in 754CE made Baghdad their capital instead of Damascus. Abbasid rule coincided with the Jewish geonic period (690–11th century), named after the Geonim, the heads of the rabbinic academies in Babylonia. Gaon meant 'pride of the community'. It is likely that talmudic practices affected the way Muslims developed their own law,

the *sharia*. Under Caliph Harun al-Rashid (786–809CE) the Jewish exilarch's office grew in pomp and stature to unimagined levels. However, Jewish life in Jerusalem declined when Damascus lost ground to Baghdad in distinct Mesopotamia.

SAADIA GAON

The greatest figure of the geonic age, Saadia Gaon was born in Fayum, Egypt, in 882CE. Saadia wrote a fearsome polemic against Karaite Jews, who rejected the Talmud and rabbinate. He translated the Bible into Arabic, opening it up to Arabic-speaking Jews; and he wrote one of the most comprehensive Jewish prayer books. Most famously he authored *Beliefs and Opinions*, regarded as the first systematic Jewish theology. Like contemporary Arab thinkers, Saadia argued that there were two ways to truth – reason and revelation (in his view, via the Torah). Saadia synthesised Jewish tradition, Greek rationalism and Muslim Mu'tazili speculative theology. He also helped 'cleanse' Judaism of superstitions, and his work still influences Jewish thought.

KARAITES AND KHAZARS

KARAITES REJECTED RABBINICAL POWER AFTER 760CE; TRIBES IN RUSSIA CALLED KHAZARS ADOPTED JUDAISM 80 YEARS LATER. LARGELY VANISHED TODAY, BOTH GROUPS REVOLUTIONIZED JEWISH HISTORY.

The talmudic dictum of 'building a fence around the Torah' helped rabbis maintain their role as arbiters of Jewish life. Yeshivas gained specific regions of control; their *gaon* (head) could appoint judges and impose or suspend a *herem* (religious ban) on transgressors. However, in the late 8th century a new movement from within the body of Jewish believers arose to challenge their authority.

BIRTH OF KARAISM
Anan ben David, a Babylonian Jew of Davidic descent, in effect declared war on Rabbanites (rabbis and their followers), allegedly after he failed to become the exilarch in *c*.760CE. Anan galvanized dormant dissident groups such as the Essenes and Sadducees, as well as schismatics led by Abu 'Isa and Yudghan in Babylonia, and Serene in Syria.

Below Karaite Jews in Odessa, from Anatole Demidoff's Voyage dans la Russie méridionale, *1854.*

Karaites argued that the Talmud had taken Jews down a false path; the only true source of Judaism, they said, was the Torah. Adherents followed its literal reading, insisting that Jews celebrate the Sabbath in the dark and not drink wine after the Temple's demise. They bowed in prayer as Muslims and biblical figures did, kept a different calendar and allowed the eating of milk and meat together.

Anan ben David's *Book of Precepts*, written *c*.770CE, considered astronomy to be witchcraft, recommended long fasts and rejected doctors and medicines because Anan reasoned that God was the only healer. Later Karaite leaders overturned his wilder views, some calling Anan 'chief of the fools'. But all Karaites maintained his core rejection of rabbinic authority.

KARAITE SEPARATISM
The Karaites gained converts when their clerics argued with the rabbis, and exploited resentment against the political clout and elitism of the yeshivas, or 'Talmudic academies'. They called themselves 'roses' compared to the rabbinical 'thorns'. Karaite authors such as Sahl al-Masliah, Yefet ben Ali, Moses Dar'i and the 15th-century poet Abraham ha-Rofe transformed Jewish literature. They adopted advanced Arab models, and replaced Aramaic with Arabic as the default secular language to holy Hebrew. But when they determined practices according to a code called the *sevel ha-yerushah* (yoke of tradition), Rabbanites mocked them for rejecting the 'manmade' Talmud, only to recreate their own tendentious oral laws.

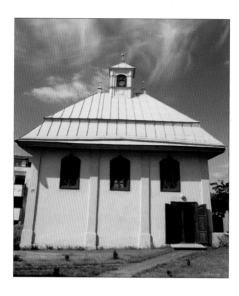

Above Karaite synagogue, Trakai, Lithuania. In the 1500s a group of Karaite Jews were invited to settle in Trakai by Grand Duke Vytautas.

The Karaites saw Diaspora existence as tragic and called for a return to the Land of Israel. Between the 9th and 11th centuries they probably outnumbered Rabbanites in Jerusalem, where they followed ritual purification rites and prayed for redemption at the city gates. Karaism spread to Fez and the Draa Valley in

---

THE KUZARI

Judah Halevi (1086–1145) wrote a book that immortalized Khazaria. *The Kuzari* was an imagined dialogue between King Bulan and a rabbi in which the pagan monarch chose Judaism over Christianity, Islam and Greek philosophy.

Originally published in Arabic and later translated into Hebrew, the book was really a polemic in favour of Jewish beliefs and a lament for Jews in the Diaspora. Halevi depicted the condition of exile as a double bind. Many Jews suffered during the Crusades that raged in his lifetime. As he wrote: 'Seir and Kedar [i.e. Christendom and Islam] may fight their wars but we are the ones who fall'.

Morocco, Spain, eastern Persia, Byzantine Asia Minor, and later to the Balkans, Russia and Poland. Invariably, Karaites lived among other Jews, but separate from them. Their spiritual leaders were *hakhamim*, or 'wise men', and their house of worship was the *kenesa*.

OUTPOSTS OF KARAITES

One of the most unusual and resilient Karaite communities lived on the Crimea. The Karaim were probably Turkic or Tatar tribesmen who converted to Karaism.

In 1392 Grand Duke Vytautas of Lithuania transplanted large numbers of Karaim to Vilnius and Trakai. There some grew wealthy from trade, and others became renowned scholars. Encouraged by their eccentric 19th-century leader, Abraham Fircovitch, the Karaim called themselves 'gentiles of Mosaic persuasion', thus absolving themselves from Tsarist charges against Jews for killing Jesus.

Small Karaite communities still exist in New York, Lithuania, Israel and, until recently, Cairo. However, polemics against them by Saadia Gaon and their own lack of cohesion, due to reverence for individualist interpretations and responsibilities, explain why they never overcame the Rabbanites. Their number dwindled from an alleged 40 per cent of all Jews to a few dozen thousand today. In 2007, however, Karaites in San Francisco celebrated their sect's first conversion ceremony since 1465, raising talk of a revival as other Jews sought alternatives to rabbinic authority.

KHAZARS CHOOSE JUDAISM

Not far from Crimea, on the estuary of the River Volga to the Caspian Sea, existed a Turkic people called the Khazars. What began as a small khanate in 652CE grew into an empire to rival the Caliphate to the south and the Rus (proto-Russians) to the north. Their royal court converted to Judaism

around 838, and their population apparently became Jewish too. Khazars rejected St Cyril's attempt to turn them to Christianity, and by the 10th century many Khazar documents were written in Hebrew.

During its heyday Khazaria formed a buffer between Christian Byzantium and Muslim powers. The empire derived wealth from its location along the silk road, and enjoyed a reputation for religious tolerance at home, while forcing tributes from neighbouring tribes, the Huns, Bulgars, Slavs and Magyars. The Khazar empire crumbled quickly towards the latter part of the 10th century, assailed by eastern Slavs and

Above Karaite synagogue, Yevpatoria, Ukraine. After Russia annexed the Crimea in 1783, Yevpatoria became a residence of the Hakham, spiritual ruler of the Karaites.

the Rus from Kiev (ironically, a city they may have founded). Khazars were probably dispersed and some suppose that this ethnically non-Semitic people formed the bedrock of the Ashkenazim, who today constitute 85 per cent of world Jewry. Recent evidence has cast doubt on such views, but Khazars undeniably shaped Jewish life in Eurasia.

Below Map of the once-Jewish empire of Khazaria, 10th century CE.

SPAIN – A CULTURAL MELTING POT

OVER THE CENTURIES, JEWS PLAYED A LEADING PART IN THE CULTURAL, SOCIAL AND ECONOMIC LIFE OF SPAIN. THEY WERE INFLUENTIAL IN THE ROMAN, ISLAMIC AND CHRISTIAN PERIODS.

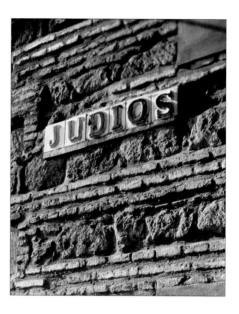

When the Romans invaded the Iberian Peninsula in 218BCE and started settling from 171BCE, they encountered a mixed population including Celts, Phoenicians, Carthaginians and Jewish families who claimed to descend from refugees of the first Temple period.

BEFORE THE ISLAMIC ERA

The Visigoths took over Spain in 551CE, after the fall of Rome, and in 587CE their king Recared (586–601CE) converted to Roman Catholicism, as did his subjects two years later. Christian rulers gave Jews the choice between conversion and expulsion in 613CE, before enslaving those who remained in 694CE. Jewish children were regularly abducted and raised in Christian homes. By the early 8th century CE, however, Spain

Below A cantor in a Spanish Sephardi synagogue reading the Haggadah to illiterate members of the community, 14th century.

Right A street sign labelled 'Judios' commemorates the fact that Cordoba was the centre of Jewish intellectual life in the Golden Age of Spain.

had split into warring fiefdoms, creating a power vacuum that Arab invaders eagerly exploited.

A NEW STATUS FOR SPANISH JEWS

It is said that one Visigoth ruler, Julian, invited Tariq ibn Ziyad to land at Gibraltar in 711CE. The name Gibraltar derives from the Arabic for 'Tariq's mountain'. Leading 7,000 converted Berbers and Arabs from North Africa, Tariq routed the Visigoth armies in the name of the Umayyad Caliph of Damascus, Al-Walid I.

Arabs, or more broadly, 'Moors', conquered Toledo and Cordoba in 711CE, Seville in 712CE and Portuguese Lisbon in 716CE. By 718CE they controlled most of the Iberian Peninsula, which they renamed Al-Andalus (land of the Vandals) with Cordoba as its capital. Moorish forces then crossed the Pyrenees into France, taking Narbonne in 720CE and Autun in 725CE, until the Frankish King Charles Martel stemmed their advance at Tours in 732CE.

Wherever they were victorious the Moors freed Jews from bondage at the hands of Visigoth rulers, and allowed them to reconstitute their communities. North African Jews began following largely Berber armies on to Spanish soil. Meanwhile, indigenous Spanish Jews became translators, advisors and diplomats to Muslim principalities, sometimes

interceding with Jewish counterparts in Christian-held territories. They were valued for their facility with languages, long residence in Spain, trading experience and their perceived neutrality, being neither Christian nor Muslim.

RENAISSANCE IN CORDOBA AND TOLEDO

Tariq's men were merely the advance guard for a much larger influx of North African Muslims. They imported irrigation techniques and crops such as rice and oranges from the Middle East, so that Cordoba flourished economically and grew into a city of 100,000 inhabitants, the largest in Europe. Spanish Muslims subdued Christian strongholds in the north and turned them into feudal holdings.

Events in distant Syria were soon to influence Spain. When the Abbasids overthrew the ailing Umayyads there in 750CE, one dynastic survivor, Abd al-Rahman I, fled to Cordoba, displaced the local ruling al-Fihri family, and proclaimed himself Emir (prince) in 756CE. Umayyads reigned in Spain until 1031, and reconfigured the social mosaic by importing cohorts from Jordan, Palestine and Damascus, and implanting them in distinct *junds*, or 'military colonies', in Iberia.

Increasingly, Spain became the cultural centre of the Muslim world and Jews contributed significantly to secular society. Their scholars translated Arabic texts into Spanish, Provençal and French, and rendered Hebrew and Greek works into Arabic. Hebrew literature also blossomed, while Latin scholarship declined, even among clerics. The Jews of Toledo contributed to mathematics, medicine, geography, poetry, botany and philosophy. The introduction of Arabic numerals and the Indian concept of zero encouraged not only the invention of algebra, but also an increasingly sophisticated commercial and banking system.

HISDAI IBN SHAPRUT

Scholars dispute when the 'golden age' truly began, but for Jews it seemed well under way in 929 when Hisdai ibn Shaprut was appointed physician to Caliph Abd al-Rahman III (891–961CE). He soon became director of customs and chief diplomat. Using his mastery of Greek and Latin, he negotiated with Abbot Johannes, emissary of Otto I, the Holy Roman Emperor, and persuaded the Christian kings of Leon and Navarre in northern Spain to sign peace treaties with the caliph.

Within his own community, ibn Shaprut was regarded as a *nagid*, or 'religious leader'. He created a centre for Jewish spiritual studies and a yeshiva, or 'academy', headed by Moses ben Hanokh of southern Italy. These institutions attracted immigrants from the East, loosened Spanish Jewry's bonds with Iraq, and supported poets and scholars such as the linguist Dunash ibn Labrat and the lexicographer Menahem ibn Seruq.

Abd al-Rahman III transformed his Emirate into a Caliphate, and ibn Shaprut served his successor, al-Hakim II (985–1021CE), as foreign affairs advisor. In 970CE al-Hakim founded a magnificent library in Cordoba called 'the jewel of the world'. He also expanded mosques, public baths, orchards, courtyards and aqueducts that served half a million people. Ibn Shaprut could, however, be despotic, as was his successor as *nasi*, or 'communal leader', Jacob ibn Jau, a wealthy silk manufacturer. Both owed their status to royal approval, and were generous benefactors to the poor.

THE SEPHARDIM

Spanish Jews came to call themselves Sephardim, after Sepharad, the name of a biblical site, which they designated as Spain. They spoke an Arabic dialect in Muslim areas and a Judeo-Spanish language called Judezmo or Ladino in Christian areas; they wrote both in Hebrew characters.

Logically, the collapse of the Hispanic Umayyad dynasty in 1031 should have marked the end of cultural advances. Anarchy prevailed as the *ta'ifa*, or smaller Muslim 'party kings', fought vicious turf wars. Jewish insecurity was highlighted when on 30 December 1066 an irate Muslim mob stormed Granada's royal palace and killed the unpopular Jewish vizier along with 1,500 Jewish families.

Above The Jewish quarter of Girona in Spain is criss-crossed with winding streets and narrow flights of stone stairs.

Yet such massacres were aberrations. Arguably the division of power between petty fiefdoms encouraged more diverse patronage of the arts and sciences. And this trend favoured talented citizens, no matter their ethnicity or faith.

Below Spain in the 10th century under the Umayyad dynasty, showing the kingdoms of Leon and the Franks.

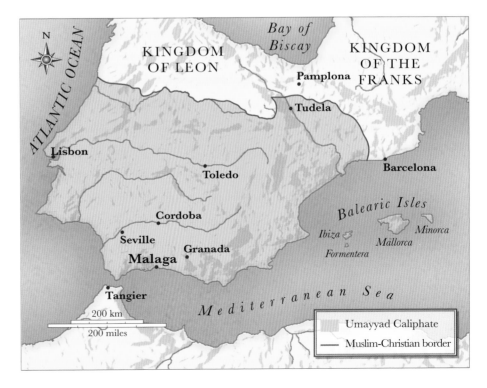

RASHI AND THE JEWS OF FRANCE

RABBI SHLOMO YITZHAKI, OR SOLOMON BEN ISAAC, BETTER KNOWN BY HIS HEBREW ACRONYM 'RASHI', IS REGARDED AS THE GREATEST EXEMPLAR OF EARLY ASHKENAZI JUDAISM, AND HIS WORDS HAVE GUIDED GENERATIONS.

Born in Troyes, the capital of Champagne province, in 1040, Rashi lived during a period of new-found confidence for European Jews who no longer depended solely on edicts from Babylonia to run their lives.

RASHI'S WORK

Rashi returned from studying in Mainz and Worms to found his own yeshiva (academy) in Troyes in 1067. His commentary on the Torah is still unparalleled for its clarity, thoroughness and accessibility for ordinary readers. He synthesized earlier sages' arguments when writing on the Talmud, imbuing his words with a passionate moral spirit that draws on consoling passages from the *aggadah*, or 'sayings'. Rashi also drew on

Below Savants at the Table of Maimonides. *From left: Joseph Caro, Isaac Alfasi, Maimonides, Jacob ben Asher and Rashi. From a Passover Haggadah.*

knowledge gleaned during his travels, and his interest in buildings, food, politics and economics. Some say he arrested a trend towards clerical elitism in Judaism and thus helped to 'democratize' the faith. He was also one of the first European Jews whose works were studied by the Sephardim of Muslim Spain.

Rashi built on foundations laid by predecessors, such as Rabbenu Gershom ben Judah of Mayence (960–1028CE) – the 'Light of the Exile'. He reinforced Gershom's ruling to outlaw polygamy, a practice that Sephardi and Babylonian Jews allowed, though seldom carried out. Such rulings marked a distinction between the three branches of Jewry.

Ashkenazi Jewry was still in its infancy and heavily influenced by rites from southern Italy. Their practices were intermingled with superstitions and coloured by popular tracts such as the 10th-century CE Josippon

Above The Rashi synagogue in Worms. He was the outstanding figure of early medieval Western Jewry.

Chronicle, a history from Adam to the age of Titus. *Minhag*, or 'local custom', differed, but generally Ashkenazi, Sephardi and Babylonian rabbis ensured that *halakha*, or 'essential religious law', stayed in harmony. An unusual feature of early medieval Jewry was the extent to which rabbis would travel to meet and debate with their colleagues, despite the fierce wars that were often fought between their home nations.

Since Charlemagne's day, urbanized Jews had established themselves as local financiers and international merchants. They generally got on well with local Christians and often formed the vanguard of new colonies. Yet while the Frankish king Louis the Pious (814–40CE) particularly favoured Jews and their mercantile skills, Archbishop Agobard of Lyons (769/79–840CE) wished to end their role in slave trading – a practice still common in Europe, and not condemned by any of the three sister faiths at the time.

PRAGMATIC SOLUTIONS

Rashi's *responsa*, or 'replies to legal questions', paint a colourful, informative picture of Jewish occupations in 11th-century northern France and the Rhine River Valley. His replies concerned particular cases but established principles on sensitive issues. He was known for his devotion to *peshut*, or 'the plain meaning of biblical texts and Talmudic edict', and warned against needless arguments and mystical excesses.

Certainly Rashi was a pragmatic community leader; for instance, he strove to find means by which Jews could lend on interest to one another, which Jewish law until then had forbidden. Often his responsa recommended making transactions through a gentile intermediary. Innovative and flexible, Rashi championed the independence of Jewish communities from each other. Most daringly, he permitted community councils to cancel or ignore 'decisions made by the ancients (i.e. prophets and sages) according to the needs of the time'.

DESCENDANTS OF RASHI

Rashi was so influential that to this day he has a separate column on every Talmud page devoted to his commentaries. The column is written in a distinctive semi-cursive hand, called 'Rashi script', although Rashi probably never used it.

Rashi's three learned daughters, Yocheved, Miriam and Rachel, helped him collate his copious writings and

engaged him in constant debate. He insisted that his girls read and study, and thus set an example to more patriarchal or chauvinist households. Yocheved's and Miriam's husbands and sons became known as the Tosafists (addition-makers), the most famous of whom was Jacob ben Meir, the Rabbenu Tam. They, too, have a small column appended to the Talmud; their methods resemble those of Christian scholastics, who were just beginning to develop at the earliest European universities.

ERUPTION OF VIOLENCE

Networks of mutual aid seem to have shielded Jews from external problems, for while western Europe was wracked by famine for much of the 10th and 11th centuries, there is little hint that the Jews of the region suffered more than other groups.

Left An illustrated copy of the first page of Rashi's commentary on the Pentateuch, produced in Italy, 1396.

Above Pope Urban II declares the first Crusade at the Clermont Synod, 1095. German woodcut, c. 1480.

Conditions deteriorated during Rashi's lifetime, when, after 1095, Christian Crusaders sent out by the Pope to capture the Holy Land killed Jews along the way, often aided by angry mobs. Jews were offered the choice of conversion or death. How should they react? On the one hand life was sacred and Jewish law regarded suicide as a desecration of God's name; on the other, martyrdom would strike a stand. In one hymn Rashi demanded that the Torah assert itself: 'If there be no Israel [Jewish people] to sing, thou art indeed silenced in every mouth and throat'. He prayed to see the Crusaders expelled from the Holy Land 'in blazing wrath'. At the same time, Rashi respected Christian zeal, and urged Jews to treat kindly those who had chosen conversion over death.

CHAPTER 5

FROM THE GOLDEN AGE TO THE INQUISITION

From the 8th century CE and for some 700 years thereafter, Spain displaced Palestine and Babylon as the central focus of Jewish life. The key that unlocked Jewish creativity was the invasion of Iberia by Arab and Berber soldiers, marching under the banner of Islam. Muslim rulers brought intellectual curiosity, economic vigour and aesthetic sensibilities that strongly influenced Christians and Jews. The 'Golden Age' of Sephardi Jewry produced great sages, linguists, scientists, physicians, diplomats, mapmakers, astronomers and mystics.

Christians reconquered the Spanish Peninsula, and in 1095 the Vatican ordered the Crusades, which soon reached Jerusalem. Jews suffered in the conflicts between Islam and Christendom, and anti-Semitic feeling reached a pinnacle when Jews were expelled from Spain in 1492. However, intrepid communities had planted seeds for survival all over the world in Norman England, Ottoman Turkey, a newly established Poland and even China and Ethiopia.

Opposite Alhambra Palace, Granada. Isabella and Ferdinand flew flags there in 1492, marking the defeat of Muslim Spain and heralding the eclipse of Jewish life on the peninsula.

Above A beautiful illuminated page from the Barcelona Haggadah of 1350, showing a synagogue service in medieval Spain.

THE GOLDEN AGE OF SPAIN

A UNIQUE CONFLUENCE OF CULTURES IN MUSLIM-RULED SPAIN INSPIRED AN EXTRAORDINARY PERIOD OF JEWISH CREATIVITY. SPANISH JEWS BECAME A BEACON FOR ALL OTHER JEWISH COMMUNITIES.

The phrase 'Renaissance man' could have been invented for Samuel HaNagid, but for the fact that he lived in Muslim Spain 500 years before the Renaissance of Catholic Italy.

SAMUEL HANAGID

Born into a Levite family in 993CE, Samuel was steeped in Jewish theology, yet also studied the Muslim Koran and spoke and wrote Arabic and Latin. In time he was elected *nagid* (prince) of Granada's Jewish community and served two successive Caliphs as *vizier* (chief minister).

Samuel was an accomplished poet, philologist, trader, rabbi, diplomat and benefactor. He was a brilliant battlefield commander, winning victories for his Muslim patrons, and becoming the first true Jewish military hero in

Below The 'Carpet page', 1260, from the Damascus keter, one of the earliest manuscripts of the Hebrew Bible that survives from Spain.

centuries. Known as Ibn Naghrela in Arabic, Samuel distinguished himself as a fine poet. His remit spread far beyond the boundaries of Spain, to Ifriqiya (Tunisia), Egypt and Iraq.

SUCCESSFUL SUBJECTS

Along with thousands of Jews, Samuel fled Cordoba in 1013 when Berbers attacked and provoked a civil war. In 1025 he became vizier to the king and later to the king's son, Badis. Samuel was an acute political observer. He wrote of the mature state in lines that anticipated the 14th-century Arab founder of sociology, Ibn Khaldun: 'When it grows full and handsome and ripe, from the tree it will certainly fall.'

Samuel had a considerable religious impact: he published an everyman's guide to the Talmud, and he commissioned dozens of scribes to produce copies of *halakhic* works which he disseminated across the Mediterranean. Samuel supported indigent Jews and struggling students. The best ruler, he wrote in one poem, was 'he who forgives his people's misdeeds and toils for the good of the poor'. Berbers, Arabs and Jews all mourned Samuel when he died in 1056.

Yet was Samuel HaNagid an exception to the rule? Outside the royal courts, Muslim subjects often envied Jews for flaunting the restrictions on *dhimmis* (non-Muslim subjects of a state governed by Sharia law) and 'favouring their own'. At times Jews suffered collectively because of such anger: in late 1066 a mob assassinated HaNagid's son Joseph, the new vizier at Granada's Alhambra palace, and killed as many as 4,000 Jews.

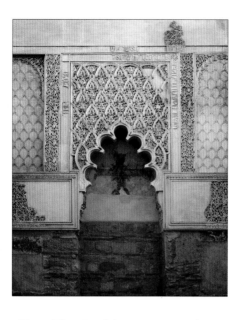

Above The Cordoba synagogue shows the fusion of Jewish, Arab and Iberian cultures that symbolized the Golden Age.

THE INFLUENCE OF ARABIC

Spanish Jews were by no means unique in their exposure to the Arabic language or tenets of Muslim faith. The archbishop of Seville, for instance, had the Christian Bible translated into Arabic because so few of his flock knew Latin. Christian scholars from France, Germany and England reportedly learnt Arabic and travelled to Seville and Toledo to study the classics and Arab algebra, geometry and trigonometry, often from Jewish tutors.

Religious Jews beyond Spain also drew on flourishing secular traditions. The writings of Ibn Sina (980–1037CE), a Persian philosopher known in the West as Avicenna, profoundly influenced both Jews and Muslims. The playful Arabic literary style *adab* helped mould Hebrew poetry and even the structure of the Hebrew language.

MUSLIM SPAIN FALTERS

After the Umayyad Caliphate collapsed in 1031 Muslim Spain split into a number of smaller kingdoms. Christian kingdoms to the north exploited Muslim divisions and reconquered formerly Christian towns, notably Toledo in 1085. The next year Morocco's powerful and religiously austere Almorabid Berbers came to the aid of Andalucians. Jewish and Muslim Spaniards were now caught between southern Berbers and northern Christians.

The Almorabids were displaced by the Almohads, and these were defeated by the Christians in 1212, effectively ending their rule over Spain. Cordoba fell in 1236 and Seville in 1248, leaving Granada as the last Muslim outpost on the peninsula.

SOLOMON IBN GABIROL

One of the greatest scholars of the period was Solomon Ibn Gabirol. Born in Malaga in about 1022, he introduced Neo-platonic ideas to Europe, where he had more influence over Christian scholastics than on his fellow Jews in Spain. His masterpiece *Mekor Hayyim*, or 'Fountain of Life', explained the universe as consisting of three elements: God, the material world, and the omnipresent will as the bridge between the two. Ibn Gabirol also wrote in Arabic two powerful yet accessible guides to ethics, *Kitab islah al-akhlaq* (Improving the Qualities of the Soul) and *Mukhtar al-jawahir* (Choice of Pearls).

The Golden Age was also stimulated by scholarly cross-pollination with Ashkenazi Jews. Jacob ben Asher (1270–1343) was born in Germany

Above Solomon Ibn Gabirol, outstanding 11th-century Andalucian Jewish poet, philosopher and moralist.

around 1270 and moved to Spain in 1303. He wrote the *Arba'ah Turim*, or 'Four Rows', a synthesis of the views of Alfassi, Maimonides and earlier Talmud writers.

Abraham Ibn Ezra (1093–1167) typified the spirit of the age. A Spanish-born rabbi, poet, astronomer, astrologer, doctor and thinker, he believed the 'angel that mediates between man and his God is intelligence'. He left Granada when the illiberal Alhomads came to power, and then wandered through France, Italy

and England, where he is thought to have died. A crater of the moon is named after him. Ibn Ezra questioned the meaning of exile. He was not the only Jew to dream of an eventual return to Zion. In 1141 Judah Halevi lamented: 'My heart is in the east, but my body stays in the west'; late in life he went to Palestine.

The Catalan rabbi and sage, Moshe ben Nahman Geronti, or Nahmanides (1194–1270) settled in Jerusalem in 1267, where he built the Ramban synagogue, so named after his familiar acronym. Almost single-handedly he re-established Jewish communal life in the holy city, which has continued since.

JEWS IN CHRISTIAN SPAIN

Nahmanides argued that Arab and Greek philosophy should be equal. He also respected Ashkenazi scholarship. In his book *Torat Ha-Adam*, the Law of Adam, the Ramban chastized other rabbis for denying the everyday experiences of pleasure and pain. He argued that humans have a special divine soul that places them above animals. He denied the truth of secular philosophy, and sought mystical meanings in biblical text, as well as professing to believe in miracles and in God's providential plans.

The Ramban lived under Christian rule, mostly at peace, until in 1263 he was summoned to defend Judaism in a 'disputation' in Barcelona. He was questioned by priests anxious to use the Talmud to prove the truth of Christianity. The Ramban debated freely and won the king's admiration – which was certainly not the case in trials in France and Germany around that time. But with hindsight, the Spanish tolerance disguised mounting prejudices against Jews and Muslims, which ultimately led to the 1492 expulsion of the Jews.

Left A synagogue in Fez, Morocco, a city which gave refuge to many Jews fleeing Spain in 1492.

KABBALAH–JEWISH MYSTICAL TRADITION

KABBALAH IS A MOVEMENT THAT DEVELOPED IN THE GOLDEN AGE OF SPAIN. NOWADAYS THE BEST-KNOWN JEWISH MYSTICAL PATH, THE KABBALAH (MEANING 'TRADITION' OR 'RECEPTION') IS AN ESOTERIC MYSTICISM.

Most forms of mysticism aim to form a perfect union with God and break the bonds of the material world. The same is true of Kabbalah. Two elements, though, set it apart from other belief systems. One is the idea that humans can help God repair a fractured world, a process called *tikkun olam*. The second idea is that the deepest mystical truths are embedded in the Bible and Talmud. Only one who knows these texts can hope to master Kabbalah. Practitioners seek to restore serenity to the individual soul by communing with God. The Kabbalah is also invoked when Jews address ethical issues, such as 'repairing the world' through everyday acts of *hesed*, or 'loving kindness'.

REACTION TO TURMOIL
Some note that Jewish mysticism typically flourishes two or three generations after a catastrophe. Kabbalah was often associated with periods of messianic fervour, and political or social insecurity, with adherents scouring its texts for hints of when the final judgement day will come.

EARLY GROWTH
Abraham Abulafia (1240–91) was a particularly compelling Kabbalist. Born in Spain, he travelled to Greece, Malta and Sicily and died in Italy, where he is credited with pioneering 'ecstatic Kabbalah'. His works include *Book of the Righteous*, *Life of the World to Come*, *Light of the Intellect* and *Words of Beauty*. He tried to spread Kabbalistic doctrines to Christians and Muslims. Other, quieter Kabbalists preached a 'practical Kabbalah'. One such trend that came to dominate in the 16th century, with the school of Isaac Luria, which evolved in Palestine during the 16th to the 18th centuries.

Jewish mysticism developed over five periods: the ancient mystics during the writing of the Talmud; the medieval Hasidei Ashkenaz tradition of the Rhineland; the Kabbalah as it developed in 13th–15th century Spain; Isaac Luria's system; and the European Hassidim who were to open up Kabbalah to the masses.

Mystical elements of Kabbalah come from the writings of the prophets and the 2nd-century CE Mishnah. One inspiration behind Kabbalistic thought is the merkavah, or divine chariot, as envisaged by the prophet Ezekiel. Kabbalists have also used Genesis or its midrashic glosses as an inspiration.

Left A Kabbalistic roll created in Paris, 1604, shows Temple implements and the ten sephirot, *or divine emanations, linked by 32 paths of wisdom.*

Above Ezekiel's vision, which the prophet said he saw in Babylon. The vivid image of a fiery merkavah, *or chariot, inspired later Kabbalists.*

NON-JEWISH INFLUENCE
Secular-minded scholars of Kabbalah detect influences from other traditions, including Gnosticism (with the eternal battle between good and evil); and its Persian religious manifestations, Zoroastrianism and Mazdaism. The Jewish idea of divine emanations in the material world appears to have affinities with the 99 names of God as explained by the Muslim mystical philosopher Al-Ghazali. Hindu and Buddhist models tally with the Jewish tree of life motif, while the Indian Jain religion's diagram of concentric circles of heaven and earth mirrors the Kabbalistic concept of seven worlds.

Kabbalah has in turn influenced Judaism's sister faiths. The Christian mystic and mathematician John Dee of England studied Kabbalah and used its ideas to devise spells, calculate the end-times or dabble in alchemy. Renaissance Christian scholars of Kabbalah included Johannes Reuchlin, Pico della Mirandola and Athanasias Kircher. Kabbalists often explain obscure texts by calculating the numerical value of letters, as do many Muslim Sufis.

Above The Tree of Life came to epitomize the Kabbalistic world view. From an illuminated Jewish book, northern France, 1290.

THE ZOHAR

By far the best-known mystical text is the Zohar, or 'Radiance'. Part-midrash (midrash means 'searching the scriptures'), part epic poem, the book addresses issues such as good and evil, interceding angels, man's role as master of virtue in bettering creation, the nature of God (part-male and part-female), and how man can ascend by steps to the ultimate 'cause of causes'.

Kabbalists attribute the Zohar to Simeon bar Zakkai of 2nd-century CE Palestine, though it was probably written by Moses de Leon of Spain (1250–1305). Within 50 years of its publication it had spread throughout the Diaspora. It was accepted as 'sacred text'. Zohar verses appear in prayer books, and most leading rabbis, including those deemed rationalist in outlook, have commented on it. Christian scholars saw in certain Zohar passages hints of the

Right Typifying Kabbalah's current resurgence, worshippers in Tel Aviv perform the tashlich ritual of throwing bread into the sea to cast away past sins.

holy trinity. According to some traditions no one unmarried, under 40 or female may read the book.

The Zohar was by no means the final mystical text. Later writings include *The Book of the Reed, The Wonder* and Moses Cordovero's *Palm Tree of Deborah*. Kabbalistic lore spread from Spain to Provence in the 13th century and received a further boost when, after 1492, Spanish and Portuguese Kabbalists dispersed to Amsterdam, Constantinople and, eventually, Tiberias and Safed.

THE TEN EMANATIONS

Before the Zohar came other works: *Sefer ha-Bahir*, the 'Book of Brightness', which includes mystical divinations with numbers and was published in 12th-century southern France; and *Sefer Yetzira*, the 'Book of Creation', written between the 3rd and 6th centuries CE. The latter addresses the ten *sefirot* or emanations of God's essence, ten being the number of divine perfection. Sometimes these elements are compounded into allied concepts. These are: crown (primordial consciousness), wisdom, love and understanding, mercy and vision, judgement and strength, compassion and symmetry, contemplation, surrender, foundation and memory, and the lower crown or kingdom of accomplishment.

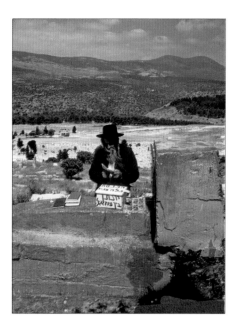

Above Blue, the pacifying colour of the spirit, adorns the tomb in Safed, northern Israel, of 16th-century Kabbalah pioneer Isaac Luria.

TREE OF LIFE

In time Kabbalists devised a diagram called the *Etz Hayyim*, or the 'Tree of Life', on which are draped representations of *sephirot*. They wrote about how the sephirot flowed from one heavenly chamber to another, so as to restore the natural state of harmony. Echoing the Creation is the concept of *tzimtzum*, the expanding power that cracks the shells of the sephirot and releases divine energy.

THE FIRST JEWS OF EASTERN EUROPE

JEWS WELCOMED INVITATIONS TO EASTERN EUROPE FROM SLAVIC RULERS WHO WANTED TO CATCH UP WITH GERMAN NEIGHBOURS AND SAW ENTREPRENEURIAL IMMIGRANTS AS THE ANSWER.

In the summer of 966CE Ibrahim ibn Yacoub, an intrepid Jewish trader and diplomat from Toledo in Spain, set off on a journey into the unknown. Travelling through the furthermost eastern lands of the Holy Roman empire, he arrived in countries we now call Poland and the Czech Republic. This region was in flux. Celts, Huns, Scythians and Goths jostled for control, towns were just being born, and the notion of swapping commodities for money, rather than bartering, was still new.

SETTLEMENT IN POLAND
Ibrahim wrote the first extensive account of Poland. That same year, 966CE, the leader of the newly arrived Polanie tribe, Duke Mieszko I, was baptized into Christianity, an event Poles regard as the birth of their nation. From the start, Jews played a vital part in the Polish story, even if their initial presence was somewhat transient. Jewish traders – Radhanites (medieval Jewish merchants) from Iraq or, like ibn Yacoub, from Spain – used Poland as a thoroughfare along the route linking China and the Orient to Western Europe.

Jews in Poland and Prague, which Ibrahim also visited, were known to sell slaves (hence 'Slavs') to Arabs and Byzantines. They developed a facility for commerce, too, and by 1170 they were running the mint in Warsaw. Jews even made Polish coins with Hebrew inscriptions.

In years to come Poland would grow into the world's largest centre of Jewish life. Some 3.5 million Jews lived in former Polish provinces in 1880 out of a global Jewish population of 7.7 million, yet very little is known about the early settlement.

One theory suggests that Polish Jews descended from Khazar Jews who fled there after the collapse of that Eastern realm. Some think

Above An old house in Kazimierz, Krakow. Its Star of David testifies to a Jewish presence that began in 1335.

Jewish communities located around Roman camps remained in 'Middle Europe' when the Roman empire collapsed. More likely, Jews poured in from the west. A number fled as persecutions mounted around the year 1000, when Frankish and Germanic Christians enthusiastically expected a second coming of Jesus a millennium after his birth. Anti-Jewish sentiment rose further in the wake of the First Crusade a hundred years later, culminating in the first great expulsion from France in 1182.

PROTECTED STATUS
As to why Jews chose remote Poland, some might have been attracted by its name: *Polin*, Yiddish for Poland, is a pun on the Hebrew expression for 'here you will live'. Poland's early rulers were also notably tolerant to newcomers. In 1203, for instance, they issued a decree allowing Jews to own land in Galicia province, just two years before Pope Innocent III declared that Jews were doomed

Left The Polish city of Krakow and surrounding hills, from Hartman Schedel's Nuremberg Chronicle, *1493.*

to perpetual servitude owing to the crucifixion of Christ. Polish authorities apparently welcomed literate and industrious Jews as 'agents of modernity' who might drag the Poles out of the dark ages, and allow them to compete with their Germanic neighbours.

Boleslav V the Pious produced a charter to protect Jews in 1264; and Casimir III 'The Great' (1333–70) guaranteed these privileges in 1334. The next year he created a new city for his Jews on an island in the River Vistula, near the capital, Krakow, called Kazimierz. In 1356 Casimir granted Jews autonomy in communal affairs; he extended these rights to the Jews of Lesser Poland and Ukraine in 1367. Privileges were extended by his successor, Grand Duke Vytautas (Vitovt; 1350–1430).

Official persecution began in Poland under King Wladislaus II (1386–1434) after 1399, and Jews found themselves the target of rioters in Krakow in 1407. Kazimierz may well have become Europe's first ghetto in 1494. This *oppidum judaeorum*, or 'Jewish city', was established 22 years before Venetians corralled Jews into a restricted area near iron foundries (*campo gheto*), from which came the term ghetto.

The onset of the Black Death fuelled anti-Jewish sentiment when comparatively few Jews perished, probably because they lived by more hygienic food practices. Economic envy from Christian traders and artisans grew, as did resentment by Catholic clergymen who felt Polish kings showed excessive tolerance to 'non-believers'. Casimir IV the Jagiellonian (1447–92) stemmed attacks on Jews; yet even he felt compelled to issue the Statute of Nieszawa (1454), which abolished ancient Jewish privileges as 'contrary to divine right and the law of the land'.

THE POLISH ASHKENAZ

It is thought that many of the Sephardi Jews expelled from Spain in 1492 eventually went to Poland, where they were probably absorbed into the Ashkenazi community. By the early 16th century, Polish Ashkenazim formed the largest Jewish community in the world. They outnumbered their cousins in the Germano-Frankish Rhineland area, the original 'Ashkenaz'.

Ashkenazim traded with gentiles but kept very much to themselves. They frequented the synagogue, studied the Torah and Talmud, and spoke Yiddish, a vernacular based

Above During the 1348 plague, pogroms in Germany drove many Jews to commit suicide, as depicted in this stylized 1880 woodcut.

on old German with Hebrew additions. After lagging behind Rashi's heirs, Polish scholars, such as Moses Isserles (*c.*1530–72), began rising to the fore.

OUTSIDE POLAND

In other parts of Eastern Europe, Jewish life could be precarious. A church synod in Breslau, chief city of Silesia, ordered Jews to wear special caps in 1267. Dozens were murdered there in 1349, more were expelled in 1360, and 41 Jewish martyrs were burnt at the stake in 1453. In 1421 Jews were imprisoned and forced to leave Austria; that same year a medieval synagogue in Vienna was burnt down together with its congregants. Jews were driven out of Eger in Bohemia in 1430, only months after co-religionists were expelled from Speyer in Germany. Despite setbacks, the seeds were planted for communities that in time became the hub of Jewry around the world.

Left Built in 1270, the Old-New Synagogue of Prague exemplifies a long Jewish presence in Czech lands.

THE AGE OF MAIMONIDES

THE GREATEST OF SEPHARDI POLYMATHS, MOSES MAIMONIDES WAS BORN IN CORDOBA. HE WENT ON TO REVIVE THE EGYPTIAN JEWISH COMMUNITY AND WROTE BOOKS THAT STILL INSPIRE TODAY.

Widely regarded as the greatest Jewish thinker since biblical times, Moses Maimonides (Moshe ben Maimon in Hebrew, and Abu Imran Musa ibn Maimun in Arabic) is also possibly the most enduring medieval philosopher of any faith. He is still studied at Jewish yeshivas, both Ashkenazi and Sephardi; his works are on the core syllabus at Al Azhar in Cairo, the supreme Sunni Muslim college; and he profoundly influenced St Thomas Aquinas, the leading Christian theologian of the Middle Ages.

EARLY LIFE
The story of Maimonides covers several zones – Spain, Morocco, Egypt, Palestine and Yemen – and must also include Christian Europe, which he never visited, but where his books

Above A contemporary bronze statue of the Rambam, Moses Maimonides, in Cordoba's Jewish Quarter.

received equal shares of admiration and opposition. An eclectic genius who wrote forward-thinking tracts on all aspects of medicine, he was also a rabbi and talmudic scholar, community leader and judge, philosopher and ethicist, and royal advisor to Caliphs.

Maimonides, often called the Rambam, was born in Cordoba in 1135, the son of a rabbi. At 13 he was forced to flee when Almohads conquered the city. The new rulers decreed that Jews unwilling to convert to Islam would be killed or exiled. For nearly a decade his family wandered from town to town, before settling in Fez, Morocco.

LOGIC AND FAITH
Despite these upheavals and his father's complaints that he was lazy, the 16-year-old Maimonides wrote a brilliant treatise on logic. In later life he called Aristotle his 'first teacher', and the Muslim philosopher Al-Farabi his second. Ibn Sina (Avicenna) was

another influence, as was his fellow Cordoban and contemporary, Muslim Ibn Rushd (Averroes) (1126–98).

Yet Maimonides was also a fully committed Jew, who believed Judaism was the highest form of monotheism. His first great work was a commentary on and digest of the 2nd-century CE Mishnah. Next came his 14-volume *Mishneh Torah*, said to be the clearest exposition of the basic tenets of Jewish faith ever written. Composed between 1170 and 1180 in his new home of Egypt, it was a comprehensive and logically organized code of Jewish law written in clear and precise Hebrew. All his other books appeared first in Judeo-Arabic.

GUIDE TO THE PERPLEXED
Even more famous than the *Mishneh Torah* is Maimonides' 'Guide to the Perplexed', first written in Arabic as *Dalalat al-Ha'irin* and translated by Yehuda Ibn Tibbon as *Moreh ha-Nevukhim*. The book is specifically aimed at educated Jews troubled by the disagreements between philosophical learning and the Torah's teachings, but it contains moral insights for all.

Below Arguably the greatest Jewish mind of his time, Maimonides lived in this house in Fez, Morocco, after leaving Spain in 1160.

Above 'The Guide to the Perplexed', the *Rambam's most famous work. Hebrew manuscript title page, Spain, 1356.*

Maimonides wrote the first statement of Jewish faith to match those of Christians (the credo) and Muslims (the shahada). These he summarized in 13 core beliefs. Within the Jewish tradition he followed the rationalist path of Philo and Saadia Gaon, and emulated the clarity of Rashi, even if he disagreed with all of them.

THE POWER OF REASON

To Maimonides all prophets had to be philosophers, and prophecy was not confined to Jews. He laboured to show that revelation and all Jewish laws had their foundation in reason. For Maimonides, only a God who transcends the universe could have created it. Later rationalists castigated this approach as contrived, while many rabbis felt it was blasphemous to demand proofs of the divine. Even the supposedly non-philosophical *Mishneh Torah* drew the ire of traditionalists, because it quoted laws without listing the rabbinical arguments that led to them. Rabbis

Right Al Hakim Mosque in Fustat, near Cairo, Egypt, where Maimonides lived in the latter part of his life.

feared that unqualified readers would claim to be experts. Maimonides countered that he had made the Talmud accessible to all and said to his critics: 'I forgive everyone who speaks ill of me through stupidity.'

MEDICAL BREAKTHROUGHS

Maimonides was prone to melancholia and suffered badly for a year, aged 30, when his beloved brother, David, died at sea. He drew on this experience to write a brilliant analysis of depression that is still studied today. His other medical writings are on diet, nutrition, gastroenterology, sexual diseases and fevers. Like his immediate Arab predecessor, Abu Bakr al-Razi (called Rhazes in the West), Maimonides observed patients and their symptoms first hand. Among those in his care was the vizier to the caliph.

HEAD OF EGYPT'S JEWS

Maimonides' Egyptian phase coincided with a political transition in the country. He arrived in Fustat in 1166, having spent several months in Akko (Acre), Tiberias and Jerusalem. In 1171 a Kurdish-origin Muslim, Salah al-Din al-Ayubi (Saladin), overthrew the Shia Fatimid dynasty and restored Egypt to Sunni rule. One of his first acts was to appoint Maimonides as *ra'is al-yahud*, or 'head of the Jews'.

Above Yehuda Ibn Tibbon translated Maimonides' Arabic books into Hebrew. Statue in Granada, erected 1988.

According to legend Saladin's great adversary, King Richard of England, wanted to use Maimonides as his doctor, but the rabbi refused.

LEGACY OF MAIMONIDES

After Maimonides died, in 1204, some rabbis in France began to condemn his works as heretical. In 1232 they persuaded the church authorities of Montpellier to burn copies of his *Guide* and the *Book of Knowledge*. The debate about Maimonides' beliefs simmered in one form or another for decades, even centuries.

In some senses, Maimonides was ahead of his time. However, he never wavered in his faith in God, even if he introduced a strong seam of rational analysis to Judaism. He believed that pursuing truth and seeking God were essentially the same task, and prescribed how to build better societies on earth. In writing about *tzedakah* (charity or justice), Maimonides defined eight stages of giving, with the highest being a donor who employs a poor person or helps him set up his own business, freeing him of the need for aid. This theory is now widely applied.

TO THE FOUR CORNERS OF THE WORLD

AS EARLY AS THE 8TH CENTURY BCE, ISAIAH WROTE OF JEWS IN CUSH, OR ETHIOPIA. SINCE ISAIAH'S TIME DIASPORAS HAVE SPREAD THROUGH CHINA, INDIA AND THE DEEPEST CAUCASUS.

One particularly engaging character of the Jewish Middle Ages was Rabbi Benjamin of Tudela in Spain, who went on pilgrimage to the Holy Land in 1165. He returned home in 1173 having visited 300 cities in Europe, the Middle East and North Africa. His famous book, the *Itinerary*, records Jewish life far and wide. He did not visit every outpost of Jewry, but his accounts bear testimony to the widespread nature of the Diaspora.

ETHIOPIAN JEWS

The Jews of Ethiopia today number more than 127,000. Since the great 'exoduses' of Operation Moses (1984) and Operation Solomon (1991), most now live in Israel. They call themselves Beta Israel (House of Israel) a term they prefer to the familiar but pejorative *Falasha*, or 'stranger'.

Below A 19th-century Ethiopian painting of Solomon receiving gold, ivory and a lion from the Queen of Sheba.

Ethiopia's strong ties with ancient Israel followed a local tradition that said Emperor Haile Selassie was the direct descendant of Menelik, a son born to King Solomon and the Queen of Sheba: thus making Ethiopian royalty the last surviving monarchy from the House of David. Although most Amharic-speaking Ethiopians are Christian, and have been since the earliest days of the faith, one theory suggests many were Jews who converted, hence the similarities between Jewish and Ethiopian Orthodox Christian rites.

The Beta Israel claim to be offspring of Moses, separated during the Exodus, or of the tribe of Dan, which fled southwards through Arabia and across the Red Sea to Africa after the united kingdom divided in the 10th century BCE. Unusually amongst Diaspora Jews, the Beta Israel, who mainly dwelt in the Gondar uplands, used the Ethiopic Ge'ez tongue as their liturgical language, not Hebrew.

Above The intrepid rabbi Benjamin of Tudela riding across the Sahara in a 19th-century engraving by Dumouza.

Despite that, their holy book, the Orit, is essentially identical to earlier sections of the Torah. Also unusually, they knew nothing of the Talmud or later Jewish festivals, like Purim or Hannukah – proof, some say, of their authentic antiquity.

JEWS OF SOUTHERN INDIA

The great Moorish traveller Ibn Battuta (1304–*c*.1368) wrote of an autonomous hilltop settlement in Malabar, five days' journey from Calicut. Some believe this may refer to one of several known communities dotted around southern India, of which the Jews of Cochin in Kerala state are the most famous. The Cochin Jews, who maintain a now much-visited synagogue, divided themselves into 'white' and 'black' communities. Known for their industriousness, hospitality and cuisine, they have apparently lived alongside Hindus, Christians and, latterly, Muslims for millennia.

JEWS OF KAIFENG

Ibn Battuta also reported entering the Chinese port of Hangzhou through a 'Jews' Gate', and encountering a vibrant Jewish community there. Even earlier, Marco Polo wrote of meeting

Right This village synagogue in Ethiopia's Gondar region once served the Beta Israel Jewish community.

Chinese Jews in Beijing around 1286. It is known that Jews habitually traded up and down the silk road to China. Some must have settled down and they presumably married into local Chinese communities, because for centuries there was a strong Jewish outpost in Kaifeng, Henan province.

The records of the Jesuit missionary and cartographer Matteo Ricci tell how he met Ai Tian, a Jewish mandarin from Kaifeng, in 1605. Westerners had never encountered Jews in the area, and Ricci assumed Ai was Christian. Hearing Jesuit Ricci was a monotheist but not a Muslim, Ai assumed he was Jewish. Ricci later corresponded with the Kaifeng rabbi and produced drawings of his pagoda-like synagogue.

Some Chinese Jews claimed descent from 6th-century BCE Babylonian exiles, and one stone monument dated 231BCE suggests a presence at the time. Certainly Jews and Phoenicians imported Far

Below India's oldest synagogue operates in the southern port of Cochin, Kerala, and reflects local architectural influences.

Eastern goods to Rome and Italy. Later, Jews from Yemen, Persia and Bukhara in Central Asia settled on the south banks of the Yellow River.

Proof of the antiquity of a Jewish presence comes in the form of a business letter written on Chinese paper in Judeo-Persian, dated 718CE. Kaifeng historical records speak of a synagogue, called *libai si*, established in 1163. More details of Jewish history, genealogy and practices appear in stelae, or stone tablets, dated 1489, 1512 and 1663. The middle stele proudly boasts that Jewish soldiers were 'boundlessly loyal' to the Song dynasty emperor of the day.

MOUNTAIN JEWS

With a population of 101,000 as of 2004, the so-called Mountain Jews of the Caucasus constitute another rare subset of international Jewry. They call themselves Juhuro, speak a language called Judeo-Tat, differ in many traditions from other Ashkenazi and Sephardi Jews, and for most of their history they lived in Azerbaijan and Dagestan, mainly Muslim areas of the former Soviet Union.

Most Juhuro immigrated to Israel during 1970–90, though some settled in Moscow and the USA. As to their origins, they may descend from hardy Jewish military colonists posted to mountainous regions by

Persia's Parthian and Sassanid rulers, or they may be local Tats converted to Judaism. One radical theory states that all Tats were once Jewish, but that most adopted Islam in the Middle Ages. Traditionally farmers and gardeners, the Juhuro were famed for their vineyards, handicrafts and skills as tanners.

JEWS IN MOROCCO

The Berber Jews of North Africa probably descended from local tribes who converted or intermarried with Jews accompanying Roman armies. During the 5th century CE a Jewish community thrived in Mauretania, south of Morocco. Two centuries later Jews escaping persecution in Spain joined them. Legend tells of a Jewish Berber warrior-queen named Kahina who repulsed Muslim Arabs around 680CE.

Many Berbers retained their Judaism after Islam triumphed. The movement caused by the Muslim conquest of Spain linked Iberian Jews to their southern brethren, and the Moroccan-born rabbi Yitzhak Alfassi (1013–73) won renown on both continents for his Torah and Talmud commentary, the Rif.

Morocco again became a haven for refugees after Spanish Christians sacked Seville's Jewish district in 1391. Within 50 years Jews had a special district, or *mellah*, in Fez.

JEWS OF NORMAN ENGLAND

IN 1066, WILLIAM THE CONQUEROR DEFEATED THE SAXONS AT HASTINGS AND IMPOSED NORMAN RULE ON BRITAIN. THIS ALSO INAUGURATED 224 YEARS OF JEWISH SETTLEMENT IN ENGLAND, WHICH ENDED IN TRAGEDY.

The vibrant Jewish community of Normandy, France, had long traded with southern England. So when King William (1027–87) invited the Jewish courtesans of Rouen, the Norman capital, to cross the Channel, many accepted gladly. Jews settled in Oxford, Lincoln, Bath, Norwich and especially London, where Old Jewry road in the City testifies to their medieval presence. Some settled in Ireland, too, and by 1232 Dublin had an established community, while Norwich became home to a small but vibrant Rhineland community.

AN OPTIMISTIC START
Norman England became the best-administered territory in western Europe. As feudal law prevented Jews from owning land or practising any profession besides medicine, they often worked as financiers, bankers and moneylenders – jobs barred to Christians, because Old Testament law forbade lending on interest to fellow believers.

Some Jews grew immensely wealthy and were therefore unpopular when times were hard. For protection they built sturdy stone dwellings. Two in Lincoln are among the earliest English homes to survive, and one may have doubled as a synagogue. Unusually for medieval society, Jewish women often worked in their own right; 10 per cent of Jewish taxpayers were female. Examples include Mildegod of Oxford, a successful innkeeper; and Licoricia, the 13th-century widow of Isaac of York, who lent to King Henry III and helped fund the building of Winchester Cathedral.

ROYAL PROTECTION
William protected his Jewish subjects, and his son and heir, William Rufus (r. 1088–1100), allowed Jews

Above Excavated in 2001 in the City of London, this medieval Jewish ritual bath, or mikveh, takes pride of place in London's Jewish Museum.

who had converted to return to their faith, against the wishes of Christian clerics. English Jews were generally spared the pogroms that bedevilled their Continental cousins after the Crusades began in 1096. Later King Henry I (r. 1100–35) allowed Jews to live in 26 cities, whereas before they were restricted to just six.

Below Jewish homes were pillaged by mobs during the reign of England's Richard I. From a painting by Charles Landseer, c.1839.

Below Clifford's Tower in York, built by William the Conqueror. Here, Jews tragically met their death in a fire after fleeing a murderous mob in 1190.

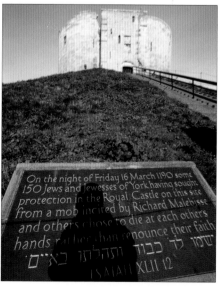

On the night of Friday 16 March 1190 some 150 Jews and Jewesses of York having sought protection in the Royal Castle on this site from a mob incited by Richard Malebisse and others chose to die at each others hands rather than renounce their faith

English Jews were unusually creative, even though they probably never numbered more than 16,000. They exported to Europe an Anglo-Norman romance about Sir Bevis of Hampton, which was reincarnated in 1507 as the *Bovo-Bukh*, arguably the first great work of Yiddish secular literature. Whimsical Anglo-Jewish illustrations of the biblical Moses, drawn in the 13th century and now held by the British Library, reveal a society that was pious, cultivated and self-assured. Rabbis Yom Tov of Joigny in York and Jacob of Orleans in London were respected as teachers, community leaders and Talmudic masters.

FROM PROSPERITY TO LIBEL

Jews also prospered under Henry II (reg. 1154–84); for example, when Aaron of Lincoln died in 1186, his 430 debtors owed him a sum equal to three-quarters of the annual revenue of the English exchequer. But conditions worsened as church authorities grew bolder, and prejudice fuelled by Crusader fervour proved more powerful than the law.

A murderous witch-hunt in Norwich in 1144 was the first of many European 'blood libels' that accused Jews of ritually killing Christian children. Another occurred at Bury St Edmunds in 1181 after a debt dispute between Jewish lenders and the local abbey. Similar outrages took place in Gloucester (1168), Bristol (1183), Winchester (1191), London (1244) and Lincoln (1255).

Crusader passions bred more violence, as in 1189, when Jews carrying gifts to Richard I's coronation were denied entry and beaten. The fiasco sparked riots in which many London Jews died, including Rabbi Jacob of Orleans. Richard the Lionheart executed three ringleaders, but new atrocities occurred when he left to fight the Third Crusade. The worst took place in March 1190 when mobs sacked Jewish houses in York and forced nearly the entire community to take refuge in Clifford's Tower. For several days some 500 Jews defended themselves valiantly, until they finally killed themselves, emulating their ancestors in Masada, Judea, a thousand years earlier.

Even Jews who accepted baptism were killed in case they might testify against defaulters. The looters deliberately destroyed records of debts stored in York castle. To prevent future recurrences, Richard's successor, John (r. 1199–1216), guaranteed Jews security, and in April 1233 Henry III formalized the system of *archae* – coffers controlled by two Jews and two Christians, which held copies of each debt owed to a Jew. This system meant that kings no longer lost money if pillagers targeted Jews, nor could murdering a Jew absolve a debtor of what he was obliged to pay.

By the late 13th century, crippling taxes had reduced Jews to penury. The 'Saladin tithe' funded war in the Holy Land, and demanded fully 25 per cent of a Jew's wealth. The Church that had once forced Jews to practise usury now outlawed the profession and retrospectively accused Jews of blasphemy. Christian bankers from Lombardy filled the vacuum and Jews found themselves dispensable.

In 1290 Edward I used the pretext of a dozen alleged counterfeiters to expel all of England's remaining 2,500 Jews. Most returned to Normandy, but after 16 years they were evicted from there, too, along with all other Jews in France. Only in 1656 were Jews formally readmitted to Britain.

THE CRUSADES AND JEWISH LIFE

IN THE FACE OF MUSLIM EXPANSION, THE LOSS OF THE HOLY LAND AND THREATS TO CHRISTIAN PILGRIM ROUTES, POPE URBAN II (1088–99) CALLED FOR CHRISTIAN MILITARY EXPEDITIONS KNOWN AS THE CRUSADES.

The Crusades were an unprecedented rallying point, a moment of European self-definition. Some Christians believed fighting would absolve them of earthly sins and prompt Christ's return. Others were motivated by baser motives: knights dreamt of ruling oriental kingdoms, while serfs welcomed the chance to escape the drudgery of feudal servitude.

CALL TO ARMS

Pope Urban II explicitly called for 'holy war' before hundreds of clerics and laity in Clermont, France, on 27 November 1095. Soon Crusader armies set off from Boulogne, Toulouse, Otranto and Flanders, accompanied by peasant militias.

European Jews were cast as the enemy within. 'Why should Christians travel to the ends of the world to fight the Saracens', asked the Abbot of Cluny, 'when we permit among us other infidels a thousand times more guilty toward Christ than the Mohammedans?'

Crusaders looted Jewish property along the Rhineland and forced Jews to convert or be put to death. Some churchmen, including John of Speyer and the Bishop of Cologne, tried to stop townsfolk from joining the melee, but invariably to little effect. Some 800 Jews perished at Worms; another thousand died in Mainz (Mayence); more were killed at Triers, Eller and Speyer. In all, about 5,000 Franco-German Jews died.

MARTYRDOM

Many Jewish mothers took their lives and their children's, wrote Soloman bar Samson, a contemporary eyewitness, rather than submitting to forced conversion or rape and murder. Jewish liturgic poetry memorialized martyrs as exemplars of kiddush hashem, or 'sanctification of God's name'.

More died when the Crusaders advanced along the Danube during 1096, though resistance was now stiffer. Five hundred Jews and 1,000 ducal soldiers repelled Crusaders at

Above Crusaders at Jerusalem's gates, from a 13th-century manuscript by Buchardus Teutonicus.

Vishehrad, near Prague in Bohemia. Henry IV of Germany (1056–1106) rejected papal calls to join the Crusade and allowed forced converts to return to Judaism. Hungary's King Coloman defended Jewish subjects from Frankish marauders.

Still, with entire communities wiped out, Jewish leaders questioned the value of royal charters of protection and began separating themselves from gentile neighbours. The Crusades also caused a huge demographic shift eastwards. By the 13th century, Rothenburg on the Tauber River had replaced Mainz, former seat of Gershom ben Judah (c.960–1040CE), as the leading Ashkenazi study centre. Other Jews settled in Slav-populated areas, especially Poland.

JERUSALEM FALLS

In 1099, Crusaders led by Godfrey of Bouillon reached Jerusalem and mounted a siege. After the Crusaders achieved victory on 15 July 1099, reported Monk Fulcher of Chartres, they had massacred so many Muslims

Left: Jews in Metz, France, were among the first Crusader victims in 1096. 19th-century painting by Auguste Migette.

Right Peasants burning down the tower of Verdun-sur-Garonne, Languedoc, where 500 Jews were hiding during the Peasants' Crusade, 1320.

and Jews that the city's streets ran ankle-deep in blood. Jews were corralled into a synagogue and burnt alive. At least 20,000 Jews were killed or captured and sold as slaves in Italy.

Baldwin I was crowned King of Jerusalem, and his successors ruled its environs in relative peace for nearly a century. His was the largest of four main Crusader 'Outremer' (overseas) principalities, the others being Edessa, Antioch and Tripoli.

FURTHER CRUSADES

French and German kings launched a Second Crusade in 1145 after a Turkish warlord, Zengi, conquered Edessa in 1144. By now, however, popular support was lacking. Crusader commanders led an unsuccessful attack on Damascus, until then a Muslim ally against Egypt, which brought Nur ad-Din to power in 1154. In 1171 his successor, Saladin, became Sultan of a united Egypt and Syria that enveloped the Jerusalem kingdom.

Saladin demolished a European army at Hattin in Galilee in July 1187. He then took Ashkelon, Gaza, Acre, Nablus, Sidon and Beirut in September, and captured Jerusalem

on 2 October 1187. One of his first acts was to invite Jews to return, which some hailed as the advent of a messianic age.

THE LAST CRUSADES

Richard I of England vowed to return Jerusalem to Christendom. In 1189 he launched a Third Crusade together with the Holy Roman Emperor Frederick Barbarossa and Philip II of France. Despite initial successes, the Crusade floundered and Richard and Saladin agreed a treaty in 1192.

A Fourth Crusade launched in 1202 failed to reach Jerusalem. A Fifth Crusade that began in 1217 ended in failure in 1221.

Eight years later, Crusaders under Frederick II retook Jerusalem with Saladin's consent. However, Muslims still controlled the Temple Mount

Left Saladin (1138–93), who reconquered Jerusalem for Islam. Painting by Cristofano Altissimo, 16th century.

and the city lay in ruins. Eventually, in 1244 Turks ousted the occupiers. By now enthusiasm for holy war was waning in Europe. The Pope refused to sanction a Crusade by Louis IX of France in 1270. In 1291 some 1,600 Christian pilgrims arrived in Acre on a papal mission and began killing local Muslims and Jews, but Mamluk forces soundly beat them, recaptured Acre, and thus ended Christian rule in the Holy Land.

Between 1290 and 1294, a concerted church campaign virtually destroyed Jewish communities in the kingdom of Naples. The original cradle of Ashkenazi Jewry was no more, and Jews who faced extermination converted en masse. Yet Ashkenazi seeds had travelled north of the Alps. There, despite further persecutions, they would later blossom into new settlements. And, in papal Rome, the pope's direct protection of Jews overrode the proselytizing wishes of his more zealous monks.

ANTI-SEMITISM IN 14TH-CENTURY EUROPE

THIS WAS A DREADFUL PERIOD FOR EUROPE'S JEWS AS PERSECUTION AND PLAGUE FOLLOWED REPEATED EXPULSIONS. DESPITE INVITATIONS TO RETURN, INCREASINGLY JEWS LEFT VOLUNTARILY FOR THE SAFER SLAVIC EAST.

Above 15th-century Jews wearing distinctive round badges, or 'wheels', on their clothing. Contemporary engraving.

In France, already saddled with debts from past Crusades, King Philip IV (1268–1314) desperately needed cash for his war against England. When punitive taxes between 1292 and 1303 failed to raise enough revenue, on 22 July 1306 he arrested 100,000 Jews, confiscated their goods, auctioned their properties and pocketed the proceeds. Then he drove them out of France with just the clothes on their backs and 12 sous (pennies) each in a purse.

There was a rash of expulsions from France in 1306, followed by invitations to return when kings found that they needed funds or, as in the case of Louis X of France in 1315, when he discovered that the Italian bankers who had replaced the Jews charged higher interest.

Below A plague scene from a 14th-century manuscript. Simple people sought scapegoats and often blamed Jews or other outsiders for their troubles.

Unlike England, France was neither an island nor a unitary state. Refugees decamped to areas beyond royal control: Burgundy, Lorraine, Savoy, Roussilon, Dauphiné and the southern papal lands of Avignon.

CHRISTIAN PERSECUTION

The French expulsions coincided with the eradication of the southern Italian Jewish community (1290–4) and the eviction of Jews from Norman England (1290). Church politics was clearly one factor behind this pattern of persecution. For centuries the Catholic Church had battled for authority against Europe's monarchs. To succeed it first had to weed out heretics. Having exterminated the Cathar Christian sect, the French clergy next targeted Jews as Europe's last 'Christ-deniers'. In 1240 a Christianized Jew, Nicholas Donin, put the Talmud on trial in what was cynically called a disputation. Defending the scriptures, Rabbi

Yehiel of Paris proclaimed: 'Our bodies are indeed in your hands, but not our souls'. In 1242 the Pope ordered monks to burn all copies of the book.

Even in places where Jews fared best, such as Rome and Provence, religious prejudice mixed with popular superstition to generate more anti-Semitism. As Crusaders fought the 'infidel' in the east, locals looked askance at the ethnic 'alien' in their midst, the Jew. Rebellious peasants targeted the Jewish moneylender or middleman who peddled goods between town and countryside. Cathedral art showed the synagogue as a blindfolded woman carrying a broken staff, alongside a youthful woman representing Christ's triumphant church. Other symbols for Jews included a brooding owl and the *Judensau*, a pig that they were said to worship.

BLOOD LIBELS

Church propaganda fanned anti-Jewish 'blood libels' across Europe after the first ritual murder accusation hit England in 1144. So potent was the myth that Geoffrey Chaucer described Jews murdering Christian children in his 1387 *Canterbury Tales*, 100 years after Jews left England.

Pope Innocent III drafted a protective 'constitution for the Jews', yet later called them 'a snake around the loins' and urged Christians to combat 'Jewish usury'. In 1298, Jews in Roettingen, Bavaria, were said to have stolen and desecrated the host (wafer) used in Catholic mass. This allegation inspired massacres in Germany and resurfaced in Lorraine and Franconia in 1338–9, when bands of *Armleder*, or 'armband-wearers', and *Judenschläger*, or Jew-beaters, murdered and pillaged at will.

Jews suffered during the Anglo-French Hundred Years War (1328–1453), and were suspected of helping the Tartars who threatened Europe. Anti-Semites targeted Jewish advisors when their royal patrons fell from grace, and in 1320 would-be 'shepherd crusaders' robbed Jews in 120 French communities. These peasants dreamt of fighting Spanish Muslims, and killed Jews who refused baptism, until the pope allowed soldiers in Carcasonne and Aragon to wipe out the zealots.

THE BLACK DEATH

The worst spur to violence was not war, politics, law or witchcraft, but disease. Two out of five Europeans died from the Black Death, a plague

that struck Europe in 1348. Superstitious people quickly blamed Templars, heretics, witches, foreign merchants, the poor, the rich and, above all, the Jews.

Pope Clement VI ruled that it was 'absolutely unthinkable that … Jews performed so terrible a deed'. Despite his words, in 1348–9 pogroms engulfed 300 Jewish communities in France, Germany, Austria, Switzerland and even relatively tolerant Krakow in Poland. Thousands of Jews died, many converted under torture, and horrors returned in 1370 when all the Jews of Brussels were wiped out.

German cities soon re-admitted Jews to fulfil essential financial functions. Now, though, they were 'serfs

Above French Jews put to the flame during the 1316–22 reign of Philip V. Illuminated manuscript, c. 1410.

of the city', no longer protected by kings and subject to short-term domiciles that could be cancelled in a trice. Many returnees were widows and orphans, forced to live outside the city gates as lepers and prostitutes. Turbulent times undermined the old Jewish bourgeoisie, and *Shtadlanim* (court intercessors for Jews) fell by the wayside. Instead, communal leadership passed to more mystical or legalistic elements.

Below A victorious Church tramples a blindfolded Synagogue underfoot. 13th-century French Christian prayer book.

MEDIEVAL SCIENCE

Levi ben Gershon (1288–1354), also known as Gersonides, was a true polyglot whose work anticipated the Renaissance. Born in France in 1288, he was a rabbi, philosopher, astronomer and mathematician. He is credited with inventing the sailor's quadrant known as Jacob's staff, which for three centuries was used to determine latitude and the local hour.

Most medieval Jewish scientists were Spanish, Portuguese or North African. In Barcelona, the astronomer, mathematician and philosopher Abraham Bar Hiyya (1070–1136) wrote the first book to introduce Islamic algebra to Europe. Isaac ibn Sid, a cantor in Toledo and amateur stargazer, updated astronomical tables.

Another intellectual trailblazer was Isaac Israeli ben Solomon, who died in Kairouan, Tunisia, in 932. A profound philosopher, skilful oculist and court physician to a Fatimid Caliph, he wrote six Arabic books on medicine, which Muslim doctors praised as 'more valuable than gems'.

MUSLIM RULERS OF THE BIBLE LANDS

MUSLIMS RULED ALL OF PALESTINE FROM 644CE UNTIL 1099, WHEN THE CRUSADERS TOOK JERUSALEM. IN 1291 THE LAST EUROPEANS WERE OUSTED AND PALESTINE REMAINED UNDER MUSLIM CONTROL UNTIL 1917.

The Crusader reign over Palestine was a 150-year-long Christian interlude in a largely Muslim story. Palestine's Jewish population waxed and waned in size during the 873 years from the Arab victory to the Ottoman takeover in 1516.

EARLY MUSLIM RULE
Arabs conquered Palestine fully in 644CE, having allowed Jews to return to Jerusalem in 638CE. In time, Arab rulers permitted Jews to rebuild a yeshiva in the holy city. Muslims became the majority population, and Arabic the dominant language.

Muslims revered Jerusalem as their third holiest city, and in 691CE Caliph Abd el-Malik built the Dome of the Rock on the presumed site of the destroyed Jewish Temples. The nearby Al Aqsa Mosque was completed in 705CE. Jerusalem was a spiritual outpost, but in 715CE Arabs built Ramle as Palestine's administrative capital. All of what Jews called the Land of Israel was absorbed into Syria, itself governed from Baghdad after 762CE.

Successive Egyptian dynasties then ruled, culminating in the Fatimids, Shia Muslims who took Ramle in 970CE. They tolerated minorities until the advent of Caliph Hakim I (996–1021CE), who in 1009 burned Jerusalem's Church of the Holy Sepulchre and later destroyed its synagogues.

Muslims held supreme political power in pre-Crusader Palestine. Under the surface, though, Jewish life showed surprising vibrancy. From the 7th to the 11th centuries, scholars known as the Masoretes formalized how to read, write, pronounce and sing sacred Hebrew texts. They also organized the Bible into chapter and verse.

CRUSADERS' RISE AND FALL
In 1099, after Crusaders captured Jerusalem, Franks, Normans, Italians and Hungarians settled in Palestine, forming a thin Christian mantle over a mainly Muslim society. The Jewish population dropped to 1,000 families.

In time, Saladin reclaimed Palestine for Islam in 1187 in a victory welcomed by Jerusalem's impoverished Jews. Ultimately the Mamluks, an Egyptian military dynasty, gained Palestine in 1260, and in 1291 evicted Crusaders from their last Palestinian enclave, in Acre.

MAMLUKS AND TURKS
Palestine was now subdivided into three sanjaks, or districts, with capitals in Jerusalem, Gaza and Safed.

Left Saladin conquered Egypt, drove the Crusaders from Jerusalem, and ruled Islam's other holy cities, Mecca and Medina.

Above A 15th-century Arabian illumination shows Mamluk soldiers on horseback.

The Mamluk triumph encouraged some Diaspora Jews to return to the Holy Land, such as the Spanish sage Nahmanides in 1267. Synagogues and yeshivas were built and the Mamluks also improved Jerusalem.

Rabbi Obadiah ben Abraham restored welfare and scholastic institutions after 1488. More Jews arrived following the Spanish expulsions of 1492, bolstering the community.

In 1516 Ottoman Turks conquered Palestine. Suleiman built Jerusalem's city walls in 1538, and the Turks were to rule for 500 years.

Below King Baldwin IV, King of Jerusalem 1174–85, drawn as a boy showing fight wounds to the Archbishop of Tyre.

THE FALL OF THE BYZANTINE EMPIRE

BY THE 11TH CENTURY, BYZANTIUM HAD BEGUN TO RESEMBLE 3RD-CENTURY CE ROME: WEALTHY AND CULTURED, YET POLITICALLY DIVIDED. IT WAS ALSO SUBJECT TO PRESSURES ON ITS BORDERS.

Life was often extremely harsh for the Greek-speaking 'Romaniote' Jews who populated the medieval Byzantine empire. Successive Emperors Heraclius, Leo III and Romanos I demanded their baptism and conversion in 640, 721 and 930CE. Basil I formally tried to ban Jewish religious practices in 873CE, and an enforced 'disputation' between rabbis and monks resulted in further expulsions in 880CE.

Resurgent Byzantine forces repelled Muslims in the 10th century, sparking an economic boom that attracted both Rabbanite and Karaite Jews. Greek became the Karaites' language and Hebrew replaced Arabic in their literature.

In the 11th century, however, Byzantium was attacked from all sides. The empire lost colonies in Sicily and southern Italy. Crusader invasions further unsettled a restive Byzantium after 1096.

INTELLECTUAL DECLINE, COMMERCIAL SURVIVAL

Earlier centuries had seen a literary flowering among Byzantine Jews. For example, many of the 200 liturgical poems by the 7th-century CE master Eleazar Kallir found their way into the Ashkenazi Jewish prayer book.

By the 11th century the Sephardi scholars of Spain had taken over as the academic vanguard of the Jewish world. Constantinople's Jews, as seen by the 12th-century Benjamin of Tudela, were barred from political and administrative office – by contrast with Jews in Muslim lands – and Greeks would beat them in the capital's streets. They 'bore their lot with cheerfulness', wrote Benjamin, but were forced to leave after 'Latins' sacked the city in 1204.

Jewish fortunes improved when Michael VIII restored the empire in 1259. Assisted by his Mongol allies, he recovered Constantinople in

Above A historical watershed: Ottoman Turks wrest Constantinople from the last Byzantine emperor on 29 May, 1453. From a 16th-century fresco.

1261, welcomed Jews back to the capital and revoked discriminatory laws in exchange for their support. No longer did Jews fear forced conversion, nor was their property stolen by greedy nobles. Indeed, by the 14th century, resident Venetian Jews enjoyed more privileges than the empire's Greek majority, due to favourable terms that Venice had negotiated with Byzantium.

FALL OF CONSTANTINOPLE

Jews felt safer under the Ottoman Turks, successors to the Seljuks, who by the 15th century occupied most of Anatolia. In 1453 the Ottomans won Constantinople after a seven-week siege, ending some 1,150 years of distinctive Byzantine civilization.

In 1472 Grand Duke Ivan III of Moscow married a Byzantine royal, and called his capital the 'Third Rome'. Russia became the new centre of Orthodox Christianity, a successor to Byzantine glory, and another potentate whose actions would profoundly shape Jewish destiny in centuries to come.

Left Rome itself might have collapsed, but Byzantium, the 'Rome of the East', survived its imperial sister's demise for another thousand years.

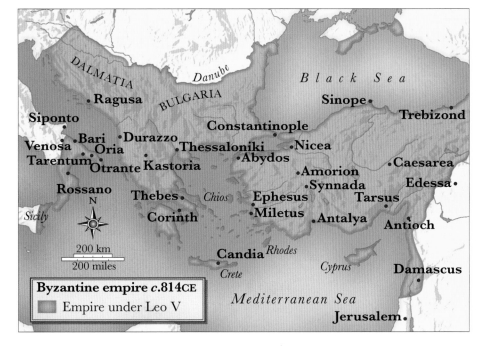

DALMATIA
Danube
BULGARIA
Black Sea
Ragusa
Siponto
Sinope
Trebizond
Constantinople
Venosa Bari Durazzo
Oria Thessaloniki Nicea
Tarentum Abydos
Otrante Kastoria
Amorion Caesarea
Rossano Synnada Edessa
N Thebes Chios Ephesus Tarsus
Sicily Corinth Miletus Antalya
Antioch
200 km
200 miles
Candia Rhodes
Cyprus Damascus
Crete
Byzantine empire c.814CE
Empire under Leo V
Mediterranean Sea
Jerusalem

SPAIN AND THE 1492 EXPULSION OF THE JEWS

FROM THE 11TH CENTURY, SLOWLY BUT SURELY, CHRISTIAN PRINCIPALITIES RECAPTURED SPAIN IN A PROCESS KNOWN AS THE RECONQUISTA. BY THE MID-1200S GRANADA WAS SPAIN'S SOLE REMAINING MUSLIM KINGDOM.

The Christian mountain enclave of Asturias became the Kingdom of Leon in 913CE, and joined its neighbour and occasional ally, Castile, in driving the Reconquista. Umayyad Andalus dissolved into 23 disparate Muslim 'party kingdoms' in 1030. In quick succession the Muslims lost Toledo in 1085, Valencia in 1092 and Zaragoza in 1118. After decades of stalemate, Christians united to defeat the Muslims at Tolosa in 1211. Cordoba fell in 1236 and Seville in 1248. Spanish Jews now found themselves mostly living under Christian rule. In time, Christian authorities started forcing Jews to convert, imposing pseudo-theological 'disputations' and officially sanctioning massacres.

JEWISH SUCCESS

Jews from France and North Africa had settled in Aragon during the reign of King James I (1213–76), encouraged by property grants and

Right Passover customs come alive in the Golden Haggadah, Spain, c.1320.

tax exemptions. Jews had also benefited from a belated intellectual flowering in Christian Spain. Toledo established a university that taught Greek, Arabic and Hebrew after 1130, and a rabbinical university was set up in Barcelona in 1267. More Jews settled in both cities after the French expulsions of 1306.

RISING ANTI-SEMITISM

However, Spanish Jewry was not immune to developments elsewhere in Europe. In 1215 the Vatican's Fourth Lateran Council instituted the 'Badge of Shame' to distinguish Jews, who were also banned from appearing in public on Good Friday.

Toledo's king and archbishop cherished their city's reputation for co-existence of Jews, Muslims and Christians, called *La Convivencia*. They persuaded the Pope to suspend

the badge law in Spain. But Aragon's King James I forbade law courts from accepting a Jew's oath in 1228; and Zaragoza saw the first Spanish 'blood libel' in 1250.

NEW LAWS AND POGROMS

Over time, petty discomforts grew into debilitating legal codes, officially approved mob violence, and finally outright religious persecution. Castile's Siete Partidas, or Seven-Part Code of 1265, allowed Jews to run synagogues and guaranteed freedom from interference on the Sabbath. While this code recommended converting Jews by 'kind words', it also claimed that Jews crucified Christian children over Easter. The Partidas banned sexual intercourse between Jews and Christians, and threatened to burn any Jew who wounded a Jewish convert to Christianity. Thus it provided later rulers with an arsenal of discrimatory powers, and sanctioned torture.

Increasingly, Jews in Spain were blamed for the plague of 1348. Henry of Trastamara unleashed his forces on Toledo's Jewish Alcana quarter in 1355, where they killed more than a thousand. Terrible

Left Auto-da-fé on the Plaza in Madrid on 30 June 1680 by Francisco Rizi, 1683.

Above Interrogation of the Jew, *Spanish altarpiece painting, 1485. Seven years later Jews were expelled from the kingdom.*

pogroms in Valencia, Seville and Barcelona in 1391 persuaded many to convert to Christianity. Some *conversos* practised Judaism in secret, so Spaniards called them *marranos* (pigs). Others became militant Christians, like Don Pablo de Santa Maria, bishop of Burgos. By now Spanish Jews faced an awful double bind. Those who kept their faith faced increasing strictures, while Jews who adopted Christianity were accused of doing so for venal motives.

THE SPANISH INQUISITION

During 1413–14 a former Jew named Jose Lorqui led 63 sessions of a disputation in Tortosa whose outcome was predetermined, unlike the earlier 1263 Barcelona disputation. Spanish Jewry's end came with the dreaded Inquisition in 1481. Spain had long resisted this method, which was designed to weed out heretics. It pried into people's lives, robbed local bishops of their authority and confiscated the property of the 'guilty' to the Vatican, not to rulers.

Nonetheless´, Queen Isabella of Castile called in the inquisitors when in 1480 she heard that leading 'New

Christians' had been caught secretly celebrating the Jewish Passover. Soon the institution reached Valencia, Catalonia and Aragon. Thousands were forced to confess their 'crimes' under torture. Many more were burnt alive in public displays called auto-da-fé (acts of faith). Those who confessed had the dubious privilege of being strangled before the pyre was lit. The Inquisition continued until the late 18th century.

FALL OF GRANADA

In 1469, powerful Jews encouraged the marriage between Castile's Isabella and Aragon's Fernando, hoping that this dynastic union might end persecution. One such advocate was Lisbon-born Isaac Abrabanel (1453–1508), philosopher, financier and advisor to Isabella. The royal couple did not wish to lose the services of their Jewish allies, but they eventually bowed to clerical pressure and expelled all Jews from Andalucia in 1483.

Now the only area where Jews could live safely was Granada. Jews had proven their loyalty in 1453 by fighting for Muslim Granada against Castile. Jews enjoyed the kingdom's hospitable and cultivated environment; Granada's sultans hosted intellectuals, built the fabulous Alhambra Palace and traded with Europe and North Africa. But its political capital was spent, and on January 2, 1492, Isabella and Fernando's armies defeated this last outpost of Muslim rule in Spain.

DISASTER AND NEW HOPE

Of the 200,000 Jews who left Spain, at least 50,000 went to North Africa or Ottoman Turkey, and another 100,000 crossed into Portugal, only to be expelled four years later. In

Right Respectful debate or thinly veiled show trial? Disputations between rabbis and monks increasingly heralded persecution. Illustration to Heinrich Heine's Disputation, *1851.*

Above Damned by the Inquisition *by Eugenio Lucas Velázquez, 1850.*

Spanish Malta, Jews had to pay 'compensation' for the effect of their departure on the economy.

Another event of 1492 was Christopher Columbus' expedition to the New World. On board was Luis de Torres, the expedition's official Arabic translator, a *converso* (a Jew who had been forced to convert to Christianity). By some accounts Columbus himself was half-*converso*. Whether true or not, he almost certainly used the maps of the Spanish Jew Abraham Crescas and the navigational tools of another Jewish scientist, Gersonides.

CHAPTER 6

THE SHIFT TO ASHKENAZ

For Jews everywhere the Spanish expulsions of 1492 seemed to snuff out a light that would never be relit. In fact, the calamity coincided with several new opportunities. That same year Columbus sailed to the 'New World', opening up previously unimagined prospects for traders. Printing technology disseminated knowledge more easily than ever before. And the Ottomans allowed Spanish exiles to settle across their empire, including Palestine.

Within two centuries, Dutch Sephardim became the first Jews to return to England, and Amsterdam produced Baruch Spinoza, arguably the greatest of early Jewish freethinkers. Yet Italy invented the ghetto, and a German reformist Christian movement known as Protestantism turned from sympathizing with Jews to deriding them. Overall, the period from 1492 saw a gradual passing of the torch from Sephardi to Ashkenazi culture, as Poland grew in stature as a Jewish centre, Yiddish flourished as a language and Rabbi Loew spearheaded a Jewish Renaissance in Prague.

Opposite The Dutch master Rembrandt (1609–69) often painted Jewish subjects, such as this striking portrait of a rabbi. Amsterdam became home to Jews, both Ashkenazi and Sephardi.

Above *Bridge to the Jewish ghetto in Venice. A sudden influx of Spanish Jewish refugees led to the founding of the first established ghetto in the world in March 1516.*

JEWS IN NEW CULTURES

THE LATE 15TH CENTURY SAW JEWS EVICTED FROM SPAIN AND PORTUGAL,
NAPLES AND NUREMBERG. YET FRESH COMMUNITIES SPROUTED IN POLAND,
THE NETHERLANDS, PERSIA, AND EVEN THE AMERICAS.

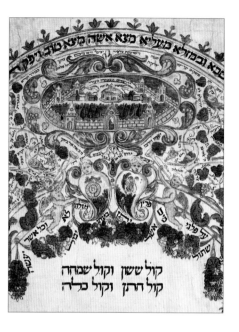

Jews survived despite the expulsions and persecution of the turbulent 16th century. They created new institutions, harnessed new technology and kept alive old traditions of scholarship. Jews thrived by creating intricate trading networks that linked their new places of refuge – Ottoman Turkey, North Africa, the Netherlands, Poland and Lithuania.

NEW HAVENS

Paradoxically, the expulsions put Sephardi and Ashkenazi Jews in contact with each other to their mutual advantage. This was especially true of the Netherlands and, later, north-west Germany, areas that came under Protestant rule and accepted 'New Christians' (converted Jews) from Spain and Portugal. As a result of this, Jews repopulated the shores of the Atlantic after years of absence, just

Below Established in 1516, the Venice Ghetto set a pattern for similar enclaves for Jews across Europe.

as the Atlantic began to take over from the Mediterranean as the prime focus of European trade.

Iberian (Sephardi) Jews also flocked to the Ottoman empire, while most German Ashkenazim moved *en masse* to Poland. Thus Sephardi–Ashkenazi co-operation grew as Poland became the chief transit for expanding overland trade between the Ottomans and central and western Europe.

THE GHETTOS

In March 1516, panicked by a sudden influx of Spanish Jewish refugees, Venice set up the world's first ghetto, so called because the area was an old iron foundry (*ghetto* in Italian). Most of the original inhabitants were of German origin; Jews from the Levant got their own ghetto in 1541. Other Italian cities set up ghettos: Rome in 1556, Florence in 1571, Verona in 1605, Mantua in 1612 and Ferrara in 1624.

The word ghetto has come to signify an area of urban depravity, but there were positive aspects: dur-

Above A beautiful ketubah, Jewish marriage contract, from Modena, Italy, 1723, with a view of Jerusalem.

ing nightly curfews Jews were protected from bigots outside the walls; during daylight hours they still traded in the city. They alone were allowed to pursue loan-banking, a trade which, although it never yielded vast fortunes, spread prosperity throughout some 300 Italian communities during the period 1300–1500. Isolated from gentile society, these Jews nurtured a distinctive culture within the ghetto.

FALSE HOPE IN PORTUGAL

By the 13th century Portugal's Jews numbered 200,000, a fifth of the total population; and King João II valued his Jewish financiers and gun-makers for most of his 1481–94 reign. After some 150,000 refugees poured across the border from Spain in 1492, however, João declared non-domiciled Jews to be slaves, and ordered that Jewish children should be separated from their parents. João's successor, Manuel, reversed these decrees, only to order all Jews to leave Portugal in October 1497. Three thousand Iberian crypto-Jews died in a pogrom in Lisbon in 1506.

In 1531 Pope Clement VII (1478–1534) began a Portuguese Inquisition aimed at 'secretly Jewish' Maranos: several thousand were imprisoned and many more fled.

SICILY, MALTA AND ITALY

The Spanish expulsions and the period leading up to them affected Jews well beyond the Spanish mainland. In 1391 some 50,000 were murdered by mobs in Majorca. After 1492, Jews were forced out of Spanish-ruled Sicily and southern Italy. Most constructed new secure lives in Ottoman territory.

Pope Alexander VI (1431–1503) allowed Jews from Sicily, Sardinia and Spain to settle in his Italian states. Many fled to papal Naples, but after it fell to Spain, Jews were evicted in 1510 and 'new Christians' (converted Jews) in 1515. As late as 1587, the duchy of Milan banished 900 Jews when it, too, came under Spanish rule. Nor were all popes so benign: in 1556 Paul IV (1478–1559) sent 24 Portuguese Maranos to burn at the stake in Ancona.

THE NEW WORLD

In 1502, on his final visit to the New World, Christopher Columbus left behind 52 Jewish-origin families in Costa Rica.

The Spanish and Portuguese began to hunt down insincere converts in their New World colonies. As early as 1515 the authorities deported one 'secret Jew' from Hispaniola (now Cuba) to face the Inquisition in Spain. Maranos were offered the choice of death or 'true conversion' at autos-da-fé in Lima, Peru (1570), Mexico City (1574), Cartagena, Colombia (1610) and Havana.

By 1640, Jews and Maranos were living safely along the Brazilian coast under Dutch rule. One town, Bahia, was even nicknamed 'The Rock of Israel'. After Portugal reconquered Brazil in 1654, resident Jews fled to nearby Surinam and Cayenne and to the Caribbean. Twenty-three Brazilian Sephardim arrived in Dutch-ruled New Amsterdam (later called New York), where they established She'arit Israel, the first Hebrew congregation in North America.

PERSIA

Meanwhile, Jews thousands of miles to the east suffered too. In 1511 the usually downtrodden Shia sect took over Persia and established its first empire since the Fatimids ruled Egypt. Their clerics forced Persia's new Safavid rulers to discriminate against Jews and Christians.

Above Lorenzo de Medici (1449–92), ruler of Florence, who protected his Jewish subjects from expulsions.

Respite came when the urbane Abbas I (1588–1629) invited Jews to settle in his new capital, Isfahan, in 1592. They welcomed his peace treaty with the rival Ottoman Caliphate and his expansion of seafaring trade with Europe, in which they played a pivotal role.

Next, Shah Abbas II of Persia (r. 1642–66) drove Jews from Isfahan in 1652 on grounds of 'ritual impurity', and forced 100,000 Jews to adopt Islam. Confronted by a Jewish delegation in 1661, Abbas relented and allowed Jews to revert to their old faith, as long as they wore a distinctive patch.

Life improved for Jews in 1730 when Afghan invasions destroyed the Safavid dynasty. Many became physicians, pharmacists and international merchants. However, they never reached the intellectual heights of their co-religionists in a Europe where the Renaissance promised new hope.

Left The current building for Congregation She'arit Israel, New York City, for a community established in 1654.

INTELLECTUAL STIRRINGS

DURING THE RENAISSANCE AND THE REFORMATION, JEWS REMAINED THE ONLY RELIGIOUS MINORITY WITHIN CHRISTENDOM. THE ADVENT OF PRINTING LED TO INCREASING INTEREST IN HEBREW TEXTS.

Europe of the 15th, 16th and 17th centuries was a ferment of change. The Italian Renaissance encouraged artistic individualism, rational inquiry and renewed interest in long-neglected classics. Protestants in Germany and France challenged the 1,200-year-long dominance of the Roman Catholic Church and were soon to split the continent apart. Other truth-seekers rejected Christianity altogether.

Meanwhile, scientific break-throughs allowed for voyages of discovery and helped create Europe's first overseas empires. In time the new mercantile class began seeking greater domestic freedoms. Europeans often oppressed the peoples of Africa, Asia and the Americas, however, and colonial rivalries led

Below Solomon and the Queen of Sheba, c. *1555, by Tintoretto, an Italian Renaissance artist fascinated by Jewish and biblical themes.*

to bloody wars abroad and at home. In addition, developing colonies demanded slaves, which led to a trade in human cargo that shamed their liberal and Christian values.

EUROPE'S SOLE MINORITY

Throughout this period Jews remained the only religious minority within Christendom. The changes around them had decidedly mixed effects on their community, for while attacks on Church authority created space for free expression, challenges to religion threatened their faith as well. Anti-Semitism refused to disappear despite the spirit of liberalism.

Jews who initially welcomed Protestantism, for instance, were shocked when Martin Luther took to Jew-baiting. Even the great Dutch humanist Desiderius Erasmus of Rotterdam wrote: 'If it is the part of a good Christian to detest the Jews, then we are all good Christians'.

Above The first book printed in Lisbon, the Book of Abraham, *published in Hebrew by Eliezer Toledano, 1489.*

PRINTING REVOLUTION

One escape from isolation came via printing, which democratized knowledge and defied borders. After Johann Gutenberg made the world's first Bible with movable type in 1445, Jews produced at least 180 Hebrew printed titles between 1472 and 1500. Most were religious works.

The first printing press of any language in the Orient was a Jewish firm, which printed Hebrew books in Constantinople in 1493. Italy became the centre for Hebrew printing, although many master printers were German Jews. The Jewish Soncino family, for instance, originally hailed from Bavaria and settled near Milan. They also printed in Brescia, Rimini, Pesaro, Constantinople and Salonika.

Perhaps the most accomplished craftsman of all was Daniel Bomberg, a Christian from Belgium, primarily active in Venice between 1516 and 1549. He printed the entire multi-volume Talmud between 1520 and 1523 in Venice and set the pagination standards for Talmuds for all time. The technical advance of printing spread Jewish knowledge like wildfire.

Left Galileo explaining his daring scientific insights at Padua University; from a painting of 1873, Mexico.

OFFICIAL CENSORSHIP

Catholic governors were worried about dissident literature being spread, so they introduced tight censorship and ordered Talmuds and other Jewish books burned in 1554. Production resumed 11 years later, but only once copies were vetted to rid them of negative references to Jesus or gentiles.

Censorship was not unknown to Jews. Conservative French rabbis persuaded Dominicans to burn copies of Maimonides' 'Guide' in

Below: Jewish Kabbalist holding a 'tree of life' diagram of divine attributes; from a book of magic, Portae Lucis, *1516.*

Montpellier, France, in 1233. Nine years later they watched as thousands of Talmuds were set ablaze in Paris by papal order, aware that they had precipitated this self-inflicted tragedy.

THE RENAISSANCE

A 15th-century revival of interest in Greek and Latin classics soon spawned curiosity in texts in Hebrew, which Italian and later German scholars came to regard as the third of the great 'classical literatures'. For Jews, literature, music and the sciences presented better chances for creative expression. One Jewish pioneer was the court composer Salomone di Rossi, who wrote European-style melodies for the ancient synagogue liturgy.

FREE THINKERS

The Renaissance encouraged Italian Jews to broach taboos and to discuss ideas with gentile interlocutors. Azaria di Rossi, for instance, revisited contentious issues of belief first raised by the 1st-century Egyptian Jewish philosopher Philo. Leone Modena taught Christians about Jewish practices and did much to demystify Jews in the public eye.

One of the most daring Jewish thinkers was Solomon Ibn Verga (*c.*1450–*c.*1525). He wrote *The Rod of Judah*, sometimes called the first

secularist Jewish history since Josephus. A dedicated rationalist, Ibn Verga criticized the Talmud and mocked Maimonides, chided Jews for being 'twice naked' by neglecting political and military science, and blamed anti-Semitism on Jews who 'show themselves lords and masters, therefore the masses envy them'.

The Renaissance spirit also took hold in Holland under Calvinist Protestant rule, where the established *ma'amad*, or 'executive body of the Sephardi community', had no truck for dissent. Uriel da Costa set an example to other Jewish freethinkers. Born in 1585 in Oporto, Portugal, and raised as a Jesuit, he reconverted to Judaism and fled from persecution to Holland. He questioned the Oral Law and wrote scathingly about the ritualistic 'Pharisees of Amsterdam', who excommunicated him. Da Costa rejoined the community in 1640, but killed himself after being forced to receive 39 lashes in the synagogue by way of 'recantation'.

Below An anti-Semitic pamphlet from Frankfurt, 1601, shows a ritual murder and Jews suckling a pig.

JEWISH COMMUNITIES IN GERMANY

BY THE 16TH CENTURY, THE HOLY ROMAN EMPIRE SEEMED LIKE A THROWBACK TO MEDIEVAL TIMES, WHEN RELIGION AND MONARCHICAL DYNASTIES, NOT NATIONALITY, DEFINED EUROPE.

Germany was not a distinct state until the mid-19th century. Before that, the Holy Roman empire encompassed most of what is today Germany, as well as Switzerland, Austria, Slovenia, Belgium, Luxembourg, the Czech Republic and Holland, plus parts of France, Poland and northern Italy. Far from being a truly united entity, the empire comprised hundreds of smaller kingdoms, principalities, counties and free imperial cities.

EASTERN EXTREMITIES
From a Jewish perspective, greater Germany was particularly uninviting in the 15th century: Jews were expelled from Vienna, Linz Cologne,

Below Built in 1175, this synagogue in Worms, sometimes called Rashi's Chapel, is the oldest in Germany.

Right Martin Luther, the dynamo behind the Protestant Revolution, at first inspired hope in Jews. Danish altarpiece, 1561.

Augsburg, Bavaria and Styria, southern Austria, in 1496. Increasingly Jews moved eastwards, through the empire's extremities to Moravia, Bohemia and on to Poland.

Jewish fortunes revived by the late 16th century: the Emperor Maximilian II (r. 1557–76) allowed Jews to return to towns in Bohemia, and in 1577 his son, Rudolph II, gave them a charter of privileges. Poland, meanwhile, emerged as the new Ashkenazi heartland; some Jews made fortunes there and further east, effectively running vast Ukrainian and Lithuanian estates that provided grain to expanding western Europe.

THE PFEFFERKORN AFFAIR
Jews discovered friends in unexpected places, such as Johannes Reuchlin, a German Christian humanist and Hebrew scholar inspired by the winds of change emanating from Italy. In 1509 Johannes Pfefferkorn, a Jewish-born Dominican monk in Cologne, declared: 'Whoever afflicts the Jews is doing the will of God'. He sought to kidnap Jewish children and raise them as Catholics. He also won imperial approval to confiscate all Jewish books, especially the Talmud. Soon Jewish tomes were set alight in Frankfurt; while 38 Jews were burned in Berlin on trumped-up charges of child murder. Reuchlin argued for the Jews, forcing the emperor to rescind his edict in 1510. The controversy raged for years.

THE REFORMATION
For more than a millennium, Roman Catholicism reigned in most of Europe. As the Byzantine empire drew to a close in 1453, Greek or Christian Orthodox pockets in western Europe, such as Ravenna in Adriatic Italy, died out. The Church of Rome isolated and eliminated competing trends, like Gnosticism and Arianism in the 3rd century, the Cathars in the 14th and Hussites in the 15th. All were called heresies, and several movements were ostracized precisely because they seemed to be too close to Judaism.

With the pope at its head the Catholic Church seemed impregnable. However, a string of corrupt popes weakened it, and resentments came to the boil in the 16th century. Disgusted by the offering of bogus 'indulgences', the rebel monk Martin Luther nailed his 95-point thesis to the door of the Wittenberg Palace All Saints' Church in late October 1517. So began the Protestant Reformation, which was to revolutionize Europe. At first Jews welcomed the new religious trend: they were no longer the only non-conformists in Europe, and some imagined that Protestants would be their natural allies. Luther published a pamphlet stressing the links between Jews and

Right A historical turning point? When thugs looted Frankfurt's Jewish ghetto in 1614, Habsburg Emperor Matthias hanged the instigators and restored Jewish property.

Christians, called *Christ was Born a Jew*. And while his aim was always to convert Jews, he insisted that this should be done with gentleness.

THE PROTESTANTS TURN

Jews soon learnt Protestants could be just as anti-Semitic as Catholics. When Jews rejected Luther's advances he issued a virulent attack on them in 1543, recommending a programme of arson, expropriation, hard physical labour and ultimately, 'if we are afraid that they may harm us', driving them 'out of the country for all time'.

After reforms in 1356, German emperors had given local princes or imperial 'electors' the right to tax Jews. Once Jews could appeal directly to the emperor; now they had to contend with the whims of local fiefs. Eventually, however, in 1614, Emperor Matthias (r. 1612–19) stood up against anti-Semites and hanged the ringleaders of a pogrom in Frankfurt. He then ceremonially restored the Jews to their homes.

Below The vast and sprawling Holy Roman empire was generally inhospitable terrain for Jews.

Generally, Jews fared better in the northern German states of the Hanseatic League. Semi-autonomous from the empire, the League afforded opportunities for trade with Scandinavia and the Baltic states. By the 16th century Jews from Spain and Portugal migrated to the region. They soon forged lucrative links with fellow Sephardim in Holland and Ashkenazim in Germany.

THE RISE OF COURT JEWS

Jews also benefited from the Thirty Years War, which erupted in 1618 between the Holy Roman empire and an array of foes, both Catholic and Protestant. Almost single-handedly one Jew, Jacob Bassevi of Prague, saved the imperial Habsburg army from bankruptcy with loans and a food-supply network in eastern Europe. Some Jews profited from supplying the opposition; other Jews became contractors to Swedish forces. In sum, the war brought about two changes. First, Jewish communities who used to suffer from any conflict were now treated better than others. Second, there were 'court Jews' who funded capital projects in peacetime as in war, who advised rulers, and who capitalized on these factors to safeguard the interests of poorer Jews.

Below This painting by Flemish artist Sebastien Vrancx depicts the Thirty Years War, 1618–48, during which some Jews shrewdly gained influence.

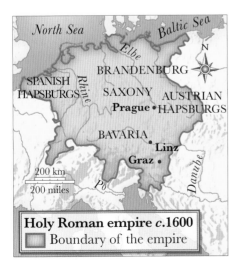

North Sea
Baltic Sea
Elbe
Rhine
N
BRANDENBURG
SPANISH HAPSBURGS
SAXONY
Prague • AUSTRIAN HAPSBURGS
BAVARIA
Linz
Graz •
200 km
200 miles
Po
Danube

Holy Roman empire c.1600
Boundary of the empire

Jews in the Ottoman Empire

After Muslim Turkey threw Spanish Jews a lifeline in 1492, Sephardim revived Jewish communities across the Ottoman-ruled Balkans, eastern Mediterranean and North Africa.

To the beleaguered Jews in 15th-century Spain, the sight of offshore sailing masts belonging to the Ottoman fleet was particularly reassuring. Between 1490 and 1492 the naval commander Kemal Reis sent ships to hug the Iberian coastline, picking up load after load of refugees and transporting them to Turkey and the Ottoman provinces. Even after Granada fell to Christian Spaniards, Reis bombarded the ports of Almería and Málaga on behalf of fellow Muslims suffering in Spain, and in 1506 he rescued the last consignment of Jews and Arabs who wished to escape the Spanish Inquisition.

BAYEZID'S INVITATION

Whereas Christian nations accepted Jews begrudgingly, Sultan Bayezid II (r. 1481–1512) made it Ottoman policy to welcome them. He was keen to engage worldly-wise entrepreneurs in building up his nascent empire. Adroitly calculating that Christianity's loss could be Islam's gain, he openly invited the Jews to immigrate, and he said of Spain's king, Ferdinand: 'Can you call such a king wise or intelligent? He is impoverishing his country and enriching my kingdom'.

Turkey's existing 50,000 Jews generously helped their brethren, performing 'unlimited great deeds of charity, giving money as if it were stones', reported the chronicler Rabbi Elijah Capsali. About 150,000 arrived, of whom 40,000 settled directly in Constantinople. Jews also came to Salonika in Greece, whose Jewish population rose to 20,000 by 1553; to Izmir (formerly Smyrna); and to Adrianople, now Edirne in European Turkey, site of an earlier influx of Ashkenazim from France and Germany. Adrianople's rabbi,

Above Ambassadors paying homage to the Ottoman Sultan Suleiman the Magnificent; from a 16th-century manuscript about his campaigns.

Isaac Sarfati, even posted letters to communities in Hungary, Moravia and the Rhineland praising the liberality of the Sultanate.

Once ensconced as citizens of the empire, Sephardi Jews did well, establishing the first Gutenberg press in Constantinople in 1493, and working as skilled craftsmen, iron-casters and makers of gunpowder.

OTTOMAN RULE

During the reign of Suleiman the Magnificent (1520–66) the Ottoman empire controlled Asia Minor, Egypt, North Africa, the eastern Mediterranean and all of the Middle East apart from Persia. In fact the dynasty originated as a small *beylik* (principality) abutting Byzantine territory. After Mongols vanquished Anatolia's powerful Seljuk Turks, the Ottomans began their inexorable rise, led after 1281 by Osman (known as Ottoman to Europeans).

Left Simple yet dignified, the Etz Hayyim synagogue in Chania, Crete, a Greek island long under Ottoman control.

Above Once a haven for Jews under Turkish rule, Safed houses this synagogue named after a famous rabbinical resident, Joseph Caro.

The first Jewish community under their control was Bursa in north-west Anatolia, taken in 1326. Osman's son, Orhan, allowed Jews to build the Etz Hayyim (Tree of Life) synagogue, and Jews immigrated from as far as Arabia. In swift succession the Ottomans took over parts of Romania and Bulgaria, Serbia, Albania, Macedonia and Greece, most of which had small Jewish populations.

Having captured Byzantium in 1453, Sultan Mehmet II (1432–81) confirmed Moses Kapsali as chief rabbi. The Greek-born Kapsali was known for both his impartiality as a civil magistrate and tax supervisor, and also for his friendship with Mehmet and Bayezid II. Scrupulous in matters of religion, he defended normative Judaism against Karaite attack and youthful rebels. Mehmet encouraged Jews from Crete and the provinces to live in Constantinople.

Right Sephardi Jews breathed new life into the Ottoman empire, which by the 1500s included Jerusalem and Mecca.

In 1556 he sent a Jewish regiment called 'Sons of Moses' to fight rebel Christian forces in Belgrade. Leading the enemy army was the monk John Capistrano, a notorious persecutor of Jews in Italy, Sicily, Bavaria, Silesia, Austria and Poland.

SEPHARDIM DOMINATION

Supremely confident that they originated from the most refined culture in Europe, Sephardi Jews set up their own synagogues. Soon a familiar pattern was repeated, but with a difference: in the past there had been rivalry between Babylonian rite synagogues and Palestinian; now it was Spanish versus indigenous. Ottoman authorities asked synagogues to collect taxes, so they became fiscal bodies as well as spiritual and communal centres and schools.

In places where each community had its own synagogue (Italian, Sephardi, Ashkenazi, Romaniote), an umbrella *kehillah*, or 'Hebrew community', came to represent them all. Moreover, ad hoc Jewish general assemblies administered internal affairs, while Ottoman Jewish law courts enjoyed more autonomy than their equivalents in Christian Europe. Ottoman prestige

rose among European Jews, too, when Palestine fell to Turkish hands in 1516.

JOSEPH CARO

The Ottoman subject who made the greatest impact on Jews was rabbi and mysticist Joseph Caro (1488–1575). He was born in Spain, moved as a child to Portugal and lived in Adrianople, Salonika, Constantinople, Safed and Jerusalem. Probably even more than Moses Maimonides, Caro determined the authoritative code of law and practice for generations of Orthodox Jews. His magnum opus, *Beth Yosef* (House of Joseph) was an overview of 32 authorities on Talmudic rulings. Caro intended to rationalize the rapidly diverging Sephardi and Ashkenazi approaches to law.

His much shorter abridgement of *Beth Yosef*, entitled *Shulkhan Arukh* (Prepared Table), achieved immortality. Published in Venice in 1574, it was to be 'carried in one's bosom and referred to at any time and any place'. Critics found it didactic; Caro himself suggested it was mainly for simpletons or beginners. However, aided by the printing revolution, the 'Table' gained popularity in both Ashkenazi and Sephardi households.

Ottoman empire in the 1500s
---- Extent of the empire

500 km
500 miles

TURKS AND JEWS IN THE HOLY LAND

THE OTTOMANS ELEVATED THE OFFICE OF CHIEF RABBI AFTER TAKING PALESTINE IN 1516, AND ALLOWED JEWS SUCH AS DONA GRACIA HITHERTO UNPARALLELED INFLUENCE IN IMPERIAL AFFAIRS.

Unlike his predecessors who were obsessed with European campaigns, Selim I the Grim (r. 1512–20) turned east after taking the Ottoman throne in 1512. He defeated Shah Ismail of Shia Persia in 1514, took Palestine and Syria in 1516, occupied Egypt in 1517 and gained possession of Arabian territories from the Mamluks.

At a stroke Selim became steward of Islam's three holiest cities – Mecca, Medina and Jerusalem – and declared himself Caliph over all Muslims. Ottoman rule reunited Jewish communities in the Balkans, North Africa and the Middle East. Significantly, from a Jewish perspective, Turks ruled the Land of Israel and Jerusalem, and would do so for another 400 years.

Below Jewish doctors often served the Ottoman court; drawing by the French geographer Nicolas de Nicolay, 1568.

CHIEF RABBI OF THE LEVANT

In 1452 the Ottomans had established the office of chief rabbi, and after 1517 the officeholder became in effect Exilarch of the Levantine Diaspora. Formally this included Palestinian Jews, too. The incumbent rabbi was Elijah Mizrahi, a Romaniote Jew. He was proficient in Arabic, Hebrew, Italian and Greek, wrote a famous commentary on Rashi's Torah, accepted Karaites as students and as a mathematician reputedly discovered how to extract the cube root.

The Ottomans set up the *kakhya*, or 'office for secular administration', headed by Shealtiel, a Turkish-speaking Jew. Jews were recognized as a separate ethno-religious community, alongside Greek Orthodox, Armenian Christians and others. However, Muslims outnumbered the minorities, Jews and Christians had to pay protection and head tax, and the Chief Mufti held a cabinet post, unlike the spiritual leaders of the Christian and Jewish communities.

Generally 16th-century sultans favoured Jews over Christians, and several rose to positions of power, such as Mehmet II's minister of finance, Hekim Yakup Pasha, and Murad II's physician, Ishak Pasha. Selim followed the trend by appointing Abraham Castro master of the mint and *nagid*, or Jewish community leader, in Egypt. Closer ties came during the 1520-66 reign of Suleiman the Magnificent, who rebuilt Jerusalem's city walls. He won popularity when his troops captured Rhodes in 1522, freeing and gaining fighters from 4,000 Jews whom the ruling Knights Hospitaller had been using as slave labourers.

Above Sultan Selim the Grim, who took Palestine and Syria in 1516, thus uniting Eastern Jews under one rule.

FAMILY RELATIONS

The Jewish pair who wielded the most power was Don Joseph Nasi, born as the Portuguese Marano João Micas around 1524, and Dona Gracia, his aunt and mother-in-law. They turned a precious-stones enterprise into a banking empire. Cultured and charming, Gracia left Portugal via England for Antwerp, mingled with European nobles and arrived in Venice in 1545. Turkish diplomats intervened when she was denounced as a Judaizer. She arrived in Constantinople in 1553 and was reunited with her nephew, having arranged escape passages for other Portuguese Maranos.

In Constantinople Don Joseph regularly met foreign ambassadors and counselled sultans on matters of policy, especially concerning the Middle East. He became a *muterferik*, or 'gentleman of the royal retinue', and Duke of the island of Naxos. In 1560, he and Gracia were allowed to develop a Jewish colony at Tiberias, near the Sea of Galilee, to the betterment of all its inhabitants.

Joseph, now Lord of Tiberias, encouraged Suleiman to attack Cyprus, a Venetian possession. At the subsequent naval battle off Lepanto

Above Born in Portugal, Dona Gracia became in her day the most influential woman in the Ottoman empire.

in 1571, however, a combined fleet of Spanish, Venetian and papal ships humiliated the Ottoman navy. Turkey secured Cyprus in 1573 and Tunis the next year, but Joseph, blamed for his Lepanto miscalculation, was never named king of Cyprus.

JEWISH DIPLOMATS

Turkey used Jews to negotiate with European political figures. Joseph's rival, Solomon Ashkenazi, represented Turkey in peace talks with Venice, despite Venetian reluctance to meet a Jew. He later got Venice to cancel a threat to expel its Jews. Don Joseph called for an embargo of the Adriatic port of Ancona, after the Inquisition began targeting the

LADINO: THE SEPHARDI LINGUA FRANCA

As Yiddish is to Ashkenazim, so is Ladino to the Sephardi Jews – a much-loved hybrid language filled with pathos, wit and charm. Again, like Yiddish, the number of its speakers has sadly dwindled; only about 80,000 Jews in Israel and a few thousand others outside still understand Ladino. The sole surviving Ladino newspaper is printed in Istanbul (formerly Constantinople).

Also known as Judeo-Spanish, Judezmo, Spanyol, or Haquitiya in Spanish Morocco, the word Ladino derives from 'Latin'. The language is based on medieval Castilian with lashings of Hebrew, Aramaic and a little Turkish, Arabic, French and Italian. Until recently Ladino was written in Hebrew characters, using a cursive 'rabbinic' typeface. Its heyday came after the 1492 expulsion, and the first Ladino Bible translation appeared in the 1700s in Constantinople. The most famous Ladino work was *Me'am Lo'ez* (1730), a retelling of Bible stories. There was a strong oral rather than written culture until the 19th century. Ladino is being revived as a literary language in academic circles and, in a curious reversal of normal practice, it might as a result be catching on again as a spoken language. This is partly driven by a revival in Ladino music.

Portuguese Maranos living there. The embargo was opposed by Italian Jews who feared papal retribution and ultimately failed. Yet it signalled an early use of economic power as a political weapon.

SAFED VERSUS JERUSALEM

Palestinian Jews benefited economically after the Ottoman conquests of 1516–17. Contacts grew with Jews in Syria and Egypt, and soon 1,500 Jewish families were living in Jerusalem. By the late 16th century some 15,000 Jews were drawn to Safed, both by its holiness and its

trade with nearby Damascus. Their prosperity, though, stoked resentment in a poorer Jerusalem.

One wealthy Safed spice dealer, Rabbi Jacob Berab, also harboured millennial ambitions. He wanted to revive the Great Sanhedrin, and persuaded Joseph Caro and others in Safed to reinstate the Temple custom of *smicha*, or 'priestly ordination by the laying on of hands'. But Jerusalem rabbis declared that such practices were forbidden until the Temple was restored.

DECLINE AFTER SULEIMAN

After Suleiman died in 1566, Muslims in Tiberias protested against Jewish plans to build city walls, and local governors imposed burdens on residents, especially Jews. Meanwhile, the Ottoman conquest of Hungary in 1526 had brought thousands of Ashkenazi Jews into the Turkish fold. Most felt comfortable, yet Christians perceived a Muslim threat to their security, and often cast their suspicion at the Ashkenazi population of eastern Europe.

Left A 1517 etching of the Ottoman capture of Erzerum, which opened the gateway to the Middle East.

THE DAWN OF THE ASHKENAZI ASCENDANCY

ASHKENAZI COMMUNITIES GREW IN SIZE AND SELF-CONFIDENCE AS THEIR MEMBERS FOUND NEW ROLES IN 16TH-CENTURY PRAGUE, KRAKOW AND PREVIOUSLY OBSCURE LANDS EAST OF GERMANY.

Precisely when Ashkenazi Jews separated from Sephardi Jews is hard to say. Some attribute the break to 1000CE, when Ashkenazim outlawed polygamy while Sephardim still allowed it. Others believe the rift dates from the adoption of the Ladino language by Sephardim and Yiddish by Ashkenazim, possibly around the same period.

In 1571 Rabbi Moses Isserles of Krakow appended notes to Joseph Caro's definitive legal summary, the *Shulkhan Arukh*. His glosses were called *Mappah*, a 'table-cloth' to dress the Sephardi Caro's 'prepared table'. They defined Ashkenazi customs such as avoiding rice over Passover. Since then, the Ashkenazi *Shulkhan Arukh* has come with the *Mappah* attached. It denotes a connection to the world of Sepharad yet also a declaration of independence from it.

*Below Torah binders (*Mappah *in Hebrew) indicate vibrant cultural creativity among Ashkenazi Jews.*

A JEWISH RENAISSANCE

By the 16th century, Mediterranean Jews were beginning to be outnumbered by their fellow Ashkenazim, with most living in Poland and eastern Europe, rather than their original heartland of Germany. Many reasons explain Poland's attraction: though Jews were temporarily expelled from Krakow in 1494, Poland's Jagiellon monarchs usually favoured Jews as economic entrepreneurs who could develop their empire's hinterland.

In 1501 King Alexander of Poland readmitted Jews to the Grand Duchy of Lithuania, and he appointed Jacob Polak as Poland's first chief rabbi in 1503. After 1551 Jews got to elect their own chief rabbi. The royal court and rabbis granted Jewish councils the power to tax their flock. This benefited the crown, which kept 70 per cent of takings, leaving 30 per cent for communal welfare and official salaries.

Rabbis approved easy access to credit finance, which allowed Jews to join forces with Polish landowners and develop wheat-growing areas in the east. Jews leased estates, ran tolls, distilleries and mills, imported wine, cloth, soap and furs, and created entire townships anew, known as *shtetls* in Yiddish. Jews also came to dominate river traffic to Baltic ports and exported grain by sea to western Europe.

In 1534 King Sigismund I (1467–1548) abolished the law that forced Jews to wear special clothes. In this freer atmosphere, Jews felt encouraged to start the first Hebrew printing house – in Lublin, 1547. Twenty years later they founded the first Jewish university/seminary in Poland.

***Above** An etching of Prague's Jewish Town Hall, c.1898, symbolizing the autonomy Jews enjoyed in Bohemia.*

16TH-CENTURY PRAGUE

Rabbi Polak was credited with inventing *pilpul*, the Talmudic system of study that involves what some call needlessly hair-splitting argumentation. Other Ashkenazi centres preferred a less insular approach to learning, one that was more relevant to the outside world and the scientific changes spawned by the Renaissance.

One such place was Prague, whose Jewish roots began in the 10th century, and where 3,000 Jews lived at the end of the 16th century. The community included some especially creative figures, such as Judah Loew ben Betzalel (1525–1609), rabbi, Talmudic sage and community leader. The Maharal, as he was known, was both a mystic and a devotee of rational science and philosophy. He was associated with the Golem, a mythical creature of mud who protected Jews after being brought to life by uttering the word *emet*, or 'truth'.

Isaiah Horowitz (c.1565–1630) became rabbi of Frankfurt and Prague, leaving for Palestine in 1620. A philanthropist, he survived a kidnapping in Jerusalem when ransomed by the Turkish pasha. His *Shnei Luhot Ha-Berit*, 'Two Tablets of the Covenant', is a classic compendium of ethics and mysticism that promotes joy in every action, and converts evil into good.

A different sort of Prague figure was Marcus Meisel, who provided the Holy Roman (German) Emperor Rudolph with art and scientific equipment. Meisel also financed Rudolph's war against Turkey. An archetypal court Jew, he protected his community, paved roads, built synagogues and cemeteries, provided charity for the poor, and won the right to bar police from entering the Jewish quarter.

COUNCIL OF FOUR LANDS
The growth of the Jewish population of Poland was dramatic: under 30,000 in 1500, about 150,000 by 1575, and as many as 450,000, or 4.5 per cent of Poland's population, in 1650. By then Polish Jews constituted about half of the world's Jews.

In 1580 Polish monarchs granted Jews a measure of political autonomy unprecedented in Europe until then. The resultant Council of Four

Lands was an autonomous assembly which lasted for nearly 200 years. It consisted of 70 delegates drawn from the *kehillot*, or 'Jewish communities', of Greater Poland, Little Poland, Ruthenia and Volhynia. The Council met half-yearly, and at times also included Podolia, now a region of Ukraine.

Above Jews displaced from Germany, Hungary and elsewhere found havens in Poland and its environs.

Ukraine remained open to the Jews even after Ivan the Terrible, Tsar of Russia (1530–84), barred them from his territory. By 1648 there were 115 Ukrainian Jewish settlements which farmed taxes, advised magnates and governments, and ran entire colonies. However, Christian Ukrainian peasants despised the Catholic Poles, and even more so the Jews who served as their middlemen. From 1648 to 1654 Ukrainian pogroms killed perhaps 100,000 Jews. This disaster devastated the Council of Four Lands, which ceased operating in the first partition of Poland in 1764. Thereafter, most Polish Jews came under the authority of Moscow.

YIDDISH: THE LANGUAGE OF THE ASHKENAZIM
'Glitch', 'chutzpah', 'shlep', 'nosh' and many other colloquial words derive from Yiddish. The language fuses German dialects with Hebrew, Slav and Romance languages. It probably began when Jews left France and Italy for the Rhineland in the 10th century. There they met Jews who still used Aramaic and French Jews who spoke Laaz, a Latin-based argot. Yiddish was probably first written down *c.*1270, and rendered in Hebrew characters.

During 1250–1500, Yiddish

Above Performance in Berlin by the Moscow Art Theatre, 1935, of a play by Yiddish writer Peretz Hirschbein.

acquired words and grammar from Polish and Russian. Eastern Yiddish displaced Knaanic, a Slavic Jewish dialect. In France and Germany, Old or Western Yiddish faded in the 1600s as urban Jews began using national languages, and 18th-century intellectuals preferred Hebrew as the 'authentic' Jewish language. Detractors saw Yiddish as a crude patois, but supporters hailed it as the essence of Ashkenazi folk culture. The 19th century saw a boom in Yiddish literature; until assimilation, the Holocaust, Soviet oppression and the promotion of Hebrew in Israel nearly suppressed it. Yiddish today is enjoying a revival, mainly spoken by ultra-Orthodox Jews.

GLÜCKEL OF HAMELN
In faraway Hamburg, near the former epicentre of Ashkenaz, the first named Jewish female author of modern times, Glückel of Hameln (1646–1724), wrote in her memoirs of other crises – the false messiah Shabbetai Tzvi and the expulsion of Jews during the Polish–Swedish war. Glückel's stoical account written in Yiddish suggests the indomitable spirit that allowed Jews to survive.

JEWISH LIFE IN HOLLAND AND BARUCH SPINOZA

JEWISH TRADERS PROBABLY ACCOMPANIED ROMAN SOLDIERS IN ANCIENT TIMES, AND A FEW ASHKENAZIM LIVED IN THE NETHERLANDS AFTER THE 12TH CENTURY, BUT THE 1580S SAW THE GREAT EXPANSION OF JEWISH LIFE.

Modern Dutch Jewry, began when 20,000 vendors and scholars, including Maranos, left Antwerp for Holland in 1585. More Jews came after Dutch cities offered charters for settlement in 1604, including Don Samuel Palache, representative of the Sultan of Morocco.

Holland gained its first Sephardi rabbi just as Amsterdam was becoming the centre of world trade. Jewish merchants refined sugar, sold tobacco and silk and came to dominate the diamond-polishing industry. They accompanied Dutch expeditions to the Americas and held shares in the East India Company. Families such as the Machado, Pereira, de Medina and Suasso provisioned Holland's army and benefited when Holland spearheaded European opposition to France after 1672. Dutch Jews were also celebrated as book printers at a time when Holland was attracting foreign philosophers such as John Locke and René Descartes.

Left The Jewish Bride, *a tender portrait by the Dutch master Rembrandt van Rijn, 1667.*

DUTCH FREEDOM?

Many Jews discovered the Dutch republic's reputation for freedom was not entirely deserved: guilds still barred Jews from key trades and the city of Utrecht refused to admit them. Nor was the Jewish community liberal: the Sephardi freethinker Uriel da Costa took his life in 1640 after a public recantation at the Portuguese synagogue in Amsterdam.

BARUCH SPINOZA

Unlike da Costa, who was brought up as a Jesuit in Portugal, Benedict (Baruch) Spinoza was raised in a Jewish environment. Born in 1632 to Maranos (crypto-Jews) from Portugal, he studied the Torah and Talmud under Menasseh Ben Israel, who persuaded England to welcome back Jews. He also studied Kabbalah and the Jewish philosophers, Maimonides, Gersonides and Crescas.

Far from being an atheist, as he was accused of being, Spinoza devoted his life to the 'intellectual love of God', a view expressed in his posthumous *Ethics* (1677). His *Theologico-Political Treatise* (1670) was controversial since it was a systematic critique of Judaism and organized religion. He saw God as part of nature and thought the idea of a God who hears prayers or has a divine universal plan was absurd.

Turning to Judaism specifically, Spinoza wrote that Torah laws 'have no relationship with happiness'. They were obsolete after the Temple's destruction and constituted 'statutes

Above The pioneering Dutch-born philosopher Baruch Spinoza left his Jewish faith and helped lay the foundations for the Enlightenment.

that were not good and by which none could live'. Religion should guide us towards an ethical life, he believed; but rabbis were more concerned about self-preservation, and Christian persecution merely hardened their stubbornness.

HERETIC OR NOT?

In July 1656, Sephardi community elders issued a *herem*, or 'act of excommunication', against Spinoza, in terms that still chill: 'Cursed be he when he lies down and cursed be he when he rises up… the anger and wrath of the Lord will rage against this man'. Only much later did some suggest that Spinoza preempted the Hassidic belief that 'all is in God' – called pantheism.

Baruch Spinoza headed a circle of rationalists while supporting himself as a lens-polisher. He died in 1677, still shunned by the Jewish community. Even detractors, however, respect his intellect. In one Hassidic tale a pupil tells his rabbi about Spinoza's belief that there is no basic difference between humans and animals. 'In that case', replies the rabbi, 'why have no animals produced a Spinoza?'

JEWS IN ENGLAND – THE RETURN TO ALBION

OFFICIALLY, THE 1290 EXPULSION ORDER WAS NEVER RESCINDED AND ENGLAND REMAINED 'JEW-FREE' FOR 366 YEARS. HOWEVER, A STRANGE SEQUENCE OF EVENTS SUBSEQUENTLY LED TO THEIR READMISSION.

England had not been officially open to Jews since 1290, but after 1492 several Maranos from Spain and Portugal made their homes in London. Rodrigo Lopez, royal physician to Queen Elizabeth I, was a prized member of this community before he was accused of plotting to poison the monarch and was executed in 1594. (Two years later William Shakespeare wrote *The Merchant of Venice*, reputedly basing his depiction of Shylock on Lopez.)

ROYAL SPIES AND TRADERS

In 1635, the Portuguese merchant Antonio Fernandes Carvajal (*c.*1590–1659) settled in London and revived a Marano community that had dwindled after the Lopez scandal. He won a contract to supply corn to the English army, ran ships to the

Below Built in London in 1702, the Bevis Marks Sephardi Synagogue is a miniature of the Esnoga in Amsterdam.

Right Menasseh Ben Israel, the Dutch Sephardi rabbi who convinced Cromwell to readmit Jews to England.

Caribbean, Brazil, India and the Canaries, and annually imported £100,000 in silver.

England was engaged in a fierce trading war with colonial rivals, so Carvajal and his fellow Maranos used their contacts to spy on Spanish ambitions in the New World. Grateful British authorities agreed to waive the usual strictures on foreigners and make Carvajal a denizen in 1655. They turned a blind eye to the fact that he and other nominally Catholic Portuguese worshipped at a secret synagogue in London's Creechurch Lane.

CROMWELL'S SUPPORT

In 1649 King Charles I was executed following the Second English Civil War, and Oliver Cromwell became Lord Protector in 1653. Cromwell listened favourably when Menasseh Ben Israel travelled from Holland in 1650 and presented him with his tract, 'Hope for Israel'. In it the Madeira-born rabbi and printer argued – somewhat fancifully – that Native Americans were the lost Hebrew tribes, and England was the only place on earth without Jews. Readmitting them would hasten the coming of the Messiah, and also prove a financial and strategic asset.

Although readmission was never formally agreed, it became accepted. By 1690 about 400 Jews, mainly Sephardim from Holland, had settled in England. Their first synagogue was the now officially consecrated

house in Creechurch Lane. In 1702 a new synagogue in Bevis Marks, City of London, opened.

IN THE CITY

The City accepted Jews as bankers and brokers, even though anti-Semitic sentiment lingered. When Dutch prince William of Orange invaded England in 1688 he became King William III of England, and many Jewish financiers left The Hague to help create London's new stock market.

Parliament passed a Jewish Naturalization Act in 1753 after Tory MPs raised an outcry about 'abandonment of Christianity'. A number of Sephardim chose to baptize their children to gain fair chances.

LIFE OUTSIDE LONDON

While Sephardim entered parliament as Christians – in time they saw Benjamin Disraeli elected as Prime Minister in 1874 – Ashkenazi newcomers from Germany and the Hanseatic League began settling in England. Most were small traders who lived in coastal towns such as Plymouth and Bristol. Slowly, new congregations emerged in Leeds, Manchester and Edinburgh. And mass migration of poorer immigrants from Russia, Poland and Romania followed, although full emancipation only came in 1858.

CHAPTER 7

A CHANGING FAITH

Disasters have typically inspired messianic hopes of redemption among Jews. This was certainly true after Ukrainian pogroms and Polish wars engulfed mid-17th-century Europe. From Cairo to Amsterdam, Jews flocked to the cause of a charismatic rabbi from Turkey named Shabbetai Tzvi, who drew from the mystical Kabbalah tradition of Safed, Palestine.

When Shabbetai proved to be a fraud, new trends emerged to fill the void. One was Hassidism, a return to Orthodox faith infused with spiritual joy that rejected elitism and intellectualism. Another was the Haskalah, a Jewish variant of the European Enlightenment, which defined Jews as a nationality worthy of full civil rights. The Haskalah in turn inspired the modernizing Reform Judaism movement, while revolutions in 18th-century America and France seemed to promise an age of equality. The historian Leopold Zunz said Jews made a dramatic transition from a prolonged Middle Ages straight into the modern era. But when Tsarist Russia corralled Jews from a dismembered Poland into a vast Pale of Settlement, such dreams of tolerance and progress became delusions.

Opposite A 17th-century Turkish folk art depiction of a rabbi holding a Torah aloft, chanting the traditional words: 'This is the Torah Moses set before the Children of Israel'.

Above *The First Great Sanhedrin, supreme court of the Jewish people, which Napoleon granted to Jews in France, symbolizing his scheme to be patron of a Jewish national revival.*

A CRISIS OF FAITH

BATTERED BY WARS AND POGROMS IN UKRAINE AND POLAND,
EUROPEAN JEWS EAGERLY LOOKED TO TURKISH RABBI SHABBETAI
TZVI, ONLY TO DISCOVER HE WAS A FALSE MESSIAH.

From his vantage point in late 16th-century Prague, Rabbi Judah Loew was relieved that the expulsions of the Middle Ages had come to an end. But his optimism was to prove misplaced: at least 100,000 Jews were slaughtered in the Ukraine during 1648–54 in the so-called Chmielnicki massacres. The upheaval also generated impossible messianic expectations, which, once dashed, set Jews back for decades if not centuries.

JEWS BETWEEN TWO FAITHS
Mid-17th-century Europe felt threatened by Muslim Ottomans. The Ottomans had besieged Vienna in 1529 and taken most of Hungary and

Below: Chief Rabbi Jacob Loew's grave in Prague's Old Jewish Cemetery, Czech Republic, where his nephew Rabbi Judah Loew, the Maharal of Prague, is also buried.

Transylvania by 1546. They fought Poland to stalemate after a 15-year-long war that ended in 1606, and launched a campaign against Venice in 1645. Many Christians suspected their Jewish neighbours were acting as a Turkish fifth column.

However, the great Ukrainian pogroms arose not out of any Muslim–Christian clash, but from a vicious fight within Christendom. In 1569 the newly created Polish–Lithuanian Commonwealth took over large parts of Ukraine where Catholic Polish landlords encouraged Jews to run their estates. By now some 75 per cent of the world's Jews may have lived in Greater Poland.

But Ukraine's peasants were Orthodox Christian, not Catholic, and felt closer to Russians than to Poles. In addition, the Cossacks of central Ukraine, a militant caste, yearned for independence. Most Ukrainians therefore despised the Polish nobles and hated their Jewish administrators with even greater venom. In 1648 the Cossack commander Bogdan Chmielnicki (*c.* 1595–1657) rebelled against the Polish yoke, telling peasants that the Catholics had sold them 'into the hands of the accursed Jews'. He quickly repulsed Commonwealth forces and declared himself 'sole autocrat of the Rus' in 1649.

Churches were burnt, priests and nobles slaughtered and estates pillaged. Nearly a million are thought to have died. Proportionately, Jews suffered worst, with 300 population centres destroyed and more than 100,000 killed. Though contemporary estimates of up to 500,000 are probably exaggerated, the killings surpassed in brutality the pogroms

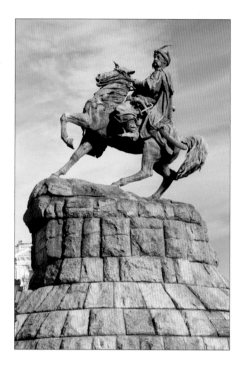

Above *Hero to some, villain to many – statue completed in 1888 of Bogdan Chmielnicki, in Kiev, Ukraine.*

of the Crusades and of the Black Death, and dispelled illusions that eastern and central Europe had adopted Enlightenment values.

Tsarist Russia absorbed a weakened Ukraine in 1654 and then attacked Poland. Russian troops killed 100,000 Jews mercilessly during the resultant Russo-Polish war (1654–67). Finally 'The Deluge', or series of 'misfortunes' following the Swedish invasion and occupation of the Polish Commonwealth (1655–60), created yet more havoc.

FLIGHT NORTH AND WEST
The gruesome four-way war between Ukraine, Russia, Poland and Sweden drove thousands of Jews westward, reversing a trend of eastward migration that had prevailed for two centuries. Many Ashkenazi refugees settled in Amsterdam alongside the existing Sephardi community. Others fled to Lithuania in the north, where local communities raised ransoms to redeem fellow Jews kidnapped by Tartars, the temporary allies of the Cossacks.

MESSIANIC STIRRING

Increasingly, Jews turned to mysticism for solace. Could these torments, they wondered, be the apocalypse that preceded the coming of the Messiah? Rumours began to pour in about a Kabbalistic 'system' that explained the mysteries of the world. The creators of this system were Rabbi Isaac Luria (1534–72), a friend of Joseph Caro, and his disciple Haim Vital (1543–1620). Both lived in Safed, in Galilee, the highest city in Ottoman-ruled Palestine and spiritually almost on a par with Jerusalem.

Luria likened the state of exile to *tzimtzum*, or God's 'withdrawal' or 'contraction' from the world at the tumultuous act of creation. Each human soul, he said, contained a *nitzotz*, or 'spark' of the divine. To move from exile to redemption, everyone, and especially Jews, should practise *tikkun olam*, or 'repairing the world', by gathering the sparks that escaped on the first day, according to Genesis. Humanity could thus achieve global harmony, explained Luria, by appeasing God through good acts, or *mitzvot*.

Jews outside Safed began reading into Luria's beliefs a radical explanation and a possible cure for historical disasters. While 'purer' Kabbalists warned against the vulgar mixing of Lurianic mysticism with ideas of a coming saviour, many felt the genie was out of the bottle.

THE FALSE MESSIAH

The man who most dramatically and disastrously inspired public passion was Shabbetai Tzvi, a Sephardi Jew born in Smyrna (Izmir), Turkey, in 1626. The son of a trading agent for Dutch and English firms, Tzvi oscillated between ecstasy and gloom, which would suggest symptoms of extreme manic depression.

Expelled from Smyrna, Salonika and Constantinople, Tzvi fled to Palestine where he visited a Lurianic Kabbalist called Nathan of Gaza (c. 1643–80) in the hope of a cure. Instead Nathan, an Ashkenazi, persuaded Tzvi that he was the foretold messianic descendant of David. Together they 'revealed' themselves on 31 May 1665: Tzvi rode around Gaza on horseback, appointing ambassadors to summon the lost tribes of Israel, while Nathan became his prophet and 'holy lamp'.

Jews in Poland, Holland, Germany, Syria, Greece, Egypt and even England were swept up in the year-long, intense craze and spread Tzvi's message. Tzvi returned to Smyrna, broke into the main synagogue and announced the date of redemption – 18 June 1666 – when he would depose the Sultan and divide the world into new kingdoms.

SHABBETAI'S APOSTASY

Nathan announced that the Lurianic system was now overthrown and that Israelite armies were gathering in the Sahara to greet the messiah. Many Jews sold all their goods and did penance in preparation for their

Left Shabbetai Tzvi, the false messiah, blessing Jews in Smyrna, Turkey, from a contemporary woodcut, c. 1665.

Above Nathan of Gaza, Shabbetai's chief ally, is blamed for dashing the hopes of a generation of Jews.

'return to Zion'. Others deliberately contravened the holiest Jewish laws and indulged in sexual lewdness.

Understandably perturbed, Ottoman officials arrested Tzvi when his ship entered Turkish waters, and jailed him in Constantinople. In September 1666 a Polish Kabbalist denounced him as an impostor. Faced with the choice of conversion or death, Shabbetai Tzvi became a Muslim, renamed himself Aziz Mehmed Effendi and was appointed the Sultan's official gatekeeper.

A shocked Jewish world fell suddenly silent, and the Sultan exiled Tzvi to Albania for his safety, where he died in 1676. Shabbateanism survived in pockets thanks to Nathan the master publicist, who explained that Tzvi's apostasy merely disguised his descent into evil to restore the last lost sparks. But most Jews felt badly deceived.

As to why mass obsession took root, it seems that crisis and upheaval so troubled a vulnerable 17th-century group that they readily believed a delusional mystic's utopian promises.

HASSIDISM

IN THE 18TH CENTURY, THE BA'AL SHEM TOV FOUNDED HASSIDISM, A RELIGIOUS AND SOCIAL MOVEMENT THAT FLOURISHES TODAY. HE TAUGHT THAT A PURE HEART IS MORE IMPORTANT THAN MUCH STUDY.

Rabbis seemed powerless to protect their flocks after the calamities of the 17th century, including the Ukrainian Chmielnicki massacres, the Russian and Swedish invasions of Poland, and the Shabbatean crisis. A century later, another 'false messiah', Jacob Frank, led followers into apostasy when he converted to Catholicism in 1759. Furthermore, the Polish Diet (parliament) ended the Jewish Council of Four Lands in 1764, and many Jews died in Ukraine's 1768 Koliyiv-shchyna rebellion. In 1772 Austria, Prussia and Russia were planning the dismemberment of Poland itself.

But this time another movement offered comfort to Jews seeking guidance and leadership. Also centred around Podolia, where Frank was born, Hassidism reinvigorated Jewish life with its passion. Its name derived from the Hebrew root, *hassid*, meaning 'piety' or 'loving kindness'. Hassidism addressed the same concerns as the Shabbateans and Frankists, but, unlike them, it never attacked the basic tenets of Jewish faith.

Left The Ba'al Shem Tov – untutored, charismatic founder of Hassidism, who challenged the rabbinical establishment.

THE BESHT

Israel ben Eliezer (1698–1760), the founder of the Hassidic movement, is better known by his nickname, the Ba'al Shem Tov, or 'Master of the Good Name', or by the acronym Besht. Born in Okopy (now in Ukraine), he settled in the Podolian town of Mezhbizh in 1740. He was orphaned young and not formally educated. He worked as a clay digger and innkeeper, and wandered alone in the Carpathian Mountains.

Known as a healer, soothsayer and holy man, the Besht appealed to ordinary Jews who lived in scattered villages and resented the didactic pronouncements of the *yeshivot*, or 'seminaries', of northern Europe. Many of those attracted to Kabbalah found the door to its wisdom barred by 'specialist' practitioners. Meanwhile, Jews who returned to Ukraine after the restoration of Polish rule in the 1690s were open to new ideas.

The Besht preached sincere love of God and fellowship among men. To the lay person he conveyed his ideas through his earthy personality and beguilingly simple parables; to the more learned, such as his disciple Meir ben Tzvi Hirsch Margolioth, he provided deeper spiritual insights.

The Besht wrote nothing himself, but his disciples transmitted his ideas orally and later set them down as an integrated system of beliefs. Soon dynastic Hassidic 'courts' spread across Ukraine, Belarus, Galicia and central Poland, and *magids*, or 'wandering teachers', inspired devotees by their force of personality.

Above The Besht's tomb in Mezhbizh, Ukraine, now a place of pilgrimage for Hassidic devotees.

RABBI DOV BER

After the Besht died, his mantle passed to Rabbi Dov Ber of Mezhirech (1710–72), an extreme ascetic whom the Besht persuaded to participate in society. Enemies of Hassidism accused Dov Ber of neglecting Torah study and introducing forbidden new rituals. In fact, Hassidism drew on Isaac Luria's Kabbalastic idea that God is to be found in all aspects of life and thus can be served in performing even mundane activities. The Hassidim stressed *devekut*, or the attempt to bridge the gap between God and man. That this could be achieved with the help of song, dance and even tobacco and alcohol infuriated more mainstream rabbis. They also practised *kavanna*, or 'concentration in prayer', and valued *tikun olam*, or 'repairing the world'; through acts of help and kindness. In that way, they said, people could gather the shards of goodness in a fractured universe.

WONDER RABBIS

Rabbi Dov Ber, in his turn, inspired Elimelech of Lizhensk, Levi Yitzhak of Berdichev, Menachem Nahum of Chernobyl, and the Besht's grandson, Rabbi Boruch of Mezhbizh. After Dov Ber's death, his four disciples subdivided Europe into distinct territories. In time, this led to the creation of Hassidic courts

Above Not the usual Hassidic headgear! – Orthodox Jews celebrate Purim in Jerusalem, 2005.

and even 'dynasties'. They spread the message with tales of *wunder-rebbes*, 'wonder rabbis', who explained their essential beliefs in a charming and accessible way. Within half a century Hassidism claimed the adherence of up to half of all Jews in eastern Europe, despite the fierce opposition of established rabbis, particularly in Lithuania, where Elijah Zalman tried to get Hassidim banned as heretics.

THE SCHOOL OF CHABAD

An acronym from Chochma, Binha and Da'at, Chabad stands for Wisdom, Understanding and Knowledge. By the 19th century the Chabad movement had its own courts and dynasties, the largest of which was based around Lubavich in Russia. Today, Lubavich Hassidim, headquartered in New York, are the most influential Hassidic sect in the world. They actively seek out wayward Jews, whom they bring back to Judaism as *hozrei b'teshuva*, or 'returnees to faith'.

INTO THE BALKANS

Hassidism also spread south across the Carpathian mountains and into Ruthenia, Romania and Hungary. The Teitelbaum family spawned many sects, including the famous Satmar Hassidim. Hassidic beliefs generally did not suit educated German Jews and faced resistance from Orthodox and Reform Jews.

THE VILNA GAON, 'DEFENDER OF ORTHODOXY'

Elijah Ben Shlomo Zalman (1720–93), usually called the Vilna Gaon, signed two orders of *herem*, or 'excommunication', against the earliest Hassidim, in 1772 and 1781. However, his true role in Judaism was more positive. Known in adulthood as the *gadol ha-dor*, or 'giant of his generation', he began as a child prodigy who mastered even the more obscure branches of rabbinical literature. The Vilna Gaon regarded secular study as necessary, though only in so far as it aided understanding of Jewish sources. He opposed the casual study of Kabbalah (mysticism) yet was himself an adept Kabbalist who believed in the power of spells and charms. Though not a rabbi by appointment, the Gaon was the acknowledged spiritual leader of Lithuanian Jewry, which under his steerage became the acme of religious scholarship.

His main disciple was Haim of Volozhin (1749–1821), who in his book *Nefesh ha-Haim* (Spirit of Life) accused Hassidim of idolatry for venerating their rabbi-leaders. Haim also took issue with established practice in yeshivas, by outlawing *pilpul*. At Volozhin he established a rota so that someone would be studying the Torah and Talmud at all hours. His life's motto was 'Man must participate in the sufferings of others and help them'.

Similarly the trend made few inroads among Sephardi Jews, despite the proximity of the southern Hassidic heartland to Turkey and the Black Sea, and the fact the earliest hassidim adopted a Sephardi *nusach*, or 'prayer rite'. Only with the creation of the State of Israel have some *Mizrachi*, or 'oriental', and Sephardi Jews joined Hassidic sects. Even so, many social historians believe that Hassidism rescued Orthodox Judaism.

HASSIDIC CUSTOM

In their distinctive gabardines and Homburg hats, fur *shtreimels*, or 'large caps', Hassidic men are familiar sights in London, New York, Jerusalem and Bnei Brak near Tel Aviv in Israel. Women dress modestly, though children put on colourful costumes for the festival of Purim. Many theories abound about the origin of the costume. Some say Hassidim imitated Polish nobles of the day; others say this was typical east European Jewish dress, only most non-Hassidim have since abandoned the custom. Yet

Right A rabbi in traditional Hassidic dress stands beside the door of Yosef Caro's synagogue in Safed, Galilee.

others suggest an oriental influence, and compare the long black satin robe called the *bekishe* to Shia imams' garb in Iran. Other aspects – the *pe'ot* 'sidelocks', and *tzitzit*, or 'side-tassels' – are normative Orthodox requirements, shared with other *haredim*, or 'ultra-Orthodox Jews'. Small differences in clothing (sock length, buttons, ties or no ties) distinguish one sect from another. That they exist in such large numbers is almost miraculous, given the devastation suffered in World War II.

PALESTINE – A MESSIANIC OUTPOST

KABBALAH MYSTICISM DREW JEWS TO 16TH-CENTURY SAFED, YET THEY FORMED A MINORITY OF PALESTINE'S TOTAL POPULATION. WITHIN 300 YEARS, OTTOMAN NEGLECT LED TO ARAB REVOLT.

Perched on a hill overlooking the Sea of Galilee, Safed is one of the four holy cities to Jews, alongside Jerusalem, Hebron and Tiberias. Under Ottoman rule in the 16th century, it rapidly grew into the largest and most developed town in Palestine with the second-largest Jewish population in Asia. It also acted as a magnet for some of the greatest scholars in Jewish history. Here the Kabbalah, the main Jewish mystical tradition, truly developed – a phenomenon that gave comfort and guidance to millions, but also, in the wrong hands, spawned the false messiah movements that imperilled the Jewish faith everywhere.

Below Ceiling of the Abuhav Synagogue, Safed, built in the 16th century and full of mystical Kabbalistic imagery.

Right Mohammed Ali, Pasha of Egypt, whose actions sparked revolt in Palestine after 1834.

RABBI ISAAC LURIA – THE LION

More than any other, Rabbi Isaac Luria (1534–72) revolutionized Jewish thought with his new system of the Kabbalah. Known as the Ha-Ari, or 'The Lion', he was born in Jerusalem in 1534 to an Ashkenazi father and Sephardi mother. He studied Torah in Egypt, made a living as a spice merchant, and arrived in Safed in 1569 where he studied directly under the great Kabbalist, Moses Cordevero (1522–70). Yet while this teacher was a master of close textual analysis of the Zohar, the prime book of Jewish mysticism, his pupil went in another direction.

EXILE TO REDEMPTION

Rabbi Luria described how in the imperfect world after Creation, the *shekhina*, or 'divine presence', known as the indwelling spirit or the feminine aspect of God, is itself in exile. Redemption would come when exile ended. For many Jewish listeners, such ideas had relevance in the real world and excited messianic expectations. On a national level they suggested there would be a Jewish return to Palestine, or the Land of Israel.

Gentle-natured and intuitive, Luria wanted his doctrines kept secret, in case they were misinterpreted. Luria wrote little himself, but his protégé Haim Vital recorded his thoughts and fashioned Lurianic Kabbalah into an intricate system of moral and spiritual empowerment. After Luria died during an epidemic in 1572, aged 38, his disciples disseminated his works via the printing presses of Safed, Vilna, Constantinople and Livorno.

RISE AND DEMISE OF SAFED

Beyond the mystical, Safed became a thriving industrial centre based on manufactured cloth, which in the still-new Ottoman empire was a novelty. Wool was imported from Macedonia in the Balkans and

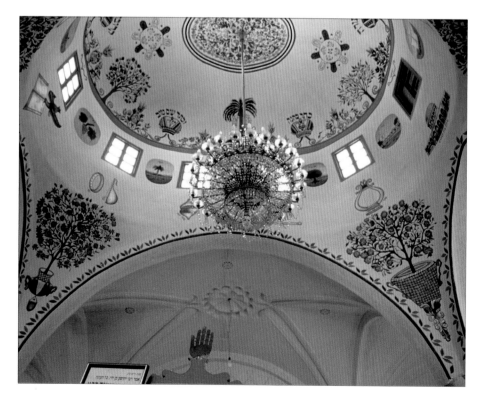

then shipped to the town of Safed by way of Sidon and Tripoli. In Safed, master weavers turned the wool into cloth that after dyeing was ready for export. Safed families also traded in food and spices with Lebanon and Syria, where there were active Jewish communities. Within Safed, Jews ran a close-knit welfare and administration system that tried to conform to Torah and Talmud precepts.

After the initial boom, problems began to emerge: Safed, like Jerusalem, Tiberias and Hebron, lacked an agricultural hinterland, thus limiting chances of expansion. New sultans neglected provincial towns, and some Turkish or Arab governors of Safed distrusted the town's Jews. Security deteriorated and robbers stalked the highways. In the mid-17th century an influx of zealous Shabbatean devotees, who had given away their worldly belongings, further strained Palestine's battered economy.

Below A 16th-century Torah scroll and traditional casket associated with Rabbi Isaac Luria, in Safed.

ASHKENAZIM IN PALESTINE

Poor Jews in Jerusalem badly needed aid, so *shlichim*, or 'emissaries', were sent from the Holy Land to wealthier Diaspora communities in Alexandria, Constantinople, Izmir and Ashkenazi centres. Diaspora Jews regarded *hallukah*, or 'donating charity', as an honour. Some, such as the esteemed Rabbi Isaiah Horowitz, personally immigrated; he settled in Jerusalem in 1620.

In 1740 the Muslim ruler of northern Palestine invited Haim Abulafia (1660–1744), Rabbi of Izmir, to rebuild the city of Tiberias. That same year the Ottoman Sultan Mahmud I allowed Christians to worship in Jerusalem, and come under the jurisdiction of their European homelands. Perhaps it was this ruling that encouraged more pious Ashkenazim to settle in 'Eretz Israel': first Hasidim from Belarus, Ukraine and Poland, and then, after 1780, Perushim, the 'separated ones' or disciples of the anti-Hassidic Vilna Gaon of Lithuania. By now Jerusalem had eclipsed Safed in importance.

SEEDLINGS OF JEWISH AND ARAB NATIONALISM

As of 1609 Palestine was subsumed within the province of Greater Syria; though Jerusalem was treated as a

Above Johann Gutenberg at work – his printing revolution of 1447 profoundly altered Jewish society too.

separate *sanjak*, or a district under a military governor. Most inhabitants of Palestine were neither Turkish nor Jewish, but Sunni Muslim Arabs. Like their Jewish co-residents, Palestinian Arabs loathed the Ottoman tax collectors; unlike them they often protested vigorously.

Their largest revolt came after the Egyptian ruler Mohammed Ali, a former Ottoman vassal, wrested Syria and Palestine from a weakened Turkey in 1831–41. In May 1834 Arab sheikhs from Nablus, Jerusalem and Hebron refused to offer Ali conscripts; they briefly took Jerusalem, Safed, Tiberias and Haifa. Ali and his son, the Egyptian army commander Ibrahim Pasha, eventually crushed the uprising. Arab historians call it the 'Syrian Peasant Revolt', although others detect the first strains of a specifically Palestinian Arab nationalism.

For their part, Jews also harboured nationalist dreams but they felt that return from exile should come from a divine agency. They generally favoured Ottoman rule of law, which helped bind one Diaspora community to another.

JEWS OF NORTH AFRICA AND THE MIDDLE EAST

FROM TIMBUKTU IN AFRICA TO BUKHARA IN CENTRAL ASIA, JEWS WERE DYNAMIC TRADERS, WHILE SEPHARDI IMMIGRANTS REVITALIZED ANCIENT LEVANTINE COMMUNITIES.

The Sephardi Jews who were exiled from the Iberian Peninsula at the end of the 15th century generally felt safe under Ottoman rule. They no longer needed to fear persecution, or hide their identity in public. However, later sultans and governors proved less accommodating than earlier ones, economic slowdown hampered scholastic development, and wars between Europe and Turkey interfered with ties between Jews in both zones. The first challenge facing Sephardim in the 16th century was how to co-exist with the old Jewish communities of North Africa and the Middle East.

Jewish merchants of the Ottoman empire from the 16th to the 19th centuries, transported merchandise to the great cities of Salonika and Constantinople, just as they had done under the Romans 1,500 years earlier. Jews were invaluable to commerce with Europe because many could speak German, French, Italian and Spanish.

Old Jewish firms in Muslim ports like Basra and Alexandria imported foreign products and exported raw materials. New Jewish-run industries, especially weaving, boomed in Salonika, Safed, Izmir and Algiers.

CAIRO

The Ottomans took Cairo in 1517, a year after occupying Jerusalem. There they encountered a mixed Jewish community, which included Sephardi descendants of the 12th-century Spanish scholar Maimonides. Spanish rabbis came to dominate synagogues, with only limited local *mughrabi* opposition. Sultan Selim I (1512–20) appointed Abraham Castro head of the Egyptian mint.

Sephardim settled in Alexandria, Cairo and Rosetta, as well as Damascus and Aleppo in Syria. They founded new yeshivas (rabbinical seminaries); poetry and rabbinic scholarship flourished to the benefit of Egypt and Palestine. Trade was revitalized in the

Above A 19th-century African Mizrah showing the direction of Jerusalem and blending Islamic art and Jewish symbols.

16th century as peace returned to the eastern Mediterranean and Maghreb (North Africa). Some immigrant Sephardi Jews benefited from the capitulation agreements that Sultan Suleyman (1520–66) signed with Venice and France to protect foreign citizens.

TUNISIA

Talmudic sages had arrived in Tunisia in the 2nd century and Jews built an esteemed yeshiva in Kairouan soon after Muslim Arabs established it as their fourth holiest city in 670. Spanish raids in the 16th century drove Jews inland and to the mountains, where they took refuge with Berber tribes. Only in the 17th century did Tunisia return to Ottoman control, and even then Tunisian *beys* (governors) enjoyed autonomy.

In the 17th and 18th centuries Italian Jews from Leghorn (Livorno), known colloquially as Grana, joined indigenous Judaeo-Arabic Jews and earlier refugees from Spain in the 'Berber states' of Tunisia, Algeria and

Left Lighting the candles in the ancient El-Ghriba synagogue on the Tunisian island of Djerba.

Right Jewish Wedding in Morocco, *Eugène Delacroix, 1841.*

Tripolitana (part of today's Libya). They were very European in their dress, attire, speech and habits. In Tunisia they enjoyed the company of the forcibly converted Spanish Muslims who were expelled from Spain in 1609, and who, like the Grana, spoke Spanish.

By contrast, the Jews of the island of Djerba claim descent from Israelites who fled Babylonian persecution. They held to customs that probably originated in First Temple times. Their El-Ghriba Synagogue, the oldest in Africa, is still active and attracts Jews and other pilgrims.

JOURNEY TO TIMBUKTU

Evidently, a thriving Jewish community once existed in the vital trading entrepôt of Timbuktu, Mali. Southern Moroccan Jews imported gold and salt from inner Africa through the city, and many settled there, including Sephardi refugees from Spain. Most later converted to Islam, though pockets remain who proudly recall their Jewish roots and are reviving Judaic traditions in the 21st century.

Below Jewish children in Hara Sghira, Tunisia, learn the Hebrew alphabet.

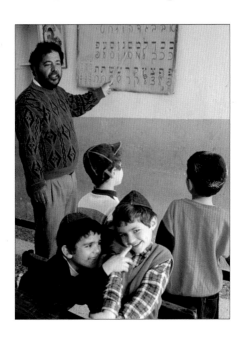

YEMEN

Jews were already established in Yemen in the 5th century, and in medieval times regularly sought rulings from Maimonides when he lived in Fustat in Cairo. Jews in Sana'a, the capital, kept close contact with the academies in Iraq. The port of Aden also became a vital transit point for lucrative Jewish trade with India.

The Turks conquered Yemen in 1546, but soon lost control of Sana'a to local sheikhs and Zaydi Shia imams who accused the Jews of helping the foreigners. During this period of incessant revolts and forced conversions, the great Yemenite Jewish poet Shalom Shabazi wrote his finest works, such as *Im Nin 'Alu* and *As'alk*.

PERSIAN JEWRY

Shia Persia lay outside the Ottoman realm, and resisted the Constantinople Caliphate's presumption to represent all Muslims. Many Persian Jews had generally suffered under the Shia regimes of the Safavid dynasty, so they welcomed the new Sunni dynast, Nadir Shah (1736–47). He settled numerous Jews in Mashad, a city where the community thrived as rug merchants. They bolstered state coffers by trading in silk and gems with other Jews in Mirv, Khiva, Samarkand and Bukhara in Central

Asia, and Herat in Afghanistan. Many thousands migrated to these imperial outposts as well as to Kurdistan, Egypt and India. Politically, Persian Jews served as negotiators between Sunni Turkestanis and Shia Iranians and had their own representatives in local government.

The fragility of Persian Jewish life was shown when the Qajar dynasty, which ruled Iran from 1796 until 1921, restored Shia ascendancy. They persecuted minorities and in 1839 – a century after Nadir Shah – forced the Jews of Mashad to convert to Islam. Elsewhere Jews were quarantined in separate neighbourhoods.

Paradoxically, Qajar excesses attracted the attention of Jews in the West who threw lifelines to their brethren in Persia. In 1865 French Jews represented by the educational association Alliance Israelite Universelle, and Sir Moses Montefiore, an influential English Sephardi philanthropist, interceded with ministers in Tehran to better the lot of Persian Jewry. This pattern was repeated in Ottoman territories.

Despite a promising start at the beginning of the 16th century, therefore, the Sephardim had to call on all their resources of ingenuity and perseverance to survive in often unstable conditions in North Africa and the Middle East over two centuries.

THE PARTITION OF POLAND

IN 1700 THE POLISH COMMONWEALTH DOMINATED CENTRAL EUROPE. BY 1800 POLAND HAD DISAPPEARED, AND JEWS WHO LIVED THERE FOUND THEMSELVES DIVIDED BETWEEN AUSTRIA, PRUSSIA AND RUSSIA.

A tiny band of Western Jews had played a key role, albeit unintentionally, in events leading to Poland's demise. These 'court Jews' of Germany and Austria were urban cosmopolitans who became closely connected to Europe's new breed of absolutist monarchs.

Absolutism arose out of the centralization of the state that began in the France of Cardinal Richelieu and Mazarin in the early 18th century. The new rulers attacked crafts guilds and church privileges that stood between the sovereign and the individual. They also mistrusted Jews, who seemed doubly alien in their language and religion. The absolutist strain showed itself even in liberal guise, during the French Revolution. Many Jews hoped to be considered equally Jewish and French, yet the state granted Jews everything as individuals, and nothing as a 'nation'. Court Jews realized, however, that there was

space within this secular ideology for advancement. Guilds that barred Jews were now powerless, as religious denomination was no longer a hindrance to entry. An individual's worth depended on his or her contribution to the state's well-being, not upon birth, faith or origin.

CONTROLLED SOCIETIES

Instead of excluding Jews from society, as in medieval times, absolutists wanted to make them 'useful' to the state treasury. A 1750 Prussian regulation ensured that Jews had to register their homes and businesses, and that their weddings were supervised. If they obeyed, they were 'protected'; if not, they could be demoted to 'useless' citizens and deported. In practice the new dispensation made privileged Jews richer and other Jews poorer. The latter were forced to work as old-style moneylenders, pedlars or pawnbrokers.

The Edict of Toleration issued in January 1782 by the Holy Roman Emperor of Austria, Joseph II (1765–90) best illustrated absolutism at work. On the one hand, his law decreed that Jews no longer had to wear demeaning badges of ethnic identification or pay the onerous *leibzoll* (body tax) when they entered an area that customarily banned them. On the other, they had to adopt German-style forenames and surnames and were liable for state military service. In addition, Jews were barred from using Hebrew or

Left German, Polish and East European spice boxes to mark the end of Sabbath, 18th–19th centuries.

Above Catherine the Great, Empress of Russia, 1762–96, under whose reign a million Polish Jews became Russian subjects when borders changed.

Yiddish in commercial and communal records, and rabbis lost their juridical autonomy.

Although discriminatory, the law marked an advance. All Jews had been evicted from Vienna in 1670 (though most soon returned) and they had faced severe persecution under Maria Teresa in Bohemia and Moravia in 1745. Emperor Joseph had argued that toleration would serve the 'betterment of Jews' and would make them 'less harmful' to general European society. Other Enlightenment figures followed the ideas of the English social theorist John Toland, whose book *Reasons for Naturalising the Jews in Great Britain* (1714) argued that Jewish culture is intrinsically positive and productive. Toland believed that the Jewish masses, not only the rich, could benefit from the general community.

COURT JEWS

The new Court Jews applied themselves systematically to their tasks and were openly rewarded as a result. Samson Wertheimer (1658–1724), chief rabbi of Hungary and Moravia, and financier to Austrian Emperor Leopold I (1658–1705), for example, made large loans to government during the war with Turkey and purchased numerous palaces and gardens. He also built hospitals, distributed charity in Europe and Palestine, and helped establish 40 Jewish congregations in Hungary.

LOOMING CRISES FOR POLES AND JEWS

The heyday of the Polish empire was long past; in fact, Poland never completely recovered from the Chmielnicki uprising of 1648–54, or the invasions of Russia and Sweden that followed. Powerful nobles, moreover, refused to cede power either to King Stanislaus II (1764–95) or to Commonwealth citizens. They blocked attempts at reform and created a crisis of administration. By the mid-18th century Poland was threatened by neighbours on three sides: Prussia in the north, Austria in the south, and Russia in the east.

THREE PARTITIONS

The three partitions of Poland effectively severed connections between Jewish communities in both towns and regions. The first, of 1772, awarded much of White Russia

(Belorussia), to Russia, while Austria gained Galicia, and Prussia received Pomerania. Parliament duly passed a progressive Polish constitution in 1791 and some nobles and intellectuals began calling for Jews to receive civil equality. However, Empress Catherine of Russia sabotaged the venture by sending in troops to reinforce the old order. This prompted the second partition, of July 1793, whereby Russia gained half of Volhynia, all of Podolia and the remaining part of Ukraine. Prussia, meanwhile, seized Greater Poland (Poznan).

The Kosciusko Uprising erupted in 1794 when Poles tried to defend their rights against their new Russian imperial masters. One Jewish merchant from Lithuania, Berek Joselewicz, formed a Jewish Brigade. Their 500-man unit was an entirely new concept for the age, and a sign that some Jews, at least, were willing to take up arms for the cause of society as a whole. The unit was wiped out just east of Warsaw, but their bravery and commitment, both as Poles and as Jews, impressed many gentiles.

Left Interior of the Remuh Synagogue, first built in 1554, one of the oldest Jewish structures in Krakow, Poland.

Above Fiddler on the Roof, by Carl Spitzweg, 1880 – often taken as symbolizing the precarious nature of Jewish life in eastern Europe.

Although the uprising collapsed, Joselewicz survived to fight in the Napoleonic Wars, leading to the third Polish partition of 1795. Now Prussia gained the remainder of Poland, including Warsaw; Austria took Galicia and Krakow; and all of Lithuania and its 250,000 Jews passed over to Russia.

RUSSIAN RULE

At a stroke, nearly a million Jews came under Russian rule. At first Empress Catherine defined Jews as part of the town population and even granted them the municipal vote. However, the Russian statute of 1804 reiterated that Jews needed to be 'improved' before they deserved political rights, and ordered Jews to leave all villages within four years, lest they corrupt the peasants by selling them alcohol. It seemed as if history had again played a cruel trick, for just as western Europe was embracing the Enlightenment, eastern Jews found themselves ruled by despotic Tsars. Some nobles and intellectuals began calling for Jews to receive civil equality.

REVOLUTIONARY TIMES

DESPITE THEIR SMALL NUMBERS AND ALMOST ACCIDENTAL ORIGINS, JEWS
FOUGHT IN AMERICA'S 1776 WAR OF INDEPENDENCE. SOON AFTERWARDS,
THE FRENCH REVOLUTION ENCOURAGED HOPE IN THE OLD WORLD, TOO.

Today the United States of America houses seven million Jews, the largest single Jewish community in the world. By contrast there were barely 2,000 Jews in North America when English settlers declared their independence from Britain in 1776.

NEW WORLD STIRRINGS
A desire for liberty inspired the earliest Jewish migrants to North America. Jews were admitted as burghers (town citizens) and in 1654 they set up their first congregation, She'arit Israel, or 'Remnant of Israel', in New Amsterdam. The city was renamed New York in 1665, and ceded to the English in 1674.

Meanwhile, Rhode Island, founded as an outpost of religious freedom in 1643, attracted 15 Sephardi families from the West Indies to its

Below Touro Synagogue, Rhode Island, built in 1763 and the oldest Jewish house of worship in the USA.

Right John Adams, a founding father of the USA, whose ambiguous views on Jews reflected that of many Americans.

leading town, Newport, in 1658. Almost immediately they set up Congregation Jeshurat Israel and built the first permanent synagogue in North America in 1763. It was named Touro after its dynamic spiritual leader, Isaac Touro.

OLD TESTAMENT PURITANS
Mid-18th-century North America was a patchwork quilt of mostly coastal European colonies – French, Spanish, English, Swedish and Dutch – dotted among a majority population of Native Americans. Most of the English settlers were devout Nonconformist Protestants called Puritans, and although there were hardly any Jews among them, they felt strongly attached to Jewish mores. They likened their departure from England to the flight of the Israelites from Egypt, with the king

cast as pharaoh and America as the Promised Land. Hebrew was widely taught at Yale, Harvard and Princeton universities, and nearly half the 1655 legal code of New Haven quoted from the Hebrew Bible, or Old Testament.

SEEDS OF REVOLUTION
English settlers steadily edged out European rivals, especially after New England colonies united as the Massachusetts Bay Colony in 1691. However, tensions with the mother country culminated in the 1773 tax revolt known as the Boston Tea Party, and finally the Declaration of Independence of 1776. Jews fought on both sides in the resulting war, but overwhelmingly for the rebels. As a community, Jews anticipated more freedom to worship, less interference and better opportunities away from the monarchy.

GUARANTEES OF FREEDOM
Pious and God-fearing though America's founding fathers were, their constitution chose to separate church from state and guaranteed freedom of worship. Legislation did not mention Jews specifically, which was almost an advantage. In Europe, 'enlightened despots' were pushing through supposedly emancipating

Above Decree instituting freedom of worship in France, 1799, showing non-Catholic recipients, including a Jew.

laws that often forced integration. Such rulings reinforced historical prejudices about a dominant culture and religion, which were absent in American law.

American politicians nonetheless felt ambivalent about Jews. John Adams, for instance, wrote that they were 'the most glorious nation that ever inhabited the earth.' Yet he also remarked: 'It is very hard work to love most of them', and he hoped their 'asperities and peculiarities of culture' would be worn away.

LIFE IN THE *ANCIEN REGIME*
In France, life was precarious under the royal system that preceded the 1789 Revolution. Formally France had been closed to Jews since 1394, but for pragmatic reasons successive kings ignored the presence of Jewish communities. Paris did not object, for example, when Maranos fled Spain after the Inquisition and introduced chocolate-making to the south-western town of Bayonne.

Maranos still faced discrimination when they revealed their Jewish identity, and, despite royal proclamations that guaranteed Jews security after 1550, it briefly became illegal to harbour or even speak to them in 1615. The community's make-up changed when anti-Semitic troubles in Provence drove Jews northwards and the Sun King Louis XIV annexed Alsace and Lorraine from Germany. France simultaneously gained a large number of Ashkenazim and a fierce local strain of anti-Semitism. The royal court did, however, abolish the poll-tax on Jews in 1785 and allowed them to settle anywhere in the country.

Intellectuals had nurtured ideas of 'liberty, equality and fraternity' since the early 1700s. After the Revolution of 1789, France's new rulers sought to put the ideas into practice and challenge the monarchies of the day. Many European regimes fell in France's post-revolutionary wars, which, to many Jews, seemed to offer new hope for freedom.

PARTIAL LIBERATION
The Revolution of 1789 had a dramatic effect in France and beyond. That August, the new National Assembly declared that 'no man shall be molested for his beliefs', and in September 1791 it enfranchised all Jews. Revolutionary leaders such as Count Mirabeau and Abbe Gregoire argued strongly for Jewish emancipation. When France's revolutionary army expelled the Pope from Rome in 1798, it broke down the ghetto walls and revoked local laws that restricted Jews.

NAPOLEON'S REFORMS
Throughout this period, reformers were puzzled by two questions: were Jews a religion or a people; and, depending on that answer, should they be accepted or forced to change? Napoleon, who seized power in 1799 and crowned himself emperor in 1804, saw Jews as a distinct nation. Yet he also wanted Jews integrated into France, so he convened an Assembly of Jewish Notables in 1806, dubbed the New Sanhedrin, and in 1807 he classed Judaism as an official religion of France. Two years later, however, he concentrated all Jewish affairs in the hands of a central consistory in Paris. Napoleon's 'Infamous Decree' of 1808 annulled debts owed to Jews, leading to widespread bankruptcy. Thus, what began with emancipation ended with restrictions reminiscent of medieval times.

Below Napoleon reinstates Jewish rights, in an idealized depiction by François Louis Couché, 1806.

THE RUSSIAN PALE OF SETTLEMENT

DRAMATIC BORDER CHANGES MEANT THAT, OVERNIGHT, JEWS OF POLAND AND LITHUANIA FOUND THEMSELVES UNDER RUSSIAN RULE. GIVEN THE TSARS' FIERCE REPUTATION, THIS PROVOKED MUCH FEAR.

From a small, landlocked 15th-century Christian principality, cut off from Western civilization, Russia grew into the largest country on earth. Today it covers nearly 6.6 million square miles, stretching from the Baltic in northern Europe to the Sea of Japan in the East. Still larger was the Tsarist empire of which Russia was the rump: it accounted for fully one-sixth of the earth's land surface.

JEWS OF OLD RUSSIA
Small pockets of Jews had existed in what is now Russia, possibly even from First Temple times. Some 4th-century Armenian cities had Jewish populations of up to 30,000; other Jews lived in the Crimea; and the large Khazar khanate adopted Judaism until the Rus (proto-Russians) of Kiev defeated them in 969.

Below Founded in 1794, the multi-ethnic southern Russian port of Odessa became a magnet for Jews.

Kiev had a Jewish quarter from the 11th century and there are records of their contacts with fellow Jews in Babylonia. Persian Jewish traders, the Radhanites, traversed Russian territory along the route from Europe to China, and other Jews may have lived in parts of north-eastern Russia during the 12th century. In the 14th century Lithuanians took over parts of western Russia, where they granted privileges to Jews. However, under Ivan IV the Terrible (1533–84) Russia recaptured territory and began treating Jews harshly, forcing some to convert.

The Duchy of Muscovy – the kernel from which Russia grew - shook off its Tartar overlords and laid claim to all ethnic Russian lands in 1480. Soon afterwards it declared its capital, Moscow, an Orthodox Christian 'Third Rome' and barred entrance to any 'enemies of faith' – Jew, Muslim, pagan or even Catholic.

Above The Pale was a place of confinement and state restrictions, yet it also incubated a vibrant Jewish culture.

POLISH JEWS IN RUSSIA
When Moscow captured part of Ukraine in 1727 it cleared the area of Jews. For most Polish and Lithuanian Jews the threat of Moscow seemed notional until the first partition of Poland in 1772 gave Russia large swathes of formerly Polish land. The largest transfer of land and people occurred with the second (1793) and third (1795) partitions, when at a stroke Russia 'inherited' nearly a million Jews.

From the start, Russia discriminated against her newly acquired Jewish subjects. By 1791, though, she had learnt that Jews could benefit trade and administration, so she encouraged them to settle in southern territories that Russia had wrested from the Ottomans. When Lithuania passed to Russia in 1795, Tsar Alexander I (1801–25) added it to an area known as the Pale of Settlement.

LIFE IN THE PALE
The Pale was a zone within which Jews could live but not leave. The dimensions of the Pale stabilized around 1812. It included two provinces adjoining the Black Sea: Bessarabia (now Moldova) along the Dnieper in the west, and Taurida in the east.

Right Traditional life. Riding to market in Piaski, eastern Poland, 1979, once part of the Jewish Pale of Settlement.

The former included the towns of Kishinev and Khotin, and the latter, Sebastopol and Yalta on the Crimean Peninsula. Ultimately the Pale continued in one form or another until the fall of Tsarist Russia in 1917.

FORCED ASSIMILATION

After 1794, Jews in the Pale paid double rates of taxes compared to Christian town dwellers. At times they were banned from certain major towns, including Kiev and Sebastopol. They were also encouraged to live in *shtetls*, or 'small towns', and excluded from running inns or living in the countryside, where as estate managers many had made their living. All these policies increased destitution, and Jewish charities struggled to support the needy.

Conversely, Russia opened public schools to Jews in 1804 in the hope of encouraging them to assimilate, learn Russian and become 'useful' subjects. Many Polish and Lithuanian Jews carried passes allowing them to trade in Russian cities beyond the Pale. Furthermore, other Jews lived semi-secretly in Russian towns, confident that inefficient officials would not enforce the law or might ignore them for a fee.

NICHOLAS I'S CRACKDOWN

When Tsar Nicholas I (1825–55) took power, tolerance gave way to a commitment to destroy Jewish life. In his first year as tsar, Nicholas ordered all Jewish males aged 12 or over to be conscripted into the Russian army where they would spend decades of their life. He had in mind social engineering on a grand scale, whereby Jews would forget their religion and stop speaking Yiddish. He also encouraged Jews to resettle on agricultural land in southern Russia.

Because Jews had not flocked to state schools as intended, in 1844 Moscow decided to create special schools for Jews 'to bring them nearer to Christians and to uproot their harmful beliefs which are influenced by the Talmud'. At the same time the Government disbanded Polish-style Jewish communal structures and replaced them with a state-approved system. Jews could no longer wear traditional clothes or grow *pe'ot*, or 'sidelocks', of Orthodox Jews. Exemptions from the worst restrictions were granted to 'useful' Jews, such as the wealthier merchants.

A RUSSIAN THAW

When Nicholas died he was replaced by the apparently more amenable Alexander II (1855–81). Alexander had abolished serfdom in 1861, but he was less liberal regarding minorities. He forbade Jews from hiring Christian servants, restricted their travel rights and insisted they could own no land. In short, his rule did not bring the hoped-for emancipation that Jews west of Russia were, by then, starting to enjoy.

Right Bust of the Vilna Gaon, fulcrum of the 18th-century Jewish community, in present-day Vilnius, Lithuania.

JEWS OF LITHUANIA

Separated from Russia itself, Lithuania was home to a now thriving Jewish community with a distinctive identity. Some, it seems, came originally from Babylon and Palestine around the 8th century, but probably most were descended from German Ashkenazim who fled eastwards after the 12th century. Their population grew rapidly, up to 250,000 in 1792. Living alongside them was a sizeable population of dissident Karaite Jews, mostly transported to Troki in Lithuania from the Crimea.

18TH-CENTURY MODERNITY

UNTIL 1800, MOST EUROPEAN JEWS WERE BARRED FROM CLUBS, UNIVERSITIES, POLITICAL OFFICE AND MANY OCCUPATIONS. SLOWLY, AS MONARCHIES BEGAN TO LOSE THEIR GRIP, JEWS STARTED TO LIBERATE THEMSELVES.

A century of European intellectual creativity led acculturated Jews to expect social acceptance. So they were disappointed to learn that several Enlightenment thinkers had deep anti-Jewish prejudices. Voltaire, for example, called Jews 'the greatest scoundrels who ever sullied the face of the globe…our masters and our enemies… the most abominable people in the world.'

On the other hand, the German playwright, freethinker and critic Gotthold Lessing consistently defended Jews against attack. As his model for the learned and humane Jewish sage in his play *Nathan the Wise*, he chose his friend Moses Mendelssohn (1729–86), the leader of what became known as the Haskalah (Jewish Enlightenment).

MOSES MENDELSSOHN
Born a hunchback and the son of a poor rabbi and scribe, Moses Mendelssohn learnt Torah, Talmud and Maimonides as a child, as well

Above Moses Mendelssohn (left) plays chess with dramatist Gotthold Lessing, 1771; painted in 1856.

as the secular disciplines of Latin and mathematics. He was highly regarded in German circles and his philosophical work *Phaedon* earned him the title the German Socrates. However, Jewish critics said that by trying to make Judaism acceptable to Christians, Mendelssohn merely encouraged assimilation. He remained an Orthodox Jew all his life, but all his grandchildren were baptized after his death, including the brilliant composers Felix Mendelssohn and Fanny Mendelssohn-Bartholdy.

THE HASKALAH
Arising from a desire to counter anti-semitism by showing the value of Jewish learning, the Jewish Enlightenment was known as the Haskalah. Jewish *maskilim*, or 'followers of Haskalah', were also aware that there may be faults within Judaism and Jewry. The Haskalah thus pulled in two directions: towards assimilation into general society, and towards defining a Jewish identity to complement and perhaps replace religion as a binding force. Haskalah ideas inspired the birth of Reform Judaism, which sought to modernize worship and allow Jews to adopt the culture wherever they lived.

Mendelssohn felt that gentiles would only embrace Jews as equals if they engaged with current intellectual developments. Born in Dessau, Saxony, he wanted to share Hebrew literary treasures with non-Jews and with Jews who knew no

Left Fanny Mendelssohn-Bartholdy (1805–47), composer, sister of Felix and granddaughter of Moses Mendelssohn.

Hebrew. He tried to revive Hebrew as a spoken language, and translated the Hebrew Bible into the finest German. At the same time he believed Judaism should shed its medieval superstitions and overly ritualistic elements. Like Maimonides before him, he saw no contradiction between religious belief and critical reason, and his works *Jerusalem* and *Morning Hours* explain Judaism as a coherent ethical system.

MENDELSSOHN'S LEGACY
Moses Mendelssohn generously supported *maskilim*, including Solomon Maimon (1754–1800), a Lithuanian-born philosopher whose 1790 work *Transcendental Philosophy* was praised by Emmanuel Kant as the most penetrating of all critiques. In 1784 neo-Hebraists in Germany, Austria and Poland founded an influential periodical called *Ha-Me'assef* (The Collector), while Leopold Zunz (1794–1886) launched a methodical approach to studying Jewish history and literature called *Wissenschaft des Judentums*, or 'The Science of Judaism'. His followers included David Luzzatto in Italy (1800–65) and Salomon Munk in France (1803–67).

THE REFORM MOVEMENT

THE 19TH-CENTURY MOVEMENT CALLED REFORM JUDAISM MARKED THE MOST RADICAL DEPARTURE FROM TRADITIONAL JEWISH BELIEF AND PRACTICE TO DATE, AND SPREAD FROM GERMANY TO ENGLAND AND THE USA.

Reform developed out of Haskalah and aimed to integrate Jews into Europe, bring Judaism up to date with scientific developments and win back those who felt alienated from traditional religion. The idea was to jettison 'obsolete' ritual such as dress codes that attracted suspicion from outsiders, while maintaining and promoting Judaism's ethical core. Reform was thus a natural and perhaps inevitable response to long-brewing cultural developments in Western Jewish society.

NEW METHODS

Reform Jews held services in local vernacular languages. They called their synagogues temples and imitated churches by using choirs and music. Men and women were seated together in prayer, not divided by a *mechitza*, or 'barrier', or segregated into upper and lower floors.

Services were generally shorter and more disciplined affairs than those held in traditional 'shuls' or 'shtiebls'. The centrepiece was a sermon delivered by a rabbi attired in churchlike garb. As in a church, the pulpit assumed prominence.

DOCTRINAL REVOLUTION

Reform abandoned what it saw as obsolete laws that only applied in Temple times. Followers questioned that the Torah came from heaven and they rejected the belief in a personal Messiah, resurrection of the dead, return to the Holy Land and the rebuilding of the Temple. They emphasized the prophetic and lyrical (psalm) tradition rather than the legalistic Talmud and Pentateuch.

Reformists also saw Jews as loyal citizens of their states, rather than as a nation in exile.

THE SPREAD OF REFORM

Israel Jacobsohn was the first rabbi to introduce ceremonial reforms in a synagogue established at Seesen, Germany, in 1810. Another pioneer institution was the Hamburg Temple of 1818. Samuel Hirsch gave the movement a philosophical basis, and the great Haskalah scholar Abraham Geiger lent his support. Perhaps the most important Reform journal was *Allgemeine Zeitung des Judenthums*, edited by Ludwig Philippson.

Although mainly an Ashkenazi phenomenon, Reform appealed to those Sephardi Jews detached from traditional practices. The first Reform synagogue in London began as a breakaway from the Sephardi flagship

Below Shielded from street view, as then required by Austrian law, and built in 1824–6, Vienna's Stadttempel (city temple) later adopted the Reform liturgy.

Above Abraham Geiger, Reform rabbi pioneer and expert on Judaic influence on Christianity and Islam, 1865.

synagogue, Bevis Marks, in 1841. Other synagogues appeared in Bradford and Manchester, and Reform spawned satellite congregations in Hungary and the USA where it is now the largest US Jewish denomination.

DEBATE AND CRITICISM

At German Rabbinical conferences in the 1840s a split developed between those who wanted profound change and a majority who worried that Reform was becoming estranged from mainstream Jews. One prominent radical was Samuel Holdheim (1806–60), whose Berlin temple transferred the Sabbath from Saturday to Sunday to match Christian practice. Most congregations decided not to go so far. Some traditionalists, now defined as Orthodox, feared that Reform was halfway towards conversion to Christianity or lapsing into atheism.

In between the two poles were responses that adopted certain Reform features – such as a quizzical attitude to divine authorship. Examples include the Neo-Orthodox school of Samson Raphael Hirsch in Frankfurt, the Neologs in Hungary, and, later, the US Conservative and Reconstructionist (synagogue) trends.

JEWS AND COMMERCE – THE ROTHSCHILDS

IN THE 19TH CENTURY THE ROTHSCHILD NAME EXEMPLIFIED WEALTH AND SUCCESS, AND SO IT REMAINS TODAY. THEIR STORY IS ONLY ONE CHAPTER IN THE STORY OF JEWISH FINANCIAL PROWESS.

Above Baron Lionel de Rothschild, banker, and first professing Jew elected to Britain's parliament, 1836.

From modest origins in the back streets of 18th-century Frankfurt am Main the Rothschild family rose to become the byword for financial ingenuity and commercial success worldwide. Apart from their original banking venture the family's interests have embraced such diverse fields as art patronage, politics, diplomacy, textiles, scientific innovation, oil exploration, engineering works, wine-making and philanthropy. And, while the Rothschild saga is exceptional, it throws light on the challenges and achievements of other Jewish enterprises, large and small.

THE FIRST ROTHSCHILD

The story begins with Mayer Amschel Rothschild (1744–1812), a coin and art dealer who was appointed Crown Agent to the Principality of Hesse-Hanau in 1769. In 1785 Mayer's

Below Five sons of Mayer Rothschild, each of whom ran a bank branch in a major European financial centre.

employer, Prince William, inherited the largest private fortune in Europe. In time Mayer used his hard-won post to launch his own career in banking after working at the Oppenheim banking house in Hanover. By 1785 he could afford a large house, which he shared with his wife, Guttele Schnapper, and their five sons.

In the early 1800s Mayer expanded his business and set up interdependent banking branches in five major cities, as a deliberate policy of spreading influence and facilitating pan-European links. One son headed each branch: Frankfurt, Vienna, London, Naples and Paris. The bank adopted a crest showing five arrows shooting out in different directions.

INDEPENDENT FINANCIERS

Initially the Rothschilds followed the example of earlier court Jews, like the Wertheimers and Oppenheimers, except that they spread their interests and acted independently, not so much servants of a prince but masters of their own affairs.

By transcending borders while keeping the business within the family, the Rothschilds arguably founded the first transnational corporation. Thus they insured themselves against the dangers of a change of ruler, as had happened in 1737 when Joseph Oppenheimer's patron, Duke Karl Alexander of Wurttemberg, died and jealous rivals sent Joseph to the gallows the next year.

The Rothschilds' early achievements owe much to a happy twist of fate: the moving of the Anti-Napoleonic League's financial centre to Frankfurt from Amsterdam, which

had fallen to France. After the Congress of Vienna (1815), which marked Napoleon's defeat by English and Prussian forces, the Rothschilds extended their business into most European states. They made loans to governments, issued state bonds, liquidated inflated paper currencies, founded floating public debts and funded post-Napoleonic war (1815) reconstruction projects. The Austrian emperor made all five brothers peers by 1822, and from 1815 to 1828 their capital rose from 3.2 million francs to 118.4 million.

ENGLISH BRANCH

Nathan Mayer Rothschild played a pivotal role in his family's banking success, though he was originally sent to Manchester as a textile merchant in 1798, aged 21. He sold English cloth to Europe until Napoleon's blockade threatened English exports. In 1811 he founded the brokering house N.M. Rothschild. The Rothschild family was soon handling most English financial dealings with the Continent. Nathan's branch funded the British war effort against Napoleon and supplied Wellington's troops with gold before the Battle of Waterloo in 1815.

Between 1818 and 1835 Nathan Mayer issued 26 British and foreign government loans. In 1824 he floated the Alliance Assurance Company and the following year he helped the Bank of England avoid a liquidity crisis. His own dedication to work was legendary and his marriage to the well-connected Hannah Barent Cohen afforded him a network of business contacts. Like his father he was famously discreet, and used similarly cautious agents to courier funds through Napoleonic France. Above all, he understood the value of accurate and speedy information. His private intelligence service learnt the outcome of the Battle of Waterloo a day before the British Government.

Two of Nathan's descendants were path-breakers in British politics, the first being Lionel de Rothschild, who in 1858 became the first professing Jew to enter parliament. In fact, he was first elected in 1847, 11 years earlier, but he refused to take the Christian oath of entrance and so was barred from the chamber. Only when parliament allowed him to swear on the Hebrew Bible did he take his seat. In 1885 Sir Nathan Mayer

Below The Rothschild Family at Prayer *by the German Jewish painter Moritz Daniel Oppenheim.*

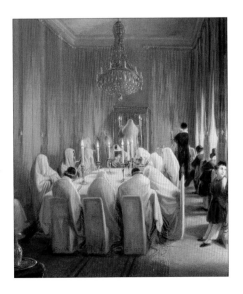

Right Waddesdon Manor, Buckinghamshire, the Rothschild country estate built 1874–89.

Rothschild II entered the House of Lords as the first Jewish peer and established a baronetcy in his family's name.

THE INDUSTRIALISTS

The Rothschilds realized the potential of technological innovation. Salomon Rothschild (1774–1855), head of the Vienna banking branch, built Austria's first railway system. James Mayer de Rothschild (1792–1868), founder of the French branch, played a dominant role in transforming 19th-century France into a major industrial power. He financed mining enterprises and helped found the French railway consortium Chemin de Fer du Nord in 1845. Other Rothschilds backed the newly formed mining conglomerate Rio Tinto Zinc in 1873 and advanced the British Government the money needed to purchase the Suez Canal in 1875.

BEYOND BANKING

Nathan's son Nathaniel (1812–70) moved to Paris, set up a second French branch and acquired a vineyard whose Château Mouton Rothschild wines are among the best in the world.

After the Russian pogroms of the 1880s, Baron Edmond James de Rothschild (1845–1934) set up the Jewish Colonization Association that established 12 settlements in Palestine. Baron Lionel Walter Rothschild was the addressee of the 1917 Balfour Declaration that committed Britain to establishing a 'national home for the Jewish people' in Palestine.

VENTURE CAPITALISTS IN A CHANGING WORLD

Apart from the Rothschilds, Jewish families such as the Warburgs, Mendelssohns and Bleichroeders pioneered merchant banking to meet changing economic needs. Railways were a fruitful source of enterprise: during 1850-70 Samuel Poliakov developed Russia's network, while the Paris-based Maurice de Hirsch (1831–1896) made a fortune in Turkey, Austria and the Balkans. Jews also capitalized American railroads and developed joint stock institutions such as Deutsche Bank, founded in 1870.

Such entrepreneurship built on older traditions of financial innovation. In medieval Baghdad and Cairo Jews had devised *jahbadhiyya*, a system that distributed risk by tying state loans to the savings of the entire Jewish merchant class. Spanish Jews spread to Venice and France other Islamic ideas, such as the cheque (*sakh*) and bill of exchange (*suftaya*). Jewish refugees boosted the prosperity of 16th-century Livorno, Italy, as well as Marseilles, Bordeaux and Rouen in 17th- and 18th-century France. The Henriques family helped found the Bank of England in 1694 and the Ashkenazi Goldsmid banking family joined their Sephardi brethren in the City of London.

In time other Jews realized the potential of a consumer culture. Levi Strauss (1829–1902) invented denim jeans in the US and built a thriving textile business; while in Manchester, England, the Belarus-born Michael Marks (1859–1907) and gentile Thomas Spencer formed in 1894 Marks & Spencers, one of the first major retail chains.

CHAPTER 8

REVOLUTION AND EMANCIPATION

While Jewish civil emancipation proceeded at a snail's pace after the 1815 Congress of Vienna, access to education created a generation of individual Jews whose contributions to art, music, science and politics became considerable. By the late 19th century formal emancipation was achieved, but anti-Semitic factions still survived. Within the community, Orthodox and conservative leaders worried that new liberties might encourage total assimilation, even the disappearance of Judaism itself. Meanwhile in eastern Europe, Jews lacked the opportunities enjoyed in Paris, Berlin or London. Thousands of Russian and Polish Ashkenazi Jews left for America, the 'golden land'. Likewise, Sephardi Jews began deserting an Ottoman empire in decline. Of the Jews who stayed behind, many believed that the betterment of their people was impossible until the whole of society changed. Jews thus flocked to ideologies including Marxism, socialism, and nationalism. Gradually a new strand emerged, Zionism, which sought to 'solve the Jewish problem' by transplanting Diaspora Jews back to the historic Land of Israel, in Palestine.

Opposite An Ashkenazi Rabbi of Jerusalem, *by G.S. Hunter. As the 19th century unfolded, figures of Orthodoxy came under attack from within the Jewish community.*

Above A bustling street scene in New York, 1890s. Jewish immigrants from Russia and Poland flocked to the city that seemed to offer a chance for new beginnings.*

EMANCIPATION AND REVOLUTIONARIES

THE FRENCH REVOLUTION RAISED JEWISH HOPES OF ACCEPTANCE INTO CIVIL SOCIETY. BUT THE FIGHT FOR EMANCIPATION WAS LONG AND HARD, WHICH LED SOME JEWS TO ADOPT MORE RADICAL APPROACHES.

The forces unleashed in the French Revolution could not be contained within the country's borders. By August 1792, France declared war on Austria and the republican Girondin party wanted to spread revolution to the whole of Europe. In the spirit of Jacques Rousseau, the Continent would 'be forced to be free'. The major emissary of this new freedom was Napoleon Bonaparte.

Jews throughout Europe greeted Napoleon as a liberator, and many joined French troops and local radicals as they literally tore down the ghetto walls. Some dreamt that the Russian Pale of Settlement – arguably the largest ghetto of all – would fall, too, as French troops marched towards Moscow in 1812.

Below The Berlin Revolt of 1848, in which Jews died fighting for their freedom alongside Christian citizens.

It was not to be: Napoleon failed in Russia and ultimately lost the Battle of Waterloo in 1815.

THE OLD ORDER RETURNS

Coinciding with Napoleon's last defeat, the Congress of Vienna (1814–15) restored many royals to power. While Jews retained their liberties in Belgium and Holland, in Austria and Italy's papal states, ghettoes were re-established. In Germany – still a loose confederation of 39 states – Jews gained some rights in 1815, though not yet full freedom.

EMANCIPATION IN ENGLAND

English emancipation continued at a gentler pace. As early as 1740, parliament allowed 'foreign Protestants and others' in Britain's American colonies to be naturalized after seven years' residence. In 1753, parliament voted for naturalization in England itself, but backed down after a public outcry.

Above Ferdinand Lassalle, a Jewish socialist who advocated general social change above specifically Jewish concerns.

Only in 1826 could Jews become full citizens. Isaac Goldsmid was the first Jew to receive a hereditary title in 1841. A parliamentary act in 1845 allowed Jews to enter municipal office, and in 1855 Sir David Salomons was elected as London's first Jewish Lord Mayor. Fuller political emancipation only arrived in 1858 when Lionel Rothschild was allowed to sit in the House of Commons without taking a Christian oath.

REFORM AND REVOLUTION

Across the Channel, France adopted a constitutional monarchy in July 1830, and soon officially recognized Judaism. Four years on, Jews sat in the French parliament.

Yet not all European Jews welcomed the prospect of emancipation. Traditionalists feared losing the autonomy that preserved religious life. Some supporters of the Haskalah (Jewish Enlightenment) warned that integration might erode Jews' identity.

Many Jews felt that tolerance was not enough, and society needed radical reform. They joined Christian co-citizens in a spate of revolutions that rocked Paris, Berlin, Vienna, Budapest, Rome and Venice in 1848. They demanded equal rights and written constitutions. It seemed that Enlightenment values had triumphed: Europe's rising middle class came to accept Jews in public office (until then a taboo). Emperor Franz Joseph of Austria (1848–1916) stated in 1849: 'political and civil rights are not based on religion'.

The philosopher Karl Marx came from a Jewish family that had converted to Christianity. His grandfathers were rabbis in Trier and Holland. In 1848 Marx (1818–83) published his *Communist Manifesto* and announced an ideology that would alter the course of history. Marx attacked Jewish traders as a group that 'worshipped money', and later extended his critique to the entire capitalist class. Many Jews defended his apparently anti-Semitic attack as an ironical plea for the economic liberation of Jews.

EMANCIPATION ACHIEVED

Many of the gains of 1848 were temporary: in 1851 Prussia abolished its liberal constitution, which had promised greater democratic free-

Below Paul Reuter (1816–99), son of a German rabbi, set up Reuters News Agency in London, 1851, spurring on the communications revolution.

HEINRICH HEINE

'Where one burns books, one will, in the end, burn people.' So said Heinrich Heine, the archetypal combination of German patriot and radical Jewish humanist. Born in Düsseldorf in 1797, he yearned for 'the emancipation of the whole world'. He was an early devotee of revolutionary socialism and probably influenced the young Karl Marx.

Paradoxically, he lampooned Jews who chose conversion, 'the entrance ticket to European society', yet he became a Christian himself in 1825. Heine once blamed Judaism for developing 'the fault-finding with human beings'. And he had no respect for Reform Jews who tried to turn 'a little Protestant Christianity into a Jewish company'. Later he rejected Marx as a 'godless self-god', feared the 'dark iconoclasts' of revolution and revisited Judaic themes in essays, stories and his 'Hebrew Melodies' poems. A peerless German stylist, Heine personified European Jewish intellectual creativity, yet also, some say, self-doubt.

Above Heinrich Heine as portrayed by Moritz Daniel Oppenheim. Both painter and subject were Jews who found acceptance in German society.

doms for all Germans; in 1853 Austria banned Jews from acquiring real estate or moving to certain areas. True emancipation only arrived with the unification of Italy in 1861 and Germany in 1871.

Legislation for Jewish equality was passed in France first, in 1791, then the Netherlands, Greece, Canada and the Ottoman empire by 1839. Britain, Germany, Austria-Hungary, Italy, Spain, Bulgaria, Serbia, Spain and finally the Russian empire had followed suit by 1917.

JUDAISM MODERNIZED

Liberal views influenced change in European Jewry. Many Orthodox Jews looked to combine social integration with religious observance. Neo-Orthodoxy was a movement inspired by Frankfurt Rabbi Samson Raphael Hirsch (1808–88) and his ethos of *Torah im derech Eretz* ('Torah in the way of the land'), which taught secular alongside religious subjects.

OTHER REVOLUTIONS

Yet more social changes were afoot in the 19th century. New technology and mass production soon led to an economic revolution, and Jewish capitalists were to play a vital role in industrializing Britain, France and America.

From the 1830s, German Jews built up machine, oil and copper enterprises. In Russia, Jewish industrialists developed not only food, textile and tobacco industries, but also river-shipping, metals, mining and urban expansion. Even so, discrimination after the 1870s barred Jews from the Russian bureaucracy, and educational restrictions meant that there were virtually no Russian Jews in the liberal professions.

Beyond Russia, Jews had largely won their civil freedoms. Yet the rise of nationalist parties with explicitly anti-Semitic platforms showed that, while the legal battle had been won, a political struggle was just beginning.

THE OSTJUDEN AND YIDDISH CULTURE

YIDDISH, THE LANGUAGE OF ASHKENAZIC JEWRY, BECAME THE CHIEF VEHICLE FOR SPREADING INFORMATION IN JEWISH EASTERN EUROPE. IT WAS THE GLUE THAT BOUND A SECULAR SENSE OF 'JEWISHNESS', CALLED *YIDDISHKEIT*.

In western Europe, Yiddish was increasingly regarded as uncouth; the *maskilim*, or 'enlightened ones', of the Jewish Haskalah, spoke German or French among themselves, and wrote learned books in 'purer' Hebrew. By the 20th century, certain elements in Western Jewry professed disdain for the *Ostjuden*, or 'Eastern Jews', under the Russian yoke.

A minority, though, felt nostalgia and even envy towards their Eastern cousins who seemingly maintained a surer sense of who they were, for all their poverty and political deprivation. Some of the most Jewishly creative places in Europe were precisely those areas where *Ostjuden* and refined Western *maskilim* met, such as the 'borderland' cities of Vienna and Budapest in the Austro-Hungarian empire.

Below Red Guards, Moscow, 1917. At first, many Jews welcomed the Russian Revolution as a chance for change.

MATURATION OF HASSIDISM

Once dismissed as a passing phase, Hassidism (a populist expression of Jewish Orthodoxy) had put down deep roots in eastern Europe by the 19th century. Most sects were usually headed by a *rebbe*, or rabbinic 'master', whose authority often over-ruled that of the local town rabbi.

Hassidic ways had economic implications, as ordinary followers set up mutual self-help societies and funded *tzadikim*, 'righteous ones' who claimed to mediate between God and the common people. Hassidism entered the USA with the great immigration wave of the 1880s, but the movement found unfertile ground. Many Jewish newcomers welcomed America's freedom from European strictures, whether these were official, anti-Semitic or religious. Only much later did New York become the main destination for Hassidic survivors of the Holocaust.

Above Russia before the Revolution. Jews attacked by Russian thugs, 1903, from a contemporary Italian newspaper.

EASTERN EUROPE

The prevailing ethos east of the Dnieper River was more traditional, but eventually the *haskalah* (Jewish enlightenment), spread from its birthplace in Prussia to Austrian Galicia (culturally Polish Jewish) and on to Tsarist Russia. Eastern Haskalah assumed its own distinct character: rather than attempting to reform Judaism or seek political emancipation – a hopeless cause in Russia – Eastern *maskilim* (Haskalah enthusiasts) concentrated on regenerating their communities on a secular basis.

By the late 19th century some Western Jews, who had felt it their duty to educate the Ostjuden about civilized practices, hired east European *maskilim* to teach their children the rudiments of Judaism. Eastern Haskalah served as a bridge to a West that was losing connection with the wellsprings of Jewish tradition.

THE MAY LAWS

Optimists thought that Russia was becoming more liberal when, in 1862, Jews gained equal rights

Right Klezmer bands were a regular fixture of Ashkenazi life in both eastern Europe and America. This one stands ready at a welcoming party, c. 1920.

in Congress Poland, which essentially had been a semi-autonomous puppet state under Tsarist rule since 1815. However, both Poles and Jews suffered when Russia crushed a revolt and incorporated Poland more firmly into the Tsarist realm three years later. Much worse was to follow under Tsar Alexander III (r. 1881–94). Pogroms erupted throughout western Russia and Ukraine and dragged on for three years. Although the authorities did not officially encourage the violence, they did little to stop it.

RADICALIZATION IN RUSSIA

New pogroms, anti-Jewish mass attacks, erupted in 1903–6, coinciding with the abortive 1905 revolution, and yet another wave occurred in 1918–20, during the civil war that followed the Bolshevik Revolution. All told, tens of thousands of Jews died in the period to 1920, during which time two million Jews chose to emigrate, mostly to the USA.

For those who remained in Russia, radicalism set in. Broadly they joined one of four groups: universalist and atheist Marxists; Narodni peasant revolutionaries (who generally did not welcome Jews); the Bund, an all-embracing Russian socialist association specifically for Jewish concerns; or Zionists who laboured for an emancipated Jewish society only in Palestine.

HUNGARY – BETWEEN TWO WORLDS

The distinct worlds of Western Jewry and the Ostjuden touched in Hungary, a land living partly in the shadow of Austria, and blessed with a vast variety of Jewish types: Carpathian mountain Jews, urban German speakers, and Orthodox

Jews who preferred speaking Hungarian to Yiddish. Despite enduring residual prejudices from gentile Magyar nationalists, the Jewish population grew and fostered ties with Jews in neighbouring Serbia and Bosnia.

Hungarian Jews took advantage of the 1783 Edict of Tolerance, the brainchild of Emperor Joseph II (1765–90), and entered universities in search of secular education. Hungary's still-small Jewish population was replenished by the influx of Jews from Poland, Slovakia and Moravia. By the end of the 19th century, some 350 Jews had joined the titled nobility. A quarter of all university students and more than 40 per cent of Hungarian bankers, intelligentsia and artists were Jews, even though they made up just 5 per cent of the general population.

City dwellers favoured Reform practices, imported from Germany; and some Orthodox concocted a Hungarian moderate version of reform called Neolog. By contrast, Hassidic sects separated themselves to safeguard Jewish tradition. They set up dynasties in several towns and introduced a new flavour to Hungarian Jewry.

Meanwhile, in Austro-Hungarian Bohemia, Jews thrived because of the combined effect of the Industrial Revolution and weak local nobility. Families such as the Porges built cotton, calico and linen printing factories and spawned Jewish banking clans in Vienna. In the 1840s the Emperor ennobled the Porges, a sign that economic success could bring social respectability without any need to convert from the Jewish faith.

LITERATURE IN YIDDISH

East European Jews took to literature and theatre with alacrity. They wrote mainly in Yiddish, so their output was for Jewish 'domestic consumption'. Early pioneers included the playwright Solomon Ettinger (1802–56) and folklorist S. Ansky (1863–1920), who built on Ostjuden oral story-telling traditions. Ansky's 1914 Yiddish play *The Dybbuk* has been dubbed an Ashkenazi *Frankenstein* and a metaphor for the nature of Jewish life. He also wrote in Russian, while his contemporary Israel Zangwill (1824–1926) used English. Both men's use of the locally dominant language demonstrated the speed of Jewish acculturation. Yet they preserved a sense of Ostjuden culture.

THE SPECTRE OF ANTI-SEMITISM REVIVED

HOPES FOR JEWISH EMANCIPATION IN RUSSIA WERE SUDDENLY DASHED BY AN OUTBREAK OF VIOLENCE AFTER 1881. EVEN IN THE WEST, MEDIEVAL SUSPICIONS ABOUT JEWS REVIVED.

Above Caricature of notorious French anti-Semite Edouard Drumont, from a French satirical journal, 1893.

The 1881 pogroms in Russia altered Jewish history profoundly. They were to lead to the birth of political Zionism – the campaign to create a Jewish national state in Palestine – and the growth of American Jewry. They also led indirectly to the Russian Revolution. However, as an instance of official and popular anti-Semitism, the pogroms were not unique.

ATTACK FROM THE RIGHT

Rightists still feared that Jews were eternal aliens. Even the supposedly enlightened Frederick the Great of Prussia decreed in 1750 that 'extraordinary' Jews (such as Court Jews) could not pass on their privileges to the next generation. 'Ordinary' Jews were barred from professions, and could not allowed to marry or settle in further numbers 'until a careful investigation [had] been made'.

Below The Dreyfus affair of 1894 exposed an underlying cultural anti-Semitism that shocked French liberals.

In France, Edouard Drumont published a two-volume racist book, *La France Juive* (1886) whose popularity encouraged him to found the Anti-Semitic League and a daily paper, *La Libre Parole* (1896).

Envy of successful Jewish families such as the Reinachs (who included prize-winning lawyers, politicians, archaeologists and classicists) fuelled French rightist dislike for Jews. A string of malicious conspiracy theories followed the Comptoire d'Escompte banking crisis (1889) and the Panama corruption scandal (1893), which both involved Jews.

ANTI-SEMITISM ON THE LEFT

Diverse groups castigated Jews on economic grounds. In 1891 the Russian Jewish thinker Leon Pinsker noted: 'For property holders, [the Jew is] a beggar; for the poor, an exploiter and a millionaire'.

Some radicals saw Jews as financial protectors of oppressive state structures and nobles. Late 19th-century Russian Narodniks and anarchists jointly attacked nobles and *Zhids* (pejorative Russian for Jews). Often there was a nationalist element at play.

THEOLOGY AND SCIENCE

Theologically, some atheists and secularists blamed Jews, the first monotheists, for all the evils of religion. Enlightenment thinkers of the 18th century set this trend when they criticized Jewish beliefs, in what might have been an attack on Christianity itself. The charges stuck, and a century later fused with a new strand of racial anti-Semitism, to emerge as an offshoot of social Darwinism.

Ernest Renan, a French philosopher and analyst of religion and nationality, along with like-minded academics, saw Semites in general and Jews in particular as an 'incomplete race' with an 'inferior level of human nature'.

GENTILE FRIENDS

To balance the record of anti-Semitism, Jews also found allies, especially in Britain, such as the parliamentarian and historian Thomas Macaulay, and Walter Scott, whose 1820 novel *Ivanhoe* sympathizes with the plight of Jews in medieval England. Lord Byron's 1815 book of songs, *Hebrew Melodies*, praises Jews' persistence despite exile; and was set to music by a Jewish composer, Isaac Nathan, called the 'father of Australian music'.

Inspired after meeting a learned book cataloguer at the British Library, George Eliot took lessons in Hebrew, visited Palestine in 1869 and often frequented synagogues. Her last novel, *Daniel Deronda* (1878), features an admiring portrayal of a fictitious Jew who rediscovers his identity; his yearning for, and eventual return to,

Palestine inspired many Jews to become Zionists. Similar themes appeared in Prime Minister Benjamin Disraeli's novels *Alroy* and *Tancred*.

PROTECTING JEWS' RIGHTS

The murder of a French capuchin friar in Damascus in 1840 (the Damascus Blood Libel) led to the torture and death of three Jews. Two prominent Jews, Sir Moses Montefiore and Adolphe Crémieux, intervened to stop more bloodshed. The affair led to the creation of the Alliance Israélite Universelle in 1860, a coalition dedicated to safeguarding Jewish rights worldwide.

RUSSIAN RESTRICTIONS

Despite the positive movements of Alliance Israélite, the Tsar's May Laws of 1882 re-imposed cruel restrictions on Russian Jews. They were prevented from entering secondary schools, universities and mining institutes, and were dismissed from government services. These laws, whose prime instigator was Konstantin Pobedonostsev, revealed both economic envy and religious prejudice. They stayed on the statute books until 1907 and provided the basis for other acts of discrimination. In 1886, fines were imposed on Jewish families whose sons failed to report for military service; in 1888 Tsar Alexander III (r. 1881–94) rejected recommendations to extend Jewish rights; and in 1891, 20,000 legally resident Jewish artisans were expelled from Moscow.

Considered together, legislation and pogroms encouraged the greatest movement of Jews to date: between 1881 and 1920, two million Jews left Russia. Some went to Palestine, others to Britain, but overwhelmingly they settled in the United States.

Above French poor hitting a Jewish capitalist, probably a response to the Panama affair, 1893.

So, paradoxically, the Russian laws encouraged the still-nascent Zionist movement, and they also quite unintentionally gave birth to the modern American Jewish community, which in the 20th century became by far the largest and most influential in the world. Within Russia they radicalized more secular-minded Jews, and thus contributed to the revolutions of 1905 and 1917.

THE DREYFUS AFFAIR

The Jews of France felt more secure than most as the 19th century drew to a close. However, in 1894 a Jew from Alsace, Col. Alfred Dreyfus, was falsely accused of betraying military secrets to Germany, and convicted of treason. The trial created an uproar, pitting pro-Dreyfus liberals and republicans, notably the campaigning journalist Emile Zola, against anti-Dreyfus clerics and the social and political old guard. It took 12 years before Dreyfus was exonerated and freed from exile on Devil's Island, by which time France had passed pivotal legislation separating church from state, and safeguarding civil rights.

PROTOCOLS OF THE ELDERS OF ZION

'The Protocols of the Elders of Zion' is one of the most potent, influential and longest-lasting of anti-Semitic tracts. It was a forgery concocted by Russian secret police in the late 19th century and based on the wording of a pamphlet directed against Napoleon III, originally written by a French lawyer, Maurice Joly, in 1864. The Protocols pretends to be a master-plan by secret Jewish leaders plotting to undermine all other nations, socially, morally, economically and politically. Though reprinted during the 1905 Russian Revolution, it reached its peak of popularity during World War I and the 1917 Bolshevik Revolution, when rightists persuaded themselves that Communism was entirely a Jewish conspiracy. The document was disseminated in France by clerics who feared Jewish and Masonic influence; and in England where *The Times* launched an investigation into its authenticity in 1920. From the foundation of the independent State of Israel in 1948 it gained a readership in the Arab world, as a putative 'explanation' of Zionism. Indeed, it is probably no coincidence that its original publication coincided with the first Zionist conference in Basel, Switzerland, in 1897. Philip Graves, a reporter for *The Times*, exposed the forgery in 1921.

Above Illustration of Jew with snakes for hair from 1937 Protocol, a forgery that revealed a supposed Jewish plot to control the world.

THE 19TH-CENTURY POPULATION BOOM

AN EXTRAORDINARY GROWTH IN JEWISH POPULATION OCCURRED IN THE 19TH CENTURY. BY 1880 THERE WERE AROUND 7.7 MILLION JEWS IN THE WORLD, MOSTLY IN RUSSIA, ALTHOUGH INCREASINGLY IN THE USA.

Improved health standards, high birth rates, better nutrition and relative peace in central and eastern Europe probably accounted for the unprecedented increase in Jewish numbers during the 19th century. As of 1880, nine-tenths of the world's Jews lived in Europe. Around 3.5 million dwelt in the former Polish provinces under Russian rule. The first Russian empire census of 1897 recorded 5.2 million Jews, of whom all but 300,000 still lived in the Pale of Settlement. Another 1.3 million lived in Poland proper, where they made up 14 per cent of the population.

Ashkenazim thus outnumbered Sephardim and Mizrahim (oriental Jews) by a ratio of 9:1. There was also growth in western European Jewry.

Below: Jewish neighbourhood, Lower East Side, New York, c. 1900. Eastern European Jews transplanted their culture to an American urban setting.

WESTERNIZATION

In 1820 some 223,000 Jews lived in Germany, but while that represented a significant rise on previous years, the biggest shift of all began 60 years later, in the USA. There the population rocketed, rapidly turning America into an important new centre in Jewish life. Most of the two million Jews who left Tsarist Russia settled there. In the first 15 years of the 20th century, Jews accounted for 10 per cent of all immigrants to the United States. Jewish Americans numbered 2.5 million in 1914.

By then, a quarter of all Jews in the world lived in 11 cities. By far the largest population lived in New York, with an astonishing 1.35 million Jews. London, another immigrant magnet, had more than 150,000. That left sizeable urban communities in other American and European cities including Chicago, Warsaw and Vienna. Occupational expectations

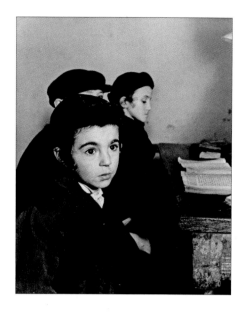

Above Roman Vishniac's 1930s photograph of a heder, *or religious class typical of those in eastern Europe.*

gradually changed: the grandparents' generation tended to be Torah observant Jews who worked in small trades as salesmen, cobblers or tailors. Parents took advantage of new freedoms and economic expansion to run larger-scale enterprises, often in mass retailing. But genuine social respectability arrived with the third generation, when their children went to university and became lawyers, accountants or doctors.

IMMIGRANT IDENTITIES

Immigrant Jews of the first two generations cherished their membership of institutions called *landsleitsverreine*, or 'fellow countrymen associations'. Jews from certain towns, such as Krakow, would gather together, in their new cities. By the third generation, however, bonds to the old country had weakened, and Yiddish gave way to English in the USA, Canada, Australia and South Africa, or Spanish in Argentina and Mexico. Now Jewish immigrants felt equally American (or Australian or Chilean) and Jewish, but no longer so strongly Litvak (Lithuanian Jewish), say, or Polack (Polish Jewish).

THE USA – A NEW PROMISED LAND

WHEN EARLY 20TH-CENTURY YIDDISH WRITERS SPOKE OF *DI GOLDENE MEDINE*, THE 'GOLDEN LAND', THEY MEANT THE USA. IT WAS A PLACE OF OPPORTUNITY, LARGELY FREE OF 'OLD EUROPE'S' PREJUDICES.

The Anglo-Jewish author Israel Zangwill famously called America a 'melting pot' in which former identities would dissolve and people would emerge as equal citizens. Many Jews thought America signalled the end of 'Diaspora persecution', even if it was not exactly the biblical 'promised land'. Jewish women were important to American social activism, and included such figures as Rebecca Gratz, educator of poor women, and Lillian Wald, a healthcare pioneer.

SETTLING IN THE USA

The first wave of Jews to the USA were Sephardim from Brazil and Holland; the second wave were educated German Jews; and the third and largest were Yiddish-speaking eastern Europeans, originally fleeing the 1881 pogroms in Russia.

Below An American gold prospector wearing Levi's jeans.

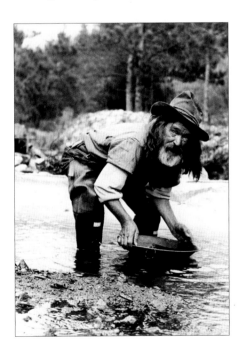

Uncomfortable with indigenous religious liberality, some 'third wave' traditional Jews created an Orthodox Congregation Union in 1898. Many others joined the Reform and Conservative movements, which seemed closer to the American ethos, while others clung to Yiddish culture even if they lost their faith.

Between 1800 and 1860 America's Jewish population had leapt to more than 100,000. This growth inspired the creation in 1843 of the *B'nai Brit*, or 'Sons of the Covenant', America's first nationwide Jewish secular organization.

JEWS IN THE WILD WEST AND IN CONGRESS

The great 19th-century move west attracted entrepreneurs such as the Gratz family of Philadelphia, who developed the new terrain with their expertise in banking, insurance and railroads. Likewise, the German-born Levi Strauss (1829–1902) found a ready market for his invention, hardy denim jeans, among the prospectors in the 1848 California Gold Rush.

Meanwhile, in New York, Mordecai Manuel Noah (1785–1851), an eccentric playwright and newspaper editor, led the Democrat Party's political machine. Noah fought to abolish slavery, and also campaigned for a Jewish homeland on an island in the Niagara.

Jews were also represented in the Deep South: as early as the 1670s Sephardim had settled in Charleston, South Carolina. Florida railroad pioneer David Levy Yulee (1810–66) became the first Jew elected to Congress in 1845. Jewish senator

Above Emma Lazarus was an American Jew born in New York City. Her poem 'Colossus' welcomed immigrants at Ellis Island with: 'Give me your huddled masses yearning to be free.'

Judah Benjamin (1811–84) became war secretary in the southern Confederate cabinet.

REFORM AND CONSERVATIVE JUDAISM

The Bohemian-born rabbi and organizational dynamo Isaac Mayer Wise (1819–1900) effectively founded modern American Reform Judaism in Cincinnati after 1854. Samuel Hirsch (1815–89) from the Rhineland then brought a more philosophical perspective as president of the Conference of American Reform Rabbis in 1869. The flagship Hebrew Union College, created in 1875, soon signalled that American Reform was set on a path distinct from its European roots.

Others balked at Hirsch's radicalism, yet found Orthodoxy too constraining. In 1886 they set up New York's Jewish Theological Seminary to promote their values. Called Conservative Jews and later inspired by the scholastic Rabbi Solomon Schechter, they founded synagogues after 1913 and by the mid-20th century they formed America's largest Jewish denomination.

DIASPORAS OF THE SOUTHERN HEMISPHERE

FOR CENTURIES, JEWISH HISTORY TOOK PLACE EXCLUSIVELY NORTH OF THE EQUATOR. WITH 18TH- AND 19TH-CENTURY COLONIAL EXPANSION, NEW COMMUNITIES AROSE IN THE SOUTHERN HEMISPHERE.

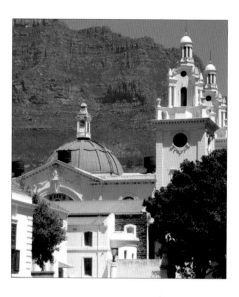

Many Jews travelled to the Southern Hemisphere after the 1881 Russian Pogroms. Few, if any, Jews lived there already and it was hard to lead a traditional Jewish life. Immigrants exploited economic opportunities in frontier societies that could ill-afford the old prejudices of Europe and soon established new Jewish communities, schools and institutions.

SOUTH AFRICA

There were few practising Jews among the Dutch who settled in South Africa in 1652. More arrived in the 1820s after Britain took over the Cape Colony, and larger numbers followed with the diamond and gold-mining boom in the late 1800s.

Initially, most Jews came from Britain. As travelling salesmen they connected remote farmsteads with larger towns; a bilingual Yiddish–Zulu lexicon helped them trade with Black Africans. A few became the wealthy heads of mining finance houses, like Alfred Beit, Barney Barnato, Lionel Phillips and Solly Joel.

Many more Ashkenazim came from Lithuania and Latvia after 1881, and Jews made up 23 per cent of all immigrants to the Cape 1885–1915. These 'Litvaks' tended to gravitate to Cape Town and Johannesburg where, considerably poorer than the gold magnates, they worked as tailors or small shopkeepers. They encouraged their children to train for the professions, and set up their own Board of Deputies in 1904.

AUSTRALIA

The first Jews in Australia arrived as convicts in 1788. Their descendants bought a burial plot in 1820; in 1832 they formed a congregation under Aaron Levi; and in 1844 built their first synagogue in Sydney. Tasmania was probably the next place of settlement. Gold rushes attracted immigrants to Melbourne in the 1850s, and Perth in the 1890s. One prominent Australian-born Jew of the period was the architect Nahum Barnet, who built synagogues, department stores, factories and theatres.

Above Great Synagogue and Jewish Museum in Cape Town, South Africa.

SOUTH AMERICA

Portuguese traders and smugglers in the Rio de la Plata most likely included a few Sephardim, but French Jews established the first true Argentinean community after the country won independence in 1810. A large post-1881 influx of 'Rusos' boosted the Ashkenazi proportion of the population to 80 per cent, while others came from Morocco.

Baron Maurice de Hirsch considered Argentina an alternative Zion and bought farmland in Santa Fe and Entre Rios provinces. Soon Yiddish-speaking gauchos were herding cattle. Over time, their *communas* (small towns) began resembling east European *shtetls*. By 1920, most of Argentina's 150,000 Jews lived in larger cities.

A liberal 1824 constitution and a booming trade in rubber made Brazil the second largest Latin American destination for Jews. Mexican Emperor Maximilian I encouraged German Jews to come to his kingdom, and Sephardi Jews fleeing an ailing Ottoman empire made new homes on the continent.

Left Consecrated in 1877, Mikve Israel Synagogue in Melbourne symbolizes Jewish roots planted in Australia.

JEWS OF THE LATE OTTOMAN EMPIRE

WITHIN A SLOWLY STAGNATING EMPIRE, SALONIKA REMAINED A
MAGNET FOR JEWISH IMMIGRATION, A HUB OF SCHOLARSHIP AND
INNOVATION, AND A VIBRANT MOSAIC OF CULTURES AND CLASSES.

In 1683 the Turks alarmed Europe when they laid siege to Vienna. Yet two months later they were repelled, after which the Ottoman empire began its gradual decline. Constantinople's reluctance to industrialize hampered its economy, and from the 16th century European trade vessels bypassed the Ottomans, sailing direct to India and the Americas. By the 19th century, Western officials mocked Turkey as 'The Sick Man of Europe'.

DECLINE AND SURVIVAL

Wars deprived Turkey of parts of Greece, Hungary and the Black Sea, and the Congress of Berlin of 1878 further chipped away at the empire. Despite this, belated reforms enhanced civil rights and five Jews sat in the Ottoman parliament by 1887. Some Jews benefited from laws, first introduced in 1536, that privileged foreign traders. Yet the overall effect was negative; Jews in Egypt, for example, felt relieved when the former Ottoman province

came under British protection in 1882. The Young Turk revolt of 1908 briefly offered new hope, until in 1914 the empire erred fatally in backing Germany in World War I.

SALONIKA

Ruled by Turks since 1430, Salonika in north-eastern Greece – today, Thessaloniki – became the mainstay of Sephardi Jewry. New immigrants enriched the community: Hungarians after 1376, Bavarian Ashkenazim in 1470, Jews from Venice and Sicily, and most of all Spanish exiles and Maranos, especially after 1492. By 1514 Jews formed more than half the population, and Salonika, an early hub of Hebrew printing, was dubbed the 'Mother of Israel'

Jews were pivotal to the wool and silk trades. After 1515 they provided the Ottoman army with uniforms. Many also worked as miners, jewellers, dockers and fishermen. In 1680 the Jewish communities united to elect one assembly. By 1900 they made up 80,000 of the city's 173,000

Above Jewish porter in the Greek city of Salonika, late Ottoman period.

inhabitants. Sephardim dominated: local dishes and songs bore an Iberian flavour; gentile Greeks, Armenians and Turks came to speak their Ladino language; and the busy port closed for the Sabbath.

Jewish colleges taught astronomy, medicine and sciences from the 1500s. An Alliance Israélite school in 1874 encouraged liberal attitudes. More Jews became lawyers, doctors and bankers, and Emmanuel Carasso and Marcel Samuel Cohen were prominent Young Turk leaders. During 1880–1910 secular Ladino theatres and newspapers flourished, along with socialist and Zionist clubs. But Orthodox stalwarts often clashed with wealthy families who favoured the French language and Western values.

Jews began leaving Salonika after Greece captured the city in 1912, and fire destroyed homes and businesses in 1917. In 1943 the Nazis deported 95 per cent of those who stayed, up to 56,000 people – almost all perished in Auschwitz.

Today descendants of Ottoman Jews live on in Istanbul, New York, London, Paris and Israel.

Left Dolmabahçe Palace, home to the last six Ottoman sultans, in Constantinople (now Istanbul).

JEWS IN 19TH-CENTURY ART AND CULTURE

WHEN UNIVERSITIES OPENED TO JEWS, DOZENS OF NEW CAREER CHOICES WERE UNLOCKED, AND CREATIVITY BLOSSOMED IN THE FIELDS OF MUSIC, OPERA, ART, SCIENCE, POLITICS AND SOCIAL CAMPAIGNING.

The mid-19th century saw an explosion of creativity by Jews in the arts, music, politics and science. According to one theory, analytical skills honed through religious study were concentrated within enclosed Jewish societies. Once the ghetto walls came down, Jews were bound to excel in other fields.

UNIVERSITY LIFE

Jews began to enter university in the 1760s in America, the 1780s in Hungary, and the 1830s in England. They soon flocked to the professions, becoming doctors, lawyers and scientists. In Russia and Romania universities still barred their entry, but Jews from those countries won university places in Vienna, which became an intellectual and scientific magnet. Jews, many of central European origin, won a disproportionate 48 of the 171 Nobel Prizes in physics between 1901 and 2001.

SCIENCE AND INVENTION

Generally, 'culturally neutral' scientific departments welcomed Jews more than arts faculties. Where prejudice lingered, as in medical schools that still prevented them from becoming surgeons, Jews pioneered fields of epidemiology and social medicine. Chemist Fritz Haber (1868–1934) won a Nobel Prize in 1916 for synthesizing ammonia.

The Industrial Revolution further enthused Jews. In Germany, Siegfried Marcus (1831–98) built the world's first petrol-driven vehicle while other Jews were innovative in aeronautics. The social sciences offered fertile ground for Jewish talent, such as the early English economist David Ricardo (1772–1823), the American anthropologist Franz Boas (1858–1942) and the German sociologist Emile Durkheim (1858–1915).

THE CHALLENGE OF ART

Art challenged Jews for two reasons: suspicion of the 'graven image' from within Jewish culture, and resistance to Jews entering the elite salon. Even so, named Jewish artists emerged in the 19th century. A few adopted a cautious approach, such as the Dutch naturalist Josef Israels (1824–1911). Others expressed a radical spirit, such as the Franco-Caribbean impressionist, Camille Pissarro (1830–1903), or the leader of Berlin's avant-garde school, Max Liebermann (1847–1935). Even more daring were the abstract painters and sculptors of Paris on the eve of

Left Camille Pissarro's Woman Wearing a Green Headscarf, *1893, illustrates his pointillist style.*

Above Marc Chagall's The Red Jew, *painted in 1915 and blending modernity with [Jewish] antiquity.*

World War I. Jewish art patrons often acted as adventurous 'taste-makers', like Paul Cassirer (1871–1926), the promoter of Van Gogh and Cézanne.

MUSICAL SUCCESS

Of all the arts, music seemed least alien to Jews because of their long tradition of sacred and secular music. Jews with musical skills could leapfrog social barriers, even in Russia, where by the late 19th century all four violin soloists in the anti-Semitic Tsarist court were of Jewish origin.

Jews revealed a surprising affinity for Western classical musical forms. In Germany, Felix Mendelssohn (1809–47) won fame for his violin concerto and Wedding March theme. His sister, Fanny (1805–47), composed 466 pieces. And the Bohemian–Austrian Gustav Mahler (1860–1911) daringly blurred divisions between symphony, song and concerto. In 1897, Mahler was appointed director of the imperial Vienna Opera.

Nonetheless, there was resistance to Jewish success. In 1850, Richard Wagner wrote an essay translated as 'Jewishness in Music', which lambasted Jews for producing shallow, artificial works that betrayed a lack of true 'German spirit'. Perhaps it is

Above Born Jewish and baptised Anglican, Benjamin Disraeli was twice prime minister of Britain.

no wonder that the Mendelssohns were raised Protestant and Mahler converted to Catholicism.

THEATRE AND OPERA

Unlike Germany, France seemed receptive to artistic expressions of Jewish identity. *La Juive* ('The Jewess') by Jacques Halévy (1799–1862), for instance, became a regular fixture of the French operatic repertory after 1835. Giacomo Meyerbeer (1791–1864) pioneered grand opera, and the German-born French composer Jacques Offenbach (1819–80) helped create the operetta form. Yiddish theatre allowed east European Jews to laugh through tears, to lampoon pompous authority figures, whether the Tsarist commissar or local rabbi, or just to escape harsh reality. While few gentiles knew this tradition, in the West Jews began taking to the mainstream stage. Emancipation now freed the previously suppressed talents of Jewish women, including Rachel (Eliza Felix, 1820–58) and Sarah Bernhardt (1844–1923), both universally celebrated actresses.

Right Henrietta Szold, social campaigner, in Kiryat Anavim, Palestine, c.1935.

MAINSTREAM POLITICIANS

Conversion offered an entry to a political world otherwise barred to 19th-century Jews. The leading example was Benjamin Disraeli (1804–81), the only person of Jewish parentage to become British prime minister. His father, an Italian Jew and historian, baptized his son after a dispute with his synagogue, but the later Conservative statesman never denied his Jewish identity.

In France, Adolphe Crémieux (1796–1880) was twice minister of justice. In 1827 he helped repeal the last pre-revolutionary legislation that disadvantaged Jews. Meanwhile, in Germany Ludwig Borne (1786–1837) became a satirical political writer and campaigner for emancipation, and Gabriel Riesser (1806–63) advocated both Jewish rights and German nationalism while serving in successive Prussian governments. He later became the first Jewish judge in Germany.

SOCIAL ACTIVISTS

Other Jews eschewed conventional politics for social activism. In the USA, Samuel Gompers founded the American Federation of Labour, and Henrietta Szold (1860–1945) taught immigrants English and founded the Hadassah Jewish women's organization in 1912. Later she founded hospitals and social services for Jews and Arabs in Palestine, and helped to rescue Jews from Nazi persecution in Europe in the mid-20th century.

ACADEMICS

Jewish academia flourished across a range of disciplines after universities opened to Jews. Iuliu Barasch (1815–63), born into a Hassidic family in Brody, Galicia, was a pioneer of medical science. Herman Cohen (1842–1918) and Ernst Cassirer (1874–1945) were leading neo-Kantians; the latter founded a 'philosophy of culture'. Henri Bergson (1859–1941) pioneered the philosophy of time and creativity, Other Jews were prominent orientalists, such as the Hungarian Ignaz Goldziher (1850–1921), a founder of modern Islamic studies in Europe.

Knowledge gained in the old world soon crossed the Atlantic: the German-born Franz Boas (1858–1942) was called the father of American anthropology. Nor is it possible to imagine sociology without Emile Durkheim (1858–1915), logic without Edmund Husserl (1859–1938) or psychology without Sigmund Freud (1856–1939).

POLITICAL ZIONISM

ONE OF MANY IDEOLOGIES THAT TRIED TO ANSWER JEWISH YEARN-
INGS, POLITICAL ZIONISM GRAFTED MODERN NATIONALIST IDEAS ON
TO THE ANCIENT CONNECTION OF JEWS TO THE LAND OF ISRAEL.

Coined by the publicist Nathan Birnbaum, the expression 'Zionism' derives from Mount Zion, which adjoins the Old City of Jerusalem. At its simplest, Zionism acknowledges Jewry's attachment to the Land of Israel that broadly covers present-day Israel and the West Bank of the River Jordan. Some draw a distinction between spiritual Zionism, which has underpinned the Jewish religion since the Babylonian Exile, and political Zionism, which crystallized in Europe in the late 19th century.

TOWARDS A JEWISH NATIONALISM

Increasingly, followers of the *Haskalah* (Jewish Enlightenment) defined themselves as a nation, not a religion. And as every nation should have a land, so should the Jews, they concluded. The German Jewish philosopher Moses Hess (1812–75)

exemplified this ideology. He wrote in his 1862 book *Rome and Jerusalem* that Jewish national feeling was unquenchable and could only be expressed by physically returning to Palestine. If necessary, Jews should sacrifice emancipation in the Diaspora for this cause.

ODESSA AND THE 1881 POGROMS

Few noticed Hess's book until two men from Odessa, Leon Pinsker (1821–91) and Ahad Ha-Am (1856–1927), revived its ideas. Odessa on the Black Sea was one-third Jewish and housed some 150,000 of the most secular, educated and assimilated Jews in Russia. The pogroms of 1881 shattered dreams of integration and prompted Pinsker to write *Auto-emancipation*, in which he declared: 'For the living, the Jew is a dead man; for the natives, an alien and a vagrant; for

Above Confident, elegant, romantic yet controversial, Theodor Herzl galvanized the nascent Zionist movement. The text above the picture bears his famous words, 'If you will it, it is no fairytale.'

the patriot, a man without a country; for all classes, a hated rival'. Jews would only enjoy respect when they liberated themselves, he said.

Pinsker headed *Hovevei Tzion* (Lovers of Zion), which founded Rishon le-Tzion as the first Zionist settlement in Palestine in 1882. Baron Edmond de Rothschild began to help, and Russian Jewish students, called *Bilu*, started the first *aliyah*, or 'ascent', or wave of immigration.

THEODOR HERZL AND THE DIPLOMATIC PATH

Hovevei set up an Odessa Committee in 1890 to plan Jewish farming in Palestine, but lacked political direction. Ultimately it was Theodor Herzl (1860–1904) who filled that need. Earlier he had mused about 'solving the Jewish problem' through mass conversion. While reporting from Paris in 1895, he heard crowds baying for Jewish blood at the court

Left 'In Basel I founded the Jewish State', wrote Herzl in 1897. Here he is with delegates at the fifth Zionist conference in the same Swiss city.

martial of Alfred Dreyfus, a Jewish colonel falsely accused of treason. Now convinced that even cultured France was irredeemably anti-Semitic, he wrote his monograph *Judenstadt*, or 'Jewish State', in 1896, which argued that the Jewish Question was national in essence, not individual; Jews could only enjoy true freedom if they governed themselves, preferably on 'ancestral soil'.

Judenstadt became Zionism's manifesto and Herzl, a man of rare panache and regal bearing, gained messianic status among some east European *Ostjuden*. Most Jews, however, were less enthusiastic. Most Jewish philanthropists rebuffed him as a dangerous dreamer.

THE BASEL CONFERENCE

In 1897 Herzl and his colleague Max Nordau convened the first Zionist conference in Basel, Switzerland. There they created an organization and a 'national fund'. Two trends quickly emerged within Zionism. General or political Zionism followed Herzl's diplomatic path, while Ahad Ha-Am persisted with cultural Zionism. Aaron David Gordon (1856–1922) later led practical Zionists who saw settlement in Palestine as a way to create a 'new Jew' through the dignity of labour.

Herzl wrote in his diary after the conference, 'In Basel I founded the Jewish State… Maybe in five years, certainly in fifty, everyone will realize it'. At the time it seemed an extraordinary prediction; Zionism was only one of dozens of Jewish ideologies.

NEW TRENDS

Gradually a third stream, known as Labour Zionism, became dominant in the early 20th century. It consisted of divergent elements, including a romantic back-to-nature trend called Po'ale Tza'ir (Young Worker) and a more Marxist grouping, Po'ale Zion (Worker of Zion).

Above Jewish men and women pray at the Western Wall, Jerusalem, c.1905.

A fourth stream emerged, Religious Zionism, which opposed both the secularists who dominated the Zionist movement and the anti-Zionists who made up most observant Jews. In 1902 this group held its first conference in Vilna under its leader, Rabbi Yizhak Reines. Finally Nordau and others who came to despair of gradualism advocated what they called Catastrophic Zionism.

THE UGANDA OPTION

Herzl envisaged a Jewish-ruled yet pluralist Palestine, a bourgeois European-style utopian paradise in the Levant, as seen in his 1902 novel *Altneuland* (Old-New Land). Even fellow Zionists mocked its naïve dream of Jerusalem as a capital of world peace, or its belief that Arabs would welcome Jewish settlement.

When Britain's foreign office offered Herzl a tract of land in Uganda/Kenya, he agreed immediately. The seventh congress in 1905, however, rejected the Uganda Option, by which time Herzl had died of exhaustion in July 1904.

Ultimately, Zionism's fate depended on external factors, the collapse of Ottoman rule and Britain's acquisition of Palestine. The challenge was reconciling the national feelings of Jews and the land's indigenous Arab majority. As early as 1891 Ahad Ha-Am warned in *The Truth from Palestine* that it was not, as some imagined, 'a land without people'. The Marxist Zionist, Ber Borochov, dreamt of Jewish and Arab workers uniting; however, Ha-Am noted that if any Arab felt oppressed by Jews, 'rage will stay alive in his heart'.

JERUSALEM – BEYOND THE CITY WALLS

During 1537–42 the Ottoman Sultan Suleiman built Jerusalem's majestic walls and eight gates, which still define the Old City today. Within those walls are Muslim, Christian, Jewish and Armenian quarters. At the centre stands the Temple Mount, or Haram al-Sharif, site of two Muslim mosques and believed by Jews to be the location of the twice-destroyed Temple. Every day religious Jews pray to God for 'remembrance of Jerusalem Your Holy City' and the 'return of the Divine Presence to Zion'.

After 1700 Polish and Moroccan Jews began filling up the Jewish quarter; soon the Old City became overcrowded. In 1860 Sir Moses Montefiore, an English Sephardi benefactor, won approval for Jewish suburbs to be built outside the walls, the first being Mishkenot Sha'ananim. Soon Muslim and Christian Arabs built their own neighbourhoods, though by the 1870s Jews probably constituted the majority of the city's population.

Early Zionists felt ambivalent about the city, because it was a centre for religious Jews who depended on charity and rejected their secular venture. To Zionists, these long-established Jews paradoxically represented the worst aspects of 'non-productive' Diaspora life.

CHAPTER 9

WORLD WARS AND THE HOLOCAUST

More than 20 million people died in World War I between 1914 and 1918, and when fighting ceased, both Jews and Gentiles understandably longed for peace. The interwar years saw individual Jews flower in the arts, sciences and politics as never before. The more radical welcomed Russia's 1917 Communist Revolution, especially when it outlawed anti-Semitism and abolished the pernicious Pale of Settlement.

Yet many ordinary Germans believed that Jews had betrayed the fatherland. Increasingly they backed Adolf Hitler's ultra-nationalist Nazi Party, which vowed to exterminate 'non-Aryans' and, during World War II (1939–45), almost succeeded. In 1942 the Nazis began the industrialized murder of 6 million Jews, including 150,000 children. Called the Holocaust, or Shoah in Hebrew, this systematic genocide virtually destroyed 1,500 years of European Jewish civilization. Recalled in monuments, museums, novels and films, it remains a benchmark for mankind's capacity for evil.

Opposite Shoes at the former Nazi extermination camp of Auschwitz, Poland. Up to 1.5 million men, women and children, mostly Jews, were murdered there in 1942–4. The Holocaust marked a nadir in human history and nearly wiped out Jewish life in Europe.

Above Prisoners are led through the gates of Theresienstadt concentration camp, c. 1942. Inscribed above the entrance is 'Arbeit macht frei' ('Work will set you free') – a supremely cynical motto.

EUROPE AT WAR

SOME 1.5 MILLION JEWS SERVED AS SOLDIERS IN WORLD WAR I,
THE CONFLICT THAT TRANSFORMED EUROPE AND INDIRECTLY LED
BRITAIN TO PROMISE JEWS A 'NATIONAL HOME' IN PALESTINE.

Even before World War I broke out, life was turbulent for Jews in eastern Europe. Violence against Jews during Russia's 1905 uprisings led to 154,000 Jews moving to the USA during 1905–6. Smaller numbers went to France and Britain. In 1904–14 40,000 mainly socialist, east European Jews moved to Palestine. This Aliyah, or 'ascent', laid foundations for the Zionist labour movement, the Hebrew press and the *kvutzot*, or 'communal farming settlements'.

THE PATH OF WAR

Austria's Archduke Franz Ferdinand's assassination in Sarajevo, Bosnia, on 28 June 1914 led to the most murderous war to date. By August, a series of alliances had been activated, with the Entente Powers – Britain, France, Serbia and imperial Russia – fighting the Central Powers of Germany and Austria-Hungary, Ottoman Turkey and Bulgaria.

Hopes of swift victory faded as trench warfare came to western Europe. The technology that enabled mass production of electric lighting, telephones, radio, railway networks and cars now drove the world's first truly industrial war. The conflict was fought on land, sea and air and across six separate fronts. Over four years, 65 million troops were mobilized, 8.5 million killed, 21.2 million wounded, and 7.8 million taken prisoner or listed as missing in action. Another 13 million non-combatants probably died through hostilities and disease.

SOLDIERS ON ALL SIDES

All leading German Jewish intellectuals – except Albert Einstein – signed a petition supporting German war aims. Some 100,000 Jews fought for Germany, proportionately more than any other ethnic, religious or political group, and about 12,000

Above A.J. Balfour, British Foreign Secretary, whose 1917 Declaration pledged a national homeland for Jews.

died in battle. Jews from European colonies also enlisted, and Algerian Jewish soldiers were particularly noted for their courage in battle.

Jews in England and America felt uncomfortable joining any alliance with Russia's anti-Jewish Tsar. Despite this, 50,000 Jews served in the British forces, of whom five won the Victoria Cross and 50 the Distinguished Service Order. Many worked in labour corps in Middlesex, Egypt and the French trenches, while a few joined the Zion Mule Corps.

The Russian Imperial Army fielded 400,000–650,000 Jewish troops, more than any other nation; possibly 100,000 Russian Jews died in the conflict. Early in the war, Russian officials expelled Jews from the Pale of Settlement.

After 1915 some 40 per cent of Russian Jews came under German and Austrian military rule. Most welcomed their better treatment yet regretted being cut off from brethren to the east. By 1917, 3.4 million Jews remained under Russian rule, 700,000 of them beyond the Pale.

Left Europe in 1914, showing the disposition of forces before a war that was to claim 21 million lives.

America's entry into the war in April 1917 ultimately tipped the balance and resulted in an Entente victory, but not before a late eastern push by Germany encouraged war-weary Russians to force their Tsar to abdicate in February 1917.

A WAR TO END ALL WARS?

Europe was transformed when the Great War ended with the armistice of 11 November 1918. Gone were the Ottoman and Austro-Hungarian empires and the German Second Reich. New states including Czechoslovakia and Yugoslavia emerged, and Poland was independent for the first time in 100 years.

The war had turned America into a global superpower, and US President Woodrow Wilson promoted a League of Nations to prevent future conflict. Yet the same Versailles Treaty that created the League in 1920 so harshly punished Germany, it virtually guaranteed another war.

BALFOUR'S DECLARATION

Barely noticed amid the clamour of war was a letter that Britain's foreign secretary James Balfour wrote to

Below Jewish soldiers from Austria, Hungary and Poland at prayer, military camp, 1914, first year of World War I. By the Jewish painter O. Ehrenfreund.

THE WAR IN PALESTINE

Although Zionists and many Jews backed Turkey and Germany over the Allies, dissidents saw an opportunity to plan a future Jewish state by backing the Allied powers. In late 1914, Vladimir Jabotinsky and Joseph Trumpeldor persuaded Britain to create the Zion Mule Corps, a Jewish transportation unit. This disbanded in 1915, but inspired the 1917 establishment of the Jewish Legion.

Palestinian Jewish spies were siphoning information to Britain on Turkish movements, as French troops were mobilizing in Syria and Lebanon. Jews and Arabs, French and British, were all fighting against a Turkish enemy.

Above Pte Nathaniel Friedlander, a Jewish barber from London, after signing up to fight with the Army Service Corps, 1915.

Eventually, on 11 December 1917, Britain's General Allenby entered Jerusalem and accepted a Turkish surrender. In 1918 a Jewish Legion battalion led a British crossing of the Jordan River into Palestine. So ended 500 years of Ottoman rule over the Holy Land. Allied and Arab forces took Damascus, Beirut and Aleppo by the end of 1918.

Lord Rothschild on 2 November 1917. In it, Balfour stated that his government 'views with favour the establishment of a Jewish national home in Palestine'. The Balfour Declaration, brief and unspecific though it was, marked the first Great Power approval for a Jewish political entity on 'ancestral soil' in 1,900 years. The letter crowned years of diplomacy by Chaim Weizmann and

Nahum Sokolow of the World Zionist Organization. Weizmann's technical assistance to Britain's war effort also helped clinch the agreement. Yet most European Jews remained sceptical about Zionism. And five days after Balfour signed his letter, Russian Bolshevik militants launched a Marxist revolution that raised Jewish hopes for a more promising solution.

Below United in death: German soldiers, one Jewish, one Christian, buried side by side at a French war cemetery.

JEWS AND THE BOLSHEVIK REVOLUTION

RUSSIA, HOME TO HALF THE WORLD'S JEWS, WAS STILL A SEMI-FEUDALISTIC STATE IN THE EARLY 1900S. THE 1917 REVOLUTIONS MARKED A DRAMATIC SHIFT, BUT THE JEWS WERE LATER TO SUFFER UNDER COMMUNIST RULE TOO.

By the 1900s, Russia's Jewish socialists were deeply divided. Many belonged to the leading Marxist Social Democratic Party, which was itself split between moderate Mensheviks and radical Bolsheviks. For their part, Socialist Zionists, called Po'ale Zion, or 'Workers of Zion', threw their weight behind the 1917 October revolution.

REVOLUTION, WAR, AND THE END OF THE PALE

The Bund, a Jewish Labour Union, had been founded in 1897 to achieve equality for Jews in the Russian empire. Bundists also led the 1905 revolutionary uprisings, which resulted in limited political reforms.

Below Born to a Jewish family, Leon Trotsky embraced Marxism and helped lead the 1917 Russian Revolution.

However, a backlash led to 500 Odessa Jews being killed in a single day, and Marxists boycotted elections to a Duma (parliament) that was soon dissolved anyway.

Russia entered World War I on 1 August 1914, woefully unprepared and allied with Britain and France against the Central Powers. Fighting largely took place in areas where Russian Jews lived. Tsar Nicholas II took personal command of forces in September 1915, but by 1917 crippling losses caused them to reject rule by the 'Little Father of the People'. In March 1917 Nicholas was forced to abdicate. Russia's new provisional government abolished the Pale of Settlement.

STORMING THE KREMLIN

Exiled Bolsheviks stole back into Russia on board a 'sealed train' from Switzerland in April 1917, led by Vladimir Lenin (1870–1924) and his chief aide, Grigory Zinoviev (born Hirsch Apfelbaum, a Jew by origin, 1883–1936). Defying orthodox Marxist qualms, in October Lenin seized St Petersburg and Moscow and within weeks the centralized empire fell to his Bolshevik cadres.

Their astonishing success would have been impossible without the organizational skills of Leon Trotsky, born in 1878 as Lev Davidovich Bronstein. His father was an illiterate Jewish Ukrainian farmer.

In January 1918 the Bolsheviks banned other parties and declared a Soviet Republic. Mensheviks were tolerated as allies temporarily, but were outlawed in 1921.

Above The future is red – 1924 propaganda poster of Bolshevik revolutionary leader Vladimir Lenin.

RUINOUS CIVIL WAR

In March 1918 Trotsky signed the controversial Brest–Litovsk peace treaty with Germany, which pulled Russia out of the war and ceded Poland and the Baltic States. By now a vicious civil war had erupted between Bolsheviks, or Reds, and Counter-revolutionaries, or Whites, a motley coalition of monarchists, liberals and local nationalists backed by Allied powers. This conflict raged for four years and included rightist pogroms that killed more than 70,000 Jewish civilians. More Jews now backed the Bolsheviks, even though some renegade Red troops had also ransacked *shtetls* (Jewish villages).

JEWS IN NEW RUSSIA

Dozens of Jewish-origin Bolsheviks now wielded power over the largest nation on earth. Lenin was himself part-Jewish, and four of his politburo's seven members had Jewish blood, including Zinoviev, Trotsky and Lev Kamenev. Another Jew, Adolph Joffe, chaired the St Petersburg Military Revolutionary

Committee that overthrew the provisional government. Jews even ran their own Communist party cell, the *Yevsektsiya*.

Soviet rule brought changes for ordinary Jews, initially for the better. In July 1918 the Communists passed a decree 'recognizing the equality of all citizens, irrespective of race or nationality', and Lenin unequivocally proclaimed in 1919: 'Shame on accursed Tsarism which tortured and persecuted the Jews'.

With the Pale gone, Jews could, in theory, live anywhere. Jews formed soviets (workers' councils). The Kremlin decided to transform Jewish pedlars and petty artisans into farmers, to integrate Jews into society and eradicate anti-Semitism. By contrast with trends everywhere else, Jews left cities for the countryside. By 1930 some 230,000 Jews were working on farming communes in Belarus, Crimea and Ukraine.

FREEDOM EXTINGUISHED

Soon Communism revealed a darker side. The authorities penalized small Jewish shopkeepers and artisans as 'bourgeois elements' and closed churches, mosques and synagogues

alike after 1921. The Evseksia summarily crushed all other Jewish organizations and ran 'community trials' against 'backward and chauvinistic' Jewish religious practices, before it, too, was disbanded in 1930. As the Russian-born Zionist Chaim Weizmann noted, the revolutionaries 'could not understand why a Russian Jew should want to be anything but a Russian'.

Joseph Stalin gradually monopolized power after Lenin's death in 1924 by sidelining, arresting or expelling rivals, notably including Kamenev, Zinoviev and Trotsky. Agricultural collectivization led to rampant famine, especially in Ukraine, which killed millions. Show trials after 1934 purged most old Bolsheviks, including thousands of Jewish origin, and former tolerance of Yiddish cultural autonomy gave way to enforced assimilation by the late 1930s. But at least the physical survival of Jews was not threatened by communist rule, as it was in Nazi Germany and fascist Europe.

Left Capturing the excitement of a new era, this Bolshevik poster calls on foreign workers to join the Revolution.

Above Soviet Jewish collective farmer Michael Gefen and wife Sheina tend their homestead in Birobidzhan, 1935.

BIROBIDZHAN

The USSR's politburo wanted to assign a homeland to each nationality, including the Jews. Communism opposed Zionism so Palestine was no option. In 1928, the USSR set up the town of Birobidzhan at the end of the Trans-Siberian railway, to be the capital of a Jewish Autonomous Region, Yevreskaya. Yiddish and Russian were its official languages, and Jews were encouraged to farm and work in factories. However conditions were poor, Hebrew and religious instruction were outlawed, and, though the Kremlin boasted 150,000 Jews would live in Birobidzhan by 1937, few actually did. Only 25,000 were there in 1974, and 4,000 in 2008.

Birobidzhan experienced a slight revival after the fall of the Soviet Union, but it never fulfilled its aim of becoming a Marxist 'alternative Zion'.

THE INTERWAR YEARS

AFTER THE DEVASTATION OF WORLD WAR I, THE LEAGUE OF NATIONS WAS ESTABLISHED IN 1919 TO GUARANTEE GLOBAL PEACE. IN FACT THE RESULT-ANT TREATIES CREATED MORE PROBLEMS THAN THEY SOLVED.

From a Jewish perspective the inter-war years presented a portrait of contrasts. On the one hand individual Jews thrived as never before; on the other, hatred against Jews mounted. And after Nazis took over Germany in 1933, both individuals and communities across Europe faced the real threat of annihilation.

JEWISH DELEGATES TO VERSAILES

The Paris peace talks of 1919 aimed to establish a new world order where all peoples had a voice. In this spirit, Jews sent a deputation called the Comité Des Delegations Juives, claiming the support of 12 million people worldwide. Led by US lawyer Louis Marshall and Russian Zionist Leo Motzkin, the Comité demanded protection for Jews as a nationality, albeit a stateless one. In the event Jews were acknowledged as a semi-autonomous minority.

The Versailles Treaty of 1919 rec-ognized a host of new states, including Poland, Lithuania, Czechoslovakia and Yugoslavia. Austria was stripped down to its core area, Hungary won its independence and Germany's Weimar Republic had to cede eco-nomically valuable land to neighbours.

Versailles was hardly ideal for Jews. Before 1914 they had lived with other minorities in ramshackle empires but now they felt exposed. Versailles compelled eastern European states to sign minority rights treaties following Comité advice, though Poland, Hungary and Romania sub-verted this requirement by targeted taxation, or laws to improve trade and sanitation. Furthermore, rifts between pro- and anti-Zionists undermined the Comité and simi-lar bodies such as the Jewish Agency and World Jewish Congress.

THE STAB IN THE BACK

Conspiracy theorists in Germany's ultra-nationalist *Freikorps* group spread the myth that Jews had stabbed Germany in the back by forcing the fatherland to surrender just when it was about to win the war. Meanwhile, rightists in Russia and beyond blamed the Jews for the 1917 revolution and subsequent ruinous civil war; even though most ordinary Jews were apolitical resi-dents of the Pale, remote from events in Moscow and Petrograd.

JEWISH REVOLUTIONARIES IN GERMANY

In November 1918, as Germany sank to military defeat, Jewish socialist Kurt Eisner overthrew the Bavarian monarchy and founded a 'people's republic'. When he was assassinated the next February, other

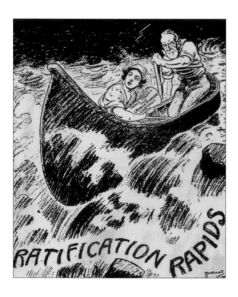

Left The League of Nations was the brainchild of President Woodrow Wilson, seen here reassuring a nervous USA.

Above Socialist firebrand Rosa Luxemburg, murdered in 1919 after an abortive coup in Berlin.

Jewish revolutionaries, Ernst Toller, Gustav Landauer and Eugene Leviné, established a short-lived Soviet republic there in imitation of the Bolsheviks in Russia.

The best-known Jewish radical of all was the Polish-born Rosa Luxemburg (1871–1919). Formerly the co-founder of the Lithuanian Social-Democratic Party, she moved to Germany in 1898 and soon rejected the parliamentary approach. Her inveterate foe was another Jew, the revisionist Marxist Eduard Bernstein, a Social-Democrat leader and Reichstag member during 1902–18 and 1920–28. Luxemburg took a bolder stance: a fiery critic of imperialism, nationalism and even Bolshevik 'bureaucracy', she co-founded the Spartacist League in 1914, which unlike mainstream socialists opposed the war and supported spontaneous uprising by the masses. Army officers murdered her in January 1919 after a failed Spartacist coup attempt in Berlin. The leftist Jewish historian Isaac Deutscher later called her assassination 'the first triumph of Nazi Germany'.

Neither Rosa Luxemburg nor most Marxists of Jewish origin cared much for Judaism. Nor did most German Jews support their views.

Above The old world meets the new? Erich Lessing's painting shows a Polish Jewish soldier reading a newspaper to his countrymen, 1920.

None the less, the prominence of Jewish revolutionary leaders allowed rightists to tar the whole community with the 'radical' brush.

JEWISH LIFE IN POLAND

Having been missing from the map of Europe since the partition of 1816, Poland was reborn as an independent nation under Marshal Joseph Pilsudski on 11 November 1918. Thousands of Jewish shopkeepers, professionals and petty capitalists voted with their feet and moved there. By 1924, Poland had nearly 3 million Jews, more than 10 per cent of its population. Jews made up about a quarter of all schoolchildren and university students. Polish Jews generally felt well disposed towards Pilsudski, who named himself dictator in May 1926 and implemented the terms of the 1919 Minorities Protection Treaty.

Poland's Jewish urban dwellers increasingly spoke Polish and revelled in a buoyant national culture, whereas poorer rural Jews stuck to Yiddish and cherished traditional ways. Jewish political parties now entered the *Sejm*, or 'Polish parliament', initially as a national council in co-operation with other minorities. After 1928 some Jewish parties joined the government

list – a new phenomenon that split Jewish votes and eroded the community's independence.

Leftist and Zionist Jewish groups competed with each other more productively in Poland and Lithuania by building networks of secular schools. Instruction was either in Yiddish or Hebrew and the development marked a breach with previous tradition.

THE MARCH OF FASCISM

All Europe suffered from the Wall Street stock market crash of 1929, and as unemployment and inflation ran rampant, fascism grew in Austria, Hungary and Poland. Fanatics began to follow the model set by Benito Mussolini's Italian Fascists who took power in October 1922. Fascism venerated the state, rejected capitalism and Marxism in equal measure, and marked, in Mussolini's words, the clear, final and categorical antithesis of democracy, plutocracy, freemasonry and the principles of 1789. Every state in Europe was under democratic government in the 1920s; by 1940 only four democracies had survived.

At first fascism was not explicitly anti-Semitic, but it provided an environment within which racism could thrive. Ultimately Nazism, the Germanic variant of fascism, transformed racism into a commanding ideology, dragged the world into a second world war, and all but destroyed the Jews of Europe.

AMERICA – PROGRESS AND PITFALLS

World War I helped establish American centrality in world affairs, and Jews became an integral part of US society. The first Jewish state governor, Moses Alexander of Idaho, was elected in 1915; Louis Brandeis became the first Jew in the US Supreme Court in 1916; and in 1917 Jews made up 5.7% of the US Army, greater than their 3.25% representation in the population.

New organizations arose to articulate Jewish interests: the American

Above Ku Klux Klan devotees, Long Island, New York State, 1930.

Jewish Joint Distribution Committee in 1914, and the American Jewish Congress (AJC) in 1918. Reconstituted under Steven Wise in 1924, in 1936 the AJC propelled the creation of a World Jewish Congress. Brandeis, Wise and Felix Frankfurter were powerful advocates for Zionism; and immigrants benefited American science, industry and popular culture.

However, an influx of comparatively unskilled workers strained the economy and led to new quotas. The 1924 Immigration Act capped entrants by area of origin to 2% of any donor country's community present in the USA in 1880, thus targeting Asians and eastern and southern Europeans, including Jews. Latent anti-Semitism came to the fore, with car tycoon Henry Ford disseminating the Protocols of Zion, and others backing the 1924 act on grounds of racial hygiene. Following the 1929 slump, the racist Ku Klux Klan added Jews as another enemy of America, and anti-Semitic organizations, some sponsored by Germany after 1933, lambasted President Roosevelt's New Deal as a Jew Deal. In 1938 the Catholic radio priest Charles Coughlin launched a propaganda campaign against Jews. Despite this, when war erupted in September 1939 most Americans united against Nazi aggression.

HITLER TAKES POWER – NAZISM GROWS

FOR JEWS, NO COUNTRY REPRESENTED CIVILIZED ASPIRATIONS MORE THAN GERMANY. YET IT WAS HERE THAT THE MOST BARBARIC AND DEVASTATING ANTI-SEMITIC ONSLAUGHT WAS DEVISED AND REALIZED.

In 1921 the novelist Jakob Wasserman proclaimed, 'I am a German and a Jew in equal measure – one cannot be separated from the other.' That same year the Berlin-born Jewish satirist Kurt Tucholsky wrote: 'Germans have two passions: beer and anti-Semitism. The beer is 28 proof but the anti-Semitism is 100 proof.'

Many Germans believed that Jews had betrayed the nation in war and were steering it to disaster in peace. They blamed Jews for the June 1919 Versailles Treaty, which limited their army to 100,000 soldiers, confiscated territories and colonies and imposed reparations of $32 billion. And they despised the Weimar Republic – instituted on 11 August 1919 – as a Jewish tool, which had wilfully dismantled the monarchy and handed Germany to the socialists.

Below In command – Adolf Hitler addresses a stormtrooper rally, Dortmund, 1933.

Above An early harbinger of coming genocide – sign designating area for Jews, Berlin Park, c.1935.

NAZISM AND ANTI-SEMITISM

Adolf Hitler's skill lay in turning this minority viewpoint into a mainstream belief and eventually using it to gain absolute power. In 1920 he became *führer*, or 'leader', of the small National Socialist German Workers' Party, better known as the Nazis. From the outset, anti-Semitism was his central motif. 'It is our duty', he said in 1920, 'to whip up and to incite in our people the instinctive repugnance of the Jews'.

Born in Linz, Austria, in 1889, Adolf Hitler fought in World War I and, like millions of ex-soldiers, thought that politicians had 'sold them out' in 1918. Hitler fostered the *Sturmabteilung*, or SA, a cohort of brown-shirted stormtroopers under the fanatic Ernst Röhm, and won the crucial backing of the veteran war hero Erich Ludendorff.

Hitler and Ludendorff instigated a coup in a Munich beer hall in 1923. When it failed, Hitler was charged with treason and jailed for nine months in Landsberg prison, where he began writing *Mein Kampf*, or 'My Struggle'. The book signalled his view that 'Aryans' were the 'master race', and that 'parasitical' Jews caused all Germany's misfortunes and were the enemy of civilization everywhere.

Some Nazis adopted anti-Christian occultism as symbolized in the swastika sign. What made Nazism so potent was its blend of elements, and its exploitation of human psychology. It appealed to Germany's growing petty middle class who envied the wealthy above them, feared the proletariat below and had most to lose from economic recession. Anti-Semitism, once thought uncouth, became more acceptable as political hysteria increased.

HITLER WINS POWER

Most Jews supported the Weimar Republic and welcomed the ascent of Walther Rathenau as foreign minister in 1922. His assassination by right-wing army officers on 24 June 1922 prompted economic panic and the German mark fell from 350 to 4,500 per dollar in four months. The Wall Street Crash and global recession of 1929 hit Germany hard. By 1932 half her factories stood idle and millions were jobless. In 1932,

Above Mein Kampf *('My Struggle')
– Adolf Hitler's manifesto, in which he
expresses his hatred against the Jews.*

14 million German voters backed
the Nazis, and Hitler was appointed
Chancellor on 30 January 1933. In
March the Nazis gained 44 per cent
support in elections, and Hitler
authorized the first concentration
camp, at Dachau, for political opponents. Four days later he used a fire
at the Reichstag – thought to have
been started by Nazis – as the pretext to rule by decree.

LEGISLATING HATRED

Hitler lost little time in putting *Mein
Kampf* theories into practice. In April
1933, he ordered a boycott of Jewish
lawyers, doctors and shopkeepers and
forced a bill through the Reichstag
that sacked Jews from the civil service. Paul von Hindenburg wanted to
exempt loyal Jewish war veterans
from the law but was rebuffed.

Non-Nazi institutions rushed to
satisfy Nazi policy with remarkable
speed. In May students burned books
by Jews, Communists and other
'degenerates', and in July universities began purging Jews from their
faculties. By June 1935 Germany's
leading medical journal openly compared Jews to the tuberculosis bacilli.

In August 1933 Propaganda
Minister Joseph Goebbels began
barring Jews from working in broad-
casting, cinema, music and the press.
Before long, no Jews could attend
theatres, film-houses or concert-halls.
Having banned rival parties and trade
unions, Hitler crushed the SA on the

TALENTED JEWISH REFUGEES

The Third Reich's race legislation prompted the flight of some of Europe's
most talented Jews. The composer Kurt Weill left in 1933, and writer Stefan
Zweig in 1934. By the time the Nazis annexed Austria in 1938, flight was far
harder. The novelist Herman Broch was rescued by James Joyce and others; and the father of modern psychology, Sigmund Freud, left Vienna for
London in June 1938. Philosopher Ludwig Wittgenstein had to pay off
officials to get papers to leave for Britain in August 1939. He and Hitler
were, paradoxically, classmates at a high school in Linz. Predictions of German
weakness due to a Jewish 'brain drain' were overstated, although the flight
of 29 Jewish nuclear physicists was to prove a massive blow to Germany
when the Allies produced the first atomic bomb. Most famous of all refugee
scientists was Albert Einstein, who left Berlin in 1932 and in 1933 helped
set up the International Rescue Committee to assist opponents of Hitler.

Night of the Long Knives in June 1934
and declared himself *führer* of Germany
after von Hindenburg died in July.

NUREMBERG LAWS, 1935

Already, before 1935, Jews could not
use hospitals, were barred from higher
education, and had to adopt middle
names – Sara and Israel. They had
identity cards stamped with a J. But
anti-Jewish legislation really started
with the Nuremberg Laws of 15
September 1935. Their purpose was
apparently to cease attacks on Jews
by party members, as this harmed the
German economy, and to standardize
the treatment of Jews, based on a
pseudo-scientific racial rationale. Now,
Jews were no longer citizens, but 'subjects', stripped of their political rights.
The Law for the Protection of German
Blood and Honour banned Jews from
marrying non-Jews in order to 'preserve the German people'. Jews were
categorized as full Jews or first- and
second-class mongrels, according to
how much Jewish blood they had.

The Nuremberg Treaty established
a legal framework for uprooting Jews
and reducing them to poverty. Public
areas were declared *judenrein*, or 'Jew-
free'; individual Jewish 'criminals'

Right Young Jews prepare to leave
Nazi Germany for Palestine in
February 1938.*

were sent to concentration camps in
1937; Jewish businesses were liquidated
or 'Aryanized' in 1938; and up to
17,000 Polish Jews were deported
to the border in October 1938.

Many German Jews persuaded
themselves Nazism was a passing
phase, but it became increasingly
obvious that trying to ride out the
storm would no longer work. About
a third of German Jews emigrated.
The Confessing Church stood
against racism in 1935, as did some
Catholic canons. However, most dissidents were exiled, incarcerated or
killed. There was no united resistance against the Nazis. Matters
worsened as Germany took more
European territory in the 1930s.

WORLD WAR II BEGINS

THE GERMAN DRIVE FOR *LEBENSRAUM*, OR 'LIVING SPACE', ULTIMATELY SPARKED WORLD WAR II. AS MORE COUNTRIES WERE CONQUERED, SO MILLIONS OF JEWS FELL PREY TO LETHAL NAZI LEGISLATION.

At first, the Nazis only coveted lands lost in 1918. They acquired the port of Danzig after 1933, and overran the coal-rich Saar region in 1935 and German Upper Silesia in 1937. Facing mere rebukes from France, Britain and the League of Nations, Hitler felt emboldened to fuse his native Austria with Germany, although the 1919 Versailles Treaty had expressly forbidden this.

On 12 March 1938, German troops invaded Austria and arrested 70,000 leading Jews, Communists and Social Democrats. Hitler then declared Germany and Austria one, entered Vienna and Linz in triumph and applied racial legislation against Austria's 190,000 Jews, about three-quarters of whom lived in Vienna.

Below Internees building Dachau, Germany's first concentration camp, under the watch of an SS guard, 1933.

EVIAN CONFERENCE

By 1938, about 150,000, or nearly one-third, of Germany's 500,000 Jews had emigrated; and more Jews left from occupied Danzig, Saar, Silesia and Sudetenland. In July 1938, US President Franklin Roosevelt convened a nine-day conference to address the refugee issue at Evian-les-Bains, France. All told, some 811,000 Jews managed to find new homes abroad during the period 1933–43: 190,000 went to America, 120,000 to Palestine and 65,000 to England.

NIGHT OF BROKEN GLASS

The true nadir arrived with the cross-continental pogrom against Jews in Germany and Austria on 9–10 November 1938. Dubbed *Kristallnacht*, or 'Night of Broken Glass', this onslaught saw 1,000 synagogues destroyed, dozens of Jews

Above Kristallnacht, November 1938, when looters ransacked Jewish shops with the connivance of the regime.

killed, businesses looted, properties resold at forced auctions and wealth stolen by Nazi thugs. Five days later Germany closed all public schools to Jewish children.

Kristallnacht shocked the world and hastened the likelihood of war. Responding to pleas from British Jews, Britain agreed to rescue 10,000 unaccompanied Jewish children in what was called the *Kindertransport*. A similar initiative in America was sadly blocked at Congressional Committee stage.

THE FALL OF POLAND

Adolf Hitler's final gamble was his non-aggression pact with the Soviet Union of 24 August 1939, which effectively neutralized Germany's 'eastern front'. The way was now clear for Hitler to invade Poland on 1 September 1939. Some 20,000 Jews died in the initial incursion, and bombing destroyed up to 95 per cent of Jewish homes in 120 centres. Poland was divided into two zones, German in the west (with 2.1 million Jews) and Russian in the east (with 1.37 million Jews). From

Above Lithuanian soldier marching a group of Jews to forced labour in Nazi-occupied eastern Europe.

October 1939 Nazis began corralling Jews into urban ghettos, with the Warsaw Ghetto holding 380,000 and Lodz, 160,000. Conditions were appalling: Jews, nearly a third of Warsaw's population, occupied just 2.4 per cent of the city's area. Thousands died of disease and starvation as Jews were only allocated 253 calories of food per person, compared to 2,613 for Germans. Jews were forbidden to step outside the ghetto and any Pole caught aiding a Jew was killed on the spot.

Within the ghetto Jews ran a *Judenrat*, or 'Jewish Council', and police, schools, libraries and theatres to keep up spirits, until the Nazis forced councillors to choose who should fill quotas for deportation to death-camps. The decision drove many an official to suicide.

WORLD WAR

Hitler's 1939 Polish invasion triggered World War II, which led to Germany invading Norway and Denmark in April 1940, and France, Belgium, Holland and Luxembourg in May. All but Britain fell before the German *blitzkrieg*, or 'lightning war'. Meanwhile, Italy and Japan joined Germany in a Tripartite Axis Pact in September. In July 1939 the Nazis had shut down the *Reichvertretung der Juden in Deutschland*, or 'National Agency for Jews in Germany', a compulsory organization of all Jews in the Reich headed by Rabbi Leo Baeck, and replaced it with a National Association directly run by the Gestapo. Jews in conquered countries were subjected to Nazi race laws, and wartime exigencies meant that emigration was no longer possible.

FRANCE AND ALGERIA

From July 1940 France was divided into a German-occupied zone in the north and the puppet Vichy regime in the south, which collaborated with the Nazis and deported thousands of Jews to German camps.

The Crémieux Decree of 1870 had naturalized Algerian Jews, but that status was revoked when 117,000 Jews felt the weight of the racist Vichy laws in Algeria.

THE RUSSIAN FRONT IN 1941

Having conquered most of mainland Europe, Adolf Hitler turned his attention eastwards. On 22 June 1941, he breached his non-aggression pact with the Soviet Union and launched Operation Barbarossa, which caught millions of Jews in a fatal dragnet. Nazis decapitated Jewish leadership by murdering any Communist commissars they found, and killing all but one or two of Lithuania's 300 communal rabbis.

RESISTANCE FIGHTERS

During April–May 1943, Mordechai Anilewicz (1919–1943) led the first armed Jewish resistance to Nazism in the Warsaw Ghetto uprising. Somehow the residents resisted for five weeks, before succumbing to Nazi soldiers, who razed the site at the cost of 7,000 Jewish lives. The remaining 50,000 were sent to concentration or extermination camps.

Later the Vilna Ghetto rose up and resistance groups formed in Bialystok, Minsk and Kovno ghettos. In Poland, Jews commanded 4 of the 12 partisan units parachuted in in 1944. Despite such bravery, nothing could stop the murder of millions known as the Holocaust.

Below A searing image of infamy: Nazi troops round up Jews after crushing the 1943 Warsaw ghetto uprising.

HOLOCAUST – FINAL SOLUTION

THE HOLOCAUST IS REGARDED AS THE ARCHETYPAL EXAMPLE OF MAN'S CAPACITY FOR WICKEDNESS. FROM A JEWISH PERSPECTIVE, NAZI RACIAL GENOCIDE PROVED MORE LETHAL THAN ANY ANTI-SEMITISM IN HISTORY.

The Holocaust, or *Shoah* in Hebrew, destroyed Jewish human life on a scale never seen before, eliminated Europe as a leading centre of Jewish civilization, and left an irreparable wound on the Jewish psyche.

Jews were not the only sector of European society to suffer the Holocaust. An estimated 500,000 Roma and Sinti gypsies were also killed, as were homosexuals, mentally and physically disabled people, the 'Rhineland bastards' (offspring of Germans and African soldiers from World War I), and political opponents, including dissident churchmen. Yet Jews were pursued with unparalleled fanaticism and died in far greater numbers.

THE 'FINAL SOLUTION'
SS chief Heinrich Himmler created *Einsatzgruppen*, or 'action forces' before the war to round up and kill Jews, gypsies and Communists.

Above The view that greeted US soldiers after they liberated Buchenwald concentration camp, April 1945.

Now their commandos killed Jews on the spot as they ploughed through Ukraine and the Baltic states *en route* to Moscow. Officials sought a more comprehensive approach. On 31 June 1941 Hitler's deputy, Hermann Goering, entrusted the Reich Security overseer, Reinhard Heydrich, with implementing 'a complete solution to the Jewish question', affecting an estimated 11 million Jews throughout the German sphere. Jewish emigration was totally prohibited on 31 October 1941. In January Heydrich convened a conference at Wansee, near Berlin, to co-ordinate the logistics of total extermination. Heydrich was assassinated in May 1942 but the policy lived on.

A NETWORK OF CAMPS
In Germany the prototype concentration camp was Dachau, set up near Munich in 1933. All extermination camps, a 1942 innovation, were located outside the Reich. The six most infamous were in Poland: Auschwitz, Chelmno, Belzec, Majdanek, Sobibor and Treblinka. Others were located in Croatia (Jasenovac), Ukraine (Janowska) and Belarus (Maly Trostenets).

Prisoners sent to such camps were not expected to last more than 24 hours. Conditions were also atrocious in 'conventional' camps – 70,000 died in Bergen-Belsen and 56,000 in Buchenwald. In 1942 Germany began mass deportations from ghettos at a bewildering pace, as part of Operation Reinhard: 300,000 Jews were shipped over just 52 days from the Warsaw Ghetto to Treblinka, where in total 750,000 Jews were killed.

GAS CHAMBERS
As early as 1933 the Nazis had used carbon monoxide to achieve the 'euthanasia' of physically or mentally handicapped people. But this method was inefficient – hence gas chambers using faster-acting Zyklon B were invented.

Left Jewish women and children marked with the yellow star are forced on to cattle truck trains to the death camps.

The selection process, as to who would die immediately or be forced to work, took the form of a pseudo-medical inspection. Jews selected for death were sent to take 'showers' in rooms that were actually gas chambers, and died within 25 minutes. The Nazis tattooed prisoners with a number on their arm; no one was addressed by name; and badges distinguished groups – yellow star for Jews, pink triangle for homosexuals.

AUSCHWITZ

Based on an old Polish military barracks near the town of Ozwickiem, Auschwitz mutated in 1942 into the largest death camp of all. It became a fully fledged city with street lighting, railway tracks and electrical and plumbing systems. An additional site was added, called Birkenau, plus a factory at Mona. Thirty freight cars of Jews arrived every day.

After victims died, a unit called the Sonderkommando purloined gold teeth, shoes, bones, even human fat which was sent to soap factories, and hair, for stuffing pillows.

Below Prelude to the Holocaust: German soldiers face a synagogue set ablaze by locals after the Nazis occupied Lithuania, 1941.

THE STATISTICS

The following are estimates of the numbers of Jews killed in the Nazi Holocaust and the percentages of each country's pre-war Jewish population who died.

Poland	3,000,000	90%
Soviet Union	1,250,000	44%
Hungary	450,000	70%
Romania	300,000	50%
Germany/Austria	210,000	90%
Netherlands	105,000	75%
France	90,000	26%
Czechoslovakia	80,000	89%
Greece	54,000	77%
Belgium	40,000	60%
Yugoslavia	26,000	60%
Bulgaria	14,000	22%
Italy	8,000	20%

All suffered collective punishment if anyone escaped, and many froze to death standing in punishment grounds. Attached to Auschwitz was a unit that experimented on live human beings. Allied airplanes overflew Auschwitz, but were ordered to bomb more militarily valuable targets. Overall, some 1.5 million Jews perished at Auschwitz.

HUNGARY AND GREECE

In April 1944 the Holocaust reached Hungary, on the back of the Nazi invasion. Until then, Hungarian Jews bore burdens but their lives were safe. Immediately Adolf Eichmann, one of the major organizers of the Holocaust, began sending Jews to Auschwitz; 380,000 arrived over six weeks and 300,000 died. Even when the Soviet Army stood at the gates of Budapest, the Germans managed to arrest 40,000 Jews and sent them on a death-march to Auschwitz.

THE FEW WHO HELPED

Certain German-occupied nations distinguished themselves by resisting, such as Finland; Denmark, which

Above Raoul Wallenberg, the Swedish diplomat who risked his life to save thousands of Jews in Hungary.

smuggled most of her Jews to neutral Sweden; Italy, which flouted German deportation edicts; and above all Bulgaria, where resolute government action saved 50,000 Jews. It is also said that King Mohammed of Morocco personally refused to hand over Jews to the Vichy overlords.

A few brave individuals helped Jews at great personal cost. In late 1942 Jules Géraud Saliège, Archbishop of Toulouse, publicly protested against Vichy French deportations. 'All is not permissible against them. They belong to mankind. They are our brethren as are so many others. No Christian can forget that', he wrote.

Another saviour was Raoul Wallenberg, a Swedish diplomat in Hungary who saved perhaps 15,000 Jewish lives by issuing false papers.

French Protestants and Catholics in Le-Chambon-sur-Lignon hid Jewish children during 1942–44. And Oscar Schindler, a Sudeten German industrialist, rescued almost 1,200 from certain death by getting them transferred from Auschwitz to work in his factories. Sadly, such cases were the exceptions; most people just averted their gaze.

THE AFTERMATH OF GENOCIDE

WHETHER THE HOLOCAUST WAS THE ZENITH OF CENTURIES OF ANTI-SEMITISM, OR A WARTIME ABERRATION, WHEN STANDING BEFORE THE MURDER OF SIX MILLION JEWS, PERHAPS THE MOST FITTING RESPONSE IS SILENCE.

One by one, the death camps were liberated by Allied troops: Auschwitz by the Red Army on 27 January 1945, Buchenwald by the US Army on 11 April, and Bergen-Belsen by the British Army on 15 April.

NUREMBERG TRIALS

From November 1945 to October 1946, an International Military Tribunal put 24 pre-eminent Nazi leaders on trial within the US occupation zone. The location was Nuremberg, doubly fitting because it was the site of the Nazi mass rallies and the Nazis' first systematic racial legislation. Questions were raised about the complicity of ordinary Germans and whether personnel acted on orders from above or on their own initiative.

Below '*Never again' was the pledge made at the Nuremberg International Military Tribunal, where Nazi perpetrators of crimes against humanity were put in the dock, January 1946.*

PSYCHOLOGICAL TRAUMA

Jews, too, faced troubling questions: notwithstanding a few uprisings, why had so many been led 'like lambs to the slaughter'? Thousands felt guilty for surviving when relatives had perished, or strove to hide the degradation from their children. Memories of impossible moral choices, like having to decide which child to surrender to the Gestapo, deepened their trauma.

Mostly, Jews felt cheated by Western civilization and the allure of its supposed 'enlightenment'. Survivors who returned to their countries were often shocked by their reception. When in July 1945 200 Jews arrived in Kielce in Poland, local anti-Semites launched a pogrom that killed 42 of them. This massacre convinced Jews that they had no future in Europe. Many tried to escape to America, while thousands joined the *Beriha*, or underground 'flight', of 1944–8 to southern Europe, *en route* to

Above A memorial to the 1.5 million dead at Auschwitz, constructed from desecrated Jewish tombstones.

Palestine. An estimated 50,000 reached Palestine during these years, despite a British bar on entrance.

DISPLACED PERSONS CAMPS

Among the eight million people displaced by World War II were some 50,000–100,000 Jewish camp survivors. Another 150,000 Jews soon joined them after fleeing anti-Semitism in Romania, Poland, Russia and Hungary. From October 1945 the newly established United Nations set up a relief administration to run displaced persons (DP) camps in Germany. Meanwhile, the group *Sh'erit Ha-Pletah*, or 'surviving remnant', met in congress at Munich in February 1946 and elected representatives for Jews who had nowhere to live.

BEHIND THE IRON CURTAIN

The Kremlin ignored the anti-Jewish nature of Nazi actions. If anything, Russian anti-Semitism increased after the war. In August 1952, 13 leading Yiddish poets were executed. Jews were called 'rootless cosmopolitans' and 'American agents' in the official press. Soon hundreds of Russian Jews lost their jobs or were arrested, the zenith being the supposed 'Doctors'

Above Jewish women and children at Belsen concentration camp, Saxony, where British troops found 60,000 barely alive survivors.

Plot' against Stalin. During the Cold War, Soviet authorities banished Jewish activists to the Gulag, and effectively barred ordinary Jews from various professions and universities.

Europe's post-war division into an American-sponsored western bloc and a Russian-backed eastern bloc also had adverse ramifications for Jews. Jews in eastern Europe found themselves subject to the same strictures as those in the USSR. They could not leave since Communist governments barred emigration. Worse, Jews were purged from Communist parties throughout the region, culminating in the arrest and execution of Czech party secretary Rudolf Slansky and 11 other leading Jews in November 1952.

PERPETRATORS, VICTIMS AND BYSTANDERS

During genocide, argued the historian Raul Hilberg, everyone is a perpetrator, victim or bystander. To blame German culture uniquely ignores non-German bystanders. A survey of 1941 shows that even before the Holocaust got under way, various peoples were persecuting Jewish citizens. French police arrested 4,000 Parisian Jews and interned them in urban Drancy, near central Paris. Over three years, 65,000 were deported from there, of whom only 2,000 survived. Likewise, Lithuania's 'Order Police' began exterminating Jews as soon as the Soviets left; and in September 1941 Ukrainian collaborators helped Nazi *Einsatzgruppen*, or deployment groups, shoot 33,771 Jews and dump their corpses at Babi Yar, a ravine near Kiev, in the largest single massacre of the Holocaust.

MEMORIALS

As early as 1945, Zionists met in London to plan a project to commemorate the Shoah (Holocaust in Hebrew). The result was the complex known as Yad Vashem (hand of God), which was built over 200 acres in Jerusalem. An avenue recalls the 'Righteous' gentiles who risked their lives to save Jews from death.

People also recall the Holocaust's acts of quiet courage, such as when prisoners held secret religious services, even when many asked, 'Where was God in Auschwitz?'

Israel has long held an annual Holocaust Day; now the UN and other nations do the same. In America, several museums mark the genocide. Berlin's Jewish Museum, opened in 2001, features a poignantly empty Holocaust Tower. Berlin also inaugurated a sculptural Memorial to the Murdered Jews of Europe in 2005.

BIRTH OF ISRAEL

The United Nations was founded in 1945 to banish genocide and replace war with dialogue. No doubt these factors hastened the decision to set up the State of Israel in the former British Mandate of Palestine in 1948. To many Jews, the fact that only three years elapsed between the Holocaust's end and the birth of the first Jewish state in 1,900 years was a miracle. But even this triumph cannot lessen the worst disaster to befall Jews in their history.

Below Displaced persons encampment, Bamberg, where thousands of survivors spent the immediate post-war years.

CULTURAL RESPONSES TO THE HOLOCAUST

INITIALLY STUNNED BY THE ENORMITY OF THE HOLOCAUST, ARTISTS GRADUALLY BEGAN TO CREATE WORKS OF DIGNITY AGAINST EVIL, AND LASTING MEMORIALS TO EUROPE'S OBLITERATED COMMUNITIES.

In 1945 a philosopher of German Jewish origin, Theodor Adorno, responded to the Holocaust with the line: 'To write poetry after Auschwitz is barbaric'. Many shared his views: what use was Western culture, which German Jews had eagerly embraced, when the cattle-wagons started rolling? Adorno soon admitted he might have been mistaken. After the war, cultural expression served as witness to arguably the greatest humanitarian crime in history. In the longer term it helped Jews come to terms with loss and begin their recovery.

POETRY OF ANNIHILATION

In June 1941, Nazis overran Vilna, shot 10,000 Jews and corralled another 20,000 into two ghettos. Witnessing the liquidation of the smaller ghetto on Yom Kippur, the Yiddish poet Avrom Sutzkever wrote from his hiding place: 'I lie in this coffin the way I would lie in a suit made of wood, a bark tossed

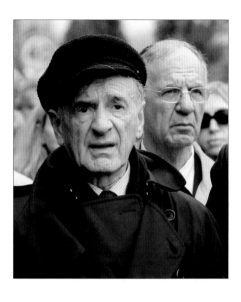

Above Nobel Peace Prize laureate and Holocaust survivor Eli Wiesel at Auschwitz, 60 years after liberation.

on treacherous waves, a cradle, an ark.' Sutzkever transplanted the image of baby Moses into this nightmarish world.

CULTURAL RESISTANCE, WORDS OF TESTIMONY

Sutzkever smuggled guns into the ghetto and conducted play readings and arts events throughout this grim era. Likewise, Mordechai Strigler, future editor of the New York Yiddish daily *Forverts*, or 'Forward', taught Jewish children in Maidanek and Buchenwald and organized literary evenings during which prisoners 'whispered poems and bits of history in order to keep their minds from dying.'

IMMORTAL WORKS

Even more than poetry, prose has been the prime vehicle of commemorating the Holocaust. The three outstanding authors are Primo Levi, Eli Wiesel and Anne Frank. All three personally experienced the trauma of the time. Anne Frank was sent to Auschwitz and then died in Bergen-Belsen after being captured from her hiding place in Amsterdam while still a young girl. Her poignant *Diary* survived and has entranced generations in many languages ever since. Eli Wiesel, born in Sighet, Romania, won a Nobel Peace Prize in part for his classic Holocaust memoirs, *Night*, first published in Yiddish in Buenos Aires.

Left Letter by Anne Frank, dated October 1942, when she was 13. She hid in Amsterdam before being sent to Auschwitz. Her diary is still widely read.

Levi, scion of an old Piedmontese Jewish family, was a chemist who survived Auschwitz and wrote several engrossing works in Italian, starting with *If This is a Man*. Later titles, all translated, include *Periodic Table* and essays *The Drowned and the Saved*. Throughout his work, he expresses the indomitable human spirit and the lunacy of war.

MUSIC

Since the 1990s concerts have featured recently recovered musical works by Jews murdered in the camps, thus recalling their creativity and defying their exterminators. The Soviet composer Dmitri Shostakovich set his Symphony no. 13 to Yevgeny Yevtushenko's fierce poem *Babi Yar*, commemorating that 1941 massacre. Neither man was Jewish, yet both were criticizing alleged Soviet denial of Jewish suffering in the crime. And in 2007 the Israeli Lior Navok composed the powerful *And the Trains Kept Coming*, an oratorio based on real documents of the Holocaust period.

CINEMA

American and British films just after the war alluded to Hitlerite anti-Semitism, yet few broached the actual calamity of the Holocaust. Exceptions were *The Stranger* (1946) directed by Orson Welles, which featured footage of the camps; and *Ostatni Etap*, or 'Last Stop', directed in 1948 by Wanda Jakubowska. Herself a Polish-Jewish former Auschwitz inmate, she said she only survived because she felt compelled to document what happened there. One of the most powerful Western documentaries was *Night and Fog* (1955) directed by Frenchman Alain Resnais.

Hollywood films tended to focus on particular cases and were arguably all the more powerful for doing so. One example was *The Pawnbroker* (1964), directed by Sidney Lumet, about a traumatised Jewish survivor who suffers flashbacks about his murdered family while running a shop in Harlem. Another was *Sophie's Choice* (1982), based on William Styron's 1979 novel and directed by a Jewish New Yorker, Alan Pakula; the film featured the agonizing dilemma of a mother (in this case a Polish Catholic) forced to choose which of two children to surrender to the gas chambers.

BETWEEN SHOAH AND SCHINDLER'S LIST

In 1985 *Shoah*, French-Jewish director Claude Lanzmann's compelling 9.5-hour-long documentary, set a benchmark for viewing the Holocaust in a literal and non-declamatory way. Two years later the celebrated veteran French director Louis Malle brought out *Au Revoir, les Enfants*, or 'Farewell, Children', reprising memories from Malle's own childhood when Jewish pupils were smuggled into his Catholic school, until they and their priest teacher were captured and sent to their death in the camps.

Right A still from The Pianist, *a 2002 film directed by Roman Polanski, himself a child survivor of the Krakow ghetto.*

Right Deported to Auschwitz in 1944, Primo Levi survived the camps and wrote outstanding much-loved books about the Holocaust.

Most famous of all was Steven Spielberg's 1995 film *Schindler's List*, adapted from Thomas Keneally's 1982 Booker Prize-winning novel, *Schindler's Ark*. Praised and criticized in equal measure, the film dramatizes the life of Oskar Schindler, a German businessman who used slave labour from Auschwitz and saved thousands of Jews. In 2002 Roman Polanski, himself a former child camp survivor, produced the acclaimed and unusually restrained Holocaust-based film, *The Pianist*.

ACADEMIC WORKS

From the 1960s, academic Holocaust literature has multiplied, as new data emerged and the number of first-hand witnesses dwindled. Possibly the most definitive work remains Raul Hilberg's monumental 1961 tome, *The Destruction of European Jewry*.

Inevitably the subject tends to controversy: the French pseudo-historian Roger Garaudy has denied the Holocaust happened, while the English David Irving minimized its extent and downplayed Hitler's role. Today, Holocaust denial is a crime in Austria, Germany and France.

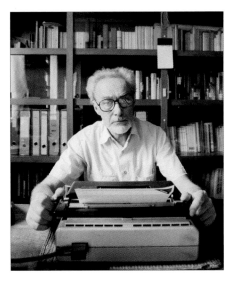

RESPONSES IN ISRAEL

For many Jews the most powerful cultural response to the Holocaust was a strong and confident State of Israel. That said, there was a certain ambivalence in early years: as the author Moshe Shamir suggested, 1950s Israelis were taught that European Jewish culture destroyed by the Nazis deserved its fate.

The trial of Adolf Eichmann in 1962 for crimes against humanity and war crimes, allowed survivors to give voice to a formerly taboo subject. On Yom Ha-Shoah (Holocaust Day) the siren sounds for a full minute, and Israelis of diverse backgrounds express a shared memory, standing still in their usually busy streets, homes and workplaces.

CHAPTER 10

ZIONISM, JERUSALEM AND ISRAEL

Political Zionism was one of several ideologies that gained credence among Jews in the late 19th and early 20th centuries. Nor was it initially the most popular. In 1948, however, just three years after the Holocaust wiped out a third of all Jews, the United Nations acceded to Zionist pressure and promulgated Israel as the first Jewish state in 1,900 years. Since then, Israel has outgrown its austere beginnings, revived Hebrew as a living language, and fulfilled the Biblical prophecy of 'gathering in the exiles', including most Jews from Europe and the Middle East. Triumph came at a cost, however. Israel has endured numerous wars and is blamed for dispossessing Palestine's indigenous Arabs. In addition, its acquisition of territories after 1967 encouraged settlers whose messianic fervour has stoked controversy. None the less Israel is today culturally vibrant and economically powerful. Demographically it has probably overtaken the United States as the major centre of modern Jewry.

Opposite Israeli flags flutter at a religious ceremony held at the Western Wall, Old City of Jerusalem. The men wear tallit and tefilin according to ancient Jewish custom.

***Above** David Ben-Gurion, the first Prime Minister of modern Israel. He became premier two days after Israeli independence in May 1948.*

ZIONISM – THE NATIONALIST DIVIDE

TURKISH MILITARY DEFEAT AND BRITAIN'S BALFOUR DECLARATION ENCOURAGED ZIONISTS TO REVIVE THEIR FADING MOVEMENT. DESPITE RESISTANCE, THEY PRESSED FOR A NATIONAL HOME IN PALESTINE.

Two events in 1917 rescued Zionist fortunes: the Balfour Declaration of 2 November, which expressed British governmental support for establishing a 'national home' for Jews in Palestine, and General Allenby's British military conquest of Jerusalem on 11 December. The prime mover behind the Balfour Declaration was Chaim Weizmann. As head of a Zionist delegation to the Versailles peace talks of 1919, he proclaimed that peaceful Jewish autonomy alongside Arabs in Palestine was both possible and necessary. In April 1920 the San Remo conference awarded Britain with mandates to govern Mesopotamia (Iraq) and Palestine, with the Balfour Declaration incorporated into the latter's charter.

Below A Labour Zionist poster for May Day, 1945, proclaims in Hebrew: 'Workers of all peoples, unite!'

Not all Jews were convinced that Zionism answered their most perplexing questions. Was Jewish nationalism really the best option? If so, was Palestine the place to locate it? And if Zionism was the way, which type should prevail out of the many contending strands?

ORTHODOX VERSUS SECULAR VIEWS

Until 1789 Jewish political and religious identity had essentially been one; after the French Revolution, Jews gained civil rights and members of the Haskalah (Jewish Enlightenment), began to redefine themselves in social and national as well as religious terms. Secular Zionism grew out of such views, yet drew heavily on imagery from the Torah, Talmud and daily prayer liturgy – nostalgia for the days of Jewish kings, rediscovering ancient Jewry's agrarian past and the mystical concept of redemption and negating the disharmony of exile.

Most Orthodox Jews prayed daily for a return to Zion, which they believed lay in the Creator's hands alone. They saw political Zionism as blasphemous because it was driven by humans, not by God's hand. They felt that the resultant community would be secular, not religious, so not a truly 'Jewish state'.

RELIGIOUS DISSENTERS

Denial of Zionism on religious grounds inspired the first truly global Orthodox political group, World Agudat Yisrael (Jewish Union), founded in Kattowicz, southern Poland, in 1912. A smaller contin-

Above Theodor Herzl with Zionist delegation on board Imperator, *on the way to Palestine, October 1898.*

gent of religious Zionists had already since 1902 organized themselves as Mizrachi – an acronym standing for 'religious centre'. They argued that faith without national spirit was only 'half Judaism'. Mizrachi affiliated with other Zionists, relocated to Palestine in 1920 and set up a youth wing, Bnei Akiva, nine years later.

At the opposite end of the religious spectrum, Reform Jews opposed Zionism for different reasons. They saw Judaism as a system of ethical principles and nothing more; nationality ought to depend on where one lived, not ethnic ties. Nazi oppression made many German Reform Jews reappraise that position.

BRITAIN'S VIEW

There are many theories as to why Britain backed Zionism, such as its desire to guard Middle East routes to India, or to ward off German or French aspirations. The Anglo-Jewish establishment was itself split down the middle on the Zionist issue. The leading Liberal politician Edwin Samuel Montagu considered Zionism a 'mischievous political creed'. The deliberate ambiguity of the Balfour Treaty's phrase 'national home' – not 'state'

– is often attributed to Montagu's watering down of the more strongly phrased original promise.

REBELLION

Before Balfour, diplomatic disappointments had deepened rifts within the Zionist movement. Some accused Theodor Herzl (1860–1904), the founder of political Zionism, and his successors of defining Zionism too negatively, as a cure for the disease of anti-Semitism. Frustrated at lack of progress over Palestine, the British Zionist Israel Zangwill had split from the Zionist movement at the 7th Congress of 1905 to lead his breakaway Territorialist group, which sought alternative homelands in Africa, Asia and Australia, but the group withered away in 1925. There were also differences between activists in Palestine versus the bureaucrats in Berlin and London; and between political Zionists, who stressed settlement before all else.

SOCIALIST ZIONISTS

More successful was a socialist party called *Po'alei Zion*, or 'Workers of Zion', and the young Russian-born David Ben-Gurion became its chief activist. To his left were Zionists of a more fiercely Marxist hue, who saw their trend as part of a global class struggle. After 1909 some young socialists began setting up *kibbutzim*, or 'collective farming colonies', and championed what they called 'Hebrew labour'. They co-operated with Arthur Ruppin, who in 1908 had founded the Zionist Organization's Palestine Bureau.

ARAB RESISTANCE

A few Palestinian Arabs welcomed the economic boost brought by Jewish immigration, but when the influx grew their suspicions increased. Arabs disliked the alien nature of Zionist socialism and felt that the 'Hebrew labour' policy discriminated against them in the workplace. Palestinian Arab newspapers such as *Karmil* (founded in 1908) ran campaigns against selling land to Zionists, and *Filastin* (1912) decried increased Jewish immigration. Above all, Arabs feared that Europeans might usurp or outnumber them.

Between 1873 and 1914 the Ottomans replaced the old administrative unit, *Jund Filastin*, or 'Palestine Province', with three separate *vilayets*, or 'governorates'. Most Palestinian Arabs, however, referred to themselves as part of Greater Syria. In

Above David Ben-Gurion signing the State of Israel document, 14 May 1948, marking the end of the British Mandate.

January 1919 their delegates attended a General Syrian Congress in Damascus that rejected Zionism, as well as a French mandate over Syria. They wanted to see Palestine incorporated within a united independent Syria and join the Arab delegation at the Paris Peace Talks.

Also in January, Chaim Weizmann met Emir Faisal, Sharif of Mecca and putative Arab leader. The two signed agreement for mutual cooperation, but this proved void when Britain and France, in Faisal's view, reneged on promises to grant him a kingdom.

A US commission of inquiry led by Henry King and Charles Crane in 1919 interviewed Jews and Arabs and provided a report that opposed major Jewish immigration. It also advised against a Jewish national home in Palestine, which could lead to 'dispossession of non-Jewish inhabitants'. Their views notwithstanding, the perils of anti-Semitism in 1920s Europe and especially the rise of Nazism in the 1930s continued to drive thousands of Jews to Palestine.

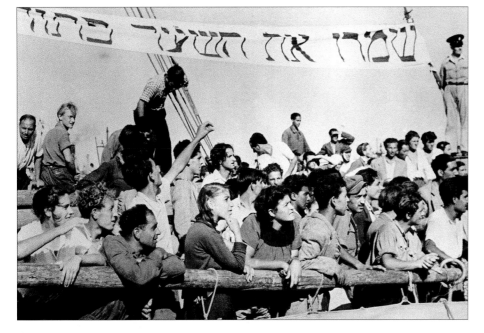

Left Some 450 Jewish refugees arrive at Haifa, 1946, onboard the Haviva Reil. *The slogan reads: 'Keep the gates open, we are not the last.'*

EARLY DAYS IN PALESTINE

SINCE 1922 AND AFTER SEVERAL WAVES OF JEWISH IMMIGRATION, PALESTINE'S BRITISH GOVERNORS FOUND THEMSELVES CAUGHT BETWEEN TWO ACRIMONIOUS COMMUNITIES, JEWS AND ARABS.

Zionism was always more than an immigration movement or political trend. Its more radical ideologies aimed to transform Jewry. To 'normalize', individual Jews should re-engage in simple handicrafts and farming and leave the world of the cerebral and mercantile. The most extreme Zionists wished to negate the Diaspora experience altogether.

THE ALIYOT

Zionism was from the start a collective enterprise, and as such it spawned distinct waves of immigration (*aliyah* in singular, *aliyot* in plural), each with its own unique characteristics. The First Aliyah (1882–1903) consisted of 25,000 mainly Russian Jews who were set on becoming farmers. They founded the first 28 *moshavot*, or privately owned rural settlements.

The Second Aliyah of the years 1904–14 was better organized and clearer in ideological intent. Its *halutzim*, or 'pioneers', established the collectivist kibbutz, set up Hebrew printing presses and the first

Hebrew high school in 1906, formed the Hashomer guards, and in 1909 created the first all-Jewish city, Tel Aviv, as an offshoot of ancient Jaffa.

POST-WAR DEVELOPMENTS

After the interregnum of World War I, revolution in Russia and pogroms in Hungary and Poland, a Third Aliyah of over 40,000 began in 1919, boosting Palestine's Jewish population to 90,000 by 1923. They established a defence group, the Haganah, in June 1920. Five months later they founded the Histadrut, an organization that quickly assumed a pivotal economic role as monopolist employers, trade union congress and even a health and welfare system.

With the Bolsheviks restricting Russian emigration after 1923, and America tightening up immigration after 1924, a Fourth Aliyah (1924–8) brought in a quite different sort of immigrant. Half of these 67,000 newcomers were middle-class Poles, including artisans and shopkeepers; they were less ideologically commit-

Above *Founders Square in Tel Aviv commemorates the 69 people who founded the city in 1909.*

ted than predecessors, and many found life in the Levant trying. By 1927 twice as many Jews left Palestine as arrived. Yet this fourth wave did create industries that stood Palestine in good stead later on.

PALESTINE MANDATE 1922

In 1921 Britain had excluded from the proposed Palestine mandate all the territory east of the Jordan River; Transjordan henceforth became a separate area. What remained was a land of some 10,000 square miles, about the size of the US state of Maryland. Its population was divided in 1922 between 84,000 Jews, settled mainly along the coastal plain, and Arabs, 71,000 of whom were Christian and 589,000 Muslim, generally in the hinterland. Cities such as Jaffa, Haifa and Jerusalem had mixed populations; otherwise Jews and Arabs tended to live separately.

In 1923, the Jewish Agency took over from the Zionist Commission as the putative government of Jews in Palestine. Chaim Weizmann held the central ground as president of the World Zionist Organization (1920–31 and 1931–46). The rising power in

Left *President Dr Chaim Weizmann addressing the Knesset (Israeli parliament) flanked by David Ben-Gurion (right) and Moshe Sharett (left) the first two prime ministers of Israel, 1949.*

Above The first kibbutz was Degania Alef, by the Sea of Galilee, built by Romanian Jews in 1909.

the new Yishuv (Jewish residents in Palestine) were the Labour Zionists. David Ben-Gurion led the largest Labour faction called *Mapai* after 1930. Under their guidance the essential features of the 'state to come' took form: kibbutzim, Histadrut, or General Federation of Labour, Jewish National Fund, the Hebrew University (founded in Jerusalem in 1925) and the adoption of the Hebrew language.

1925 also saw a long-simmering dispute come to the boil with the emergence of Vladimir Jabotinsky's Revisionist trend. Revisionists insisted that only an 'iron wall' military policy would convince Arabs that Jews were implacable in their intentions.

ARAB REVOLTS

All British attempts to create a joint Arab and Jewish executive failed. Arabs mistrusted Jewish intentions and saw them as colonial usurpers. Anti-Zionist Arab riots broke out in Jerusalem in 1920 and Jaffa in 1921.

Worse violence followed in 1929 in Jerusalem, Safed and Hebron, where some 67 unarmed religious Jews perished. The 1929 riots transformed the Haganah's status: it grew to encompass nearly all Jewish adults and youths, and its cadres began training programmes, set up arms depots and even made their own weapons.

Most tumultuous of all was the 1936–9 Arab Revolt. It caused 5,000 Arab and a few hundred Jewish deaths, and pitted forces loyal to the Mufti, Hajj Amin al-Husseini, appointed 1921, against the British and rival clans. Jews took advantage of Arab–British clashes to build 50 new 'stockade and watchtower' settlements. In 1931 Revisionists created a militant offshoot of Haganah, called Irgun, which after 1936 stepped up 'retaliatory actions' against Arabs and attacked Mandate forces after 1939.

BRITAIN'S CALCULATIONS

Determined to appease Arabs, the October 1930 British Passfield White Paper recommended limiting Jewish immigration. With violence in Palestine still raging, in 1937–8 the Peel and Woodhead commissions recommended splitting the territory into a small Jewish state and a large Arab one. Finally, a White Paper of 17 May 1939 dropped the partition idea and restricted Jewish rights to purchase land.

Most galling from a Jewish perspective was the paper's decision to limit Jewish immigrants to 75,000 in total. During 1933–9, Nazi persecution in Germany and beyond threatened the lives of all European Jews. With gates shut in Britain and America, Palestine had seemed like the only feasible refuge.

DEMOGRAPHICS IN PALESTINE		
Year	Jews	Arabs
1800	6,700	268,000
1880	24,000	525,000
1915	87,500	590,000
1931	174,000	837,000
1947	630,000	1,310,000

In 1933 Zionists created Youth Aliyah to help young threatened Jews. In 1934 the Haganah and the He-Halutz movement began chartering ships to bring refugees over illegally; after 1938 the British Navy began firing on illicit vessels. The number of Jews in Palestine rose during 1936-9 from 250,000 to 475,000 as a consequence of Fifth Aliyah immigrants from eastern Europe and Germany. Most new *olim* were neither Zionist nor Socialist. In time, their entrepreneurial spirit and cultural sophistication would add distinctive elements to the Zionists' 'state to come'. The advent of World War II put the Palestinian question on hold, yet, with hindsight, only postponed an inevitable clash between growing numbers of Jews and Palestine's Arab majority, each of whom dreamt of their own independent state.

Below The establishment of Tel Aviv, 1909, on sand dunes north of Jaffa.

JEWS IN A CHANGING MIDDLE EAST

THE MIDDLE EAST, CRADLE OF CIVILIZATION, IS ALSO THE BIRTHPLACE OF JEWS. ABRAHAM GREW UP IN TODAY'S IRAQ; JACOB'S DESCENDANTS SPENT 400 YEARS IN EGYPT; AND PALESTINE, NOW ISRAEL, LIES AT THE REGION'S FULCRUM.

Some half a million Jews lived in the Arab Middle East (Mashriq) and North Africa (Maghreb) by 1900. Though they represented a generally poorer minority of global Jewry, improved education hinted at a better future. However, within 70 years they had fallen to a few thousand.

ARAB NATIONALISM
Why did a century that began so promisingly end in the depletion of entire communities? Four political developments may explain this phenomenon: the liberation of Arab countries from Ottoman rule after 1918; European interference and mandates; the gradual winning of Arab independence; and, above all, the creation of the State of Israel.

In the late 19th century, some 'emancipated' Mizrahim, often known as 'Arab Jews', adopted leftist stances. Other Mizrahim identified with the mandate powers of the day (especially France in North Africa), but they paid for this as Arab nationalism grew. With the exception of Yemenite Jews, most chose not to go to Palestine until after 1948.

From the early 1920s Arab nationalism regarded Zionism as a threat. Such feelings often fed anti-Jewish sentiment. By making life hard for their Jews, Arab rulers contributed to their migration to Palestine and later Israel. Thus, paradoxically, they reinforced the population of the very state they wished to demolish.

In March 1945 the newly established Arab League pledged to fight Jewish statehood in Palestine and to defend Palestine's Arabs. In November 1947 the UN General Assembly voted for partition. After the 1948 war, fury at the fate of Palestinian Arab refugees often found expression in anger at local Jews. Each successive war – in 1956, 1967 and 1973 – saw an upsurge in anti-Zionism, causing yet further Jewish emigration to Israel from Arab League states.

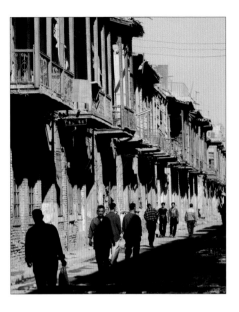

Above *Intricate wooden latticework and high ceilings distinguish the houses of the Bataween district of central Baghdad, once home to Iraqi Jews.*

MOROCCO'S HISTORY
More than 265,000 Jews lived in Arab-ruled Morocco by the mid-20th century. Jewish success, however, stoked instances of local envy and occasional wildfire pogroms. In 1438 Jews were confined to a *mellah*, or 'special quarter', in Fez, a pattern repeated elsewhere in the realm. Even before 1492, Sephardim and Maranos had begun arriving from Spain and Portugal, and settled in Tangier, Rabat, Meknes, Safi, Mogador, Marrakech and Mazagan. Sephardim influenced Moroccan musical forms, architectural latticework, and cuisine, including *pastilla*, a pigeon pie that is one of the Moroccan–Jewish signature dishes.

European trading influence grew in the 18th century, and France ruled Morocco as a protectorate after 1912. During World War II Sultan Mohammed V defied the Vichy regime's Nazi-inspired racist laws against Jews and pointedly invited all of Morocco's rabbis to his 1941 coronation.

The first Arab–Israeli war stoked anti-Jewish sentiment with dozens killed in Oujda and Djerada in June

Below *Signing of the Arab League charter, 1945, which pledged to defend Arabs of Palestine against Zionists.*

208

1948. Many Jews left for Israel and France in a trend that accelerated after Morocco won independence in 1956. Another 80,000 Jews departed over three years after bars on emigration were lifted in 1961, leaving behind 35,000 Jews by 1971 and less than 17,000 today.

IRAQ – ANCIENT COMMUNITY DEPLETED

Jews of Iraq claimed to be the world's oldest continually existing Jewish community and until 1040 their exilarch (grand communal leader) was respected as head of all Eastern Jewry. The opening of the Suez Canal in 1869 and education at Alliance schools spawned a generation of Jewish lawyers, doctors, entrepreneurs and administrators. In 1922 Great Britain created modern Iraq out of three former Ottoman

provinces, the mainly Kurdish Mosul, Sunni Baghdad and Shia Basra. Most of Iraq's 150,000 Jews now lived in Baghdad and called themselves *Yahud ibn Arab*, loosely, 'Jewish Arabs'.

After British troops quelled a revolt by Nazi-backed army officers, Iraq's only pogrom erupted in June 1941 and 180 Jews were killed. This two-day *farhud* shocked the community and made many consider leaving for Palestine. After 1948, Iraq banned emigration, as did most other Arab League members. Despite growing popular prejudice, Baghdad's rulers still valued Jewish economic contributions. But in March 1950 they agreed that Jews could leave if they surrendered their citizenship and sold their property. They were surprised when 85,000 registered to depart. Iraqi and Israeli

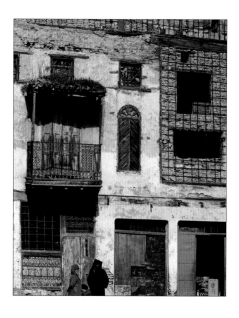

Above The Mellah of Fez, Morocco, established as a Jewish quarter in 1438.

authorities co-ordinated Operation Ezra and Nehemiah, a massive airlift that carried 120,000 to Israel over 18 months in 1951–2.

JEWS AND ARABS IN BAGHDAD

Jews had lived in Baghdad ever since it was founded as the capital of the Arab Muslim Abbasid dynasty in 762. The yeshivas of Sura and Pumbedita relocated to the city where Jews worked as goldsmiths and shopkeepers. They experienced intellectual creativity and peace with their Arab neighbours.

Baghdad later became the arena of a struggle between Sunni Ottomans and Shia Persians. Local Jews helped the Ottomans oust the Persians on 31

Above The Caliph of Baghdad receiving Jewish leaders, 937CE.

December 1534. The Turks ruled until 1623 and again from 1638 to 1917.

Conditions had declined by the early 19th century, but one English traveller praised Baghdad's rabbis and Jewish philanthropists for creating a virtual Jewish welfare state within a state, thus ensuring no one went poor.

Baghdad's Jews grew in number from 20,000 in 1860 to 50,000 after 1900. They set up printing presses, ran newspapers, hospitals and schools and became prominent musicians on Iraqi radio. As late as 1947, 10 of the 17-strong Baghdad Chamber of Commerce were Jews. Jews also ran 28 educational institutions, 60 synagogues and two hospitals offering free treatment to the poor. However, at times of trouble prominent families left, often for India. After the anti-British revolt of 1941 and the creation of Israel, anti-Zionist feelings were often conflated into anti-Semitism. The final demise of the Baghdadi Jewish community came with the public hanging of 11 Jews as alleged Israeli spies in 1969.

SCANT HOPE OF RETURN

Since the US conquest of Iraq in 2003, Jewish exiles have voted in Iraqi elections from their new places of residence, in Britain, America and even Israel. There was talk of allowing tourists to visit the burial places of the Jewish prophets along the Tigris and Euphrates rivers. However, the post-2003 conflict has spoiled these plans. Iraqi authorities have also rejected calls by the World Organization of Jews from Arab Countries for compensation of properties lost. Virtually no former Iraqi Jews have chosen to return, and the same applies in most Arab countries, including Egypt and Tunisia.

Few Jews have gone back to live in Morocco – though many visit even on Israeli passports. Today, Mizrachi culture persists in Israel, often in hybrid or modern guise. Mizrahim and Sephardis make up an estimated half of Israel's Jewish population. Mostly, however, memories of old Jewish Baghdad, Marrakech and Cairo are preserved in museums or online.

PALESTINE DURING WORLD WAR II

ZIONISTS WERE PULLED IN DIFFERENT DIRECTIONS DURING THE WAR. MANY FOUGHT WITH BRITISH UNITS, OTHERS TERRORIZED BRITISH TARGETS IN, OR SMUGGLED REFUGEES INTO, PALESTINE.

In early 1939, with world war looming, Britain hosted a last ditch attempt to solve the Palestine problem. London hoped to reconcile the competing demands of the Jews who had been promised a homeland in the Balfour Declaration and the Palestinian Arabs who were resident in the region.

Concerned that Arab nations might side with Germany and Italy, on 17 March, London released the McDonald White Paper, which dropped the Peel partition plan of 1938 and vowed to establish an independent and unitary Palestine by 1948. The paper also restricted Jewish immigration to 75,000 over the five-year period, 1940–44. Palestine's Jews did not welcome a

Below Erwin Rommel, the 'Desert Fox' who dreamt of leading German forces through North Africa to Palestine.

unitary state where Arabs would outnumber them by 1.2 million to 550,000. However, Jews feared Germany more than they resented Britain for breaking past promises.

PALESTINE'S JEWS IN WORLD WAR II

In late 1940, 26,000 Jews and 6,000 Arabs joined a British infantry division in Palestine nicknamed the 'Buffs' (the East Kent Regiment). Britain also helped create the Palmach in May 1941, a strike force of the Zionist militia, Haganah, to counter Nazi threats to Syria and Lebanon. Even the militant Irgun, the Revisionist Zionist underground, ceased sniping at Mandate forces and supported Britain's war effort.

BEHIND ENEMY LINES

Palestinian volunteers showed remarkable courage in Europe, despite criticism that they should have acted sooner. In 1943 the Budapest-born Hannah Szenes, a poet and playwright, was one of 33 who parachuted behind enemy lines in Slovakia and the Balkans, teamed up with anti-Nazi resistance fighters and sought out beleaguered Jewish communities. In June 1944 she crossed into her native Hungary, but was captured, tried and executed in November. In September 1944 the British formed the 5,000-strong Jewish Brigade, which fought in Italy and helped Jews in German Displaced Persons (DP) Camps after the war. Their military skills were passed on to Haganah, or the Socialist Zionist underground militia.

Above Three young Jewish survivors of Buchenwald concentration camp, en route to Palestine.

SMUGGLING IN 'ILLEGALS'

Haganah cadres now started smuggling in *ma'apalim* ('illegal Jewish refugees) from war-torn Europe. Over 100,000 tried to enter Palestine on 120 boats in an operation dubbed 'Aliyah B', and 70,000 succeeded. There were setbacks too: the British blockaded the coast and interned 50,000 would-be immigrants in Cyprus, Mauritius and Atlit prison, Palestine.

In November 1940 Haganah seized an illegal vessel, the *Patria*, with 1,800 refugees on board. When the British threatened to divert the refugees to Mauritius, Haganah saboteurs bungled an attempt to disable the ship and it sank off Haifa, killing 267. Survivors stayed in Palestine as 'an act of grace'.

OPTING FOR STATEHOOD

As the attempted annihilation of Europe's Jews entered its final stage, Zionist and non-Zionist Jewish groups agreed on a common strategy. At an emergency meeting in New York's Biltmore Hotel in May 1942, delegates declared the goal of a Jewish state, or 'commonwealth', in all of Palestine, which exceeded the terms of the Balfour Declaration.

Above Jewish pilot training school near Rome in November 1948, when the newly formed Israel Air Force was still in combat against Arab foes.

SEASON OF TERROR

In 1940 the Polish-born Revisionist Abraham Stern had formed Lehi, an underground unit also dubbed the Stern Gang. Lehi attacked British forces during the war, unlike fellow Revisionists in Irgun.

With war still raging in Europe, on 1 February 1944 Irgun declared its own 'revolt' against Britain. Its leader was Menachem Begin, who served in the Polish army in 1941. At first, Irgun sabotaged police stations and tax offices in Tel Aviv, Haifa and Jerusalem. Irgun and Lehi soon moved from sabotage to terror, and in August 1944 Lehi tried but failed to assassinate the British High Commissioner for Palestine, Harold McMichael. Two Lehi hit-men shot dead Lord Moyne, British Minister Resident in the Middle East, on 6 November 1944 in Cairo. This was a step too far for the Jewish Agency. They barred Lehi and Irgun members from jobs, and, in what was dubbed the Saison (season), Haganah and Palmach helped the British round up dissidents.

ANGLO-AMERICAN COMMISSION

The appalling images of Nazi death camps after World War II ended in May 1945 had radicalized Jewish feeling. Operation *Beriha* began siphoning 'illegals' from eastern Europe to Palestine via secret land routes. Lehi and Irgun blew up oil pipelines in Palestine, and after July the Haganah suspended the Saison and joined its former foes in a joint Resistance Movement that launched 19 attacks over ten months.

An Anglo-American committee of inquiry spent four months in 1945–6 interviewing Jews in Displaced Persons (DP) camps in Vienna and Arabs in Cairo. Their unanimous report of April 1946 proposed the immediate entry of 100,000 Jews into Palestine; an end to the land purchase restrictions of 1940; and the eventual establishment of a bi-national state under United Nations trusteeship. Britain's premier Clement Attlee said Jews could only enter Palestine when Zionist and Arab militias were disarmed. Even so, 1,500 Jews were let in each month after October 1946, half from detention camps on Cyprus, to the anxiety of Palestine's Arabs.

ANGER AT THE BRITISH

Fury over British policies prompted the worst act of Jewish terrorism, the Irgun's July 1946 bombing of Jerusalem's King David Hotel, site of the Palestine government secretariat and British military headquarters. In total, 91 people died. A curfew was imposed on the Jewish area of Haifa.

One of Britain's last acts during its mandate over Palestine helped push the UN towards making Israel independent. When in July 1947 the chartered ship *Exodus* entered Palestinian waters with 4,500 Holocaust survivors from European Displaced Person (DP) camps on board, British naval vessels trailed and eventually boarded the ship. Encountering aggressive resistance to their taking over the vessel, British soldiers resorted to force. Three passengers were killed and 30 wounded. Would-be illegal immigrants were eventually sent back to DP camps in Germany, and the *Exodus* became a media *cause célèbre*, symbolizing Jewish desperation to reach Palestine.

Below King David Hotel bombing, 1946, when Jewish saboteurs destroyed the British Army HQ, killing 91.

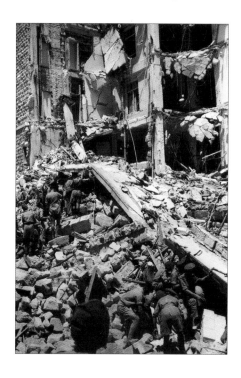

THE REVIVAL OF AN ANCIENT LANGUAGE

APART FROM THE CREATION OF THE STATE OF ISRAEL, SOME SAY THAT THE REVIVAL OF HEBREW IS THE GREATEST SINGLE ZIONISTS ACHIEVEMENT. IT IS NOW WIDELY SPOKEN, AND A FOUNT OF VIBRANT SECULAR LITERATURE.

The founder of modern Zionism, Theodor Herzl (1860–1904), envisaged a Palestine where Jews all spoke German. Opposed to Herzl, a growing movement preferred Hebrew as the Jewish people's lingua franca, and their view prevailed. There was a problem, however: few Jews spoke Hebrew as a living language.

BEN-YEHUDA AND HEBREW

The foremost champion of modern Israeli Hebrew was Eliezer Ben-Yehuda (1858–1922). He insisted on speaking only Hebrew to all Jews even before he arrived in Palestine in 1881. When his son Itamar was born the next year, he and his wife Deborah decided to raise him as the first all-Hebrew-speaking child in modern history. This caught on with other families in Jerusalem, and Ben-Yehuda then pioneered educational

Below New immigrants learning Hebrew at an ulpan *class, an indispensable part of the Israeli absorption process.*

instruction in Hebrew with the head of Alliance Israelite schools in Jerusalem. From 1884, he edited a newspaper, *Ha-Tzvi*, and he and his family also compiled a dictionary. In 1890 he set up what later became the Hebrew Language Academy.

LINGUISTIC SOCIAL ENGINEERING

In 1905, Zionists founded a language committee to popularize Hebrew as the national tongue of Palestine's Jews. Those who spoke French, German, Arabic, Russian, Yiddish, Ladino and Hungarian were moulded into a single monolingual community. Hebrew became the cultural binding agent of the Zionist ideological project.

Hebrew none the less faced challenges: few were qualified to teach it at first, and Orthodox Jews felt awkward speaking *lashon kodesh* (holy language). Also, there was confusion over pronunciation. In the end, language officials favoured a broadly Sephardi (Spanish Jewish) and Mizrachi (Oriental) system, despite the Ashkenazi origin of most early Zionist settlers. In practice, Hebrew developed organically, with speakers borrowing from French, Aramaic, Arabic and English, and purists faced a struggle to keep Hebrew true to its Semitic roots.

LANDMARKS

During the Second Aliyah period, Hebrew was used in schools and adopted for public meetings, even by the World Zionist Organization in Europe. Haim Nahman Bialik (1873–1934) became the great

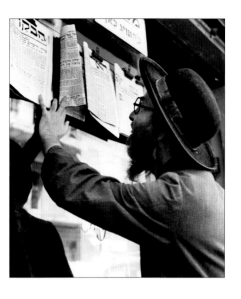

Above An Orthodox Jew peruses a Hebrew newspaper in Jerusalem's Me'a She'arim neighbourhood.

Hebrew national poet of the era, and Yiddish writers such as Sholem Aleichem and Isaac Leib Peretz also wrote in the tongue. Hebrew's battle to become a language of 'higher culture' climaxed in 1913, when the Yishuv rejected a bid by a German-Jewish association to use only German at a proposed college of engineering. The resultant Haifa Technion chose Hebrew, as did the Hebrew University in Jerusalem, which opened in 1925. By then Hebrew had been recognized alongside Arabic and English as one of Palestine's three official languages.

Throughout the Mandate period and after Israeli independence, Zionists fought a campaign against Yiddish, the natural language of most Ashkenazi immigrants. Under the slogan *Ivri Daber Ivri*, or 'Jewish person, speak Hebrew', a League of Language Defenders disrupted meetings in Yiddish. Learning Hebrew rapidly became a crucial aspect of integration. This sparked tensions among Yiddish-speakers. Gradually, Hebrew displaced other Jewish tongues. The Yiddish–Hebrew battle became an existential and symbolic struggle between two 'authentically Jewish' languages.

ORIENTAL IMMIGRATION TO ISRAEL

FROM THE START OF STATEHOOD IN 1948 UNTIL THE END OF 1967, 567,654 JEWS LEFT ARAB LANDS, MAINLY TO SETTLE IN ISRAEL. THEY HAVE ENORMOUSLY AFFECTED THE NATURE OF ISRAELI SOCIETY.

The first mass airlift into Israel involved 45,200 Yemenite Jews and was nicknamed Operation Magic Carpet. Jews flocked to the British-ruled port of Aden from remote northern Yemen and Hadramaut. While few had even seen cars before, they appeared unfazed by the British and US planes sent to collect them. They believed these were the divine 'wings of eagles' on which the Lord would gather up the scattered of Israel as predicted in the books of Exodus and Isaiah. The secret operation involved 380 flights between June 1949 and September 1950, and took place with the tacit approval of Yemen's new ruler, Imam Ahmad bin Yahya.

In Israel the newcomers met descendants of Yemenites who had arrived with the First and Second Aliyot (or waves of immigration), during 1882–1914.

Below A transit camp, where many Oriental Jewish immigrants spent their first years on Israel's land.

A DIFFERENT OUTLOOK

The conditions of departure varied considerably. In Iraq, Jews were initially forbidden to leave, while in Egypt they were expelled after 1956. Most Jews from Yemen and Iraq were airlifted out; those from Morocco took sea voyages. Jews of the Levant generally fell victim to the Israeli–Arab conflict, whether or not they were Zionist. Beirut was the only Arab capital city whose Jewish population increased after 1948.

For the most part, Jews of the Middle East were not very receptive to Zionism. It seemed bizarre that in Israel they were expected to relinquish their long-held religious values and customs.

THE SECOND ISRAEL?

At first, newcomers were housed in deserted Arab property. When numbers grew, *ma'aborot* (transit camps) were built, tent cities that later became permanent 'development towns', often in the remote Israeli

Above Born in 1957 in Tel Aviv to impoverished Yemenite parents, Ofra Haza won international fame as a singer whose stunning voice blended rock with traditional Eastern melodies.

south. Mizrachim arriving in Israel made little attempt to create their own political parties. They went along with existing structures. Some sensed official cultural prejudice and central government neglect. Riots in Wadi Nisnas, Haifa, in 1959 were a prelude to the formation of the radical leftist Sephardi youth group the Black Panthers in 1971. At that stage only 3 per cent of top posts were held by Sephardim, who represented nearly 60 per cent of Israeli Jews. The rightist opposition Likud party won power for the first time in Israel's 1977 elections, largely on the basis of a wave of Sephardi support.

In recent years, intermarriage has led to a blurring of the divisions between older inhabitants and the newcomers. Mizrachim have begun to fill senior state positions. Benjamin 'Fuad' Ben-Eliezer from Iraq, and Amir Perez, born in Morocco, have both led the Labour Party. From the established Ottoman-era Jewish community came Jerusalem's Yitzhak Navon, the first Sephardi president of Israel. In 2012, Shaul Mofaz, a former Iranian Jew, was elected leader of Kadima, Israel's largest political party.

THE WAR OF INDEPENDENCE

THE UN'S DECISION TO GRANT SEPARATE STATES TO JEWS AND ARABS WAS WELCOMED BY MOST JEWS, BUT REJECTED BY ARABS WHO WANTED ONE STATE. WAR SAW ZIONISTS DEFEND THE FLEDGLING ISRAEL.

On 29 November 1947 a United Nations General Assembly (UNGA) voted by 33 to 13 to split Palestine into two states, one predominantly Jewish, the other Arab. The USA and Soviet Union voted for partition, while Britain abstained. Generally, Zionists accepted UNGA Resolution 181, while most Arabs, both in Palestine and the region, rejected it.

FIRST STAGE OF WAR

Within hours of the UN vote, fighting broke out between communities. By January, Arabs were blockading Jerusalem and an Arab Liberation Army entered Palestine. By March, 1,200 Jews had been killed. On 9 April Irgun and Lehi militants invaded Deir Yassin village near Jerusalem and killed at least 100 civilians. Four days later Arabs attacked a convoy of Jewish doctors and patients and

Below A convoy bringing supplies to Jews in Jerusalem, 1948, during the siege by Jordan's Arab Legion.

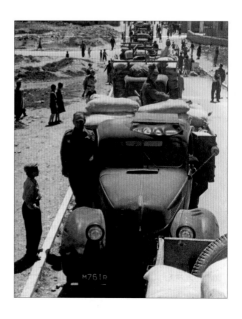

killed 80. Arab flight from Haifa and Jaffa gathered pace, and in early May Safed and Jaffa fell to Zionist forces. Most of west Jerusalem was now in Jewish hands, while the Jewish settlement of Gush Etzion fell to Arabs.

INDEPENDENCE

On 12 April 1948 David Ben-Gurion formed a provisional cabinet. War was now inevitable, and future Israeli prime minister Golda Meir made a secret deal with King Abdullah of Jordan. Zionist forces would only minimally attack areas in the eastern half of Palestine (West Bank), an area officially reserved for a Palestinian state but coveted by Jordan in exchange for control over all of western Palestine.

On 14 May 1948 the Jewish state in Palestine, now called the State of Israel, declared its independence. The declaration proclaimed 'the natural right of the Jewish people to be masters of their own fate, like all other nations' and pledged 'equality of social and political rights to all inhabitants irrespective of religion, race or sex.' Ben-Gurion vetoed any mention of specific borders. In a rare moment of concord, the USA and Soviet Union both recognized Israel.

ARAB ARMIES INVADE

As soon as independence was declared, five countries attacked Israel – Syria, Lebanon, Jordan, Egypt and Iraq. The Israelis made gains, except in Jerusalem, which fell to Jordan, and in the Golan, which fell to Syria.

Right During the war, Israeli forces rebuffed attacks from Egypt, Jordan and Syria, and gained new territory.

Above Jewish youths marching in Jerusalem on 30 November 1948, the day after the United Nations' decision to establish a Jewish State.

The War of Independence, 1948–49	
—	Armistice line, 24 February
➡	Arab forces' advance
▨	Jewish territory

Territory captured by Israel
- By July 18, 1948
- October 1948 to January 1949
- Acquired by Israel through armistice agreements

On 31 May, Israel's government announced the official disbanding of all separate pre-state Zionist militias. Their members would be subsumed within a single organization, the Israel Defence Forces (IDF), which had 100,000 troops by the year's end. While the IDF held the Syrians at bay in the north, it could not break the siege of Jerusalem until 10 June, when a secret bypass, 'Burma Road', was opened through the Judean Hills.

TRUCES AND CONFLICTS

The UN effected a truce on 11 June and sent Count Folke Bernadotte, a Swedish diplomat who had rescued 21,000 Jews during World War II, to Palestine. Bernadotte proposed that Palestine be annexed to Jordan, with a Jewish enclave attached to assist Arabs economically. Palestinian Arabs and Jews rejected the idea.

Fighting resumed on 9 July with Egyptian attacks in the south, battles in the north, assaults on kibbutzim and Israeli conquests of Lydda, Ramle and Nazareth. A second truce began on 19 July and, on 16 September, Bernadotte released his second plan. This time he acknowledged Israel as a reality, though he recommended awarding the Negev to Egypt and Jordan. His report called for 360,000 Arab refugees to be allowed to return home. The next day Lehi gunmen shot Bernadotte in Jerusalem. Mufti Hajj Amin Husseini's Government of All Palestine was declared in Egyptian-run Gaza, as was a pro-Jordanian Palestinian Congress in Amman, Jordan. Neither was truly independent. In 1950 Jordan formally annexed the West Bank, a gesture only Britain and Pakistan recognized.

The second truce ended on 15 October, after which the IDF relieved Negev settlements, took Beersheva, wiped out the Arab Liberation Army,

Right Socialist Zionists defending Kibbutz Gal-On from Egyptian forces, in the southern Negev Desert, 1948.

and, according to Israel's 'new historians', units killed civilians in several Arab villages. In December, Israel entered the Sinai Desert and in March 1949 it secured the southern Negev, including the crucial port of Eilat.

Armistice talks opened on 12 January 1949, and Israel signed agreements with Egypt, Lebanon, Transjordan and Syria. The new state added 50 per cent to the territory allocated to it under the UN plan and linked up split areas.

Many reasons may explain the course of the war including divergent interests and poor strategic co-ordination between Arab forces and secret aid from Diaspora Jewry. For the first time in almost 2,000 years there was a Jewish state, the fulfilment of long-held dreams and a place of refuge for victims of future persecution.

FIRST ELECTIONS AND THE LAW OF RETURN

Israel held its first Knesset (parliamentary) elections on 25 January 1949. In March, David Ben-Gurion became Israel's first prime minister. His coalition government included his Mapai labour party and smaller factions, including a Sephardi list, Arabs from Nazareth and a United Religious Front. Begin led the opposition and Chaim Weizmann became state president after Albert Einstein declined.

THE REFUGEE CRISIS

The 1948–9 War of Independence was seen as a victory for Jews. To Palestinians, however, it was known as the *nakba*, or 'disaster'. Their leaders had rejected the UN partition plan and lost the war, and some 725,000 Palestinians fled the country. Israel now controlled 77 per cent of historic Palestine and 60 per cent of Palestinian people became refugees.

Areas to which most Palestinian Arabs migrated included the West Bank; Gaza Strip; Lebanon; Syria; Transjordan; Egypt and Iraq.

Many of the 190,000 Arabs who stayed in Israel but left their homes are 'internally displaced'.

As of 2008, a million of Gaza's Palestinians live as refugees. The refugee question constitutes one of the 'final status issues' still at stake in Israeli–Palestinian peace talks.

In July 1950 Israel's Law of Return granted all Jews the right to immigrate as a defining principle of the nation.

Having survived possible annihilation, the young state faced the challenge of absorbing immigrants and maintaining security. Yet peace has remained elusive ever since.

JEWISH DEMOGRAPHY AFTER WORLD WAR II

SINCE 1948 OVER 3 MILLION JEWS HAVE SETTLED IN ISRAEL. YET DIASPORA COMMUNITIES HAVE SURVIVED AND EVEN BLOSSOMED, ADDING TO THE EVER-CHANGING MIX OF JEWS THE WORLD OVER.

Jewish life altered dramatically in the 20th century. Before World War II some 8.5 out of 10 million European Jews lived in a generally backward eastern Europe and developing Soviet Union. A further 300,000 Jews lived in Asia, 500,000 in Africa and 400,000 in Latin America. Some two-thirds of Jews resided in chastened conditions. After the war, three-quarters of Diaspora Jews resided in advanced countries, USA, Canada, western Europe and a now developed USSR. Comparative affluence and acceptance led Jews to adopt national languages, spelling the demise of Jewish tongues such as Yiddish, Ladino and Judeo-Arabic.

In a history with extraordinary highs and lows, the Jewish people probably experienced more upheaval

Below In 2012 US President Barack Obama hosted his fourth Passover Seder in the White House, Washington DC.

in the 20th century than ever before. The decimation of the Holocaust, birth of the State of Israel and unprecedented immigration utterly transformed Jewish demography.

There were about 4.75 million Jews globally in 1850, 8.7 million in 1900, 13.5 million in 1914 and 16.6 million in 1939. Today, Jews worldwide total 13 million, 0.23 per cent of the earth's population compared with 33 per cent who are Christians and 20 per cent who are Muslims.

QUESTIONS OF DEFINITION

The debate over who constitutes a Jew partially explains the statistical ambiguities. Normative Jewish religious law, *halakha*, defines a Jew as someone born of a Jewish mother or someone who converts to the faith.

Reform Judaism in the USA opposed intermarriage in 1909, and again in 1947. In 1950 just 6 per cent of American Jews married non-Jews,

Above Author Maxim Gorky by Isaac Brodsky, a Russian member of the Jewish Society for the Encouragement of the Arts.

but by 2000 that figure had risen to 40–50 per cent. In 1983 Reform acknowledged social changes and accepted patrilineal descent. This made it difficult for Orthodox or Conservative Jews to marry Reform Jews. In the same way, 'patrilineal Jews' wishing to settle in Israel may be accepted for citizenship by state law, but they are still deemed non-Jewish when it comes to marrying other Jews.

IMMIGRATION TO ISRAEL

Within Israel, the Jewish populace has grown at least eightfold from 650,000 in 1948. Some 1.5 million Israeli citizens are Palestinian Arabs; and in the territories occupied after 1967 there live at least 3.5 million Palestinians, Muslim and Christian, including a large proportion of refugees from pre-1948 Palestine.

SOVIET JEWS IN GERMANY

Germany attracted droves of Soviet Jewish immigrants after the unification of East and West Germany in 1990. Germany's Jewish population currently stands at about 200,000, the third largest in Europe after

France and Britain, and the fastest growing on the Continent. Former Soviet citizens now make up most of Germany's Jews, and feel under-represented on the Zentralrat, the Central Council of Jews in Germany. Founded in 1950, it is a bastion of indigenous German-speaking Jews, many of whom are descendants of Holocaust survivors. It favours Orthodox Judaism while Soviet Jews, estranged from their roots after 70 years of Communism, prefer US-style Reform founded in 1997.

MIDDLE EAST

During the 20th century, Jews in the Middle East region underwent a demographic revolution: their numbers rocketed from half a million in 1900 to more than five million in 2000, but the distribution of that population was massively skewed. In 1900 most Middle Eastern and North African Jews lived in Iraq, Yemen and Morocco, with smaller pockets in Egypt, Syria, Algeria, Tunisia and Libya. Sizeable minorities also existed in non-Arab countries, Turkey and Iran. After 1948, virtually all Arab states saw their Jewish populations rapidly diminish and in some cases disappear altogether.

Israel was the chief beneficiary, and by 2000 about 95 per cent of the region's Jews dwelt in that one country. Turkey, Iran and Morocco retain Jewish communities of more than 10,000, but these are exceptions to the rule and even there they are a fraction of their size a century ago.

EUROPE TRANSFORMED

At the end of World War II most surviving Jews on mainland Europe were found among the 250,000 located in displaced persons camps. A large number left for Israel, Britain, South America, Canada or the United States. Because Hitler never managed to invade England, Britain became by default home to the largest Jewish community in

ISRAEL AS THE JEWISH HOMELAND

Owing to immigration, Israel's population nearly doubled in its first five years. Jews leaving displaced person camps in Germany were followed by thousands from the Middle East. Absorption camps became permanent towns with persistent social problems, leading to charges of an Ashkenzi discrimination against Jews from Arab lands.

Above Israelis celebrate Independence Day with a picnic in the park, 2010.

One of the hallmarks of Israel is the way the state and rabbinate reached a 'status quo' from earliest days. Rabbis accepted national laws on most matters, but retained influence over law concerning marriages, burials and questions of identity. Most Israeli Jews are secular, but civil marriage is not allowed so non-believers still require rabbinical blessing for weddings.

Once the 1970s economic crisis was resolved, Israel adopted a more free enterprise system in imitation of America. Agriculture declined compared to industry and high technology. Unfortunately, the competitive economic atmosphere has resulted in increased disparities between rich and poor.

Most Diaspora communities cherish Israel and regard attacks on the country almost as attacks on them. Yet only a tiny minority of US, British or French Jews have emigrated to Israel. Some liberal Jews are critical of Israeli policies and some wish to distance themselves from Israel altogether.

Europe, although its size has gradually declined since the 1960s. Since then the French community has grown into Europe's largest as Maghrebi (North African) Jews flocked to Paris, Marseilles and other cities.

But Jewish populations in the Czech Republic, Slovakia, Austria, Poland and Hungary are shadows of their former selves. After the 'Iron Curtain' came down in eastern Europe, migration was banned, Zionist groups were outlawed, and only a few intrepid souls managed to get out.

NEW SELF-CONFIDENCE

In short, the Holocaust and Cold War divisions transformed the face of Jewish Europe. Other than France, the only country that saw a marked increase in Jewish population after 1970 was, of all places, Germany.

Jews worldwide worry about renewed anti-Semitism which some-times goes with anti-Zionism. Yet very few face the threats or legally sanc-tioned prejudice of the past. Most Jews feel financially secure and profession-ally fulfilled. That this should be so after the Holocaust is particularly impressive.

CHAPTER 11

JEWISH CULTURE IN MODERN SOCIETY

Most of today's 13 million Jews live in Israel and the USA. While genocide, turmoil and emigration have depleted eastern European and Russian Jewry, other European countries, such as France and Britain, have varied, creative Jewish populations; and Germany, once the birthplace of Nazism, is Europe's fastest-growing community of all. After centuries of discord, Jewish–Christian relations improved dramatically with the passage of the 1964 papal declaration, Vatican II. Jews today contribute to humanity through medicine, science and psychology; and express themselves via myriad paths, from the kibbutz and women-only prayer services to social activism, Jewish cuisine, an Orthodox revival and a plethora of hybrid identities. Individual Jews have depicted modern life in stimulating, sometimes disturbing, ways in art, philosophy and literature. Others pioneered cinema, television, orchestral music and rock bands, or invigorated traditional klezmer and Ladino musical forms. Similarly, synagogue design provides exciting contemporary casings for an ancient faith and ever-adaptable culture.

Opposite After the travails of World War II, both tragedy and hope seem to inform this striking portrait, Jewish Girl, *painted by the Italian artist Armando Pizzinato in 1945.*

Above *Moroccan Jews at a celebration honouring the medieval philosopher Maimonides. Today the UK-based Maimonides Foundation fosters relationships between Jews, Christians and Muslims.*

ISRAEL IN THE MODERN WORLD

BUFFETED BY WARS AND CRITICIZED FOR ITS ACTIONS, THE STATE OF ISRAEL HAS SURVIVED FOR 60 YEARS, ABSORBING IMMIGRANTS AND REDEFINING JEWISH HISTORY.

More than 60 years after its foundation, the State of Israel is militarily strong, economically robust and culturally vibrant. Israel probably now houses more Jews than any other nation on earth. In the words of a Second Aliyah song, Jews came to the land 'to build and be rebuilt', and in many respects that is what has been fulfilled.

HERZL'S DREAM REALIZED?
Jews from every continent have settled in the 'ancient homeland'. Reports say that Israeli Jews, 76 per cent of the population, grew by 300,000 in 2006–7, while the Jewish Diaspora shrank by 100,000. The very existence of the state has altered Jewish history. For the first time in 2,000 years, Jews can stand in the courts of nations and speak for their own national interests.

Jews outside Israel take pride in her considerable achievements in art, science, medicine and literature, on the battlefield, in trade and agriculture, and in her aid to Third World nations. They see everyday life of a Hebrew-speaking nation as a realization of Theodor Herzl's (1860–1904) dream of normalization. Religious Jews welcome the chance to live with dignity and to practise their faith on ancestral soil.

PERSISTENT TROUBLES
However, in many respects Israel remains a dream unfulfilled. Some 60 per cent of Jews still live in the Diaspora. Social disparities have grown, and inter-Jewish ethnic and religious tension remains an issue. Israel's Arab minority – descendants of those indigenous Palestinians who did not leave in 1948 – feel increasingly estranged, while Israel's conduct in the territories she occupied in 1967 has drawn wide criticism.

Most of all, Jews hoped that Israel would be a safe refuge; yet in view of the five major wars that have

Above For a nation built on immigration, the Ethiopian Jewish exodus of the 1980–90s reminded many Israelis of their raison d'être.

taken place since independence, two Palestinian *intifadas*, or uprisings, and recurrent terror attacks on its citizens, Israel has sometimes seemed like the least safe place for Jews.

The Israel/Palestine question remains one of the most vexed political issues in the world. What began as a local dispute has been cast as a clash between East and West, and it has acquired religious overtones. Some Arab analysts call it the root cause of all Middle East troubles, while growing numbers challenge Israel's very right to exist.

FROM 1948 TO 1956
Israel endured years of economic austerity and hardship as it absorbed Jewish immigrants in its first decade – 500,000 between 1948 and 1950 alone. The 1950 Law of Return opened the doors to Jews everywhere. Conversely, in that same year Israel's Absentee Property law foreclosed Arab refugees' hopes of returning, which neighbouring Arab

Left US President-elect Richard Nixon chats with Israeli ambassador Yitzhak Rabin (left) and Israeli Defence Minister Moshe Dayan (right), 1968.

leaders made a precondition for further talks. As a result, hopes receded of turning the armistice agreements that Israel signed in 1949 with Jordan, Egypt, Syria and Lebanon into full peace treaties.

Increasingly, Third World and Soviet bloc nations have portrayed Israel as an alien colonial outpost. Palestinian refugees on Israel's borders stepped up attacks as *fedayeen*, or 'self-sacrificers'. Israel's retaliations were often condemned as disproportionate. Egypt's post-1954 leader, Gamal Abdel Nasser, made 'Palestine' central to his pan-Arabist doctrine.

ROAD TO THE SIX-DAY WAR

All these factors raised tensions and set the scene for the October 1956 Suez War, in which the Israel Defence Forces (IDF) captured the entire Sinai and the Gaza Strip. However, UN and American pressure forced Israel to surrender all gains within a year.

In the 1960s Israel drew closer to Washington, and was alarmed when Egypt sponsored the creation of a Palestine Liberation Organization (PLO) in 1964. When Egypt blockaded the Gulf of Aqaba to Israeli shipping, Prime Minister Levi Eshkol (1895–1969) ordered a pre-emptive attack on Egypt, Syria and Jordan on 5 June 1967. In six days Israel defeated all Arab forces and quadrupled the size of land under its control. Up to 200,000 Palestinians became refugees.

A NEW PARADIGM AFTER 1967

In Israeli and Jewish eyes, David had defeated Goliath. Israel now held the Gaza Strip and the Golan Heights (Syrian). Most significantly it controlled the formerly Jordanian-run West Bank, what religious Jews call Judea and Samaria, the heart of biblical Eretz Israel. This included East Jerusalem's Old City with its Jewish

Quarter, Temple Mount and Western Wall. However, Israel was now cast as an occupier, which in turn bred serious internal schisms.

Liberal Israelis envisaged trading territories for peace with Arabs — essentially the idea behind UN Security Council Resolution 242, which Israel signed in 1970. Others felt that expanding Israel's pre-1967 pencil-thin 'waist' would protect against future attack. Few Israelis, though, proposed annexation, as this would enfranchise Palestinian residents and erode the Jewish nature of the state.

Positions soon polarized: in August 1967 the Arab League rejected talks while the PLO recommitted itself to armed struggle. Within Israel buoyant religious Zionists felt that God had delivered victory, and considered it sinful to return an inch of sacred soil.

YOM KIPPUR WAR

Many Israeli policy-makers believed they were invincible after 1967, although a draining 'war of attrition' with Egypt, between 1967 and

Above The Suez Canal blockaded by sunken ships, a symptom of war, November 1956.

1970, should have warned Jerusalem against complacency. In October 1973 Egypt and Syria launched a pincer attack on Israel on Yom Kippur, the Jewish Day of Atonement, and caught the IDF unawares. Israel withstood the blows and after three weeks repelled the enemy, but more than 2,600 Israelis died in combat and national morale was badly dented.

The war prompted the resignation of Golda Meir, the first female premier in the region. It also gave new impetus to Jewish civilians who planted new settlements in the territories, often defying the prime minister, Yitzhak Rabin (1922–95), and contravening international law. A new movement, *Gush Emunim*, or 'Bloc of the Faithful', used messianic religious motifs to champion the settlers. Opposition crystallized in the Peace Now movement, which wanted to return Israel to its former 1967 'green line'.

Above Six-Day War, 1967. A truck full of captured Egyptian soldiers meets an Israeli troop convoy near El Arish.

After Yasser Arafat, leader of the radical Fatah faction, won control of the PLO, international support for Palestinians grew. He addressed the UN in 1974, and the General Assembly soon passed a resolution equating Zionism with racism. Israel and the USA blamed Arafat for encouraging attacks inside Israel and against Israeli and Jewish targets abroad, including the murder of Israeli athletes at the 1972 Munich Olympics.

PEACE TREATY WITH EGYPT

In the May 1977 elections, Likud defeated Labour for the first time. The head of the new government, Menachem Begin (1913–92), was renowned for supporting 'Greater Israel'. He thus surprised critics by hosting a groundbreaking visit by Egypt's President Anwar Sadat – the first by any major Arab leader – in November 1977. Following talks at Camp David, Maryland, Israel and Egypt signed a peace treaty in 1979. Israel agreed to return all of the Sinai Peninsula to Egypt. The treaty, however, failed to initiate negotiations over Palestinian autonomy.

LEBANON WAR AND PALESTINIAN UPRISING

In June 1982, Israelis became embroiled in the Lebanese civil war. By August they had occupied Beirut, HQ of the PLO since 1971, and forced them to evacuate. The Lebanese conflict temporarily clipped the PLO's wings, but also bred a new enemy in the radical Shiite militia, Hizbollah.

Palestinians revolted against what they called 'an illegal occupation' after December 1987, starting in Gaza and spreading to the West Bank in December 1987. Less than a year into this 'intifada', Arafat hinted that he might negotiate and Jordan relin-quished its claim to the West Bank. However, Israel doubted Arafat's sincerity and the intifada continued.

FROM WAR TO PEACE

Impatient with Israel's continual settlement expansion and wary of another war, America pressured Israel and Arab states to meet in Madrid in October 1991. So began the first direct bilateral negotiations between Israelis, Jordanians, Syrians and a Palestinian delegation since 1949.

Madrid seemed to release Israel from its status as a pariah. The UN rescinded its 'Zionism is racism' vote, and Jerusalem created or restored relations with Russia, India, China and 56 other nations. Labour's Yitzhak Rabin won elections in 1992 and pledged action for peace; his foreign minister, Shimon Peres, envisaged a 'New Middle East' based on open borders and economic and cultural co-operation.

Ultimately secret discussions in Oslo led in September 1993 to mutual recognition between Israel and the hitherto shunned PLO. Palestinians gained limited autonomy in Jericho and Gaza, to which PLO

Below The West Bank settlements are a source of pride to many Zionists, but are considered by others to be illegal and an impediment to peace.

Left Yasser Arafat, Shimon Peres and Yitzhak Rabin at the Nobel Peace Prize ceremony, Stockholm, 1994, a year after signing the Oslo Accords.

ROADMAP TO PEACE

Israeli public opinion swung against Labour in late 2000s, with rightists blaming the 'Oslo criminals' for arming the Palestinians. Ariel Sharon, who won elections for Likud in 2001 and 2003, confined Arafat to Ramallah. In 2003 Sharon and Arafat accepted US President George Bush's 'roadmap to peace' that would result in Palestinian independence. But the war in Iraq diverted attention and continuing violence thwarted the plan's implementation.

Sharon's decision to evacuate settlers from Gaza in 2005 upset the Israeli right, and the next year's war with Lebanon and electoral victory of Hamas in the territories made peace a distant dream. Israel celebrated 60 years' existence in 2008, and despite war with Hamas in 2009 a possible Iranian nuclear threat, social protest in Israel and the Arab Spring, Israel has a permanent presence on the international stage.

Below In 1996 US President Bill Clinton attended the Sharm al-Sheikh summit to rally support for Shimon Peres after four horrific terror attacks.

leaders returned in 1994. That October, Israel and Jordan's King Hussein signed a peace treaty. Arafat's new Palestine Authority (PA) gained control over Ramallah, Tulkarm, Nablus and Jenin.

SETBACKS AFTER 1994

Distrust remained, particularly over expanding settlements and threats from Palestinian militants. Matters worsened when Hamas, a militant Islamic movement founded in 1988, launched a string of terror attacks in 1994.

Religious Zionists felt betrayed: and after a peace rally on 4 November 1995, Yigal Amir, a right-wing Jewish extremist, shot Yitzhak Rabin dead after a peace rally. Peres succeeded Rabin, but the peace process slowed down when Likud under Benjamin Netanyahu (1949–) narrowly defeated Labour in early 1996. During 1996–9, settlement building increased and relations with Egypt and Jordan deteriorated.

NEW UNREST AFTER TALKS FAIL IN 2000

Ehud Barak (1942–) led Labour back to power in 1999 and after failing to clinch a peace deal with Syria, he withdrew Israeli troops from southern Lebanon in May 2000. Then in July he began talks with Yasser Arafat, hosted by Bill Clinton at Camp David. For the first time Israelis and Palestinians officially addressed the 'core issues' of Jerusalem and final borders.

Israelis said Barak generously offered to give up 95 per cent of captured territories for lasting peace and security. Palestinians felt they were being cajoled into surrendering Jerusalem and refugees' rights in exchange for a non-contiguous 'bantustans', not real statehood.

The talks failed and a new *intifada* began in late September 2000, sparked by a visit by Israeli opposition leader Ariel Sharon to the Temple Mount/Haram al Sharif. Protest spread through the territories and Palestinian factions led by Hamas began suicide attacks in Israeli civilian centres.

Israel responded by sealing off West Bank and Gaza towns, setting up dozens of roadblocks and conducting 'targeted killings' of enemy leaders, including *Hamas* founder Sheikh Ahmed Yassin in 2004. By January 2008, 1,047 Israelis and 5,103 Palestinians had died in the conflict.

DIASPORA LIFE – THE USA AND CANADA

FOR MOST OF THE 20TH CENTURY, AMERICA HAD THE WORLD'S LARGEST JEWISH POPULATION. IT REMAINS A PILLAR OF MODERN JEWRY, WHILE CANADA HAS THE FOURTH LARGEST JEWISH DIASPORA COMMUNITY.

The bedrock for today's American Jewish population were the 2.5 million who arrived during 1880–1920, overwhelmingly from eastern Europe. Life was not always easy in the supposed Golden Land: during the 1890s three-quarters of Jewish breadwinners were manual labourers, but this proletariat status was preferable to the insecurities of being hawkers and middlemen in Europe.

AN EVOLVING COMMUNITY

By the 1930s more Jews took up commerce, fewer worked in industry and nearly 30 per cent were self-employed compared with the under 12 per cent national average. Jews began leaving inner cities for the suburbs and economic opportunities on the west coast. Increasingly they spoke English, not Yiddish, and entered universities and the professions, despite occasional discriminatory admission quotas that persisted until the 1950s.

Jews became 'Americanized' as their ties to their original European city or *shtetl* loosened. Yet they maintained a distinctive identity through such organizations as the long-established Bnai Brith welfare and advocacy network. Synagogue affiliation also leapt from 20 per cent in 1920 to 60 per cent in 1960. Another 100,000 Jews arrived from central Europe in the 1930s. American Jews helped rehabilitate brethren in eastern Europe and Arab countries through the United Jewish Appeal, founded in 1939. Yet they could not stop the Holocaust, which may explain why they backed the State of Israel so passionately after 1948.

CULTURAL INTEGRATION

By the 1950s, individual Jews had become leaders in mainstream literature, art, and jazz, classical and rock music, and above all in cinema and television. Jews also prospered in

Above 'Bugsy Siegel', a Jewish-American gangster who helped establish Las Vegas, in 1941.

the professions, most notably in medicine and law. In large part this derived from a veneration for education: US Jews numbered five or six million in 2004, 2 per cent of the population, yet accounted for 5 per cent of all college enrolments and more than 20 per cent of Ivy League students.

REDISCOVERED IDENTITIES

American Jewry's rediscovery of identity has taken many forms. Holocaust education has grown as a subject and about 100 universities now run regular Jewish studies courses. While comparatively few US Jews immigrate to Israel, many more involve themselves in school exchanges, educational visits, or buy a second home in Israel.

Meanwhile, those of a less Zionist bent have revived interest in the Yiddish language and klezmer music tradition of the Ashkenazic Jews of

Left Leonard Bernstein conducting Beethoven in Berlin, 1989, after the fall of the Berlin Wall. He was a hugely successful Jewish-American composer.

eastern Europe. And Jews seeking spirituality, many of whom dallied with Eastern mysticism in the 1960s, have eagerly embraced hybrid forms of worship in the Jewish Renewal and Havurah movements, or sought out fashionable Kabbalah workshops with varying levels of authenticity.

POLITICAL INTERESTS

Jews were enthusiastic unionists in the early 20th century, especially in the garment industry. A large number were anarchists or Communists, associations that came back to haunt them during the McCarthyite era. Since World War II Jews have tended to be Democrats. To date, no Republican presidential candidate has received more than 40 per cent of their vote. Despite their comparatively small numbers, Jews' traditionally high voting turnout and concentration in key 'swing states' – New York, California, New Jersey and Florida – gives them enhanced influence. Hence aspirant politicians pay attention to 'Jewish concerns'. In the 2000s more than 10 per cent of America's 100 senators are Jewish.

Below Jewish studies enter the academic mainstream: Center for Jewish Life at Princeton University.

FOOD-FEST ON MAIN STREET

Food is a classic manifestation of Jewish culture, and in few cities is this more obvious than in New York. Delicatessens serve trusted staples of the Jewish table such as chicken and matzo ball soup and bagels with lox (smoked salmon). Not to forget wurst (garlic sausage), pastrami on rye, lokshen (noodle) pudding, and the Sabbath loaves called challah.

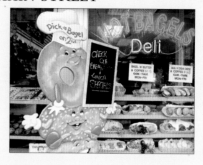

Florence Greenbaum published her *International Jewish Cook Book* in New York in 1919, featuring European, *Above Bagels and other Jewish specialities in a New York deli.*

Ashkenazi dishes. Since then, Jews from Syria, Turkey, Israel, Bukhara and Morocco have introduced such foods as couscous, hummus and falafel.

GROWTH OR DECLINE?

Every December civic squares in suburban America feature Hannukah menorahs alongside Christmas trees. Yet to some, the freedom American Jews enjoy endangers their survival. Freedom means the right to practise one's faith but also to abandon it. Some Jews, it is said, feel such harmony between American and Jewish values that they neglect their culture.

Conversely, the recent 'return to faith' trend has boosted the number of young Orthodox Jews. Likewise, refugees from Iran, Iraq, Syria and Egypt have replenished a declining Jewish community, as have migrants from Russia, Georgia and Bukhara since the 1970s and from Israel after the 1990s. Brighton Beach is a magnet for Russian Jews, Beverley Hills for Iranians and Houston for South Africans.

CANADA

Jews arrived in Canada in 1760 as British Army soldiers, and established Bnai Brith Canada in 1875 as a powerful advocate for human rights and communal defence. Canada's Jewish population rose to 100,000 by 1914, the year in which a new Jewish public library made Montreal a focal point on the Yiddish and Hebrew writing circuit.

Several Jewish organizations joined a Canadian Jewish Congress (CJC) in 1919, and a brief influx after 1924 followed when the US curbed immigration, until Canada, too, blocked entry to European migrants in 1930. Almost all the 50,000 Jews who entered Canada in the interwar years came from the USA or Britain. Only 1 per cent of Jews fleeing Nazism found refuge in Canada; xenophobia simply ran too high.

During World War II about 17,000 Jews fought for Canada. Conditions improved markedly afterwards. Canada's Jewish population grew to 260,000 by 1961, after 40,000 Holocaust survivors entered in the late 1940s, Hungarians arrived in the 1950s and francophone Sephardi Jews from North Africa settled in French-speaking Montreal. Traditionally leftist in their politics, Canadian Jews suffered from suspicion during the Cold War years.

Today, Canada's 380,000 Jews constitute the fourth largest Diaspora community in the world. Most reside in Ontario and Quebec. Some 30,000 left Montreal after French separatists threatened English-speakers, although the crisis has abated since 1985. Despite recent anti-Semitic incidents, Jews feel secure, and have contributed disproportionately to Canadian culture.

DIASPORA LIFE – GREAT BRITAIN AND FRANCE

SEPARATED BY THE CHANNEL, BRITAIN AND FRANCE NOW HAVE TWO OF EUROPE'S LARGEST JEWISH COMMUNITIES. IN BOTH IMMIGRANTS HAVE REPLENISHED ONCE-DECLINING COMMUNITIES.

The influx of Romanian, Russian and Polish Jews to Britain was so intense in the late 19th century that reportedly the Jewish Free School in London's East End had 4,000 pupils, more than any other school in the world.

A few wealthy Anglicized Sephardi and Western Ashkenazi families, dubbed the cousinhood, dominated the Board of Deputies of British Jews (established in 1760), the United Synagogue (1870), the Anglo-Jewish Association (1871) and the Maccabeans professional dining club (1891). Recent arrivals gradually acquired more power, but the old elite put up stiff resistance.

FROM ALIENS ACT TO BEATING THE BLACKSHIRTS

Some established Jewish grandees campaigned against immigration and supported the Aliens Act of 1905 that blocked entry to 'undesirable indigents'. The act left the door open to refugees fleeing persecution, and funded improved amenities in crowded urban ghettoes.

After the Great War, Jews increasingly entered the professions and many succeeded in business, such as the Sieffs who developed Marks & Spencer, and the Cohens who founded Tesco. Within a generation the children of Yiddish and German speakers were fully at home in English, and a number joined the erudite Bloomsbury group of writers and artists. In the 1930s, émigrés such as Sigmund Freud, Ludwig Wittgenstein, Isaiah Berlin, George Steiner and Albert Einstein enhanced British academia.

Even celebrated figures faced a residue of xenophobia, and proto-Nazi ideas gained currency after

Below A mural marking the 1936 Battle of Cable Street, when east London Jews beat off Mosley's Blackshirts.

***Above** Dubbed 'The Jewish Dickens', Israel Zangwill (1864–1926) also coined the phrase 'the Melting Pot'.*

Oswald Mosley founded his Blackshirts movement in 1932. Jews, Irish Catholics and anti-fascists confronted Mosley's bullies in the East End's October 1936 'Battle of Cable Street', which passed into folklore as a time when the fascists were beaten.

POLITICS AND DEMOGRAPHY

After 1945 Jews experienced a conflict of loyalties between their British patriotism and their sympathy for fellow Jews fighting Mandate authorities in Palestine.

DUTCH COURAGE

Communist dockworkers went on strike to protest against Nazi race laws in April 1941, the only such incident in Europe, and the Dutch underground hid up to 30,000 of Holland's 140,000 Jews. About 75 per cent of Jews were deported to the camps and killed, leaving a post-war community which, though safe, wealthy and well integrated, stood at 24,000 in 1954 and about 41,000 today. While most affiliated Jews are Orthodox, progressive trends have made inroads in recent years.

In the immediate post-war era, British Jews were mostly loyal to Labour. Affluence returned after austerity, and gradually more Jews gravitated to the Conservatives; Thatcher era Tories included Nigel Lawson, Leon Brittan, Shirley Porter, Edwina Currie and Michael Howard.

Jewish families moved to London's leafier north-west suburbs from the East End, where Bengali and Somali immigrants have replaced them. Provincial communities in Leeds, Bristol, Glasgow, Birmingham and Bradford declined, and only Manchester maintained its critical mass with its distinctive blend of old Sephardi Jews, children of Ashkenazi textile merchants and a growing Orthodox community.

NEWCOMERS AND SUCCESSFUL INDIVIDUALS

Small numbers of Jews arrived after 1945 from former colonies or protectorates: South Africa, Rhodesia, Gibraltar, Aden, Iraq and Egypt. Latterly pockets of Israelis have sprung up in parts of London.

The Board of Deputies and weekly *Jewish Chronicle* (established in 1841) represent Jews to the broader community and now champion interfaith harmony. Meanwhile, jurists like former Lord Chief Justice Harry Woolf have profoundly affected the British legal system.

Jews in the arts include the playwright Harold Pinter, poet Dannie Abse, novelist Frederic Raphael and actors Claire Bloom and Peter Sellers. Wolf Mankowitz, Arnold Wesker and Bernard Kops often wrote about their Jewish experience. Recently, the comedian Sacha Baron-Cohen became popular for his satirical attacks on prejudice; while the Chief Rabbis Immanuel Jakobovits and Jonathan Sacks gained wide respect for their ideas on ethics.

Right Jews dancing in the Rue des Rosiers, Marais Quarter, Paris, 2010.

Right A 19th-century neo-Moorish extravaganza, this London ark suggests a new sense of arrival for British Jews.

CHANGES IN FRENCH JEWRY

In the 30 years to 1914 some 25,000 Greek, Turkish, Polish, Bulgarian, Russian, Algerian and Romanian Jews arrived in France, reinvigorating an indigenous community of only 60,000 in 1880. Leon Blum of the socialist Popular Front became prime minister in 1936–7 and 1938. He served as premier in 1946–7, having survived Nazi incarceration in Buchenwald and Dachau, where he wrote his famous essay, 'For all mankind'.

Many Jews who fled Germany and Austria for France before 1939 perished in the Holocaust. All told, 76,000 Jews were deported to death camps from occupied France and the Vichy puppet regime in the south. France's first post-war president, Charles de Gaulle, welcomed Jews as full co-nationals, and some camp survivors, like the Romanian-born poet Paul Celan, made France their home.

CRIF, an umbrella group dedicated to preserving Franco-Jewish life, was secretly created in 1943. By the 1950s CRIF absorbed Jews arriving from North Africa, who soon outnumbered indigenous Ashkenazim.

They ensured that France had the largest Jewish population in Europe for the first time in a millennium.

France's close ties with Israel, at least until 1967, boosted the status of French Jews. Since then anti-Semitism has risen, although the act of the fanatic who murdered a rabbi and two children at a Jewish school in Toulouse in March 2012, was roundly condemned. Despite right-wing Holocaust denial, left-wing anger at Israeli policies, and degrees of tension between Jews and a few of France's six million post-war Muslims, figures like Bernard-Henri Lévi, Raymond Aron and Simone Veil have profoundly shaped public thinking in modern France.

JEWS IN GERMANY AND EASTERN EUROPE

RUSSIA, POLAND AND GERMANY WERE ONCE THE HEARTLANDS OF JEWRY. MASS EMIGRATION AND CALAMITIES IN THE 20TH CENTURY SEEMED IRREVERSIBLE, YET SHOOTS OF REVIVAL HAVE REAPPEARED.

After taking control of Russia in 1917, the Bolsheviks dismantled the despised Pale of Settlement and outlawed anti-Semitism. Jews gained access to education and new professions. Leon Trotsky, Lev Kamenev and Grigori Zinoviev reached the highest echelons of Soviet power.

Liberation came at a price: the authorities banned Torah classes, confiscated religious property and had shut down half the synagogues by 1934. Jews who backed Zionist, Bundist, liberal or social-revolutionary parties faced persecution; even the Communist Party's Jewish division, the Yevsektsiya, was liquidated in 1930.

SHTETL CULTURE
The flight to the cities loosened bonds to the *shtetl*, the semi-rural heartland of Russian Jewry. New political borders divided formerly interconnected communities on the borderlands of Russia, Ukraine and Poland. The *shtetl* structure survived

civil war pogroms and Stalinist totalitarianism. Yet what Communism did not extinguish, World War II did.

The Nazi–Soviet Pact of 1939–41 imposed a news blackout. When the Germans invaded in late 1941 it was too late for Jews living between Poland and Russia. Nazi *Einsatzkommandos* and local cohorts began the Holocaust with the mass shooting and gassing of 1.5 million Jews in western Soviet Union.

AFTER WORLD WAR II
Barred from fleeing south or west, many Jews went east, which saved lives but destroyed social cohesion. The Jewish Anti-Fascist Committee encouraged a brief cultural revival after 1943, but five years later Stalin had its leaders killed as traitors. The Kremlin barred publication of the 'Black Book', first-hand reports of Nazi atrocities against Jews, lest it detract from the preferred version of the 'Great Patriotic War'.

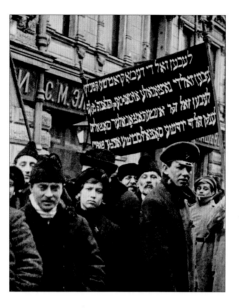

Above Jewish Socialist Workers Party supporters celebrate revolutionary times under a Yiddish banner; Russia, 1918.

NEW DISCRIMINATION
Israel's military victory in 1967 intensified anti-Zionism in Russia and officially approved attacks on Judaism itself. University quotas for Jews reduced their presence from 18 per cent of Soviet scientific workers in 1947 to 7 per cent in 1970. Under Brezhnev not one Jew was admitted to Moscow University in 1977–8. Some 250,000 were allowed to emigrate in 1971–4, after which the doors closed and 'refuseniks' (those refused an exit visa) were jailed on bogus security charges.

COLLAPSE OF THE UNION
The collapse of Communism across Europe in 1989 and the break-up of the Soviet Union in 1991 created a ripple effect on Jewish life in the region. Mass migration to the USA and Israel ensued, and some predicted the demise of Jewish life in Russia itself. Today most former Soviet Jews live in Israel, followed by the USA, with the Confederation of Independent States

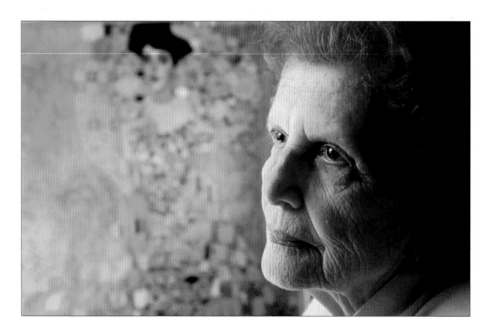

Left Austria finally returned Gustav Klimt's portrait of her aunt to Maria Altmann in 2006. In all, Nazis stole six of her family's artworks in 1938.

Above Soviet Jewish refugee families reach Vienna on their journey out of the USSR, 1979.

(successor to the USSR) taking third place. It is thought about 300,000 Jews now live in Russia, 122,000 in Ukraine and 25,000 in Belarus.

Predominantly Muslim former Soviet Central Asian states have not discriminated against Jews. However, most Jews have emigrated, leaving behind small, aging populations. Only 3,600 Jews remain in Lithuania, once the centre of Jewish religious life.

EASTERN EUROPE

Throughout eastern Europe the events of World War II reduced once-vibrant Jewish communities to fractions of their former size. Thousands left for Israel and the West. The most dramatic decline was in Poland, whose pre-war population of 3.3 million Jews, accounting for 27.2 per cent of all city dwellers in 1931, had shrunk to 5,000 by the 1980s. Many Jews who had survived the Holocaust fled Hungary after the violent suppression of an anti-Stalinist revolt in late 1956.

Czechoslovakia's Jews played a leading part in the Communist establishment in the early days, and Czech arms helped a nascent Israel survive the 1948 war. Then in 1952 party secretary Rudolf Slansky was accused

of being a crypto-Zionist, ousted, and executed along with 11 other Jews. Three years later Czechoslovakia became the chief conduit for Warsaw Pact weapons to Israel's Arab neighbours. This switch in policy fed Israel's sense of entrapment, and in part persuaded her to side with Britain and France in the Suez War of 1956.

Two organizations represent the Jews of a newly united Europe: the European Council of Jewish Communities, first established in 1968, and the European Jewish Congress, founded in 1986. Since 1996, 26 European countries have participated in an annual European Day of Jewish Culture. In an event scarcely imaginable just ten years earlier, Poland, Hungary, Slovakia, the Czech Republic, Slovenia, Latvia, Lithuania and Estonia all joined the European Union in May 2004, and Bulgaria and Romania followed in January 2007. As a result Jewish communities in the West and East began meeting each other again after decades of division.

GERMAN RESETTLEMENT

The country that truly defied expectations was Germany. Jews have settled there in large numbers. Most come from the former Soviet Union and many others are Israeli; by 2000 they outnumbered the German descendants of Holocaust survivors, who in 1950 had set up a *Zentralrat*, Central Council, to rebuild their community. West Germany taught schoolchildren about the Holocaust, and after 1952 paid reparations to Jewish survivors for wartime suffering and property stolen, totalling $25 billion by 1987. Bonn also established firm relations with Israel and offered former refugees German citizenship.

Right Once a symbol of a divided Europe, the Berlin Wall's ruins now stand for future hope of tolerance and lasting peace. Photographed in 1989.

VATICAN II
Relations between Roman Catholics and Jews took a turn for the better in 1965 with the rulings of a council called Vatican II. The key document, *Nostrae Aetate*, 'In Our Time', proclaimed: 'Jews should not be presented as rejected or accursed by God.' The Church, 'mindful of the patrimony she shares with the Jews', condemned persecution of Jews and for the first time absolved them for killing Jesus.

East Germany was less forthcoming about acknowledging wartime crimes, so Jews were wary at the prospect of reunification after the Berlin Wall came down in 1989. But Jewish life is mostly thriving.

THE AUSTRIAN CONUNDRUM
Austria saw itself as 'Hitler's first victim' and unlike Germany denied guilt for killing its Jews. There was scandal over the alleged SS wartime record of Austria's 1986–92 president, Kurt Waldheim. Vienna's Jewish population fell from 200,000 pre-war to 8,000 by the 1980s, but Jews have since made a positive impact on post-war Austrian life.

THE SPREAD OF JEWISH COMMUNITIES

GLOBALIZATION IS NOTHING NEW FOR JEWS WHO LEFT EUROPE AND THE MIDDLE EAST TO MAKE NEW LIVES IN SOUTH AMERICA, SOUTH AFRICA, AUSTRALIA, HONG KONG AND SINGAPORE.

Today four out of every five Jews live in either Israel or the United States. Of the remaining 2.3 million, 550,000 are found south of the US–Mexican border. Paradoxically most of these Spanish- and Portuguese-speaking Jews are not Sephardi but Ashkenazi.

Tighter US influx controls made South America more attractive after 1924, and drew immigrants from far and wide. This created great variety: Venezuela with its 35,000-strong half-Ashkenazi, half-Sephardi community; Uruguay with 40,000 Jews in 1980; Cuba, reduced from 12,000 pre-revolution to 1,000 today, and Guatemala, home to many German Jews. In Mexico, 45,000 European, Damascene and Sephardi Jews have largely moved from commerce to the professions. 'Judaizing' sects of *mestizos* (half-Indians) claim Jewish ties.

Below Daniel Barenboim, born in Argentina in 1942, conducting the Arab-Jewish Divan Orchestra, 2010.

Right Templo Libertad, Buenos Aires, a synagogue that symbolizes Judaism thriving south of the equator.

South American states helped pass the 1947 UN Partition Plan that created Israel, spawning strong intercontinental ties ever since.

JEWS OF ARGENTINA

Argentina accounts for nearly half the continent's Jews. Its Italian and Spanish inhabitants attracted 88,000 Jews in 1901–14, and another 74,000 Russian Jews in 1921–30 joined groups from Morocco and Syria.

Anti-Semitism rose with German encouragement in the 1930s, though 30,000–40,000 refugees from Nazism entered Argentina during 1933–43, many illegally. Post-war Argentina absorbed former Nazis and in 1966 the military junta sacked civil servants who were Jewish. In 1967 nearly half the world's anti-Semitic incidents occurred in

Argentina and 1,500 Jews are still counted as 'missing', presumed killed by the state. In 1994, 85 people were killed in a terrorist bombing on the Asociación Mutual Israelita Argentina in Buenos Aires , the centre of the Argentinian Jewish community.

Today, Jews are well integrated and contribute to society, arts and sciences, especially since the end of junta rule.

BRAZILIAN JEWS

Unreliable figures suggest millions of Brazilians have 16th-century Jewish or Marrano (crypto-Jewish) ancestry. Moroccan Sephardim founded a synagogue in Belem in 1824; but today's community of about 150,000 are mainly of Russian, Polish and Hungarian descent. Communal activities started in Porto Alegre in 1910 and soon extended to São Paulo and Rio de Janeiro, where most Jews now live. Jews also farmed on ICA communes along the Rio Grande, though by 1958 most had left for the cities. Each wave of immigrants brought its own flavour. Some 24,000 Jews arrived from west and central Europe in 1931–39 and 12,000 from Arab countries in 1957–60 joined an existing 5,000-strong Egyptian-Jewish community in São Paulo.

SOUTH AFRICA

Although South African Jews number fewer than 71,000, just 0.5 per cent of the population, their impact remains significant. The community is known for its strong Lithuanian origins. The youth groups Habonim, Beitar and Bnei Akiva nurtured Zionist ties, and per capita South African funding of Israel exceeds all other Diaspora communities. Until the recent building of yeshivas (academies), and renewed religiosity in Johannesburg, all chief rabbis were imported from Britain.

Rabbis and community heads were slow to condemn apartheid, but individual Jews helped lead the anti-apartheid struggle, including Ronnie Kasrils, Albie Sachs and Joe Slovo. For 13 years, Helen Suzman was a lone parliamentary voice against official racism.

Some 40,000 Jews had left before black majority rule was attained in 1994. Many pursued careers in Britain, including the former attorney for Nelson Mandela, now Law Lord Joel Joffe; and much earlier the future Israeli foreign minister Abba Eban, and Lord Solly Zuckerman, chief UK science advisor.

Below Consecrated in 1863, the Old Synagogue, Cape Town, is the oldest in South Africa.

Since 1994 fear of crime and reduced employment opportunities have seen Jews move to Australia. Some 80 per cent of emigrants leave with university degrees, whereas few of their Lithuanian forebears had finished secondary school. By the same token former Zimbabweans and Israelis are replenishing South Africa's otherwise aging community.

AUSTRALIA AND NEW ZEALAND

Today, South African and recent Soviet immigrants make up nearly a quarter of Australian Jews. They joined British Sephardim, who developed businesses, galleries and libraries in the 19th century. Refugees from Germany revived a community that seemed to be losing its identity. Its population grew from 70,000 in 1968 to 120,000 in 2008. Australia has 81 synagogues, numerous day schools, low intermarriage rates and an above-replacement level of Jewish children.

Far smaller in size is the Jewish community of New Zealand, which numbered just 5,000 in the 1990s. Even so, 'Kiwi Jews' included Sir Julius Vogel, twice premier in the 19th century; and the novelist, Benjamin Farjeon, who edited the islands' first newspaper. Since then there have

Above Twice Prime Minister of New Zealand, Sir Julius Vogel (1835–99) campaigned for women's suffrage.

been many prominent Jewish doctors, hoteliers, retailers, university professors and steel industrialists.

ASIA

Americans and Israelis boosted Hong Kong's Jewish population from 200 in 1974 to 4,000 in the 1990s. The first settlers were English- and Arabic-speaking Baghdadi Jewish traders, who also built a tiny, vibrant community in Singapore. One of their descendants, David Marshall, became the first premier of Singapore after independence in 1955.

In India, Baghdadi Jews represent a third wave of arrivals. Other Jews settled in Cochin in the 10th century. The Bene Israel of Bombay, known as 'Sabbath-observing oil pressers', claim descent from 3rd-century shipwreck survivors. India took in refugees from Nazi Germany and Poland, though after independence numbers fell from 45,000 to under 6,000, with many leaving for Israel. General Jack Jacob spearheaded India's victory in the Indo-Pakistan War of 1971. In 2012 he declared, 'I am proud to be a Jew, but am Indian through and through.'

DIVERSITY AND ORTHODOX REVIVAL

PROBABLY NEVER BEFORE HAS THERE BEEN SUCH DIVERSITY IN JEWISH BELIEF AND WORSHIP. WHILE THOUSANDS OF JEWS ABANDON ALL TIES TO JUDAISM EACH YEAR, THOUSANDS MORE HAVE 'RETURNED TO FAITH'.

Today there are rabbis who insist that only commitment to all 613 commandments counts as Judaism, and others who deny the existence of God altogether. Judaism has experienced schism before, between Pharisees and Sadducees, Karaites and rabbis, Sabbateans and mainstream Jews, Hassidim and Mitnagedim. Since the mid-19th century, a formerly divided Orthodox camp closed ranks against new perceived common enemies: first Reform Judaism and the Haskalah, then overt atheism, revolutionary socialism, political Zionism, and latterly Western consumerism.

Today pious non-Hassidic Jews also don the black gabardines considered typical of Hassidim, in areas of New York, Stamford Hill in London, Me'ah She'arim in Jerusalem and Bnei Brak outside Tel Aviv.

Below Circle dancing to celebrate harvest at Kibbutz Tuval, Galilee. Communal activities are a vital part of kibbutz life.

These so-called ultra-Orthodox are collectively dubbed *haredim*, literally 'those who tremble [before God]'. With the exception of the Habad movement Lubavich, they tend to live apart from other Jews.

POST-WAR RECOVERY

The Holocaust destroyed traditional centres of Hassidism, and 70 years of Communist suppression virtually extinguished the trend in western Russia, once part of the Hassidic heartland. After the Soviet Union fell, Hassidism – and particularly the Lubavich – has experienced a revival. Today, Hassidic sects, invariably named after their place of origin, are thriving in America and Israel.

The Satmar group provides a remarkable example of Hassidism's phoenix-like recovery after the Holocaust. Now probably the largest Hassidic sect of all, it derives its name from the Hungarian city of Satu Mare. Under the dynamic leadership

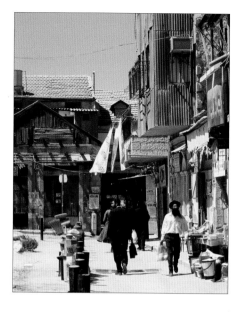

Above Jerusalem's strictly Orthodox Me'ah She'arim quarter – a throwback to 18th-century Europe.

of Rabbi Joelish Teitelbaum, who escaped Nazi persecution to Switzerland and briefly Palestine, Satmar reconstituted itself in Williamsburg, New York, and grew enormously by absorbing remnants of other Hungarian, Romanian and Transylvanian Hassidic sects.

RETURN TO FAITH

Ba'alei teshuva, signifying 'returnees to faith', represent perhaps the most remarkable Jewish religious trend of the past 20 years. Many found a

THE KIBBUTZ

Perhaps the most thorough experiment in community living anywhere, the kibbutz or Israeli communal agricultural collective posited an alternative Jewish society free from religious domination. Money was banned, gender equality stressed and no one could study or travel outside without committee permission. After banking crises in the 1980s, kibbutzim could only survive by joining the economy, and utopian dreams were largely shelved.

home in the Habad movement, another name for the Lubavich school of Hassidism. Lubavich has made a point of finding disaffected Jews seeking meaning in their lives.

Many factors account for the *ba'al teshuva* tendency: youthful rebellion during the 1960s, pride in Jewish identity after Israel's victory in the 1967 Six Day War, and disenchantment with Western social values. Some say *Ba'alei* resemble born-again Christians or Muslim *Salafi* revivalists.

SECULARISM AND RELIGION

Israel is not a theocratic Jewish state. The elected Knesset (parliament) determines all major laws, and rabbis rule over limited aspects of personal status. Today some 44 per cent of Israeli Jews call themselves secular, 36 per cent broadly traditionalist, 10 per cent religious and 10 per cent Haredi. Many strictly Orthodox men study full-time in yeshivas, and rely on working wives, charity and state remuneration to support their typically large families.

THE SETTLER MOVEMENT

Situated between the *haredim* and 'secular' Jews, are modern Orthodox Jews, called in Israel *dati leumi* or 'national religious'. Unlike the black-hatted *haredim*, they welcomed the State of Israel as 'the beginning of redemption' and preferred to integrate their faith with involvement in secular society. After 1967 the movement affiliated with the more radical beliefs of the Gush Emunim settler movement, and saw in Israel's conquest of the West Bank (location of ancient Judea and Samaria) a sign of an impending messianic age.

Extreme affiliates opposed attempts to trade land for peace; one zealot killed Prime Minister Rabin in 1995, and ten years later the Government's evacuation of Jewish settlements in Gaza prompted a minor revolt against a state that they felt had abandoned them.

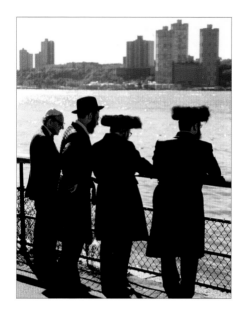

Above Orthodox Jews cast bread into the Hudson, New York, for the tashlikh *ceremony during Rosh Hashanah.*

A NEW SPIRITUAL THIRST

Young American Jews and Israelis demobbed from the army, caught up in the counterculture mood of the 1960s, felt a craving for spirituality and a new interest in Kabbalah. Out of this arose attempts to reconstruct a hybrid Judaism for the New Age: the *Havurah*, or 'fellowship', movement; Jews in the Woods, an ecological movement nicknamed 'Fruity Jews'; the Jewish Renewal Project; and the New Jewish Catalog, a popular 1970s manual of customs and practices.

ATHEIST JUDAISM?

Standing outside mainstream Judaism are movements called Jews for Jesus and Messianic Jews, both of which see Jesus as fulfilling ancient Judaic promises. Their followers like Hebrew prayers and wish to retain Jewish culture, so they choose this path, not outright conversion to Christianity. Other Jews have organized counter-missionary activity to ward off their attempts to win followers.

20th-century America has produced two innovations for Jews who felt Jewish by identity, yet believed science had disproved the existence of a personal God. Under Mordechai Kaplan (1881–1983), Reconstructionist Judaism posited Judaism as an ever-changing civilization, the result of natural human development. It has 100 synagogues and favours inclusivity for woman. Humanistic Judaism, founded in 1958 by Rabbi Sherwin Wine (1928–2007), with perhaps 40,000 active members, takes pride in Jewish cultural achievements and ethical teachings. It comes closest to overt atheism and raises again the old question, can one be Jewish and not believe in God?

Below Revellers in costume at the Boombamela New Age festival at Nitsanim beach near Ashkelon.

WOMEN IN JEWISH SOCIETY

'PATRIARCHAL' JUDAISM IS OFTEN SEEN AS CHAUVINISTIC, YET EVEN ORTHODOX JEWS NOW STRIVE FOR GENDER EQUALITY. JEWISH WOMEN HAVE CONTRIBUTED GREATLY TO THE ARTS, SCIENCES AND PROFESSIONS.

While outsiders see discrimination against women in the ultra-Orthodox community, the Bible often suggests a different attitude. Women probably sang in Temple services and prayed with men at the Sanctuary in David's time. The matriarchs Sarah, Rebecca, Leah and Rachel are venerated as 'mothers of the Jewish people'. Moses' sister Miriam was called Israel's first prophet; the judge Deborah led in battle; and Queen Esther saved Jews from destruction in Persia. For all that, the abiding impression of the Old Testament is of a man's world.

Similar contradictions apply to Jewish practice. On the Sabbath a husband sings to his wife that she is a woman of worth; and the Talmud calls on a man to love his wife as himself and respect her even more. Yet there is a daily prayer for men to thank God for not making them women, and women in Orthodox synagogues cannot be rabbis, cantors or choristers. Separated from men by a *mechitza*, or 'barrier', they may not handle the Torah nor publicly recite from it, and cannot qualify for a *minyan*, or the quorum of ten men needed for a full service. Religious women hide their hair beneath *sheitls*, or 'wigs' or 'scarves'. Perhaps most controversial today is that Jewish law restricts women's activities during menstruation.

CHECKS AND BALANCES
Defenders of Orthodoxy argue that post-Talmudic checks and balances have guarded against sexist abuse. Formally a man may divorce a woman and not vice versa; yet the medieval Rabbeinu Gershom allowed women to petition a rabbinical council for an annulment and outlawed polygamy.

Women are exempt from many Torah commands because, argue the rabbis, they are innately more spiritual than men. They ruled that running the household equalled religious ritual. Many feminists see such attitudes as anachronistic and patronizing.

Above Biblical heroine Queen Esther with her uncle Mordechai. Dura-Europos mosaic, 2nd-century Syria.

HISTORICAL COMPARISONS
In the past, Jewish women were not necessarily more oppressed than Christian and Muslim women. Jewish women were powerful independent merchants in England after 1066 and Judaism insisted that all women be literate. Apart from converts, someone is only Jewish if their mother is; the father's faith is irrelevant.

RELIGIOUS REFORM
Enlightenment values wrought significant change in certain synagogues. Reform thinkers referred back to the gender equality presumed in Genesis: 'God created man in His own image; male and female created He them'. As a result, both men and women lead services, read from the Torah and sing in choirs at American Reform and some Conservative synagogues. In 1922, Reconstructionist Rabbi Mordecai Kaplan had his daughter Judith take the first bat mitzvah, equal to the bar mitzvah for boys. However, only in 1935 was Regina Jonas ordained as the first female Reform rabbi, in Germany.

Unlike strictly observant Haredi and Hassidic Jews, modern Orthodox have gradually tried to make women feel more a part of religious services. They adopted a variant of the bat mitzvah, and since the mid-1970s

---

WOMEN PIONEERS
Increasingly, Jewish women are being recognized for their contributions. Some changed history, such as Dona Gracia who led Portuguese refugees to Turkey and Palestine, and Tannait Asenath Barzani of Mosul, yeshiva head in 17th-century Kurdistan. Women like Rahel Levin in Berlin, Genevieve Straus in Paris and Ada Leverson in London hosted salons, a practice revived by Gertrude Stein and Alice Toklas in 20th-century America. Western feminism is unimaginable without Betty Friedan, Andrea Dworkin, Erica Jong and Naomi Wolf.

Prolific Jewish women writers have included the South African Nobel laureate and enemy of apartheid Nadine Gordimer; Emma Lazarus, Lillian Hellman and Cynthia Ozick in America; Margo Glanz of Mexico and Marjorie Agosin of Chile; and Shulamit Hareven and Shifra Horn in Israel. Prominent women scientists include Rosalind Franklin, who helped unveil the DNA double helix; and Italy's Rita Levi-Montalcini, 1986 Nobel laureate for discovering the protein that makes nerves grow.

Above Hannah Arendt, political theorist and the first female professor at Princeton University, in 1960.

a Tefillah Network has arranged separate women's prayer groups and 'partnership *minyans*' where they read directly from the Torah.

FEMINISM

Jewish women were extremely prominent in the post-1960s feminist movement, but few addressed specifically Jewish concerns. A more pointedly Jewish critique started with Trude Weiss-Rosmarin, an American educationalist whose seminal 1970

Below A girl reads from the Torah for her bat mitzvah, initiation into the community equivalent to the bar mitzvah for boys.

article, 'The Unfreedom of Jewish Women', inspired a group to change Jewish laws. Tamar Ross, Rachel Adler, Paula Hyman and the Reform thinker Judith Plaskow (author of *Standing Again at Sinai*) have since amplified her views.

PROMINENT THINKERS

Jewish women often helped define 20th-century trends in society at large. They range from the cult novelist Ayn Rand to the political theorist Hannah Arendt. Susan Sontag wrote radical essays on photography and popular culture, while Yale professor Seyla Benhabib of Turkey addresses issues of globalization and multiculturalism.

AMBIGUITIES IN ISRAEL

In Israel, women serve a mandatory two years in the army. The kibbutz demanded absolute gender equality. In 1969 Golda Meir became Israel's prime minister, the first woman premier in the Middle East. Israel adopted laws of affirmative action for women in 1993. Yet women's rights, championed by politicians such as Yael Dayan and Ada Maimon, usually play second fiddle to issues of war and security.

Today campaigners fight Orthodox strictures on women's right to pray at the Western Wall; others challenge new Hebrew words that betray sexist bias; and the New Israel Fund has shelters for battered women. Women in Black have long marched in solidarity with Palestinians, and

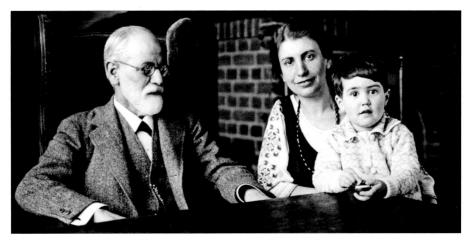

Above Pioneering child psychoanalyst Anna Freud in 1927 with her father, Sigmund Freud, and her niece Eve.

Machsom Watch monitors abuses at checkpoints in the territories. In response, rightist settlers set up their own Women in Green.

Female Israeli and Palestinian legislators jointly demanded greater women's involvement in peace brokering in 2005. Sceptics may doubt their chances, yet the record of the Four Mothers lobby, which forced Israel to withdraw from Lebanon in 2000, suggests further surprises in future.

Below Israeli woman soldier, Jerusalem, 1990. Women have been part of Israel's military since 1948.

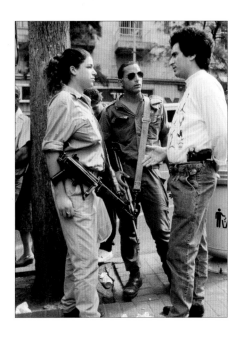

MEDICINE AND SCIENCE

THE JEWISH DOCTOR HAS LONG BEEN A RECOGNIZED FIGURE ALL OVER THE WORLD. THE OPENING OF UNIVERSITIES TO JEWS DURING THE 19TH CENTURY LED HUGE NUMBERS INTO THE SCIENCES.

In the Bible, God is called the great healer. Because mankind is seen as completing God's worldly plans, the doctor is regarded as performing divine work; Jews are obliged to value *peku'ah nefesh*, or 'preservation of life'.

Whole sections of the Talmud prescribe remedies and cures, and concern embryology, pathology and intricate examination of medical conditions. Jewish philosophers often practised medicine, such as the 9th-century master of ophthalmology and court physician to the Fatimid Isaac Israeli. Many rabbis combined their duties with medical practice. Maimonides, the most obvious example, wrote ten medical works

Below Jonas Salk (1914–95), whose invention of a safe and effective polio vaccine in 1952 has nearly eradicated the disease worldwide.

including *Aphorisms of Moshe* and *Regimen Sanitatis*, written in Judeo-Arabic. His view that a healthy body is essential for a healthy soul influenced doctors for generations.

FROM THE MIDDLE AGES TO THE 18TH CENTURY

During periods of liberality Jews studied medicine in the School of Salerno in 9th–12th century southern Italy, and at Jewish centres in 12th–13th century southern France. Jews served as physicians to Christian kings in Zaragoza, Toledo and Barcelona, and to Muslim sultans in Cairo and Cordoba. The 1492 Iberian expulsions disseminated Jewish medical knowledge to Holland, Germany, Denmark and the Ottoman empire.

MEDICINE IN EUROPE

Jews were still mostly excluded from the best European medical schools until two events dramatically changed matters: the Austrian Edict of Toleration of 1782 and the French Revolution of 1789. Jews poured into the universities and soon achieved remarkable successes. Tsarist edict still barred them from reaching their potential in Russia, and in Germany they were denied access to prestigious fields like surgery. None the less, they were pioneers in ignored areas – notably microscopy, neurology, biochemistry, haematology and psychiatry.

20TH-CENTURY BREAKTHROUGHS

Progress accelerated in the 20th century, although now the stress was on practical application of accumulated knowledge. Paul Ehrlich helped cre-

Above Hans Krebs, German-born British doctor and biochemist who won a Nobel Prize in 1953.

ate chemotherapy and invented the first effective drug against syphilis in 1910; shortly after, Casimir Funk showed how vitamin B could counter beri-beri. Partially realizing Ehrlich's dream of a 'magic bullet' to destroy bacteria, the English Nobel Prize-winner Sir Boris Chain isolated penicillin, while other Jews, Harry Eagle and Maxwell Finland, pursued the new field of antibiotics.

In America, Jonas Salk discovered the polio vaccine and in 1963 founded the famous Salk Institute for Biological Studies at La Jolla, California. Albert Sabin, a pioneer in immunology and the relationship of viruses to cancer, invented the oral polio vaccine, which largely eliminated the disease after it was publicly released in 1961.

PHYSICS

As with medicine, Jewish scientists, physicists and chemists flourished with the academic advances of the 19th century. Similarly, the advent of Nazism in the 1930s saw a decided shift in talent from old Europe to America. One early pioneer was the Breslau-born Arthur Korn, who transmitted the first photograph by wire. In the USA innovation and enterprise often went hand in hand, a prime example being Isaac Singer's famous sewing-machine invention, whose export to Britain in the 1860s boosted the still-nascent and Jewish-dominated tailoring trade.

There were few fields where Jews did not leave their mark. Abraham Sztern (1762–1842) pioneered early calculating devices, Siegfried Marcus (1831–98) invented an ignition device in 1864 and the first petrol-driven vehicle in 1870; David Schwartz (1852–97) built the first dirigible airship in 1896 (Count von Zeppelin bought the plans from his widow in 1898). Theodore von Kármán (1881–1963) pioneered supersonic aerodynamics, while Mikhael Gurevich, together with A.I. Mikoyan, built the first supersonic Soviet jet airfighters, the MiGs.

ALBERT EINSTEIN

Apart from creating the greatest upheaval in scientific thinking since Isaac Newton, Albert Einstein (1879–1955) became a prominent figure in Jewish affairs.

Einstein used his platform to criticize politicians and lambasted the abuse of science: 'In the hands of our generation these hard-won achievements are like a razor wielded by a child of three.' Einstein resigned his post at the Royal Prussian Academy of Sciences when Hitler took power in 1933 and never returned to Germany. Instead he travelled to Oxford, England, and eventually settled in

Above Two giants of nuclear physics conferring: Albert Einstein and Robert Oppenheimer.

Princeton, USA. He protested against the use of nuclear arms, although he was largely responsible for the technology that created the bomb.

A Zionist who agitated for peace between Jews and Arabs, Einstein was offered the presidency of Israel in 1948 but declined. Always proud of his Jewish roots, he was an agnostic, although he said that 'The mysterious stands at the cradle of true art and true science'.

CHEMISTRY

Jewish scientists have found chemistry a particularly fruitful field. In 1916 Fritz Haber won a Nobel Prize for synthesizing ammonia. The Austrian Karl Landsteine discovered

the basic blood groups and the Rhesus blood factor. In Israel, Aharon Katzir (Katchalski) gained world fame for his work in polymer chemistry, while his brother, Ephraim, an expert in proteins at the Weizmann Institute, created synthetic fibres for use in internal stitching, and became Israel's fourth state president (1973–8). Aaron Klug, a South African, won a Nobel for his study of the three-dimensional structure of nucleic acids, proteins and viruses.

THE LIFE SCIENCES

Jews in zoology, botany and biology included Julius Sachs, the creator of experimental botany; Lawrence Bogorad, professor of biology at Harvard; and Moses Ezekiel, one of the world's leading economic botanists. Waldemar Mordecai

Left Italian neurologist and 1986 Nobel Medicine prize-winner Rita Levi-Montalcini celebrates her 100th birthday in style.

Haffkine developed the first effective vaccine against cholera in 1892. Otto Loewi and Sir Bernard Katz won Nobel Prizes for discovering how nerves work. From 1950 to 1967 Jewish scientists won 11 of the 46 Nobels for biology.

SPLITTING THE ATOM ...

Jewish scientists, who won 48 of the 174 Nobel Prizes in the field during 1901–2004, have played a disproportionate role in atom-splitting studies, the best known of all being Albert Einstein. Another was Max Born, an early master of quantum physics and probability theory.

It was Einstein's letter to President Roosevelt that launched America's top-secret Los Alamos Manhattan Project and created the world's first atomic bomb. The Manhattan team included many great Jewish nuclear physicists, like the American Robert Oppenheimer, and Edward Teller, later credited with inventing the hydrogen bomb.

JEWISH ARTISTS AND THEMES IN ART

ART HAS LONG POSED A QUANDARY FOR JEWS: THE TALMUD PRAISES BEAUTIFUL HOLY OBJECTS BUT THE TORAH ITSELF FORBIDS THE 'GRAVEN IMAGE', THUS PRODUCING ART WAS SOMETIMES SEEN AS REJECTING JUDAISM ITSELF.

Although synagogues banned human images, Pharaoh, Moses, Egyptians and Israelites peopled the pages of illustrated Passover *haggadahs*. Calligraphy became a fine art, as did micrography, which formed patterns and pictures from tiny marginal notes in the Torah.

DAWN OF THE NAMED ARTIST

Notions of the named individual artist bypassed Jews, until Moritz Oppenheim (1800–82) began painting elegant portraits of Jewish notables and biblical themes in German Romantic tones. Polish-born Maurycy Gottlieb (1856–79) painted *Shylock and Jessica* and *Jews Praying on Yom Kippur*.

In Holland the contemplative Jozef Israels (1824–1911) was hailed as a reincarnation of Rembrandt. Max Liebermann (1847–1935) shocked German salons with his overtly Jewish painting of *Twelve-year-old Jesus in the Temple*, though he later became the doyen of genteel portraiture and landscapes.

REBELLION AND SUPPRESSION

In eastern Europe the 1881 pogroms bred not only works of despair, but also Lazar Krestin's defiant *Birth of Jewish Resistance* (1905). Not all Jews felt obliged to paint 'Jewish themes'. The work of pioneering Impressionists Camille Pissarro and Isaac Israels reflected little explicit Jewish content.

Paris fostered new trends during 1900–40 such as Fauvism, Cubism, Dadaism and Surrealism, attracting Russian Jews like Marc Chagall and Chaim Soutine and Sephardi Jews like Amadeo Modigliani (Italian) and Jules Pascin (Bulgarian). This 'Jewish School' varied in style from Modigliani's African inspirations to Soutine's anxious Expressionism; only Chagall depicted Jewish imagery. 'Were I not a Jew', he wrote in his 1931 autobiography, 'I would not be an artist at all.'

Stalinism and Nazism stamped out individual expression. In 1933 Nazis sacked Max Liebermann as president of the prestigious Berlin Art Academy. Work by Jews was judged 'degenerate'

Above *Prolific and ever innovative, the artist Marc Chagall celebrates his 90th birthday in 1977.*

and all non-representative art was considered the handicraft of Jews, even if the artist was 'Aryan'. Paradoxically, this drove creative talents into exile where they spread their radical ideas.

BRITAIN AND THE USA

A remarkable flowering of Jewish artists occurred in Britain at the turn of the 20th century. The movement's godfather was Sir William Rothenstein, an Impressionist painter and principal of London's Royal College of Art (1920–35). His most talented pupil was Mark Gertler (1891–1939), who never forgot his Jewish roots, as seen in *The Rabbi and his Grandchild* (1913).

In 1914 David Bomberg's London Group organized the first exhibition of modern Jewish artists. Two German Jewish painters arrived in Britain in the 1930s: Sigmund Freud's grandson Lucian, a leading Representational portraitist, and the earthy Expressionist Frank Auerbach. England's Cecil Roth was the first true historian of Jewish art.

American art took the lead in daring abstraction, such as the 'colour field' innovations of Mark Rothko and

Left *Jacob Epstein's powerful group sculpture* Social Consciousness, *1954, stands today in Philadelphia.*

Above The Rabbi and his Grandchild, *a compelling portrait by Anglo-Jewish artist Mark Gertler, 1913.*

Adolph Gottlieb. Pop artist George Segal (1934–) invokes classical Jewish topics, such as Abraham sacrificing Isaac.

THE SCULPTED IMAGE
Even more than painting, sculpture represented a special taboo due to its association with idols. The first Jewish pioneer was Vilna-born Mark Antokolski (1843–1902), whose early Realist sculptures depicted such scenes as 'The Talmudic Debate' and 'Jewish Tailor'. More modern in ethos, the American-born British sculptor Jacob Epstein (1880–1959) continually quoted biblical themes:

LOOTED ART
During World War II the Nazis took 100,000 art pieces from France alone; some 60,000 were recovered, of which 45,000 were returned to their owners or heirs, invariably Jews. Reparation for lost or 'looted' art is a controversial issue now and has proven a good opportunity to re-inspect some fabulous gems. Ironically Germans seemed passionate for abstract art, or art by Jews, given what Nazi propaganda called it.

ART THAT SERVES FAITH
Jews have used art from earliest times, often in the service of religion. The *mezuzah*, a doorpost prayer case, can be made of wood, ivory, metal or even sculpted coloured plastic. Ashkenazic coverings for Torah scrolls are made from embroidered cloth, and silver breastplates, and Sephardi tik boxes from wood or metal. The Torah is decorated with silver crowns and bells and a *yad*, an ivory pointer shaped like a tiny hand. Jewish craftsmen decorate the Sabbath loaf cloth, twin candlesticks and spice boxes.

Over time calligraphers and miniaturists illustrated flowers and pretty scenes on the *ketubah* or 'traditional marriage document'. Particularly beautiful *ketubot* (pl.) were made in Bohemia, Italy, Egypt, Persia, Jerusalem, Yemen, India and Afghanistan. Other objects treated artistically include kiddush cups, Hannukah lamps, Passover plates and even circumcision tools.

Adam, the Sacrifice of Isaac, Genesis, and Jacob and the Angel. Even more influential was the Cubist sculptor Lithuanian-born Jacques Lipchitz (1891–1973), who escaped Paris for America as Nazis invaded in 1941.

ART IN ISRAEL
Zionist ideologues wished to create a 'new Hebrew' on Palestinian soil. Biblical scenes inspired Jakob Steinhardt; Yemenite settlers and local Arab farmers caught Reuven Rubin's imagination. Both studied at the Betzalel art and crafts academy, named after Moses' master craftsman and founded in Jerusalem in 1906 by Boris Schatz, a court sculptor in Bulgaria. In 1965 Betzalel's gallery turned into the Israel Museum, now the world's largest repository of Israeli art. Since then, Israelis have moved from 'Jewish imagery' to more universal, individual and abstract concerns.

PHOTOGRAPHY
When US galleries admitted photographs by Alfred Stieglitz, other Jews, such as the French Surrealist Man Ray and Hungarians André Kertész and Laszlo Moholy-Nagy began turning craft into fine art. Several exploited

Right A chronicler of a lost world, photographer Roman Vishniac shot this image of a child in Warsaw, 1938.

photography's documentary potential, for example German-born Alfred Eisenstaedt and Budapest-born Robert Capa in *LIFE* magazine, or Roman Vishniac, who shot the last days of Europe's *shtetls* and Jewish quarters.

Mary Ellen Mark, Diane Arbus and Lee Friedlander intimately observed contemporary US life, and Judah Passow and David Rubinger have chronicled Israel at war and peace. Examples of creative commercial portraiture and fashion include the baroque style of Irving Penn, the psychological work of Arnold Newman, the experimentalism of Cindy Sherman (USA) and Jeanloup Sieff (France), and Annie Leibovitz's elegant, often ironic studies of celebrities.

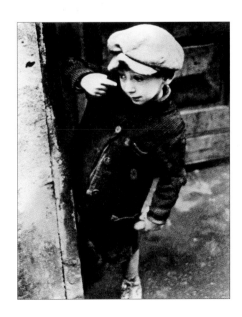

JEWISH WRITERS AND LITERATURE

IT IS OFTEN QUESTIONED WHETHER ALL WRITING BY JEWS IS BY DEFINITION 'JEWISH LITERATURE'. MANY ARGUE THAT EVEN WHEN JEWS WRITE ABOUT GENERAL TOPICS A JEWISH SENSIBILITY INFORMS THEIR WORDS.

Creative writing by Jews, even when its content is secular, has had a powerful impact on surrounding cultures: imagine German literature without Heinrich Heine or Franz Kafka, American writing without Saul Bellow or Arthur Miller, or Chilean literature without Ariel Dorfman.

THE BIBLICAL WELLSPRING

Before the 19th century, Jews concentrated on religious writing. Many wrote commentaries on what is arguably the most widely read and influential of all literary works, the Hebrew Bible. The Bible contains literary elements: plots, characterization, drama and violence, family sagas and personal rivalries. Though mostly written in prose, the Bible also includes the first instances of Hebrew poetry, in the songs of Deborah and Miriam, and the Song of Songs.

Below A scribe, or sofer*, painstakingly writing out holy verses before the advent of printing. From Rothschild Miscellany, northern Italy, c. 1450–80.*

From the Oral Tradition came the Talmud's Aggadah, Midrashic stories loosely based on the Bible, and later mystical works such as the Zohar. These inspired medieval Spanish Hebrew poets including Samuel ibn Nagrela and Solomon Ibn Gabirol, who described intimate personal feelings alongside religious themes. Peaceful times brought cultural cross-fertilization: Judah Halevi and Moses Ibn Ezra incorporated Arabic metre into their poetry, and Joseph ibn Zabara's popular *Book of Delights* showed intimate knowledge of Arab, Greek and Indian folklore.

WRITING IN YIDDISH

Early Yiddish exponents included such women as Glückel of Hameln, or were specifically aimed at women, such as the Bible compendium *Tsena u-Rena*. Abraham Goldfaden was hailed as the 'Yiddish Shakespeare'. In 1876 in Romania he founded the first professional Yiddish language theatre. He wrote 40 plays, before he died in New York. Some have dismissed his

Above Ludwig Zamenhof, who wrote the first grammar of Yiddish.

works as 'low culture', and his rival the Russian-born American playwright Jacob Gordin responded with adventurous plays like *The Jewish Queen Lear*.

L.L. Zamenhof, who gave respect to Yiddish with its first grammar book, written in 1879, was the same man who invented Esperanto. The trio of Yiddish masters were Mendele Moikher Sforim, social critic and idealist; Sholem Aleichem, much-loved author of Tevye tales (later staged as *Fiddler on the Roof*); and Isaac Leib Peretz, a modernist who believed in self-emancipation.

Since the 1970s a desire to 'return to roots' revived Jewish interest in Yiddish culture. While secular Yiddish remains mainly a studied language, the remarkable growth of Orthodox families guarantees that the argot survives in New York, London and Jerusalem.

Three institutions epitomized the extraordinary outpouring of Yiddish creativity in the 1930s: the Moscow State Jewish Theatre, founded in 1920; the YIVO Jewish Scientific Institute, founded in 1925; and after 1929, 'Young Vilna', a leftist band of artists, writers, polemicists and educators. YIVO and Young Vilna were devastated by the Holocaust, and survivors fled to the Soviet Union or America, where the Singer brothers, Isaac Bashevis and Israel Joshua, had already taken refuge.

POETIC REBIRTH IN PALESTINE AND ISRAEL

Hebrew began replacing Yiddish and Ladino as 'the' Jewish language in 20th-century Palestine, and the greatest Hebrew writers of the 1920s, Haim Nahman Bialik, Ahad Ha-Am and Saul Tchernichowsky, settled in Tel Aviv. By 1940 more books were published for Palestine's 500,000 Jews than for their 5 million American cousins.

Israeli novelists are now widely read and often raise uncomfortable issues, at times questioning Israel's founding myths. S. Yizhar wrote two novellas during the 1948 war, *Khirbet Khizah* and *The Prisoner*, which contrasted Jewish experience of pogroms with their contemporary attitudes to Arabs. Yizhar belonged to the War of Independence generation of writers, as does the nationalist poet Haim Gouri and author and playwright Moshe Shamir. The more sceptical Aharon Appelfeld is the author of *Badenheim 1939*, a darkly satirical work.

Below Topol played the lead in Fiddler on the Roof, *from Sholem Aleichem's stories about Tevye the milkman.*

Internationally recognized stars of the post-1967 generation include Amos Oz, A.B. Yehoshua and David Grossman, who trace the interplay of memory, love, friendship and responses to conflict. Newer voices have expressed fresh views, such as Etgar Keret's cartoon-like pop fables. Additionally Israeli Arabs such as Anton Shammas, Emil Habiby and Sayed Kashua have used dark humour in Hebrew to express the ambiguity of non-Jewish indigenes living in a Jewish state.

HEBREW ON STAGE

Founded in Moscow in 1917, Habimah (The Stage) was probably the first Hebrew theatre company in the world. Tel Aviv's Kameri theatre won acclaim for plays by the popular satirist Hanoch Levin and others. Smaller groups, including Arab and Jewish troupes in Akko and Jaffa, address intercommunal strife and the trauma of regional conflict.

New writers have introduced a distinctive female voice, with Orly Castel-Bloom (1960–) leading the way in her controversial urban satire, *Dolly City*. Others include Savyon Librecht (1948–), Ronit Matalon (1959–), and Dorit Rabinyan (1972–), author of *Persian Brides*. In their different ways, all describe the place of Diaspora memory in contemporary Israeli society.

WRITERS IN THE DIASPORA

Moses Mendelssohn, godfather of the Haskalah, used German and Hebrew in his essays. Later, Heinrich Heine wrote in German, followed by Joseph Roth, Franz Rosenzweig, Franz Kafka and Arnold Zweig. Writers Arthur Schnitzler and Jakob Wasserman urged fellow Jews to fully absorb German culture, until World War II changed their minds. Few Jews still wrote in German after 1945, an exception being the poetess and playwright Nelly Sachs, a 1966 Nobel Prize-winner.

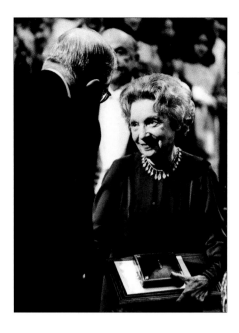

Above A Swedish poet born in Germany, Nelly Sachs shared the Nobel Prize for Literature with Israeli author Shmuel Yosef Agnon in 1966.

JEWISH THEMES

Despite his Jewish origins, Marcel Proust wrote only tangentially on Jewish issues. By contrast, the Swiss-born Jewish essayist Edmond Fleg wrote biographies of Moses, Solomon and Jesus; and Andre Schwartz-Bart's *Last of the Just*, a Jewish historical novel from the Crusades to Auschwitz, is a French classic. George Perec survived the Holocaust to write daringly experimental French literature.

Sholem Aleichem used humour to instruct 'greenhorns' how to acclimatize to American conditions. Generations later, nostalgic books appeared such as *The Apprenticeship of Duddy Kravitz*, by the Canadian Mordechai Richler, or the fictitious Hyman Kaplan, subject of short stories by New York writer Leo Rosten. By now, authors had moved from immigrant literature to the American mainstream. They wrote in English and included two authors fascinated with Zionist settlement, the poet Jessie Sampter, who went to Palestine in 1919, and the intrepid Chicago-born novelist Meyer Levin.

THE JEWISH IMAGE IN LITERATURE

By the late 18th century, Christian writers showed renewed interest in Jewish themes. Gottfried Lessing's German plays *The Jews* and *Nathan the Wise* championed dignified Jews in the face of prevailing bigotry; and romanticism about an ancient, perse-cuted yet talented people partly countered the anti-Semitic depictions of Jews of 19th-century England.

By contrast, stereotypes of Jewish swindlers persisted, perhaps the most famous being Shakespeare's Shylock in *The Merchant of Venice*. In the 19th century Charles Dickens introduced Fagin in *Oliver Twist*. Shocked when readers saw his depiction as anti-Semitic, Dickens introduced a more sympathetic character in his last completed book, *Our Mutual Friend*, called Mr Riah, 'the gentle Jew in whose race gratitude is deep'.

Above Fagin, Charles Dickens' villain from Oliver Twist, *suggested a negative view of Jews as criminals.*

Literature often treated Jews sympathetically when they were few on the ground, but when their numbers increased the mood changed. In *The American Scene* (1907), Henry James complained of 'a Jewry that had burst all bounds...There is no swarming like that of Israel'. T.S. Eliot and F. Scott Fitzgerald indulged in commonplace anti-Semitism, though by the 1930s backtracked somewhat when such views were associated with Fascism.

One writer who championed the oppressed Jews of Russia was Maxim Gorky (1868–1936). Though not himself Jewish he defended Jewish rights during the 1903 Tsarist pogroms, and after the 1917 October Revolution, which he supported, he wrote his 1918 story *Pogrom*.

Below Isaac Bashevis Singer, first Yiddish novelist to receive a Nobel Prize for Literature, in 1978.

AMERICAN WRITERS
Isaac Bashevis Singer was an exception who still wrote in Yiddish. In 1978 Singer became the first Yiddish author to win the Nobel Prize for Literature. Although located in a Jewish setting, Singer's writing discussed issues that affect all society.

Bernard Malamud's Jewish self-awareness shines through in *Dubin's Lives* and *The Jewbird*. 'Everybody is a Jew but they don't know it', he wrote, suggesting Western urbanites now share what used to be a Jewish preserve – displacement and the need to juggle multiple identities.

Canadian-born Saul Bellow, a 1976 Nobel laureate, became per-haps America's top literary stylist who dissected post-war alienation in *Herzog* and *Humboldt's Gift*. Chaim Potok's more populist books threw a spotlight on an Orthodox world long ignored by the US literati, while Joseph Heller, whose *Catch 22* was a cult best-seller, later wrote ribald works like *God Knows* about King David. Even Allen Ginsberg, Beatnik poet and Buddhist convert, drew on his Jewish roots in *Howl* and *Kaddish*.

Norman Mailer's works straddled journalism and fiction, starting with *The Naked and the Dead*, 1948, and essays on Vietnam protest, radicalism and conservatism. Probably most searing in his critique of contempo-rary Jewry was Philip Roth, with *Goodbye Columbus* and *Portnoy's Complaint*, full of sexual fantasies and jibes at a domineering mother.

ENGLISH AUTHORS
Israel Zangwill (1864–1926), known as the Jewish Dickens, wrote *King of the Schnorrers*, a comedy that shot a few broadsides at the Sephardi elite. His magnum opus *Children of the Ghetto* introduced the vibrant Jewish East End to a wider reader-ship. Later Anglo-Jewish writers have included such bold voices as Howard Jacobson, who won the

Below South African writer, political activist and winner of the 1991 Nobel Prize for Literature, Nadine Gordimer.

Above Arthur Miller, who received the Pullitzer Prize for Drama in 1949 for Death of a Salesman, *at the United States Jewish Culture Awards in 1995.*

Man Booker Prize in 2010 with *The Finkler Question*, Clive Sinclair and Linda Grant.

Commonwealth writers include the South African Dan Jacobson, who often depicts the Jewish immigrant experience, and Nobel laureate Nadine Gordimer, an early foe of apartheid (racial segregation), who won the Nobel Prize for Literature in 1991. Smaller numbers of South African Jews wrote in Yiddish, Hebrew and Afrikaans, while in India, Bnei Israel member Nissim Ezekiel was called the leading English-language poet.

RUSSIAN STARS

While in 1897 only 1.3 per cent of the Pale's Jews spoke Russian, the rest Yiddish, 100 years later that ratio was reversed. The trend accelerated after the Revolution and led to passionate writing in Russian from the likes of Isaac Babel, reporter of Jewish Odessa and the vanishing shtetl, and later Boris Pasternak, Vassily Grossman and Nadezhda Mandelstam. Born in Russia and expelled in 1972, Joseph Brodsky, Nobel laureate of 1987, settled in the USA where he stated: 'I am Jewish – a Russian poet and an English essayist'.

THE ITALIAN LEGACY

Italy's small Jewish population has produced an amazing number of authors. Giorgio Bassani in *Garden of the Finzi-Continis* showed wealthier Jews surprised by fascist race laws. Others wrote 'non-Jewish' gems, such as Carlo Levi's paean to peasant life, *Christ Stopped at Eboli*. Primo Levi strove to understand the other Jewish worlds he encountered as a prisoner in Auschwitz. Some call his understated works the most powerful Holocaust literature written. Italian Jewish authors also include Alberto Moravia, Elsa Morante, Cesare Pavese, Natalia Ginzburg and Italo Svevo.

ASHKENAZIM WRITING IN SPANISH

Latin American Jewish writers tend to display spiritual restlessness and a passion for justice. Jacobo Timerman, a Ukrainian-born Argentine and author of *Prisoner Without a Name, Cell Without a Number,* was jailed for his dissident writings. Alicia Partnoy wrote about her experiences as a political prisoner in Argentina in *The Little School.* Cultural anthopologist Ruth Behar writes about her experience as a Cuban Jewish woman.

PLAYWRIGHTS

Loved on both sides of the English-speaking Atlantic, Arthur Miller wrote plays with few overtly Jewish characters, although recognizable Jewish types. Another prolific dramatist who addressed social ills was Lillian Hellman. Her successors have since pricked the nation's conscience on issues from racism and Vietnam to AIDS and infidelity. More recently Yasmina Reza, the French-based daughter of a Persian father and Hungarian mother, both Jewish, won fame in English translation for *Art*, a pastiche of 1990s materialism.

Right British playwright and political activist Harold Pinter was awarded the Nobel Prize for Literature in 2005.

Above Howard Jacobson, celebrated Anglo-Jewish writer and columnist, who won the 2010 Man Booker Prize for Fiction, for The Finkler Question.

In Britain, leading playwrights of Jewish origin include Jonathan Miller, Mike Leigh and the Czech-born Tom Stoppard, renowned for witty philosophical dramas. Frantisek Langer was one of Czechoslovakia's leading interwar playwrights. Many musical writers of modern America were Jewish, such as Irving Berlin, Richard Rodgers, Oscar Hammerstein II and Stephen Sondheim, and Jews are well represented as directors and scriptwriters for radio and television drama series. Additionally, Jews have contributed disproportionately to cinema, perhaps the quintessential art form of the 20th century.

HOLLYWOOD AND BEYOND

CINEMA DEVELOPED FROM HUMBLE ORIGINS IN THE 1890S TO BECOME PERHAPS THE DEFINING ART FORM OF THE 20TH CENTURY, AND FROM THE START JEWS WERE INTIMATELY INVOLVED IN THE INDUSTRY.

At first promoters and producers, then directors, scriptwriters, actors and composers, by 1912 Jews had set up over a hundred production companies in California, and were pivotal to the creation of the eight super-firms.

RAGS TO RICHES

Almost to a man – and they were all men – the Jewish movie moguls were born into poverty. Carl Laemmle, the 10th of 13 immigrant children, managed a clothes shop before running a string of nickelodeons and in 1912 founding Universal, the first big studio. Louis Mayer joined the junk trade at 8, owned a New York theatre-chain at 22 and produced the epic *Birth of a Nation* in 1915, aged 30. Adolph Zukor, who founded Paramount Pictures in 1917, was born in Hungary, emigrated at 15 and peddled fur garments.

A similar rags-to-riches story applied to the Warner Brothers, sons of a Jewish cobbler from Poland. In 1927 they amazed the filmic world by harnessing new technology to produce the first 'talkie'. Starring Al Jolson, *The Jazz Singer* presented Jewish family dilemmas about tradition and assimilation to a mainstream audience. In the 1930s cinema blossomed. MGM's Irving Thalberg released *Mutiny on the Bounty* in 1936; and David Selznik produced the immortal box-office sensation *Gone with the Wind* in 1939.

FILMS ABOUT JEWISHNESS

Jewish themes became ever more rare, as moguls deliberately played down ethnic traits. The same cannot be said of Yiddish cinema, or of shorter American films that targeted Jewish immigrants. Three basic types prevailed: the ghetto melodrama, the historical pogrom saga and the vaudeville comedy. The Marx Brothers films of the 1930s used humour that was Jewish in origin, and made it universally popular, appealing to anyone who ever had to deal with petty bureaucrats.

Above A Night at the Opera – brothers Groucho, Chico and Harpo Marx hamming it up in 1935.

GERMAN CINEMA

By the 1920s, cinema had spread worldwide, and in Germany, Jewish producer Erich Pommer made *The Cabinet of Dr Caligari*, which set a benchmark for creativity. Fritz Lang directed *Metropolis*, a futuristic critique of industrial society, and *M*, a Kafkaesque murder drama starring a young Peter Lorre. Unlike their Polish cousins, German Jews fostered a cosmopolitan rather than a particularly Jewish sensibility.

Nazism decimated this short-lived flowering, and most Jewish directors, actors, producers and technicians left Germany for London, Paris, Amsterdam or Hollywood. Ernst Lubitsch had already come to America in 1923, and top directors and actors Josef von Sternberg, Billy Wilder, Erich von Stroheim, Fred Zinnemann and the Vienna-born Otto Preminger soon followed. Meanwhile German cinema produced anti-Semitic dramas such as *The Eternal Jew*.

Left Gillo Pontecorvo realized the power of cinema with his searing 1959 debut about the Holocaust, Kapo.

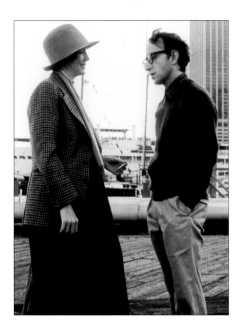

Above Woody Allen faces Diane Keaton in his 1977 MGM comedic classic Annie Hall.

ÉMIGRÉS IN BRITAIN

British cinema received a boost from talented central European Jews such as Alexander Korda. He moved to Britain in 1930 and nurtured actors and films tailored to the American market, such as *Rembrandt*, *The Scarlet Pimpernel* and *The Third Man*.

Sir Michael Balcon graduated from Alfred Hitchcock films to Ealing comedies. Canadian-born Harry Saltzman produced the edgy *Look Back in Anger* (1959) and then a string of James Bonds. Karel Reisz,

one of 669 Czech Jewish children who Sir Nicholas Winton rescued from the Nazis, defined the social realistic cinema of post-war Britain in *We are the Lambeth Boys*, *This Sporting Life* and *Saturday Night and Sunday Morning*. London-born John Schlesinger picked up the baton with *Billy Liar* and *Midnight Cowboy*. Other Anglo-Jewish directors are Michael Winner and Mike Leigh.

JEWISH THEMES

After World War II many French, Italian, Czech and Polish film directors addressed Jewish themes. In his 1959 directorial debut, *Kapo*, Gillo Pontecorvo broached the awkward subject of Jews who collaborated or adopted false identities to survive the death camps. In France, *Le vieil homme et l'enfant* by Claude Berri focused on Jews who hid in wartime. After his light-hearted *Mazel Tov*, about a Jewish wedding, he won fame in 1986 with *Jean de Florette* and *Manon des Sources*. *Soleil* (1993), by Algerian-born Jewish actor-director David Hanin, began a trend of films about the North African Jewish experience.

The Diary of Anne Frank (1959) was the first Hollywood film to focus on the plight of Jews in the Holocaust; followed by *Judgment at Nuremburg* (1961). There was renewed interest in a pre-American past: *Fiddler on the Roof* revived nostalgia for the *shtetl* while recognizing its imperfections.

Jewish women appeared in the 1970s in a non-stereotypical way in *The Way We Were* starring Barbara Streisand, *Hester Street* and *Girlfriends*. New Jewish characters emerged: gamblers, lesbians, cowboys, hit-men and even whorehouse madams.

The comedies of Woody Allen and Mel Brooks turned the comic Jewish *nebbish* (hopeless case) into a representative of late 20th-century angst. *The Frisco Kid* (1979) showed Jewish values and American pragmatism clashing in the US. Steven Spielberg and Roman Polanski viewed the Holocaust anew with *Schindler's List* and *The Pianist*.

Below Film director Steven Spielberg with the cast of Schindler's List, *1993.*

MUSIC AND MUSICIANS

THE PROPHET ISAIAH PROCLAIMED, 'MAKE SWEET MELODY, SING MANY
SONGS, THAT THOU MAYEST BE REMEMBERED'. FORBIDDEN FROM EXPRESSING
THEMSELVES THROUGH THE GRAVEN IMAGE, JEWS TOOK TO MUSIC WITH ZEAL.

The songs of Miriam and Deborah
are just two examples of early Jewish
music. It has thrived, in both sacred
and secular formats, while individual
Jews have contributed immeasurably
to Western classical, jazz, pop and folk.

The Bible and Talmud speak of
elaborate musical arrangements associated with Temple rites and
sacrifices, and even singing 'duty ros-
ters' for Levite choristers.
Performances featured 12 instruments – including pipes, whistles,
bells, horns, cymbals, *halil* flutes, the
kinnor and *nevel* lyres and the *tof*
frame-drum.

A great breach occurred when
Rome destroyed the Second Temple
in Jerusalem in 70CE. After that
calamity, Jews shunned the use of
instruments for sacred music as a sign
of mourning. This ban was soon
lifted outside places of worship.
Wedding parties stimulated religious
melodies and secular festivities wherever Jews settled.

*Below Broadway pioneers George and
Ira Gershwin were influenced by Yiddish
theatre and popular Jewish music.*

RAM'S HORN

The exception to the ban on synagogue instruments is the *shofar*, the
ram's horn, which is blown on Rosh
Hashanah, the Jewish New Year. The
shofar is meant to awaken people from
their spiritual slumber and call them
to repentance. One name for Rosh
Hashanah is Yom Teru'ah, or the 'day
of blowing'. The instrument is arguably
the oldest known to mankind.

CHANTING AND MELODY

Other than the *shofar* and organs at
weddings, all Orthodox synagogue
music is sung. One sage called
singing 'the fruit of the mouth'. The
oldest modes are reserved for chanting weekly portions of the Torah and
Prophets, and special markings written above and below the holy words,
called *te'amim*, denote their tune.

Early medieval synagogues allowed
more tuneful leeway with hymns
and *piyuttot*, or liturgical poetry. These
were and still are sung to a particular
nusah, or melody pattern, akin to the
Arabic *maqam*, Indian raga, Byzantine
hymnody or Roman plainsong. The
nusah denotes special times, so that
someone with a discerning ear can
enter a synagogue blindfolded and
immediately tell from hearing everyday prayers, like the *amidah*, whether
it is the Sabbath, a high holy day,
morning service or evening service.

CANTORS AND CHOIRS

Over time the virtuoso *hazzan*
(cantor) began to displace the more
humdrum *shaliach tzibbur*, or prayer
leader, and his role increased as
congregants' knowledge of Hebrew
diminished. The period between
the two world wars is known as the
'golden age of *hazzanut*'.

*Above Frank London and his
Klezmatics use jazz to breathe life
into old European Jewish klezmer.*

The synagogue choir, originally an
ad hoc body of harmonic responders,
grew in stature and opulence with
exposure to Western classical music.
In 1882 the Polish-born Jewish composer Louis Lewandowski scored an
entire choral service, *Todah ve-Zimrah*,
or 'Thanks and Song', for Berlin's
Oranienburgerstrasse Temple.

KLEZMER

From the 16th century, eastern
European *Klezmorim*, or 'wandering
folk musicians', and the *badchen*
(jester or compère), were staple fare
at weddings. Like their Sephardi
counterparts, Ashkenazim absorbed
local tunes and techniques into their
repertoires. Players employed plain-
tive or ecstatic ornamentation and
also mimicked the synagogue *hazzan* or fervent Hassidic *nigun* (often
wordless improvizations). The resultant mixture gives *klezmer* its
distinctive 'Jewish feel' to this day.

Since the 1970s klezmer and ladino
have revived as Diaspora Jews rediscovered their roots. Some adherents
favour hybrids with rock, folk and
jazz, such as the American group,
Klezmatics. Interestingly, some of the
most skilful klezmer practitioners are
non-Jewish Germans, like Tickle in
the Heart, or Poles, like Kroke.

Above Gustav Mahler, perhaps the greatest composer of Jewish origin, in the loggia of Vienna Opera House, 1907.

CLASSICAL COMPOSERS

Medieval Arab theorists inspired Jews to study music as a science, and in time certain Italian and Provençal Jews embraced secular music composition.

The 19th-century enlightenment led to an explosion of Jewish talent in Germany and France, with composers like Felix and Fanny Mendelssohn, Claude Offenbach, Fromental Halévy, Giacomo Meyerbeer and Gustav Mahler. Many became Christians, thus casting doubt on their definition as 'Jewish composers'. Even so, hints of *klezmer* and synagogue melody appear in the majestic orchestrations of the newly Catholic Mahler.

Arnold Schoenberg shocked audiences with atonal experimentations, and inspired numerous imitators after fleeing Austria for America in 1934. More conventional were the American Jewish composers Aaron Copland and Leonard Bernstein. Both evoked a specifically American classical oeuvre, as in Copland's *Appalachian Spring* and Bernstein's *West Side Story*. In more contemplative works such as *Chichester Psalms* and his Third Symphony *Kaddish*, Bernstein set Hebrew texts to modern music.

Jews including Philip Glass and Steve Reich pioneered minimalism and experimentation with electronics

in the 1960s. Both addressed Jewish themes – Glass in his *Einstein on the Beach* and Reich in *Tehillim* (Psalms), *Proverb*, *The Cave* (about Abraham and Hebron) and *Different Trains*, which evokes trucks en route to Auschwitz.

Jews have excelled as virtuoso performers, including pianists Arthur Rubinstein and Vladimir Ashkenazy.

JEWS AND JAZZ

From the early 1900s, black American and Jewish musicians practised and performed together in large cities like Chicago and New York. Several Yiddish tunes were reinterpreted as Jazz numbers, including *Burton on the Ritz*, derived from *Bei Mir Bist Du Shein*. Al Jolson moved from traditional Jewish music to become a leading Jazz, blues and ragtime singer.

Others who followed Jolson's Tin Pan Alley path included the songwriter Irving Berlin and Brazilian jazz diva, Flora Purim. George Gershwin bridged the chasm between 'high classical' music and Jazz with such rousing works as *Rhapsody in Blue*. The great swing clarinettist Benny Goodman was born in Chicago to Jewish immigrants and broke down racial segregation in America by working with black musicians.

Below Stan Getz (1927–91), the American saxophonist who blended Brazilian bossa nova with jazz.

Above Arthur Rubinstein, classical pianist, received international acclaim for his interpretation of Chopin.

ROCK AND ROLL

It is hard to imagine modern rock music without Jewish songwriters Jerry Leiber and Mike Stoller who helped launch the genre. Phil Spector pioneered the 1960s 'wall of sound' technique. In Britain, Brian Epstein managed the Beatles. Notable performers include Gene Simmons of Kiss, Marc Bolan of T Rex, Beastie Boys, Bob Dylan, Leonard Cohen, Ramones, Simon and Garfunkel, Paula Abdul, and converts to Judaism Sammy Davis Jr and Ike Turner.

THE SOUNDS OF ISRAEL

The sensitive songwriter Naomi Shemer drew heavily on the French chanson tradition of the 1960s, before releasing her song *Yerushalayim Shel Zahav* (Jerusalem of Gold) just before the Six Day War. It became in effect a second national anthem.

By the 1980s the singers Ofra Haza, Zehava Ben and the band Ethnix blended East and West to great effect. Hybrid forms and originality now typify Israeli music, examples of which include Yehuda Poliker, of Greek Jewish origin, who shifts from playing bazouki to hard electric rock, and Ahinoam Nini, who mixes jazz, 'indie' folk and Yemenite sounds.

247

JEWISH PHILOSOPHERS AND POLITICIANS

EVEN IN REJECTING ASPECTS OF TRADITIONAL JUDAISM, THINKERS SUCH AS FREUD AND DERRIDA SHOWED SIGNS OF ENGAGING WITH JUDAIC CONCEPTS, THUS REVEALING A SHARED JEWISH IDENTITY.

Perhaps the most revolutionary Jewish thinker of the 20th century was Sigmund Freud (1856–1939), who created psychoanalysis and explored the human unconscious. Convinced that neurosis resulted from repressed impulses and sexual drives, Freud drew on medicine, myth and dreams to explain how the mind works. Freudian terms such as the ego, the pleasure principle, paranoia, guilt feelings, subconscious, peer pressure and regression are repeatedly used and misused in everyday English conversation.

PSYCHOLOGY AND THEORY
Sigmund Freud was not a practising Jew and his books *Totem and Taboo* and *The Future of an Illusion* spoke of religion as the antithesis of reason and experience. None the less he

Below Hailed as the father of modern anthropology, Franz Boas studied people in their physical environment.

accepted that faith was part of the human psyche. All his psychologist colleagues bar Karl Jung were Jewish. Sigmund's daughter, Anna, became a pioneer in child psychology.

Freud influenced other thinkers, including Jews such as Franz Boas (1858–1942) and Claude Lévi-Strauss (1908–2009) the founder of structural anthropology. While Lévi-Strauss analysed 'primitive' societies, Raymond Aron (1905–83) and Walter Benjamin (1892–1940) cast their gaze at modern civilization. The Parisian-born Aron asked how ordinary people made sense of industrial progress and political competition.

SOCIOLOGISTS
Walter Benjamin killed himself while trying to escape Nazis on the Franco-Spanish border. Even more than Freud, this translator, essayist and philosopher wrestled with his Jewish identity. He individualistically applied the ideas of Goethe, Marx, Brecht and Jewish mysticism to current literature and aesthetics, and his prescient posthumous works *Illuminations* and *Arcades* considered the shopping mall and street life as epitomizing contemporary society. One of his last books, *Theses on the Philosophy of History*, addressed the Jewish quest for a messiah and humanity's clash with nihilism.

Another Jewish-origin pioneer of the link between words and ideas was the Austrian-born Cambridge philosopher and former 'logical positivist', Ludwig Wittgenstein. He and other Jewish thinkers such as Benjamin, Levi-Strauss and Theodor Adorno laid the basis for a post-war

Above Hermann Cohen. German neo-Kantian philosophers wrestled with Jewish topics in his many books.

school called structuralism. Its most celebrated figure was Jacques Derrida (1930–2007). Derrida pioneered 'deconstruction', a method of minutely interrogating texts for signs of true meaning obscured by written convention, which has been profoundly influential.

Below 'Philosophers have interpreted the world; the point, however, is to change it' – Karl Marx, 1875.

PIONEERS IN ECONOMICS

New thinking in economics, jokingly called 'the dismal science', also owes much to Jews. Born into an English Sephardi family in 1772, David Ricardo became one of the most influential political economists. Monetarist Milton Friedman inspired Thatcherism in 1970s Britain and President Reagan's supply-side economics in America. Academic development economist Jeffrey Sachs draws on Jewish philosophy, not least Maimonides' theory of facilitating self-help as the highest form of charity. He has advised many Latin American and post-communist states.

Finally, George Soros of Hungary has turned his billions gained in speculation to promoting 'open societies' worldwide. Soros' ideas come from Jewish philosopher Karl Popper, who championed transparency as the ultimate tool against authoritarian systems.

Interestingly, many Jews in the Marxist camp veered from narrower economic analysis to investigating social change.

NEW THINKING IN JUDAISM

Thousands of believing 19th-century Jews sought a middle path, one that married Jewish heritage with modern realities. Exposure to

Left Claude Lévi-Strauss, pioneer of structuralism, at the opening of the Musee du Quai Branly, Paris, 2006.

Western academic methods led to radical new outlooks. From the 1950s onwards French philosopher Emmanuel Levinas (1906–95) popularized Talmudic methods to a new generation of secular scholars. More mainstream Orthodox Jews responded to the Haskalah spirit and Hassidic fervour by promoting the Mussar movement of contemplation and ethical introspection started by Rav Israel Salanter (1810–83). Salanter was inspired by the writings of Moshe Chaim Luzzatto (1707–46, an Italian kabbalist and rabbi.

THE NON-JEWISH JEW AND DIASPORA POLITICIANS

And yet the question remains, is there anything specifically Jewish about thinkers on general matters who just happen to be Jewish? To Isaac Deutscher (1907–67), the Polish-born British historian, Marxist activist and biographer of Stalin and Trotsky, it was possible, indeed almost inevitable, to be a 'non-Jewish Jew'. Though an atheist and foe of Jewish nationalism, he felt himself a 'Jew by force of my

Above Seasoned diplomat and former US Secretary of State Henry Kissinger (right) conversing with Russian President Vladimir Putin in 2004.

unconditional solidarity with the persecuted, because I feel the pulse of Jewish history.'

Germany's Chancellor from 1909 to 1917 was Theobald von Bethmann Hollweg, a descendant of a prominent Frankfurt Jewish banking family; while in Italy two Jews, Sydney Sonnino and Luigi Luzzatti, became prime ministers in 1909–10 and 1910–11 respectively. France has had five Jewish-origin prime ministers in the last century, most notably Leon Blum before World War II and Pierre Mendes-France after, both from the left. For 12 years Bruno Kreisky was Austria's Chancellor, and Henry Kissinger, who arrived in America in 1938 as a refugee from Nazi Germany, rose to become possibly Washington's most influential Secretary of State during 1973–77. Perhaps most powerful of all was Benjamin Disraeli, the first and only British Prime Minister of Jewish origin in 1868 and 1874–80; he spoke proudly of his people's heritage, though he was converted to Anglicanism aged 13.

JEWISH ARCHITECTURE AROUND THE WORLD

THE QUINTESSENTIAL JEWISH BUILDING MUST SURELY BE THE SYNAGOGUE. LIKE A BAROMETER OF JEWISH HISTORY, IT REPRESENTS THE SELF-IMAGE, TRIBULATIONS AND TRIUMPHS OF THE PEOPLE.

King Solomon built Jerusalem's first Temple and fortifications in Hazor, Megiddo and Gezer *c*.970-930BC. A millennium later, King Herod transformed the smaller second Temple into an imposing Hellenistic white stone structure. Rome ended large-scale Jewish ceremonial architecture, when it destroyed the Temple ten years after its final refurbishment. Absalom's tomb in Jerusalem's Kidron Valley offers a rare hint of ancient Jewish hybrid style with its Egyptian-like up-ended siphon roof.

The first synagogue was probably built during 6th-century BC Babylonian exile, and became the chief institution of decentralized Jewish worship after the Temple's destruction. More than 400 synagogues existed in the Judea and Galilee of Jesus' day; in function and form they influenced early churches and mosques. Two Toledo synagogues show the

Below National Assembly, Dhaka, Bangladesh, by US architect Louis Kahn.

Spanish–Moorish Mudéjar imprint most powerfully. One, now the El Transito Church, has amazing floral decorations, Nasrid stucco-work and Hebrew inscriptions; the other, founded in 1180 and now the Church of Santa Maria la Blanca, features Arabesque horseshoe arches, Almohad brickwork and white inner columns.

FALLOW YEARS

Bereft of statehood, Jews generally looked inward and so did their buildings. Small-scale Palestinian gems include 2nd–6th centuries CE catacombs in Beit She'arim, Lower Galilee, with squat Roman columns topped with Levantine-figured capitals, or zodiac signs on mosaic synagogue floors at Hamat and Beit-Alpha. Outside Palestine, Syria's Dura-Europos synagogue unusually displayed frescoes of human images, and the huge 6th-century synagogue complex at Sardis, Turkey, suggested a wealthy, integrated and self-assured community.

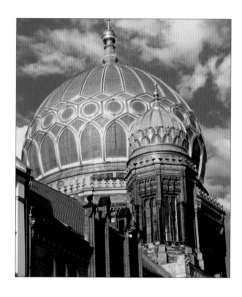

Above The Neue Synagogue, Berlin, 1866, is Moorish in style.

THE CLASSICAL PERIOD

Europe's oldest active synagogue is Prague's Altneuschule ('Old-New Synagogue'), a Gothic twin-nave structure in the Jewish quarter, finished in 1270. The Nazis destroyed many *shuls*; among those that survived are the ones in Hungary, Budapest, Florence, Trani, and, Poland's oldest, the 15th-century Kazimierz in Krakow, renovated after the war.

The Paradesi synagogue of Cochin, India, founded 1568, still operates, as does London's oldest synagogue, the Sephardis' Bevis Marks in the City, completed 1701. Possibly the finest Georgian synagogue is America's oldest, the Touro on Rhode Island.

IMPACT OF REFORM

In the 19th century, Reform Jews rejected ideas of a rebuilt Jerusalem and named their synagogues 'temples'. Men and women sat together, choirs and organs were introduced and new styles adopted: such as the Greek-temple look of Beth Elohim (1840) in Charleston, South Carolina; Byzantine in the West London Synagogue (1870); and a majestic Moorish–Gothic blend in the New Synagogue, Oranienstrasse, Berlin (1886). British Orthodox Jews developed grandiose 'cathedral synagogues',

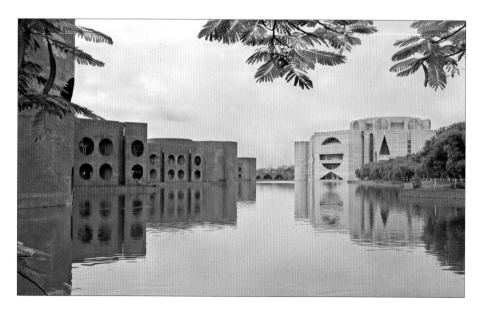

though the largest was Reform's 1929 flagship Temple Emanu-El on Fifth Avenue, New York.

TRADITION AND RENEWAL

In the 20th century, the pendulum swung from pomp and ornament towards abstraction and functionalism, and then to post-modernism. Louis Kahn's Temple Beth-El in Chappaqua, New York State, for example, imitates Poland's now lost pagoda-like wooden synagogues. Geometry reappeared in Erich Mendelsohn's 1950 observatory-style Park Synagogue in Cleveland, Ohio; in Max Abramowitz's funnel-like Temple Beth Zion, Buffalo; and in the triangles of Percival Goodman's Temple Beth Emeth, Albany, NY.

Recently, English Reform and Liberal congregations have started housing old arks and *bimahs* rescued from Czechoslovakia in modern synagogues. Equally indicative of renewal is Munich's modern Ohel Jakob synagogue, inaugurated in 2006, 68 years after Nazis destroyed its predecessor. A glass ceiling recalls the portable Tabernacle, a white stone base evokes the Temple in Jerusalem, and large windows are a sign of transparency and trust.

Below Frank Lloyd Wright's Beth Sholom Synagogue, Pennsylvania, 1954.

ISRAELI INNOVATORS

Palestinian Jewish architecture was transformed by the German and Central European influx of the 1930s. Against these Bauhaus stylists were ranged 'orientalists' who tried to incorporate local elements and reflect the people's diverse origins. Zvi Hecker drew on plant design and Arab village terracing for his 1963 Spiral House in Ramat Gan. Moshe Safdie built the Yad Vashem Museum, Jerusalem.

Architects inspired by Le Corbusier pioneered public housing in Beersheva and then developed Jerusalem. Some tried to incorporate 'Jewish emblems' such as Moses' tablets or stars of David. More successfully, the Israel Museum's 1965 Shrine of the Book pays homage to the bedouin urn that contained the Dead Sea Scrolls. Waterways in Jerusalem's outstanding Supreme Court of Justice, built by the brother and sister team of Ram Karmi and Ada Karmi-Melamed in 1992, echo the psalmist's description of justice on high reflected in law below.

MODERN ARCHITECTS

Frank Gehry and Daniel Libeskind are among the 21st century's leading architects. Canadian Gehry uses fish shapes and curves, as in Seattle's Experience Music Project, Hanover's Gehry Tower, Prague's Dancing House and Bilbao's Guggenheim Museum.

Above Tel Aviv Opera House, designed by Ya'akov Rechter, opened in 1994.

Libeskind's fractal designs and surprising use of symbolism appear in faith-related projects: the zigzag-shaped Berlin Jewish Museum; Bar Ilan University's Wohl convention centre, fashioned like a book; and the Danish Jewish Museum, whose design traces the Hebrew word *mitzvah*, or 'good deed', in tribute to Denmark's wartime rescue of Jews. Whether angular or flowing, the lines of contemporary Jewish architecture may be said to reflect the peaks and troughs of Jewish history.

Below The Shrine of the Book, Jerusalem, houses the Dead Sea Scrolls.

INDEX

Acknowledgements

To my valiant editor Joy and to my parents Hyam and Vivienne, my sister Tamara and her husband David, and my nephew and niece, Daniel and Hannah

This edition is published by Lorenz Books, an imprint of Anness Publishing Ltd, Blaby Road, Wigston, Leicestershire LE18 4SE; info@anness.com www.lorenzbooks.com; www.annesspublishing.com

Anness Publishing has a new picture agency outlet for images for publishing, promotions or advertising. Please visit our website www.practicalpictures.com for more information.

© Anness Publishing Ltd 2012

Publisher: Joanna Lorenz
Editor: Joy Wotton
Maps: Peter Bull Art Studio
Designer: Nigel Partridge
Production Controller: Wendy Lawson

PUBLISHER'S NOTE

PICTURE ACKNOWLEDGEMENTS

AKG–Images: 4bl, 27b, 31t, 35t, 36t, 40b, 42b, 48, 78t, 80b, 94b, 95b, 101, 104b, 117t, 128t, 130b, 131b, 139t, 143b, 143t, 147t, 159t, 161b, 162b, 164b, 164t, 166b, 166t, 170t, 171t, 190t, 194t, 195t, 197b, 240t; /Bible Land Pictures 51t; /Bible Land Pictures/Photo 85t, 92b, 115tr; /Bible Land Pictures/www.Bi 152b; /Bible Land Pictures/Z. Rad 4bl, 35b, 67br, 112b, 113b; /Bildarchiv Pisarek 145b, 165t, 181b, 193b, 248t; /British Library14t, 37tr, 111, 115tl, 125t, 127t, 128br; /Cameraphoto 65t; /Electa 56b, 68b, 69t; /Erich Lessing 8, 28b, 36b, 46t, 55t, 57tl, 66b, 73t, 84b, 131tr, 146t,156t, 182t, 187bl, 191t; /Gerard Degeorge 110; /Heiner Heine 138b; /Hervé Champollion 75b, 119tr; /IAM/WorldHistory Archive 151b; /Israel Images 64b, 80t, 91b, 141t, 154b, 206b, 214t; /Nimatallah 30b; /Philippe Maillard 37tl; /Pirozzi 67t; /Rabatti – Domingie 33t; /Suzanne Heid 155b; /ullstein bild 185, 196t; /VISIOARS 109t.

Alamy: /© 19th era 2 151t; /© AF archive 241b; /© Arcaid Images 5tr, 251bl; /© Arclight 123b; /© Art Directors & TRIP 147b, 175b; /© Art of Travel 140b; /© Bernie Epstein 238b; /© Carmen Sedano 10; /© David Hoffman 226b; /© dbimages 102t; /© Eddie Gerald 50t, 233b, 250t; /© Hanan Isachar 54b, 89t, 207t; /© Idealink Photography 159b; /© Interfoto 204t; /© Israel Images 81t, 83b, 212b, 214bl, 215; /© Israel Imagesi 232b, 251t; /© Ivan Vdovin 152t; /© Janice Hazeldine 225b; /© John Norman 105t; /© Laura S Goodman 178b; /© Lebrecht Music and Arts Photo Library 179t; /© Maria Adelaide Silva 104t; /© Mary Evans Picture Library 71b, 120t; /© Matthias Wassermann 108t; /© Maurice Joseph 121b; /© Mohammed Khaluf 88b; /© Nathan Benn 106t, 118b, 163t, 209t; /© North Wind Picture Archives 169, 170b; /© Paris Marais 227b; /© Peter Horree 92t; /© Peter Titmuss 178t; /© PhotoStock-Israel 71t, 83t, 121t, 206t; /© Pictorial Press Ltd 245t; /© Robert Estall photo agency 47t; /© Robert Fried 230t; /© Russell Kord 78b; /© Sally and Richard Greenhill 235bl; /© Shaun Higson colour 150b; /© Steve Allen Travel Photography 202; /© The Art Gallery Collection 93b; /© vario images GmbH & Co. KG 163b; /© White House Photo 216b; /© www.BibleLandPictures.com 47b; /©Yurij Brykaylo 150t; /©Ken Welsh 113t; /©RIA Novosti 249t; /Art Directors & TRIP 227t; /Dan Cohen 50b; /Israel Images 220t; /The Art Archive 28t.

The Art Archive: 72t, 76, 195b, 246b; /Archaeological Museum Aleppo Syria/Collection Dagli Orti 51b; /Archaeological Museum Baghdad /Gianni Dagli Orti 88t; /Archaeological Museum Tehran/Gianni Dagli Orti 58b; /Archaeological Museum Venice/Collection Dagli Orti 62t; /Bardo Museum Tunis/Gianni Dagli Orti 52t; /Basilica San Marco Venice/Collection Dagli Orti 90t; /Biblioteca Capitolare Padua/Gianni Dagli Orti 124t; /Biblioteca Nazionale Marciana Venice/Gianni Dagli Orti 95t,126t; /Bibliothèque Municipale Arras/Gianni Dagli Orti 58t; /Bibliothèque Municipale Valenciennes/Collection Dagli Orti 54t; /Bibliothèque Municipale Verdun/Kharbine-Tapabor /Coll. Jean Vigne 127b; /Bodleian Library Oxford 38t, 41t, 49, 55b, 82t, 109b, 114b, 119tl; /British Library 1 2, 30t, 53tr, 57b, 57tr, 70b, 106b,130t; /British Museum/Collection Dagli Orti 53tl; /Church of Saint Francis Tecamachalco/Gianni Dagli Orti 60t; /Collection Dagli Orti 86t,91t; /Culver Pictures 188b, 236b; /Domenica del Corriere/Collection Dagli Orti 172t; /Egyptian Museum Cairo/Alfredo Dagli Orti 31b; /Fondation Thiers Paris/Gianni Dagli Orti 149; /Galleria d'Arte Moderna Venice/Collection Dagli Orti 61b, 256b; /Galleria degli Uffizi Florence/Collection Dagli Orti 44t, 125b; /Gianni Dagli Orti 6b, 99, 119b, 174b; /Harper Collins Publishers 100t; /Hazem Palace Damascus/Gianni Dagli Orti 103tl; /Humor Monastery Moldavia/Collection Dagli Orti 86b; /Israel Museum Jerusalem/Gianni Dagli Orti 14b, 70t; /Karl Marx Museum Trier/Alfredo Dagli Orti 248br; /Kharbine-Tapabor 126t; /Library of Congress 45t; /Manuel Cohen 112t; /Moldovita Monaastery Romania 129t; /Musée Archéologique Naples/Collection Dagli Orti 56t; /Musée Condé Chantilly/Gianni Dagli Orti 73b; /Musée d'Art et d'Histoire Metz/Gianni Dagli Orti 124b; /Musée Départemental des Vosges Epinal/Gianni Dagli Orti 139br; /Musée des 2 Guerres Mondiales Paris/Gianni Dagli Orti 189b; /Musée des Beaux Arts Orléans/Collection Dagli Orti 38b; /Musée du Louvre Paris/Collection Dagli Orti 157t; /Museo Capitolino Rome/Collection Dagli Orti 84t; /Museo Civico Bolzano/Gianni Dagli Orti 68t; /Museo de Bellas Artes Zaragoza/Granger Collection 131tl; /Museum of London 187t; /National Archives Washington DC 176b, 198b; /National Library Cairo/Gianni Dagli Orti 96b; /National Museum Bucharest/Collection Dagli Orti 79; /National Palace Mexico City/Gianni Dagli Orti 137t; /Nationalmuseet Copenhagen Denmark/Collection Dagli Orti 138t; /Navy Historical Service Vincennes France/Gianni Dagli Orti 142b; /Nicholas J. Saunders 187br; /Palatine Library Parma/Gianni Dagli Orti 82b; /Palazzo Barberini Rome/Collection Dagli Orti 39t; /Palazzo Pitti Florence/Collection Dagli Orti 135t; /Private Collection/Marc Charmet 155t, 188t, 200b; /Private Collection/Gianni Dagli Orti 120b; /Rijksmuseum Amsterdam/Superstock 146b; /Russian Historical Museum Moscow/Collection Dagli Orti 158t; /Stephanie Colasanti 133, 134b, 231b; /Szapiro Collection Paris/Gianni Dagli Orti 134t; /Tate Gallery London 34t; /Tate Gallery London /Eileen Tweedy 154t, 122bl; /Topkapi Museum Istanbul/Gianni Dagli Orti 140t, 142t; /Turkish and Islamic Art Museum Istanbul/Harper Collins Publishers 100b; /Turkish and Islamic Art Museum Istanbul/Collection Dagli Orti 53b, 98; /Turkish and Islamic Art Museum Istanbul/Gianni Dagli Orti 44b; /University Library Istanbul/Gianni Dagli Orti 148; /Vezzolano, Italy 94t; /Victoria and Albert Museum London/Sally Chappell 32t.

The Bridgeman Art Library: 7t, 9, 17b, 24, 40t, 45b, 52b, 59tl, 59tr, 60b, 66t, 87b, 136b, 137bl, 144b, 167b, 174t, 216t, 231t, 239t; /Gift of James A. de Rothschild, London 22t; /The Stieglitz Collection and donated with contribution from Erica & Ludwig Jesselson 18b; /© Edifice 167t; /© Look and Learn 114t; /© SZ Photo 137br, 194b; /© Zev Radovan 27t, 32b, 39b, 65b, 74t, 75t, 234t; /Alinari 6t; /Ancient Art and Architecture Collection Ltd 26t, 29t; /Archives Charmet 25, 96t, 108b, 144t, 175t; /extended loan from Michael and Judy Steinhardt, New York 37b; /Gift of James A. de Rothschild, London 240b; /Giraudon 43t, 59b, 61t, 64t,81b, 89b, 132, 161t; /Ken Welsh 118t; /Peter Willi 69b, 180b; /Photo © Christie's Images 168; /Photo © Philip Mould Ltd, London 181t; /Seth G. Sweetser Fund 160t; /The Stapleton Collection 22b, 116b; /The Steiglitz Colleciton and donated with contribution from Erica & Ludwig Jesselson 158b.

Cody Images: 7b, 192b, 196b, 199b, 210b.

Corbis: 76t, 172b, 210t, 235tl, 235tr, 237t; /© Adrian Andrusier/Lebrecht Music & Arts 173; /© Andy Aitchison/In Pictures 222b; /© Ann Johansson 228b; /© Araldo de Luca 63t; /© Atlantide Phototravel 232t; /© Bettmann 177t, 177b, 182b, 189t, 190b, 191b, 199t, 205b, 207b, 211t, 213b, 220b, 222t, 224t, 236t, 241t, 242bl, 242t, 248bl; /© Bojan Brecelj 246t; /© Cezaro de Luca/epa 230b; /© Charles and Josette Lenars 74bl; /© Chris Hellier 93t; /© Christel Gerstenberg 136t; /© Claude Medale/Kipa 4bm; /© Colin McPherson 243br; /© Daniel Deme/epa 122t; /© Dave Bartruff 20b; /© Dave G. Houser 12; /© David Clapp/Arcaid 116t; /© David James/Sygma 245b; /© David Rubinger 213t; /© David Sutherland 5tl, 198t; /© DK Limited 107t; /© Douglas Pearson 87t; /© Ed Kashi 208t; /© epa 197t; /© Gianni Giansanti/Sygma 201t; /© Hanan Isachar 67bl, 153t; /© Hanan Isachar/JAI 251br; /© Hulton-Deutsch Collection 171b, 192t, 208b, 211b, 212t, 221, 239b; /© Ira Wyman/Sygma 243b; /© Jon Arnold/ JAI 103tr; /© Katarina Stoltz/Reuters 184; /© Kevin Fleming 225t; /© Larry Downing/Sygma 223b; /© Lebrecht Arts & Music 228t, 247tl; /© Lebrecht Authors/Lebrecht Music & Arts 123t; /© Lee Snider/Photo Images 11, 160b; /© Leland Bobbé 21b; /© Li Erben 247tr; /© Marc Garanger 229b; /© Marcus Fhrer/epa 193t; /© Melvyn Longhurst 179b; /© Michael Freeman 209b; /© Michael Nicholson 186t; /© Michel Selboun/Sygma 156b, 157b; /© Nathan Benn 117b; /© Nathan Benn 5tm, 235t; /© Nathan Benn/Ottochrome 3, 97t, 229t; /© Nicolas Sapieha 63b; /© Ocean 33b; /© Pascal Parrot/ Sygma 235br; /© Patrick Ward 122br; /© Peter M.Wilson 165b; /© Pimentel Jean/Corbis KIPA 13; /© Reuters 224b; /© Richard T. Nowitz 74br, 153t; /© Robert Holmes 135b; /© Ronen Zvulin/Reuters 115b; /© Sophie Bassouls/Sygma 242br; /© Stapleton Collection 183; /© Swim Ink 2, LLC 204b; /© Ted Spiegel 4br, 219; /© Walter Mcbride 243tl; /©Le-Dung Ly/Science Faction 250b.

Rex Features: 23, 247b; /Alinari 180t, 218; /Assaf Shillo 223t; /Chameleons Eye 217; /Courtesy Everett Collection 226t; /Everett Collection 201b, 244b, 244t; /Israel Sun 203; /Marco Marianella 237b; /Roman Koszowski 200t; /SIPA PRESS 205t, 238t, 249b.

p. 1. Aaron the first high priest pours oil into the sacred seven-branched candelabrum, the menorah; from northern French manuscript c.1280. 2. "This is the bread of affliction" reads this beautiful image from the Barcelona Haggadah, c.1340. The haggadah is read at Passover to commemorate the Jewish people's liberation from slavery in Egypt. 3. A Sephardi Jewish boy carries a Torah casket while celebrating his bar mitzvah by the Western Wall in Jerusalem. Below. The destruction of the Temple in Jerusalem, 70AD.

children 195

$36